Europe in Crisis

EUROPE IN CRISIS

Intellectuals and the European Idea, 1917–1957

Edited by

Mark Hewitson

and

Matthew D'Auria

berghahn
NEW YORK · OXFORD
www.berghahnbooks.com

First published in 2012 by

Berghahn Books

www.berghahnbooks.com

Library of Congress Cataloging-in-Publication Data

Europe in crisis : intellectuals and the European idea, 1917–1957 / edited by Mark
Hewitson and Matthew D'Auria.
    p. cm.
  Includes bibliographical references and index.
  ISBN 978-0-85745-727-1 (hardback : acid-free paper) -- ISBN 978-1-78238-924-8
(paperback : acid-free paper) – ISBN 978-0-85745-728-8 (ebook)
  1. Europe--History--1918–1945. 2. Group identity--Europe. 3. European federation.
4. Nationalism--Europe--History--20th century. 5. National characteristics, European.
6. Europe--History--1945– 7. Europe--Intellectual life--20th century. I. Hewitson,
Mark. II. D'Auria, Matthew.
  D720.E97 2012
  940.5--dc23

                                                                      2012011635

British Library Cataloguing in Publication Data

A catalogue record for this book is available from the British Library

Printed on acid-free paper.

ISBN: 978-0-85745-727-1 hardback
ISBN: 978-1-78238-924-8 paperback
ISBN: 978-0-85745-728-8 ebook

CONTENTS

꙳

LIST OF MAPS AND FIGURES

Maps

Figures

All illustrations are Michael Wintle's photographs unless otherwise stated.

ACKNOWLEDGEMENTS

The present volume is based on a selection of papers, duly revised and lengthened, presented at a conference on 'Europe before the European Community' held in London on 11–12 December 2008. The conference was made possible by the generous funding of the Centre for European Studies at University College London. The Institute for Historical Research also helped by granting us the use of its rooms. We would like to thank the anonymous reviewers of Berghahn Books for their useful suggestions and criticisms.

Introduction

EUROPE DURING THE FORTY YEARS' CRISIS

> The Persepolis of the spirit is no less ravaged than the Susa of material fact.
> Everything has not been lost, but everything has sensed that it might perish.
> An extraordinary shudder ran through the marrow of Europe. She felt in every
> nucleus of her mind that she was no longer the same, that she was no longer
> herself, that she was about to lose consciousness, a consciousness acquired
> through centuries of bearable calamities, by thousands of men of the first rank,
> from innumerable geographical, ethnic, and historical coincidences.
> – Paul Valéry, 'The Crisis of the Mind'

Like many others meditating at the time on the tragedies of war and on Europe's
future, Paul Valéry felt at once a tragic sense of uncertainty combined with the
hope that Europe could find the strength for its rebirth. Defining and understanding
the 'European soul' became central in all cultural and intellectual milieux; far from
being mere intellectual quarrels, such debates stemmed, on the contrary, from the
immediate need to banish the risk of a new war and, more fundamentally, from
the urge to avoid the complete destruction of European civilization.[1]

Even though Europe was suffering its greatest crisis, many agreed nonetheless
with Valéry that 'not all had been lost'; the crisis of 'Europe's soul' was not seen
merely as a negative result in itself, but was viewed as a phase from which, if the
right decisions were taken, Europe could emerge even stronger. In some writings
of the time, the crisis was perceived as an opportunity to stop the disintegration
of Europe, whose decay had started long before the outbreak of the Great War. As
José Ortega y Gasset wrote in 1930:

> Is it as certain as people say that Europe is in a state of decadence; that it is resigning
> its command; abdicating? May not this apparent decadence be a beneficial crisis
> which will enable Europe to be really, literally Europe? The evident decadence of the
> nations of Europe, was not this *a priori* necessary if there was to be one day possibly
> a United States of Europe, the plurality of Europe substituted by its formal unity?[2]

Crisis, in this sense, was a chance to rethink an existing state of affairs, not simply a concentrated moment of instability or a premonition of collapse.[3]

This study looks at those authors who perceived the crisis in similar terms, and sheds light on the different solutions they put forward. While many agreed that action should be taken, the answers they gave to the European question were quite different. Some turned to the past to find the roots of European civilization, referring to Christianity or to humanism in their search for a common identity. Others, on the contrary, believed that Europe had to be a collection of nations whose integrity had to be maintained; to them, the only possible project was a confederation of nation-states representing 'unity in diversity', which Europe, as the site of freedom, had to preserve. Finally, there were those who called for the creation of a federation at the expense of the independence of individual nation-states, which were considered the reason for Europe's downfall rather than the cause of its greatness.

The three main approaches proposed, respectively, a regeneration of Europe in terms of a return to its past, where the continent's cultural unity had to be sought (Part II), the preservation of a perpetual present, designed to maintain and redeem the achievements of European civilization in the face of contemporary deviations (Part III), and the generation of a new and different future, constituting a break from the catastrophe of the First World War and the conditions of the 1920s, 1930s and 1940s (Part IV). Such approaches were frequently combined in the numerous treatises and articles on 'Europe' after 1917, but one in particular – past, present or future – was usually emphasized. The first approach, which aimed to recreate a European past, derived from many sources, including a revolt against the imposition of a supposedly revolutionary or illegitimate regime at home, fear of Bolshevik or capitalist versions of modernity, a yearning for a new moral or religious order, scepticism about the principle of national self-determination, and a longing for the resurrection of multinational aristocracies and empires, especially those of Austria-Hungary.[4] In such a paradigm the nation-state was often irrelevant and what mattered was the quest for a lost cultural unity. The second approach considered Europe's 'present' – from the eighteenth century onwards – the time of its greatest achievements, thanks above all to the triumph of the nation-state, which intellectuals like Johan Huizinga and Lucien Febvre sought to reconcile with the presumed existence of a European 'culture' and the need for a European political structure.[5] It was predicated on the belief that all possible solutions to a European question had to be founded on the continuing independence of the continent's nations and on the assumption that only by preserving national differences could Europe be the locus of freedom. Finally, the third approach, which envisaged a fundamentally different future for Europe, came to rest on the programmes put forward by federalists, who outlined a solution eschewing past or existing experience. To them, the independence of Europe's nation-states was the ultimate cause of conflict and the cause of Europe's downfall.

Europe as an Idea and a Project

These ways of addressing Europe's predicament after 1917 reflect three different understandings of the relationship of Europe to its own past, its present and its future. Of course, all the authors analysed considered Europe's 'temporality' in a broader sense, since all conceived of a project for a future Europe. Significantly, all called for some sort of action at a time when the two main extra-European powers were jeopardizing the capacity of Europe to master its own destiny.[6] It could seem, precisely in this era of crisis, that Europe had either to perish or to become a 'project' – a projection of itself. The period considered is based on such an understanding. 1917 adumbrated the fall or eclipse of Europe, since it marked its incapacity – as a result of the Bolshevik revolution in Russia and the United States' intervention in the First World War – to determine its own destiny, while 1957 represented the end – or, at least, transformation and diminution – of the crisis, with the signature of the Treaty of Rome. Against a backdrop of decolonization and superpower politics, European governments appeared to have accepted the need to concentrate on their own continent, as one region amongst many, and to find new ways of coordinating national interests and policies. Importantly, none of the three approaches – oriented towards the past, present and future – clearly triumphed over the others.[7] It was arguably the very diversity of Europe's past and the variety of attachments to Europe's actual achievements which helped to preclude a clear, future-oriented federal solution to Europe's problems. Despite appearances, these different conceptions of Europe were present at the birth of the European Communities and remained significant for their future.

This volume reassesses historians' and political scientists' assumptions about the nature, role and importance of conceptions of Europe as obstacles to and catalysts of integration before and after 1957.[8] It asks whether the transition from a set of ideas about Europe to the European project was as significant or definitive as is sometimes supposed; it questions the extent to which such ideas were linked to cultural criticism and permeated by a sense of pathos as a consequence of the continent's supposed self-destruction and exposure to external threats; it enquires whether 1945 really constituted a watershed – or 'zero hour' – in either the conceptualization of Europe or the realization of European integration; and it examines whether a putative transformation of political conditions on the continent – the development of internecine ideological conflicts, the Great Depression, the partition of Germany and the establishment of the 'iron curtain' – brought about a thorough-going reevaluation of Europe's territorial scope, its shared values and culture, its existing and envisaged institutions, and its place in the world.[9] These suppositions, which are characteristic of much of the secondary literature on the topic, are in many instances warranted, but they are rarely substantiated and are sometimes unfounded.[10] At the very least, it is legitimate to ask whether, as is often assumed, the geopolitical conditions produced by the Second World War turned specific conceptions of Europe into feasible projects, or whether such ideas, already circulating in the interwar years, helped to create an understanding of what Europe was, which in turn helped to set the intellectual premises on which a project of European integration could be based.

The assumed disjunction between Europe as a project and as an idea, which is partly the result of the subsequent significance of the European Union, the incremental nature of European integration and the dominance of positive or empirical social sciences such as economics and functionalist sociology, has had several distorting effects, not least by obscuring the tardiness and uncertainty of the project of integration itself. Many scholars have succumbed to the temptation of seeking the 'origins' of European integration in failed attempts to establish a supranational organization in the late 1940s (the Council of Europe) and early 1950s (the European Defence Community and EPC), the resistance of the war years, the Pan-European movement of the 1920s and '30s, and the various 'foundations' of a purported European identity before that date, referring to etymology, geography, Christianity, the Enlightenment, the pentarchy of Great Powers, cosmopolitanism, nationalism, imperialism and, even, National Socialism, according to Richard Swedberg's analysis of the literature on Europe.[11] Such a *modus operandi* tends to overstate the importance of the different precursors of integration, isolating them from the various discourses and institutional contexts of which they were a part.[12] This study treats ideas of Europe as elements of broader debates about morality and culture, capitalism and economics, foreign policy and imperialism, and different aspects of politics relating to the welfare state, economic planning, liberal and social democracy, and sovereignty, territory and power. These debates evolved quickly, contained many inconsistencies and were subject to uneven forms of dissemination, transfer and reception, undermining the notion of origins or foundations and informing inchoate designs for a European set of institutions.

Periodization

Debates about Europe after 1917 were framed primarily by the experiences of the First World War, of course, which had widely been experienced, in Georg Simmel's phrase, as a 'cultural crisis'.[13] To many observers, the war seemed to have demonstrated Europe's capacity to destroy itself through the misuse of technology and state organization. As a consequence, it appeared, especially to those on the right, to have exposed its own civilization, which was usually associated with middle-class and aristocratic milieux, to the menace of a revolution by 'barbarians' – Bolsheviks, socialists or Jews – at home, or invasion by 'barbarians' – most notably, 'Slavs' – from abroad. Such anxieties were salient in treatises such as Hermann von Keyserling's *Spectrum of Europe* (1928), José Ortega y Gasset's *Revolt of the Masses* (1930), Arnold Toynbee's *A Study of History* (1934), and Oswald Spengler's *Decline of the West* (1918–22), which outsold all other works of non-fiction in Germany during the 1920s and early 1930s.[14] However, it is worth noting that these authors – and like-minded cultural pessimists on the left and in the centre – were also influential during the period when a 'European community' was being discussed after the Second World War, not merely after the Great War. Technocracy, the overextension of science, misreadings of the Enlightenment, anonymous bureaucratization and the standardization of culture were all targets of Theodor Adorno and Max Horkheimer's *Dialectic of Enlightenment* (1944) and Hannah Arendt's *The Origins of Totalitarianism* (1951), just as they had been the objects of Max Weber's, D.H. Lawrence's, T.S. Eliot's and Paul Valéry's criticism after the First World War.[15] There was an ongoing and understandable ambivalence about 'modernity' and 'civilization' – with 'Modernism' at once critical and constitutive – throughout the entire period between 1917 and 1957, but it did not usually entail an abnegation of the European Enlightenment, scientific progress, state building, political freedoms, welfare or industrial production.[16] The threat of communism was established in 1917 and fear of Americanization was commonplace by the 1920s, as were their respective attractions.[17] For these and other reasons, it is misleading to depict interwar discourses about Europe's cultural decline giving way to postwar plans for a European community. Multifaceted discourses ran alongside, and were connected to, more concrete planning throughout the period up to – and beyond – 1957.

The Second World War, although it was quickly succeeded on the Continent by the partitions of the Cold War and the presence of U.S. or Soviet soldiers in most states, did not constitute a caesura in the discussion of 'Europe'. The very onset or even existence of a single 'Cold War' in Europe has been challenged by historians such as David Reynolds, who has rightly pointed out that the logic of military might, ideological conflict and economic incompatibility was only manifested belatedly, and that the retention or reacquisition of empires by Britain and France continued to give them a world role until the mid-1950s.[18] The division between the Comecon countries and Western Europe largely confirmed older distinctions between the 'West' and the 'East', 'Germanic' and 'Romance' peoples and 'Slavs', and 'Europe', 'Mitteleuropa' or 'Zwischeneuropa' and 'Eastern Europe' or the 'Balkans'.[19] The United States, despite rhetorical support for a 'United States of Europe', did not push consistently for, and sometimes opposed, the creation of supranational organizations on the continent.[20] The same was true of the United Kingdom, which was still Europe's largest economy and its principal military power in the late 1940s and 1950s.[21] Such conditions left the question of European integration in the balance, with discourses about Europe continuing to play a role. Many of these discourses did not correspond to a periodization beginning or ending in 1945: fears and hopes of 'globalization' appeared much later, in the 1970s and 1980s; economic lessons had been learned from the Depression, predicated on greater coordination of national economies, but they had been discussed, and even acted upon, much earlier than the end of the Second World War, as Andrew Shennan, Richard Kuisel and others have pointed out in the French case; 'history', notwithstanding new taboos and traumas, remained vital, perpetuating antagonisms and anxieties, which helped to prevent the ratification of the European Defence Community in 1954, and initiating attempts at reconciliation, which contributed to the creation of a self-interested and limited Franco-German axis at the core of the European Coal and Steel Community in 1951.[22] Above all, the recovery and reconstruction of nation-states, together with accompanying national narratives of revival and self-sacrifice, took precedence in the 'postwar' demobilizations of the 1920s and the 1940s and 50s, as Alan Milward and Richard Bessel have indicated, with uncertain but unavoidable consequences for discourses about Europe.[23]

The diplomatic and political shifts of the post-1945 era, especially U.S. coordination of military policy in Western Europe, helped to defuse tensions and enable greater cooperation between old enemies to take place. Yet the main shifts, which were mediated discursively, took place over a longer period. The principal antagonism – between France and Germany – was deep-rooted and was arguably not overcome until the signature of the Franco-German Treaty in 1963.[24] European empires had been under threat since 1914, and in the German case colonial possessions had been seized in 1919, but they remained in place in most instances, with the exception of India, until the 1950s and '60s. The opposition between communism or socialism and capitalism or liberal democracy had been characteristic of foreign and domestic policy in Europe since 1917. Although fascism had been extirpated in 1944–45, right-wing authoritarian dictatorships remained on the fringes of Europe in Spain, Portugal and Greece, and fear of a reversion to fascism was common in former dictatorships such as Germany, Austria and Italy. When the German philosopher Karl Jaspers asked *Where is the Federal Republic Heading?* in a widely discussed book in 1966, his answer was towards dictatorship.[25] Debates about Europe were tied to such internal and external political discourses throughout the interwar and early postwar periods. The terms of debate – whether Europe should be confederal or federal, national or supranational, political or economic – remained the same.

Plan of the Book

It is the aim of this volume to examine the relationship between ideas of Europe and projects designed to create common European institutions. Such a relationship was an enduring, complex and formative one, as were the connections between conceptions of Europe and wider discourses about culture and politics. René Girault might be right in identifying a *Europe vécue* as a valid object of study, rather than a *Europe construite* or a *Europe pensée*, but it is misleading to imply that there is little left to say about an 'imagined' or 'thought' Europe.[26] Rather, the panoply of ideas and overlapping, sometimes contradictory, discourses about Europe constitute an essential and still under-researched part of our understanding of the interwar and postwar periods and of attempts, then and later, to achieve European integration. Using the methods and approaches of intellectual history, this study explores familiar and unknown aspects of the subject in a new way.[27] Part I asks how important federal and other plans for Europe's future were in contemporary discourses and in actual policy making. It has two main claims. The first is that the analysis of this particular period – never before considered in a volume on Europe – is of seminal importance in understanding the birth and, to a certain extent, the later development of the European Community (EC). The second claim is that, precisely in such a period of radical ideological oppositions, distinct approaches to the solution of Europe's crisis can be identified. All of these relate to the different ways in which Europeans conceived of their own identity. Part II looks at intellectuals whose conceptions of Europe concentrated, above all, on the past; Part III examines the works and ideas of writers and thinkers who wished to emphasize the achievements and power of Europe in the present; and Part IV analyses the writings of advocates of new projects, which were usually federal, for Europe's future. This distinction between backward-looking, synchronic and forward-looking approaches to Europe, although only a question of degree, illuminates the ways in which the historical identity of the continent and collective images of the EC were understood by contemporaries, defining different narratives, explanations, diagnoses and solutions concerning a putative 'European question'.

The volume aims to reassess the relationship between ideas of Europe and the European project; it asks whether conceptions of Europe before 1957 were pessimistic, defensive, progressive, cultural, economic or political; it questions the relevance of 1918 and 1945 as turning points in the history of the conceptualization of Europe and of European integration; and it reconsiders the impact of long- and short-term political transformations on assumptions about the continent's scope, nature, role and significance. The next section considers the limited consensus which existed in respect of 'Europe' (Chapter 3) and investigates the impact of conceptions of the continent and its future on policy making in the 1920s (Chapter 1) and in the late 1940s and 1950s (Chapter 2). The emphasis here is on interaction and transfer – and on obstacles – between the conceptualization of Europe in the public sphere and the formulation and implementation of policy. Subsequent sections examine the full and disparate range of such conceptualizations of Europe as a means of reconstructing the debates and the intellectual horizons of opinion and decision makers.

Notes

1. P. Valéry, 'The Crisis of the Mind' (1919), in idem, *History and Politics* (London, 1963), vol. 10, pp. 23–36.
2. J. Ortega y Gasset, *The Revolt of the Masses* (New York, 1993), 139. Originally published in 1930.
3. Martin Heidegger makes this point in 'Europa und die deutsche Philosophie' (1936), in Hans-Helmut Gander, *Europa und die Philosophie* (Frankfurt am Main, 1993), 31.
4. On the link between uprooted aristocrats in Central and Eastern Europe and 'Europeanism' after 1918, see Chapters 5 and 8, where Łukasz Mikołajewski points to the aristocratic background of 'East European' intellectuals such as Jerzy Stempowski.
5. See Chapters 12 and 14.
6. See, for instance, the Swiss historian Gonzague de Reynold, *L'Europe tragique* (Paris, 1933), 393.

7. On the influence of the present on historians' accounts of a European past, see S. Woolf, 'Europe and Its Historians', *Contemporary European History* 12 (2003), 323–37.

8. For an introduction to this literature, see E. du Réau, *L'idée d'Europe au XXe siècle. Des mythes aux réalités* (Brussels, 1996).

9. For a fuller survey of the literature, see Chapters 1–3. On the transition from ideas to project, see especially K. Wilson and J. van der Dussen (eds), *The History of the Idea of Europe* (London, 1993); on the pathos of the European idea, see P.M. Lützeler, *Die Schriftsteller und Europa* (Munich, 1992) and M. Spiering and M. Wintle (eds), *Ideas of Europe since 1914: The Legacy of the First World War* (Basingstoke, 2002); for examples of works which see 1939 or 1945 as a watershed, see M. Dedman, *The Origins and Development of the European Union, 1945–2008* (London, 2009), D.W. Urwin, *The Community of Europe: A History of European Integration since 1945* (London, 1994), and W. Loth, *Der Weg nach Europa. Geschichte der europäischen Integration 1939–1957* (Göttingen, 1996).

10. See, for instance, R. Girault, 'Das Europa der Historiker', in Hudemann (ed.), *Europa im Blick der Historiker* (Munich, 1995), 55–90.

11. R. Swedberg, 'The Idea of "Europe" and the Origin of the European Union: A Sociological Approach', *Zeitschrift für Soziologie* 23 (1994), 378–87. On 'origins', see classic works by F. Chabod, *Storia dell'idea Europa* (Bari, 1961), J.-B. Duroselle, *L'idée d'Europe dans l'histoire* (Paris, 1965), G. Barraclough, *European Unity in Thought and Practice* (Oxford, 1963), and H. Brugmans, *L'idee européenne 1920–1970*, 3rd edn. (Bruges, 1970). Also, H. Mikkeli, *Europe as an Idea and an Identity* (Basingstoke, 1998), 3–108; G. Delanty, *Inventing Europe: Idea, Identity, Reality* (Basingstoke, 1995), 16–129; A. Pagden, *The Idea of Europe: From Antiquity to the European Union* (Cambridge, 2002), 1–32. The classic account of the translation of ideas into policies remains that of Walter Lipgens, who stressed the divisions, lack of realism and poor connections to government of the European movements of the 1920s, and the unity of purpose and subsequent effect on the policy making of the Resistance, in *A History of European Integration, 1945–1947* (Oxford, 1982), idem, *Europa-Föderationspläne der Widerstandsbewegungen 1940–1945* (Munich, 1968), and idem, 'Europäische Einigungsidee 1923–1930 und Briands Europaplan im Urteil der deutschen Akten', *Historische Zeitschrift* 203 (1966), 46–89, 316–63. Neo-functionalists have stressed the failure to create a federal political structure (Council of Europe, EDC-EPC): E.B. Haas, *The Uniting of Europe* (Stanford, 1958), revised edn. in 2004; P.C. Schmitter, 'Ernst B. Haas and the Legacy of Neo-Functionalism', *Journal of European Public Policy* 10 (2005), 255–72; A. Wiener and T. Diez, *European Integration Theory* (2003), 45–66, and B. Rosamond, *Theories of European Integration* (2000), 50–73.

12. Scholars have already started to address this question, with varying degrees of rigour: R. Girault (ed.), *Identité et conscience européenne au XXe siècle* (Paris, 1994); R. Frank (ed.), *Les identités européennes au XXe siècle* (Paris, 2004); R. Girault and G. Bossuat (eds), *Europe brisée, Europe retrouvée. Nouvelles réflexions sur l'unité européenne au XXe siècle* (Paris, 1994); R. Hudemann et al. (eds), *Europa im Blick der Historiker* (Munich, 1995); E. du Réau (ed.), *Europe des elites? Europe des peuples? La construction de l'espace européenne 1945–1960* (Paris, 1998); E. Bussière (ed.), *Europa. L'idée et l'identité européennes de l'antiquité grecque au XXe siècle* (Anvers, 2001); H. Kaelble, *Europäer über Europa. Die Entstehung des europäischen Selbstverständnisses im 19. und 20. Jahrhundert* (Frankfurt, 2001); and G. Bossuat and G. Saunier (eds), *Inventer l'Europe. Histoire nouvelle des groupes d'influence et des acteurs de l'unité européenne* (Brussels, 2003).

13. D. Frisby and M. Featherstone, *Simmel on Culture* (London, 1998), 55–108.

14. See Chapters 4–9 and Chapter 11.

15. See especially W. Lepenies, *Between Literature and Science: The Rise of Sociology* (Cambridge, 1988); P. Fussell, *The Great War and Modern Memory* (Oxford, 1975); idem, *Wartime: Understanding and Behaviour in the Second World War* (Oxford, 1990); S. Hynes, *War Imagined: The First World War and English Culture* (London, 1992).

16. M. Bradbury and J. McFarlane (eds), *Modernism* (London, 1978), 19–56.

17. For Germany, see V.G. Liulevicius, *The German Myth of the East, 1800 to the Present* (Oxford, 2009), 130–219; M. Burleigh, *Germany Turns Eastward* (Cambridge, 2002); M. Nolan,

Visions of Modernity: American Business and the Modernisation of Germany (Oxford, 1994); E. Klautke, *Unbegrenzte Möglichkeiten: 'Amerikanisierung' in Deutschland und Frankreich 1900–1933* (Wiesbaden, 2003).

18. See especially D. Reynolds (ed.), *The Origins of the Cold War in Europe* (New Haven, 2009), 1–22, 77–120.

19. For Germany, see V. Conze, *Das Europa der Deutschen* (Munich, 2005). On Central and Eastern Europe, see M.N. Todorova, *Imagining the Balkans* (Oxford, 1997); G. Schöpflin and N. Wood (eds), *In Search of Central Europe* (New York, 1994); R. Okey, 'Central Europe/Eastern Europe: Behind the Definitions', *Past and Present* 137 (1992), 102–33; J. Rupnik, 'Central Europe or Mitteleuropa?', *Daedalus* 119 (1990), 249–78.

20. Some U.S. officials feared that the ECSC might become a 'super-cartel', but they eventually backed the initiative: J. Gillingham, *Coal, Steel and the Rebirth of Europe* (Cambridge, 1991), and idem, 'Solving the Ruhr Problem: German Heavy Industry and the Schuman Plan', in K. Schwabe (ed.), *Die Anfänge des Schuman-Plans* (Baden-Baden, 1988), 268–80; A.W. Lovett, 'The United States and the Schuman Plan', *Historical Journal* 39 (1996), 425–55. On the EDC, which Washington – in the end – opposed, see T.A. Schwartz, *America's Germany: John McCloy and the Federal Republic of Germany* (Cambridge, Mass., 1991); T.P. Ireland, *Creating the Entangling Alliance* (Westport, Conn., 1981); F.H. Heller and J.R. Gillingham (eds), *NATO: The Founding of the Atlantic Alliance and the Integration of Europe* (New York, 1992); A. Grosser, *The Western Alliance* (London, 1980); and P. Winand, *Eisenhower, Kennedy and the United States of Europe* (New York, 1993).

21. J.W. Young, *Britain and European Unity, 1945–1992* (London, 1993), 1–52, and idem, 'Churchill's "No" to Europe', *Historical Journal* 28 (1985), 923–37; S. Croft, 'British Policy towards Western Europe, 1947–1949: The Best of Possible Worlds?', *International Affairs* 64 (1988), 617–29: S. Burgess and G. Edwards, 'The Six Plus One: British Policy-Making and the Question of European Economic Integration, 1955', *International Affairs* 64 (1988), 393–413.

22. A. Shennan, *Rethinking France: Plans for Renewal, 1940–1946* (Oxford, 1989); M. Margairaz, *L'Etat, les finances et l'économie. Histoire d'une conversion 1932–1952* (Paris, 1991); R. Kuisel, *Capitalism and the State in Modern France: Renovation and Economic Management in the Twentieth Century* (Cambridge, 1981), and idem, 'Vichy et les origines de la planification économique 1940–1946', *Le Mouvement sociale* 98 (1977), 77–101.

23. A.S. Milward, *The European Rescue of the Nation-State*; idem, *The Reconstruction of Western Europe, 1945–51* (London, 1984); idem and V. Sorensen (eds), *The Frontier of National Sovereignty: History and Theory, 1945–1992* (Routledge, 1993); R. Bessel and D. Schumann (eds), *Life after Death: Approaches to a Cultural and Social History of Europe during the 1940s and 1950s* (Cambridge, 2003); R. Bessel, *Germany 1945: From War to Peace* (London, 2010); idem, *Germany after the First World War* (Oxford, 1995); D. Geppert (ed.), *The Postwar Challenge* (Oxford, 2004).

24. Recently, C. Germond and H. Türk (eds), *A History of Franco-German Relations in Europe* (Basingstoke, 2008), 137–98.

25. K. Jaspers, *Wohin treibt die Bundesrepublik?* (Munich, 1966).

26. R. Girault (ed.), *Les Europe des Européens* (Paris, 1993), and idem (ed.), *Identité et conscience européenne au XXe siècle*.

27. The methods of intellectual historians vary, of course, as this volume demonstrates, but a concern for authorial intentions, the meaning of concepts and the transfer and reception of ideas in the context of wider debates and historical circumstances is common to most approaches: D.R. Kelley, *The Descent of Ideas: A History of Intellectual History* (London, 2002); Q. Skinner, *Visions of Politics* (Cambridge, 2002), vol. 1; R. Koselleck, *The Practice of Conceptual History* (Stanford, 2002); D. LaCapra, *Rethinking Intellectual History* (Ithaca, 1983); H. White, *The Content of the Form* (Baltimore, 1987); R. Darnton, 'Intellectual and Cultural History', in M. Kammen (ed.), *The Past Before Us* (Ithaca, 1980); F. Ringer, 'The Intellectual Field, Intellectual History and the Sociology of Knowledge', *Theory and Society* 19 (1990), 269–334.

Part I

PROLOGUE

꧁꧂

'Europe', claimed Simone de Beauvoir in the memoirs which she published in 1963, was a myth, used by the United States as it sought to restore the power of Germany as a counterweight to that of the USSR.[1] Over the last two decades or so, historians, drawing on works from the 1960s and beyond, have investigated the European myth and the uses to which it has been put, in part to redirect attention from the 'founding fathers' of the European Communities to the wider cultural, intellectual, political and diplomatic context in which so-called founders lived and worked.[2] Despite such studies, however, much of the literature on conceptions of Europe and on processes of European integration arguably relies too heavily on one – or more – of three propositions: first, that ideas of Europe – or a European identity – contain enduring elements and have 'origins' which can be identified and investigated; second, that there was an important historical shift – or a 'zero hour' – during or after the Second World War which made projects for Europe seem more realizable and significant, not necessarily to the exclusion of long-established ideas of Europe but at the expense of tradition 'as a legitimizing force'; and, third, that questions of identity and culture quickly became secondary during the postwar era, displaced by planning and technocracy in practice and by neo-functionalism in theory.[3] It is intended here, not to deny, but to qualify these propositions through an examination of the persistence of ideas and the relationship between ideas and policy making during the period of 'crisis' from 1917 to 1957.

Discussion of ideas in the public sphere affected the formulation of policy. As a comparison of the long nineteenth and short twentieth centuries makes plain, contemporaries were only likely to advocate greater cooperation between European states or, even, integration in certain spheres of state activity as a consequence of a specific set of beliefs about recent history, Europe's place in the world, economic prosperity, nationalism and the nation-state. To most prewar Europeans, such cooperation – not to mention integration – would have been unthinkable. Nevertheless, it is equally obvious that 'ideas', especially those articulated by intellectuals and publicists, rarely dictated political actions. Europe was an 'invention', in Gerard Delanty's formulation, in so far as it was 'constructed in a historical process', 'a historically fabricated reality of ever-changing forms and dynamics', yet it was also the product of history's 'divisions and frontiers, both internal and external', 'interpolated in concrete configurations of power and their geo-political complexes'.[4] 'Europe', as a construction of ideas, was subject to constant contestation and transformation, as different interested parties sought to adapt it to existing or perceived conditions – or to prevent its adaptation – for their own purposes. In such circumstances, the 'origins' or enduring elements of a putative European idea or identity – 'crystallisations', in Delanty's phrase – are less significant than shorter-term relationships between participants in public debates, politics and the making of public policy in given but changing conditions.[5] Individuals' motivations and actions are incomprehensible without reference to their assumptions, ideas and beliefs, but they are not to be understood merely as their corollary. Advocates and opponents of diverse projects for Europe appear to have had very different reasons for acting as they did as a result of varying national and political perspectives, traditions and interests, not least because any European project required the establishment of new practices and institutions, in conjunction with a shift away from existing levels and spheres of government. Actors had many motives for supporting, opposing or ignoring a particular conception of or project for Europe. Many of their motives appear to have been informed by ideas which had been debated in the public sphere. The following chapters examine the ways in which ideas, interests, motives, conditions and actions intersected. Chapters 1 and 2 show how policy-makers' actions in the 1920s, the late 1940s and the 1950s betrayed a profound sense of the purported crisis of Europe, which helps to explain why they attempted to achieve European cooperation in both periods at the same time as evincing a frequent disregard for the precise, often confusing, diagnoses and prognoses put forward by intellectuals. As is demonstrated in Chapter 3, there was a broad sense amongst intellectuals that Europe existed and that it was being eclipsed, but there was little agreement about what Europe consisted of and how it might be 'saved'.

Many earlier conceptions of and projects for Europe persisted after the Second World War.[6] Certainly, the French intellectual Julien Benda was not alone in maintaining that 'the war has exercised no influence either way on my ideas or on my conception as to the manner of expressing them.'[7] Intellectuals like Benda, Jean-Paul Sartre, Raymond Aron, André Malraux, Lucien Febvre, Jacques Maritain, Emmanuel Mounier, André Gide, François Mauriac, José Ortega y Gasset, Altiero Spinelli, Benedetto Croce, the Mann brothers, Max Horkheimer, Otto Kirchheimer, Carl Schmitt, Ernst Jünger, Karl Jaspers, Isaiah Berlin, Karl Popper, John Maynard Keynes, Friedrich Hayek and Arnold Toynbee were all active before and after 1945, as were the different schools of European Marxism, political Catholicism, liberalism, social democracy, and orthodox and renegade conservatism. Such movements and thinkers continued to countenance and disseminate heterogeneous views about the future of Europe, some of which influenced decision makers. In keeping with the tenor of contemporary commentary, the actions of such statesmen and politicians in both the interwar and postwar eras were largely defensive, reacting to the menace of extra-European powers such as the USSR and United States, and to conflict and a crisis of confidence in Europe itself after the First World War – facts which seemed to have been confirmed by the Second World War, the onset of the Cold War, and the shocking revelation of the Holocaust. The 'German question' and the Franco-German axis remained central to most European policy makers in both postwar periods, with even semi-detached British observers like General Hastings Lionel Ismay – Winston Churchill's chief military assistant in the Second World War and later Secretary General of NATO – admitting that the North Atlantic Treaty Organization was not merely designed to keep the United States in Europe and the USSR out, but also to keep Germany down.[8] Many European ministers continued to combine fear and hubris with regard to the wider world, with the British Foreign Office attempting to maintain a global role until the Suez crisis of 1956, and with the Quai d'Orsay attempting to rebuild its empire – including major campaigns and loss of life in Syria, Madagascar, Indo-China and Algeria – until the late 1950s. Such uncertainty about the role of European powers was similar in some respects to that of the 1920s. It helped to produce a bewildering array of prognoses for Europe's recovery in the late 1940s and 1950s, as in the 1920s, which often clashed with plans for the 'rescue' of individual nation-states and reconstruction of national economies, and which took place in tumultuous conditions, militating towards limited, predominantly economic reform on the European level rather than political or military integration.[9]

What is surprising, it could be held, is the precariousness of decisions for and against 'Europe' in the 1920s and early '30s, and in the late 1940s and early '50s. History, agreed the liberal, 'positivist' Austrian émigré Karl Popper and the ex-socialist, conservative-minded Spanish liberal José Ortega y Gasset, had no intrinsic direction.[10] What would happen in and to Europe was, as historians of the Cold War have begun to acknowledge, difficult to predict.[11] Chapters 1 and 2 show how nationalism, traditions of the state, globalism and the priorities of domestic politics continued to stand in the way of Europeanism, despite contemporaries' newly articulated and strong attachment to the continent against the backdrop of a continuing European crisis. They reveal the fragility and reversibility of instances and processes of European cooperation and integration during the aftermaths of both world wars. Chapter 3 examines intellectuals' conceptions of the crisis of Europe, as well as the flawed quest for origins and building blocks of identity on the part of historians of a 'European idea'. This section aims to contextualize common and competing ideas of Europe by relating them to other sets of political ideas, in the domestic and international spheres (Chapter 3), and by assessing their significance in the formulation and execution of policy (Chapters 1 and 2).

❧ **Notes**

1. S. de Beauvoir, *La force des choses* (Paris, 1963), 340.
2. Recent projects include R. Girault (ed.), *Identité et conscience européenne au XXᵉ siècle* (Paris, 1994); R. Frank (ed.), *Les identités européennes au XXᵉ siècle* (Paris, 2004); R. Girault and G. Bossuat (eds), *Europe brisée, Europe retrouvée. Nouvelles réflexions sur l'unité européenne au XXᵉ siècle* (Paris, 1994); R. Hudemann et al. (eds), *Europa im Blick der Historiker* (Munich, 1995); E. du Réau (ed.), *Europe des élites? Europe des peuples? La construction de l'espace européenne 1945–1960* (Paris, 1998); E. Bussière (ed.), *Europa. L'idée et l'identité européennes de l'antiquité grecque au XXᵉ siècle* (Anvers, 2001); H. Kaelble, *Europäer über Europa. Die Entstehung des europäischen Selbstverständnisses im 19. und 20. Jahrhundert* (Frankfurt, 2001); and G. Bossuat and G. Saunier (eds), *Inventer l'Europe. Histoire nouvelle des groupes d'influence et des acteurs de l'unité européenne* (Brussels, 2003). Foundational works include F. Chabod, *Storia dell'idea europa* (Bari, 1961), J.-B. Duroselle, *L'idée d'Europe dans l'histoire* (Paris, 1965), G. Barraclough, *European Unity in Thought and Practice* (Oxford, 1963), and H. Brugmans, *L'idee européenne 1920–1970*, 3rd edn. (Bruges, 1970).
3. Recent investigations of origins and 'building blocks', some more critical than others, are H. Mikkeli, *Europe as an Idea and an Identity* (Basingstoke, 1998), 3–108; G. Delanty, *Inventing Europe: Idea, Identity, Reality* (Basingstoke, 1995), 16–129; K. Wilson and J. van der Dussen (eds), *The History of the Idea of Europe* (London, 1993), 13–82; A. Pagden, *The Idea of Europe: From Antiquity to the European Union* (Cambridge, 2002), 1–32; R. Girault, 'Das Europa der Historiker', in Hudemann (ed.), *Europa im Blick der Historiker*, 55–90; E. du Réau, *La construction européenne au XXᵉ siècle. Fondements, enjeux, defies* (Nantes, 2007), 15–32; and idem, *L'idée d'Europe au XXᵉ siècle. Des mythes aux réalités* (Brussels, 1996), 17–70. The quotation about tradition losing its legitimizing force comes from Ole Waever, 'Europe since 1945: Crisis to Renewal', in Wilson and van der Dussen (eds), *History of the Idea of Europe*, 152. Other works emphasizing a historical shift around 1945 are W. Lipgens, *A History of European Integration, 1945–1947* (Oxford, 1982), idem, *Die Anfänge der europäischen Einigungspolitik 1945–1950* (Stuttgart, 1977), and idem, *Europa-Föderationspläne der Widerstandsbewegungen 1940–1945* (Munich, 1968), notwithstanding his studies of the 1920s and 30s; D.W. Urwin, *The Community of Europe: A History of European Integration since 1945* (London, 1991); A. Bachoud, J. Cuesta and M. Trebitsch (eds), *Les intellectuals et l'Europe de 1945 à nos jours* (Paris, 2000). Elisabeth du Réau makes the point about continuities from the 1920s and early '30s to the late '40s and early '50s in *L'idée d'Europe*, 72; see also idem, *L'Europe en construction. Le second vingtième siècle*, 2nd edn. (Paris, 2007). For more on neo-functionalist theories of European integration, see A. Wiener and T. Diez, *European Integration Theory* (2003) and B. Rosamond, *Theories of European Integration* (2000).
4. Delanty, *Inventing Europe*, 3.
5. Ibid., 13.
6. On the institutional continuity of a French-sponsored, Eurocentric core of world 'culture' and 'patrimony', joining the IICI and UNESCO, both based in Paris, see Chapter 11.
7. Cited in R. Nichols, *Treason, Tradition and the Intellectual: Julien Benda and Political Discourse* (Lawrence, 1978), 155.
8. See A. Deighton, *The Impossible Peace: Britain, the Division of Germany, and the Origins of the Cold War* (Oxford, 1990). More generally, D. Calleo, *The German Problem Reconsidered* (Oxford, 1978).
9. A. Milward, *The European Rescue of the Nation-State* (London, 1992). The view expressed here is, of course, highly contested.
10. See, for instance, Andrew Shearmur's commentary on Popper's *The Poverty of Historicism* (1957) in *The Political Thought of Karl Popper* (London, 1996), 41–43; also, H.C. Raley, *José Ortega y Gasset: Philosopher of European Unity* (Alabama, 1971), 11; R. Gray, *The Imperative of Modernity: An Intellectual Biography of Ortega y Gasset* (Berkeley, 1989); and A. Dobson, *An Introduction to the Politics and Philosophy of José Ortega y Gasset* (Cambridge, 1989).
11. Especially David Reynolds (ed.), *The Origins of the Cold War in Europe* (New Haven, 1994); idem, *From World War to Cold War* (Oxford, 2006); and idem, *One World Divisible* (London, 2000).

Chapter 1

THE UNITED STATES OF EUROPE

The European Question in the 1920s

✹

Mark Hewitson

The fact that attempts at European 'integration' and 'cooperation' failed during the interwar era and succeeded in the postwar years has tended to obscure important similarities between the two periods and has led, it could be argued, to an over-estimation of the role of movements and ideas in the 1920s and early '30s, and an under-estimation of the significance of ideas after 1945.[1] The cultural assumptions and political utopianism of the Pan-European and other movements founded in the 1920s, combined with the exacerbation of nationalism and the inadequacy of the states' system, seemed to have impeded integration, with Aristide Briand's plan for a European Union, presented to the Assembly of the League of Nations in Geneva on 5 September 1929, appearing to be at once an isolated incident and a rare translation of such utopianism into the realm of high politics. 'It is partly in reaction to the ideology of "Europeanism" in the interwar era that actions in favour of European unity came about in the aftermath of the Second World War', contends Jean-Luc Chabot, one of a number of scholars who have sought to excavate and reevaluate the legacies of the interwar years: 'Drawing their lessons from the relative failure of the intellectualism of the European current prior to 1939, and benefiting equally from the self-destruction of nationalism in a totalitarian guise with the end of the second global conflict, the movements for the unity of Europe took, with Jean Monnet, paths which were mindful of the efficacy of neo-liberal technocracy.'[2] The implication of such interpretations is that an unrealistic championing of diverse ideas of Europe by the different movements during the 1920s and 1930s helped to prevent integration, and the jettisoning of 'intellectualism' by both movements and policy makers after the Second World War helped to promote it. Part of the case for contrasting the two periods – before and after the Second World War – rests on the proven failure of the European movements of the interwar years either to agree on a realistic programme of European cooperation or to convince governments to carry out their ideas.[3] Another part of the case hinges on the inability of the different governments either to impose their will on their neighbours – especially in respect of France, which had occupied the Ruhr in 1923 and had stood down in 1925 – or to overcome national rivalries and long-standing hostilities in order to achieve a degree of economic and political cooperation.[4] However, it could be proposed that certain policy makers were affected by a much broader discussion of 'Europe' and continental cooperation after the First World War, notwithstanding their reluctance openly to endorse a particular movement's point of view, and that such policy makers saw the need for a new European states' system – adumbrated by the Locarno Treaties' guarantee of western borders, signed by France, Germany and Belgium, and underwritten by Britain and Italy in 1925 – within which European cooperation could have occurred.[5] Here, I aim to reexamine these assumptions by concentrating on the relationship between the French and German governments – on which the chances of European cooperation depended – during the 1920s.[6]

By the 1930s, dictatorships outnumbered democracies on the Continent, leaving the Versailles 'system', including the League of Nations, apparently powerless to prevent Germany's remilitarization of the Rhineland, Italy's conquest of Abyssinia and the outbreak of the Spanish Civil War, all of which occurred in 1936.[7] The French writer Georges Duhamel summarized a common point of view before the Paris conference of *Le comité français de cooperation européenne*: 'An enormous, terrible silence has fallen on the genius of Europe. We have all had the impression that a European spirit has been struck by stupefaction, that the workers for a future Europe have been infinitely discouraged.'[8] After the Nazi seizure of power in 1933, there was little opportunity to unite Europe politically or economically. Even earlier, with Heinrich Brüning's nomination as Reich Chancellor in March 1930, Franco-German reconciliation – and therefore attempts at European cooperation – had been deprived of much of their impetus. The German government's response to Briand's memorandum about a European Union in May 1930 was privately hostile, with Bernhard Wilhelm von Bülow, who was about to take over as Secretary of State at the Foreign Office, accusing France of wanting 'to impose new fetters on us' and with the Chancellor suspecting the Quai d'Orsay of trying to restrict Germany's claim to 'sufficient natural living space'.[9] Robert Curtius, the new Minister of Foreign Affairs was more cautious, but he was urged by the cabinet to give the memorandum 'a first-class burial'.[10] By April 1931, Bülow had decided to conclude a German–Austrian customs union, which eventually came to nothing, rather than pursue a European customs union founded on an agreement between France and Germany.[11] In effect, the Brüning government had decided to bring the Locarno era of Gustav Stresemann to an end. French elites and public opinion subsequently lost hope in a European solution to the German question.[12]

European Rhetoric and a European Order

The relationship between France and Germany was pivotal in the 1920s to the success or failure of European cooperation, as Heinrich Mann, amongst others, pointed out.[13] It existed, of course, within the structure of the League of Nations, which Germany eventually entered in 1926, within a tangle of bilateral arrangements between France, Belgium, the Netherlands and the new states of Central and Eastern Europe – and between Germany and the Soviet Union (Treaty of Rapallo, 1922) – and within parameters which were set by the United States and the United Kingdom, both of which were reluctant to enforce the payment of reparations or to broker agreements between continental states. As could be expected, neither French nor German statesmen or diplomats aimed – at least until Briand proposed a European Union in 1929 – for the establishment of specifically European organizations or the achievement of 'European' cooperation, but they did couch their attempts at Franco-German rapprochement in European terms. Thus, Gustav Stresemann, who had briefly been Chancellor between August and November 1923 during the later stages of the Ruhr crisis and who was Minister of Foreign Affairs between 1923 and 1929, referred to 'Europe' in speeches to both nationalist audiences and more progressive ones.[14] The most notorious instance of the former, to the representatives of lost or dismembered frontier regions on 14 December 1925, made it clear that, although 'nations are always egoists', the Foreign Minister was 'not thinking of war in relation to the eastern question either, where the right of self-determination has been violated in an unheard-of way', but he was thinking of exploiting widely agreed menaces to European stability and prosperity for Germany's advantage:

> What I imagine is that if conditions once arise which appear to threaten the peace or the economic consolidation of Europe through developments in the east, and if the question arises as to whether the whole instability of Europe is not caused by the impossible way the frontiers are drawn in the east, then it may also be possible for Germany to succeed with its demands, if it has previously established ties of political friendship and an economic community of interest with all the world powers who have to decide the issue. In my opinion, this is the only practical policy.[15]

In the most famous example of the latter, progressive discourse – a rare speech by Stresemann about the international system at the University of Heidelberg on 5 May 1928 – the minister insisted that the task 'for international politics and especially for German policy' was a 'double' one: 'the securing of a free Germany with equal rights and the inclusion of such a Germany together with all other states in a stable international structure'.[16] Attitudes to war had changed, with the shift from the caste-based, standing armies of Frederick the Great to the conscript armies of the First World War, and interstate relations had altered, in line with the transformation of the social basis of states and the introduction of ideological conflict from the French Revolution onwards. Stresemann continued that whereas

Otto von Bismarck had understood such transformations, exercising moderation in his conduct of power politics in order to construct a peaceful international order, his successors had failed to understand the same lesson, permitting a 'system of international anarchy … of alliances and counter-alliances' and allowing Europe 'to tear itself apart' in 1914.[17] Stresemann's hope after 1919 was not to abandon the 'ruthless application of the principle of national power', since a majority of Germans and the French government – as it demonstrated with the occupation of the Ruhr in 1923 – seemed unwilling to accept such a change of course, but to 'create a system of international understanding based on equal rights', given that most Europeans desired peace and that 'a new conflagration would deliver our continent to utter ruin as a result of the horrifying escalation of the technology of destruction'.[18] Like many contemporary commentators, the German Minister of Foreign Affairs – arguably the most important decision maker of the 1920s – saw the need to reconfigure the critical European part of the postwar international order because of the conceptual and actual changes wrought by the First World War.

Much of the Quai d'Orsay agreed with Stresemann's aims, together with many French politicians and important sections of public opinion in France. 'It is almost as if an outstanding French statesman has died, the grief here is so general and sincere', reported Harry Kessler, a long-time resident of Paris, on 4 October 1929, after the announcement of the German minister's death: 'The French feel Stresemann to have been a sort of European Bismarck. A legend is in the making – by his sudden death Stresemann has become an almost mythical personality … He is the first to be admitted to Valhalla as a genuine European statesman.'[19] In the secondary literature, French policy makers have been criticized for attempting – inconsistently – to conciliate the *Wilhelmstrasse* instead of capitalizing on Germany's temporary weakness to impose France's 'coal and steel project' and to prevent its neighbour's future 'hegemony' (Jacques Bariéty), to separate the Rhineland from the Reich in order to create parity between the two powers and to prepare the ground for Western European economic integration (Walter McDougall), or to put France's public finances on a surer footing by redistributing the fiscal burden at home in order to free the Quai d'Orsay of the counsel of London and Washington, which were prepared to use their financial leverage – forcing France to accept lower German reparations payments in the Dawes Plan (1924), for example – on Germany's behalf (Stephen Schuker).[20] Paris, it is held, followed three potentially contradictory policies, endeavouring – in vain – to maintain Allied solidarity, to neutralize the Rhineland or sever it from Germany, and to pursue Franco-German reconciliation.[21]

In fact, though, the most influential members of the Ministry of Foreign Affairs – Philippe Berthelot, the Secretary General, Jacques Seydoux, the head of Commercial Relations, and Jules Laroche, the Director of Political and Commercial Affairs – were working towards a rapprochement between Paris and Berlin from 1923 onwards, during and after the occupation of the Ruhr, in the belief that it could be combined, as Seydoux made plain, with a shift in British foreign policy, as London abandoned its predilection for a balance of power, favouring a German counterweight to France as the greatest mainland power. London thus became more amenable to a policy of European reconstruction, especially under an anticipated Labour government: a Franco-British entente could 'be established and England will then abandon its habit of perpetually grouping all of the scattered forces in Europe against France, on the condition that France itself ceases any action which gives credence to the view that we are pursuing a policy of encirclement or dislocation of Germany'.[22] Laroche had made the same points in his memorandum, 'Propositions Concerning the Peace to be Made with Germany', on 8 March 1923:

> I feel that the Germans will give in before the end of April. This will be the critical moment. We must remember 1918 and not bungle the armistice and especially not the future accord, which should contain all the necessary guarantees, but also should be really enforceable and should foster the resumption of normal relations with Germany ... we need a conqueror's peace, but one from which peace follows and which no longer nourishes the excitement of fanatics. At the same time, we must re-establish relations with England, for we must not lose sight, alas, of the fact that our very low birth rate is a terrible danger for the future if we remain isolated and confronted with a Germany thirsting for vengeance.[23]

Despite his earlier struggle during the First World War 'to bring about victory through the economic encirclement of Germany', ignoring the crippling disease of rheumatoid arthritis from which he suffered, Seydoux had come by the early 1920s to see the necessity of coming to an agreement with Berlin, even at the cost of revealing to Poland 'that we will not support it to the bitter end'.[24] According to the French ambassador in Berlin in 1924, Paris had repeatedly received 'complete guarantees against military aggression as regards France' and had been told by the *Wilhelmstrasse* that Germany would not attack Poland, which had prompted Seydoux in February 1925 to offer Warsaw and Prague arbitration by the League of Nations 'as the most that we can promise' on the question of the Reich's eastern borders.[25] The Locarno Treaties, which resulted from such deliberations, should – in the view of the Quai d'Orsay – 'not only be a consecration of the [Versailles] treaty, but while referring to it, should go beyond it and be something new', for 'one will only construct something new if, in some way, Germany finds some advantage in it', which had been achieved for reparations 'through the Dawes Plan' and which could now be done 'for security'.[26] French diplomats were willing in the 1920s to give up the precise terms of Versailles, if not its symbolism of victory, in order to come to a workable agreement with Germany.

Most French ministers seem to have been ready to do the same, notwithstanding the charge made at the time and since that the Radical Socialist Edouard Herriot, the Président du Conseil and Minister of Foreign Affairs between June 1924 and April 1925, squandered the position that France had gained after Raymond Poincaré's decision to occupy the Ruhr in January 1923.[27] The former socialist and wartime nationalist Alexandre Millerand, who was Président du Conseil and Minister of Foreign Affairs in 1920 before becoming Président de la République

International Frontiers, *c.*1926

International Frontiers, 1914

Rhineland Zone under Allied
Occupation after 1919

1. Saar Plebiscite Area (under
   League of Nations, 1919–35

2. Limit of Rhineland Demilita-
   rized Zone after 1919

3. Danzig Free City

4. Memel Territory
   (to Lithuania, 1923)

5. Klagenfurt Territory
   (to Austria, 1920)

6. Burgenland Territory
   (to Austria, 1921)

7. Fiume Free State (1920–4)

Map 1.1. European territorial changes after 1918. Source: David Stevenson, *The First World War and International Politics* (Oxford, 1988), 264–65.

between 1920 and 1924, had already conceded immediately after the Paris Peace Conference that the literal execution of the Versailles Treaty would be impossible and that some sort of *modus vivendi* would, therefore, have to be found which was more acceptable to Germany.[28] In spite of his hard-line reputation, Poincaré, the right-wing Président du Conseil from 1922 to 1924, continued this policy, engaging in protracted talks with Berlin and London before finally ordering the occupation of the Ruhr, after deliberate German defaults on the delivery of timber reparations and the thirty-fourth default on the delivery of coal in thirty-six months. Even then, having achieved Stresemann's renunciation of passive resistance in September 1923, the French premier, who wanted to restore financial stability and to maintain legality, handed over the question of German repayments to the Reparations Commission and to what became the Dawes Committee in the full knowledge that they would seek to mediate between Paris and Berlin rather than pressing home France's advantage.[29] In his second period of office as Président du Conseil between 1926 and 1929, in conjunction with Briand as his Minister of Foreign Affairs (1926–32), Poincaré was said, as the Quai d'Orsay pointed out to London, Berlin and Brussels, to have mellowed, endorsing Briand's meeting with Stresemann at Thoiry on 17 September 1926, at which the two foreign ministers had discussed the possibility of the return of the Saarland to Germany, the disbanding of the Inter-Allied Military Control Commission charged with inspecting German factories and the *Reichswehr*, the opening of negotiations with Belgium about the return of Eupen-Malmédy, and the ending of the Allied military occupation of Germany.[30] All such points of discussion, which Briand later – under pressure from critics in the National Assembly – stressed had not been definitively agreed, were designed to conciliate Germany and tie it to a French-led security and economic settlement in Europe.[31] In this sense, Briand and his premier Poincaré, whom the Foreign Minister was sure he could win over, were close to Herriot, who argued in his treatise on *The United States of Europe* (1930) that big business was already 'being led by an irresistible movement towards a system of agreements' on a European level and that 'if Germany is prevented from resolving' the problem – created by the Versailles Treaty – of its eastern borders through arbitration and 'in a peaceable way, it will be resolved by arms'.[32] Like many French intellectuals and businessmen, the majority of leading French politicians concurred by the late 1920s, at least in private, that Germany should be connected more closely to France, even if this implied a modification of the Treaty of Versailles.[33]

An Economic Union

Behind French ministers' desire for a rapprochement with Germany were complicated negotiations concerning France's economy and currency.[34] The need to strengthen the franc had been connected from the start to the question of German reparations, with French policy makers preferring to capitalize the Reich's

future payments through the floating of reparation bonds, which could be sold to
the City of London and Wall Street in order to create liquidity in France, and in
Europe generally. Such plans were undermined by the postwar instability of the
German Reichsmark during the period of inflation and hyperinflation between
1919 and 1924, destroying the prospect of regular returns on any bond issue and
pushing French governments to demand actual assets – state railways, mines and
forests in the Saar, Rhineland and Ruhr – or specific tax revenues in advance.[35]
The failure of the Reich government to make such deliveries triggered Poincaré's
decision to occupy the Ruhr in 1923, which in turn helped to aggravate the
collapse of the franc from 5 francs to a dollar before 1914, to 15 in May 1924,
when the Cartel des Gauches won the elections, to 25 by November 1925, and to
36 by the end of June 1926. In these circumstances, the radical Minister of
Finances, Joseph Caillaux, took up the offer of the Wall Street firm Dillon, Read
and Company to supply an $800-million loan in return for the capitalization of
reparations, at the same time as asking the Chamber of Deputies for permission to
rule by decree in order to tackle the financial crisis. When the chamber rejected
the request, the franc sank to 49.2 to the dollar and the left-wing government of
Herriot was replaced in July 1926 by the National Union government of Poincaré,
which stabilized the currency. Backed by the Président du Conseil, Briand raised
the question with Stresemann of a German capitalization of reparations, in return
for an early end to the Allied occupation of Germany, only three months later at
Thoiry, because the perceived problems of the French economy remained the
same: a weak currency and inadequate tax base, making France dependent on
American loans; a lack of iron, steel, coal and, especially, coke, which was believed
by policy makers to be crucial in the smelting process; and a long-standing fear of
French economic decline and German industrial hegemony in Continental
Europe. Such reasoning prompted Briand to support the Young Plan in August
1929, which partially capitalized reparations and terminated the military
occupation of Germany, and it underpinned his plan for a European Union, which
he elaborated in the memorandum of May 1930. Arguably, a belief in some form
of Franco-German economic cooperation within a European framework, although
differing in detail, dated back to the plans of Etienne Clémentel, the Minister of
Commerce between 1915 and 1919, for a 'new economic order' in Europe, with
guaranteed supplies of German raw materials to France, and it extended to the
period after 1945, when the same difficulties of purported industrial backwardness,
shortages of capital, and a lack of coal resurfaced.[36]

The Ministry of Foreign Affairs granted economics precedence over security
from the early 1920s onwards. The policy was opposed by the military, which
gave support to the separation of the Rhineland from Germany and to what
Marshal Ferdinand Foch, the supreme commander of the Allied armies at the end
of the First World War, termed – in 1925 – the 'surrounding' of Germany with a
strong network of alliances and a refusal 'to let anyone tamper even an iota with
the Treaty of Versailles'.[37] Some ministers, such as the Minister of Finance between
1922 and 1924 Charles de Lasteyrie du Saillant, believed as a consequence that 'a

certain opposition between the two aims pursued by France' – 'on the one hand to be paid and on the other to assure its security' – had emerged, yet few of their colleagues in the Quai d'Orsay appear to have been convinced by their arguments.[38] It was much more common in the Ministry of Foreign Affairs to assume that the Treaty of Versailles, in dismantling the Ottoman, Habsburg, Russian and German empires, had led to what Seydoux implied was an unsustainable 'fragmentation of states' and to the alienation of most parties, even the democratic and republican ones, in Germany, which had left much of Eastern Europe in an exposed position between a revisionist German state and the unknown quantity – outside the League of Nations – of the Soviet Union.[39]

From this point of view, an economic agreement with Germany would bring in its train better diplomatic relations between Paris and Berlin, securing the position of France's eastern European allies, even though their borders, which had been defined by the Paris Peace Conference, would be subject to arbitration by the League of Nations. In autumn 1926, Seydoux wrote:

> I know that our smaller allies in the East are rather disturbed by what has happened in Geneva and at Thoiry. If there is Franco-German collaboration, and the signature of the steel cartel is one of the most important indicators, this means that we will talk to Germany before we act, that we will come to agreement with her, that we will do nothing against her. This radically changes our attitude to the countries on which our policy has until now relied. Basically it is a question of a complete reversal, one which should lead to peace much more surely than the old policy.[40]

The continuing loyalty of Poland and Czechoslovakia was worth risking, Seydoux hinted, for the greater goods of guaranteed western borders at Locarno, a reliable 'reparations settlement', which alone would 'give Europe the possibility of working in peace and recovering the strength which it lost in the war', and the broader financial reconstruction of Europe, which would provide France with foreign loans and restore the franc in exchange for the reestablishment of parity between Paris and Berlin, with the former no longer dealing 'with Germany as conqueror to conquered'.[41] Economic reconciliation between France and Germany would allow the rewriting of European history, the diplomat continued in a memorandum of February 1925:

> We should remind ourselves of the advantages, from which all of Europe benefited, from France's accession to the Holy Alliance, after the treaties of 1815; if after the Treaty of Frankfurt, Germany had come to an arrangement with France which the latter could accept and if the question of Alsace-Lorraine had been settled without war between the two countries, the whole history of modern Europe would have turned out differently. What we all want in Europe is peace: to succeed at making peace, we must put Germany back into circulation, bring it into the League of Nations and search for ... 'a formula which will allow Germany to find its equilibrium in Europe and to pursue, in concert with the Allies, the work of economic and financial reconstruction which, alone, will allow the binding up of the wounds of war and the

avoidance of new conflicts' … All in all, we must take Germany at its word. If we fail, the fault will be Germany's, not ours, and there will be time to revert to a sort of League of Allies which will result in the creation of an iron ring around Germany, which would set the two parts of Europe against each other yet again and would inevitably be shattered by violence.[42]

Briand's plan for a European Union, although also reflecting his own evolving political priorities, constituted the continuation of a well-entrenched diplomatic strategy during the 1920s. Since raising the question of the capitalization of reparations in his Thoiry meeting with Stresemann in September 1926, the former socialist Minister of Foreign Affairs had promoted the economic reconciliation of France and Germany, building on the successful negotiation in 1926 of the International Steel Cartel between France, Germany and Luxembourg, which was initiated by the pro-European manufacturer and founder of the Franco-German Study Committee, Emile Mayrisch, extending the scope of the Franco-German trade treaty signed in 1927, and supporting the ongoing efforts of the entrepreneur and ex-minister Louis Loucheur, who had presented a plan for the cross-border sectoral cooperation of industry and the eventual creation of a customs union to the League of Nations in September 1925.[43] For Loucheur, speaking at the League in May 1927, it was likely that cooperation had to proceed 'following the so-called horizontal method' – 'that is, by industry' – but this would subsequently 'allow the creation of the necessary profound transformations' and would 'resolve, in part, the question of tariff barriers' and 'present the possibility of a parallel and simultaneous raising of salaries, in order to return to postwar Europe the power of consumption of prewar Europe'.[44] Despite tensions between different lobbies wishing, respectively, to prioritize the concentration of industry, to form a customs union and to reconstruct the financial structure of postwar Europe, many commentators, industrialists, financiers, officials and ministers in France and elsewhere assumed that such objectives complemented rather than contradicted each other.

Accordingly, the economic section of Briand's memorandum of May 1930 emphasized 'the possibilities of an expansion of the economic market, attempts at the intensification and improvement of industrial production and, in the same way, all possible guarantees against crises of work, sources of political as well as social instability', echoing the expectation of the President of the Chambre de commerce internationale that 'a European commercial league would constitute a free internal market of a fertility at least the equal of that of the United States and its production could then compete with that of this vast country of commercial exchanges on equal terms'.[45] Initially, in his speech introducing the project of a 'United States of Europe' to the Assembly of the League of Nations in September 1929, Briand had been unequivocal in asserting that 'the association will act chiefly in the economic domain: it is the most pressing question'.[46] He also mentioned an accompanying European political apparatus, vaguely alluding to 'a sort of federal link', which recalled his reference to a 'kind of European federation' in a private conversation with Stresemann a few months earlier, but also reassuring his listeners that no participating state would lose its sovereignty.[47] His broad aim, the French minister had explained to a journalist travelling with him to Geneva, was to offset France's military concessions by reinforcing the legitimacy of interstate commitments in Europe and the League of Nations: 'We must use the moment when France is giving up military positions to secure ourselves moral positions. Despite everything I will launch the United States of Europe. Now or never is the moment to give the institutions of the League of Nations a new impulse, to awaken a movement of general enthusiasm. Otherwise, everything is finished.'[48] France was offering to modify the 'Versailles system', reconfiguring its alliances in Central and Eastern Europe and renegotiating reparations and the Allies' military occupation of Germany. In return, Briand expected the Reich to act cooperatively in the emerging European core of a reinforced League of Nations.

By the time that Briand put forward his 'Memorandum on the Organization of a Regime of European Federal Union' to the League of Nations in May 1930, he gave a much fuller description of the institutions of the union and spelled out 'the necessary subordination of the economic to the political', after lobbying by other states and in response to Stresemann's call for a clarification of the political ideas in the plan.[49] As on the occasion of his speech to the League in September 1929, when he had expressed disappointment that Stresemann had only welcomed the economic aspects of his project, Briand was seeking to ensure that the new powers being granted to Germany were counterbalanced by binding political commitments. 'The contrary order would not only be useless,' the memorandum stated, 'it would appear to the weaker nations to be likely to expose them, without guarantees or compensation, to the risks of political domination which might result from an industrial domination of the more strongly organised states.'[50] The political machinery envisaged was intergovernmental in form and similar to that of the League of Nations, with a European Conference of government representatives serving as the 'essential directing organ of the European union' and a Political Committee made up 'of only a certain number of members' maintaining continuity between the meetings of the conference.[51] 'The federal tie, without touching the sovereignty of any of the nations which could make up such an association, can be beneficial,' the memorandum went on, permitting 'the possibility, at any moment, of entering into contact' with other European powers, of making 'common resolutions' and of taking 'collective responsibility in the face of a danger threatening European peace'.[52] Gradually, Briand anticipated, a European system of arbitration and security was likely to develop, but the spread of individual agreements akin to the Locarno Treaties would have to suffice until that date. The French Foreign Minister's emphasis throughout was on the establishment of a confederal structure of states – the term 'federal' continued to have diverse connotations – to bind Germany to its neighbours and to ward off future diplomatic crises and conflicts in Europe, at the same time as concentrating industrial production, rationalizing currencies and flows of capital, and creating a larger, tariff-free market on the continent in order to counter the effects of the

Great Depression. The project can be seen as an extension of the Quai d'Orsay's policy of Franco-German reconciliation, economic cooperation and multilateral security arrangements under the auspices of the League of Nations prior to 1930. In common with many intellectuals and publicists, Briand aimed, as Austen Chamberlain put it, 'to raise a new temple of peace' from the 'blood-soaked ruins of the past'.[53]

The Structure of a European Community

The German government accepted much of Briand's initiative, just as it had proved receptive to previous advances, notwithstanding its reservations about any attempt to sanction the Reich's existing eastern borders. Stresemann's response on 9 September 1929 welcomed Briand's project as 'a great idea' which – like other great ideas – might seem 'crazy at first'.[54] He rejected the scepticism of 'pessimists in principle' and criticized proponents of autarky and protectionism vis-à-vis the rest of the world.[55] The European economy was excessively fragmented, akin to Italy before unification or Germany before the *Zollverein* and made worse by the Treaty of Versailles, he continued: 'Where is the European currency, the European postage stamp?'[56] Economic integration would improve Europe's ability to resist U.S. penetration and strengthen the position of European statesmen in negotiations. The economy and the conquest of nature would better occupy the continent's youth than dreams of a future war, in which technology would produce slaughter not heroism. The Locarno Treaties and other similar endeavours were designed to foster greater international understanding and avert conflict, Stresemann suggested. Such German support went back to the Genoa Conference in 1922, which had mooted the eventual formation of a European customs union and which had rejected a Central European bloc in favour of 'European free trade'.[57] It also recalled Berlin's backing of Loucheur's plan in 1925, urged on by most German unions, many politicians – especially SPD deputies – and much of German business, and the government's hailing of the Franco-German trade treaty of 17 August 1927 as a 'European event'.[58] Although Stresemann was principally interested in Germany's national interests, as leader of the Deutsche Volkspartei (DVP) and a prominent advocate of the war effort prior to 1918, he had long been interested in economic integration in Europe, as a former spokesman of German big business. As he put it in a newspaper article in 1925, he was looking beyond the imminent security pacts of Locarno to the development of an 'economic understanding between the great industrial nations of Europe and beyond that something like the structure of a European community, in comparison to the present system which has created a Europe reminiscent of the old Germany with its dozens of states and customs barriers'.[59] As after the Second World War, Germany – with its supply of critical raw materials (coke), its high technology industries (electricity, chemicals, transport) and its manufacture of machines and consumer goods – seemed to have much to gain from the concentration of industry, the negotiation of production quotas, the creation of liquidity and the lowering of tariffs within an emerging customs union.

Germany's strategic objectives did not clash with its economic interests, contended Stresemann, following a policy of peaceful revision inaugurated by Walther Rathenau, the liberal Minister of Reconstruction and Foreign Affairs (1921–22), Joseph Wirth, the Centre Party Chancellor (1921–22), and Matthias Erzberger, the Centre Party leader and Finance Minister (1919–20) who had argued for the signature of the Treaty of Versailles. Stresemann had been close enough to the centre of power in 1918 to witness the General Staff's disastrous overestimation of German strength. As he informed Crown Prince Wilhelm privately on 7 September 1925, in a letter which also promised the reemergence of Germany as a Great Power, the protection of German minorities abroad, the correction of Germany's eastern frontiers and a possible future union with Austria, the Foreign Minister remained adamant that he had little choice but to sign the Treaty of Locarno, since the Reich was too weak to be a credible ally – potentially in opposition to France – for the United Kingdom and too ideologically distant from the USSR to allow itself 'the utopia of flirting with Bolshevism', which would 'be quite content to have bolshevized Europe as far as the Elbe', leaving 'the rest of Germany to be devoured by the French'.[60] To Stresemann, after the experiences of the First World War, it was evident that another conflict would destroy Europe, especially Germany as its geographical centre, and would cause the collapse of Weimar's experiment in parliamentary democracy.[61] In these circumstances, the League of Nations and Locarno could constitute not merely a necessity for Germany, but a welcome shift away from the old – implicitly anti-German – states' system in Europe, as the Minister of Foreign Affairs explained to the DVP *Parteitag* on 2 October 1926, immediately after his meeting with Briand at Thoiry:

> Whatever one's private opinion about the general ideas of the League of Nations and its historical significance, it would be an act of stupidity not to recognize what a great political reality the Geneva institution embodies. An international forum has been created in Geneva which has great effects because of the very existence of its constantly prepared apparatus ... I am of the view that international life really needs new forms and is searching for new forms, and that, in Geneva, there is at least a worthwhile starting-point for such endeavours ... For me, the League of Nations is not only an aid, grasped for opportunistic reasons, for the promotion of the momentary, individual tasks of our diplomacy, and I can only hope that, in Germany, there is more and more recognition of the fact that the League of Nations embodies the very idea on whose realization the political future of Europe depends – that is, the idea of a policy of reasonable understanding and conciliation.[62]

Stresemann managed to convince the parties participating in or backing the coalition governments of Hans Luther (1925–26), Wilhelm Marx (1923–25, 1926–28) and Hermann Müller (1928–30) – the Centre Party, German Democratic Party (DDP), the DVP, the Bavarian People's Party and the SPD – of the reality of the new 'Locarno' system in Europe. Only the conservative German National

People's Party (DNVP) – 'these donkeys', in the Foreign Minister's phrase – refused, resigning from Luther's first government in October 1925 because of the signature of the Locarno Treaties.[63] As late as October 1929, in the midst of the Depression and agitation against the Young Plan, the DVP was still warning its voters that there was no alternative to 'a policy of understanding', which 'was, is and remains dependent on the recognition of the growing importance of common interests': given that all the new states created by the Treaty of Versailles contained German minorities, there was no chance of returning to the pre-1914 status quo without a 'conflict against the whole world'; since Germany had not 'rearmed', 'the possibilities of German policy are therefore limited'.[64]

For its part, the German Foreign Office, under the stewardship of the forty-two-year-old Carl von Schubert as Secretary of State, backed the Reich's new course and the Locarno system as 'the only policy opening the way to freedom' and the policy 'which had recreated a diplomatic position in the world for us'.[65] By 1926, after Germany's entry into the League of Nations, Stresemann and his officials had been let into the inner chamber of European high politics, attending a series of private meetings with Briand and Austen Chamberlain, the British Foreign Secretary. These so-called 'Geneva tea parties', of which the meeting at a restaurant in Thoiry – a French village just across the Swiss border – was the most famous, were attacked at the time – as they have been since – for their unnecessary secrecy, but they nevertheless allowed the leaders of historically hostile states to come to trust each other and to make Franco-German reconciliation the centrepiece of attempts at European cooperation.[66]

As Peter Krüger rightly points out, the Locarno system of European security, which Briand's project for a European Union (1929–30) sought to extend, was threatened and undermined largely by internal conditions, disputes about domestic policy, electoral shifts and changes of government between 1930 and 1933 within Germany itself, all of which had relatively little to do with foreign policy, despite the recurring question of 'revision'.[67] Thus, even after the accession of Brüning's right-wing government to office in March 1930, Curtius and the Foreign Office began to waver in their response to Briand's memorandum during the summer, when the Reich's ambassadors – especially Leopold von Hoesch in Paris, who had previously urged resistance against France's occupation of the Ruhr in 1923 – reported that the French Minister of Foreign Affairs was not committed to existing borders in the East or to the precedence of political over economic affairs, but merely wanted to treat them in conjunction with each other rather than handing them over entirely to experts.[68] Curtius's hesitation, in the face of his Chancellor's expressed desire to bury Briand's project, betrayed the extent to which the Locarno system, economic cooperation and a rhetoric of Europeanism had been accepted by significant political constituencies, commanding a majority of the vote until at least 1930, in Weimar Germany and elsewhere.

Clouding Curtius's judgement in 1930, as he decided whether or not to reject Briand's plan, was the worrying fact that the majority of European governments and significant sections of public opinion had already expressed support for the project. According to the German embassies there, both the press and the governments of Poland, Czechoslovakia, Estonia, Latvia, Lithuania, Romania and Yugoslavia – the new states created, or refashioned, by Versailles and allied to France – were almost wholly in favour of Briand's memorandum.[69] There was a similar reaction in the neutral states of Scandinavia, which saw the memorandum, in the words of one diplomat, as 'proof of the depth of the feeling that a way must be found of escaping the disputes which hinder the progress of Europe'.[70] The Austrian and Belgian governments, although mindful of the position of Berlin, supported the project, with Brussels, like The Hague, reiterating its unwillingness to subordinate economic cooperation to security.[71] Turkey, too, voiced its desire to enter Briand's union. Only the supposed 'victims' of the settlement of 1919–20 – Bulgaria, Hungary and Italy – clearly opposed the French proposal. The British press was divided, with *The Times* and *Daily Express* praising the attempt to create a new, more successful order in Europe, although discounting the possibility of the United Kingdom's participation, and most other newspapers opposing the idea as a potential threat to British interests. The new Labour government of Ramsay MacDonald, which had come to power in June 1929, was also hesitant, with the Foreign Office attempting to stoke up German opposition to the plan and the Treasury forcing the cabinet to tone down its initial approval: 'We ought surely to make it clear that we only accept the introduction of political influences in so far as they help to promote economic union, that we can't encourage any ideas of political union.'[72] Although eventually helping to consign Briand's memorandum to a League of Nations' committee for further study and procrastination, which was used by the German government as a means of burying the plan, the British government is unlikely, given its mixed response in 1930, to have rejected the project outright in the face of German, French and wider 'European' support.

London's response was ambiguous in part because much of British industry, many union leaders, sections of the press – including *The Economist*, whose editor Walter Layton wanted the United Kingdom to take up the cause of cooperation and avoid the 'Balkanization' of the European economy – and prominent Labour and Liberal politicians were in favour of a more integrated continental economy.[73] In the event, many businessmen and MPs, particularly those in the Conservative Party, came to prefer the consolidation of the British Empire as a trading bloc rather than the establishment of a British-led European market, but the decision was not straightforward, as the MP for Birmingham and later Tory leader Neville Chamberlain intimated: 'Alone the United States of America are vast enough, and contain sufficient resources within their own limits, to stand on their own feet, and to tower somewhat menacingly over smaller units.' 'It is the recognition of these facts, and the need for self-preservation, that has raised the idea of a United States of Europe, and has turned the eyes of the British Empire towards the old conception of an economic unity between its members,' he went on: 'We, in these islands, cannot stand by ourselves alone. If we do not think imperially, we shall have to think continentally.'[74] Most British observers in the 1920s seem to have believed that Europe would be consolidated economically, whether or not London took a lead, as the Liberal MP and leading industrialist Sir Alfred Mond told Conservative politicians in 1927, having just returned from a tour of European capitals: 'It was quite remarkable, and I should not have believed it had I not come so closely into contact with it. The idea that you must form some economic union of European countries, some form of joint action in industry … In taxation, in tariffs, and even further steps that, in order to enable Europe to go on existing against the Continent of North America, is becoming almost axiomatic, almost a passionate faith.'[75] Some contemporaries, such as the journalists of the *Manchester Guardian Commercial*, argued that London should forestall the creation of a European trading bloc, but even they tacitly acknowledged that it might come about.[76] Others used the creation of a European bloc in order to canvass support for a similarly consolidated imperial market and economy. Yet they, too, seemed to have assumed – or to be confident that they could seem to have assumed – that greater European cooperation would occur, not least because there was considerable support for it in influential sections of public opinion, business and government on the European mainland.

Conclusion

The balance of such calculations, and the decisions which rested on them, was – and remains – difficult to assess. While it is widely accepted that the various European organizations failed to gain close ties to government or to create a single, dominant current of opinion, despite acknowledgement during the 1920s by sceptics such as the British ambassador in Vienna that 'the movement has certainly made great strides', 'European' rhetoric, the idea of a European economy and a continental system of security, as long as they were not seen to be opposed to the United States or the League of Nations, appear to have had broad support. Certainly, Briand was able to claim by 1929, without fear of ridicule, that 'I know that I have the peoples behind me. European feeling is a current against which one can do nothing'.[77] Although few contemporaries of the French Minister of Foreign Affairs seem to have believed that such 'Europeanism' superseded or necessarily clashed with state sovereignty and national interests, most were convinced that Europe had been damaged by the First World War and was menaced by internal and external threats, precipitating and exacerbating different types of crisis during the 1920s. The laments and prophecies of intellectuals such as the Mann brothers, Paul Valéry, Carl Schmitt, Rudolf Pannwitz, Johan Huizinga and José Ortega y Gasset played a central part in reinforcing and interpreting this sense of crisis. In such circumstances, many leaders were convinced that economic cooperation and some form of European security system within the League of Nations – what supporters like Heinrich Mann called the 'spirit of Locarno' – offered at least partial answers to the problems which they faced.[78] There were, of course, numerous impediments to such cooperation and there was considerable contempt for the wilder ideas of 'thoroughly impractical theorists' like Coudenhove-Kalergi, but 'Europe' as a cultural entity and possible sphere of state activity, alongside others, enjoyed considerable prominence in the 1920s, eclipsed only by the installation and consolidation of dictatorships in Central, Eastern and Southern Europe during the 1930s.[79]

Notes

1. See the literature listed in the Introduction, and Chapters 2 and 3.
2. J.L. Chabot, *Aux origines intellectuelles de l'Union européenne: l'idée d'Europe unie de 1919 à 1939* (Grenoble, 2005), 325.
3. Karl Holl, 'Europapolitik um Vorfeld der deutschen Regierungspolitik. Zur Tätigkeit proeuropäischer Organisationen in der Weimarer Republik', *Historische Zeitschrift* 219 (1974), 33–94, and Jürgen Hess, 'Europagedanke und nationaler Revisionismus. Überlegungen zu ihrer Verknüpfung in der Weimarer Republik am Beispiel Wilhelm Heiles', *Historische Zeitschrift* 225 (1977), 572–622, disagree about the relative likelihood and significance of 'Europeanism' in the interwar era, with Hess emphasizing the inevitability of national interest, but they agree about the potential significance of the movements, their damaging inability to cooperate with each other, and their failure to enlist the German government.
4. Some scholars argue that a successful French strategy after 1919 was the only chance of a durable peace, in opposition to British and American appeasement of Germany, but the Quai d'Orsay was unable to impose a stronger and more consistent policy because of internal failings and the weakness of France's economic and military position; see J. Jacobson, 'Strategies of French Foreign Policy after World War I', *Journal of Modern History* 55 (1983), 78–95, for a summary. For a criticism of France's and Belgium's inability to overcome their national differences and cooperate economically, see E. Bussière, *La France, la Belgique et l'organisation économique de l'Europe* (Paris, 1991).
5. For arguments in favour of a 'shift' of international system after 1919, and especially after 1924, see P. Krüger, 'Das doppelte Dilemma: Die Aussenpolitik der Republik von Weimar zwischen Staatensystem und Innenpolitik', *German Studies Review* 22 (1999), 247–67, and idem, *Die Aussenpolitik der Republik von Weimar* (Darmstadt, 1985). For scepticism about Locarno's significance, given different interpretations of it by various governments, see J. Jacobson, *Locarno Diplomacy: Germany and the West* (Princeton, 1972).
6. For a recent work on the significance of Franco-German relations, see C. Germond and H. Türk (eds), *A History of Franco-German Relations in Europe* (Basingstoke, 2008), 75–124.
7. See S. Payne, *A History of Fascism, 1914–1945* (London, 1996), 3–22, 71–289.
8. E. du Réau, 'La France et l'Europe d'Aristide Briand à Robert Schuman. Naissance, déclin et redéploiement d'une politique étrangere (1929–1950)', *Revue d'histoire moderne et contemporaine* 42 (1995), 561.
9. Cited in J. Wright, *Gustav Stresemann: Weimar's Greatest Statesman* (Oxford, 2002), 485.
10. A. Rödder, *Stresemanns Erbe. Julius Curtius und die deutsche Aussenpolitik 1929–1931* (Paderborn, 1996), 113–19; H. Graml, *Zwischen Stresemann und Hitler. Die Aussenpolitik der Präsidialkabinette Brüning, Papen und Schleicher* (Munich, 2001); W.G. Ratliff, *Faithful to the Fatherland: Julius Curtius and Weimar Foreign Policy* (Berne, 1990); F. Knipping, *Deutschland, Frankreich und das Ende der Locarno-Ära 1928–1931* (Munich, 1987).
11. K. Holl, 'Europapolitik', *Historische Zeitschrift* 219 (1974), 39.
12. E. du Réau, 'La France et l'Europe', *Revue d'histoire moderne et contemporaine* 42 (1995), and idem, *Edouard Daladier, 1884–1970* (Paris, 1993); J.-B. Duroselle, *La Décadence, 1932–1939* (Paris, 1979); Y. Lacaze, *L'Opinion française et la crise de Munich* (Berne, 1991).
13. See Chapter 13.

14. P. Krüger, 'Zur europäischen Dimension der Aussenpolitik Gustav Stresemanns', in K.H. Pohl (ed.), *Politiker und Burger: Gustav Stresemann und seine Zeit* (Göttingen, 2002), 194–228; J. Hiden, *Germany and Europe, 1919–1939*, 2nd edn. (London, 1993).
15. Cited in J. Wright, *Stresemann*, 344–45. See also H.A. Turner, Jr, *Stresemann and the Politics of the Weimar Republic* (Princeton, 1963).
16. Wright, *Stresemann*, 416.
17. Ibid., 416–17.
18. Ibid.
19. Ibid., 503.
20. Jacques Bariéty, *Les relations franco-allemands après la Première Guerre Mondiale* (Paris, 1977), 140–44; W.A. McDougall, *France's Rhineland Diplomacy, 1914–24: The Last Bid for a Balance of Power in Europe* (Princeton, 1978), and idem, 'Political Economy versus National Sovereignty: French Structures for German Economic Integration after Versailles', *Journal of Modern History* 51 (1979), 4–23; S.A. Schuker, *The End of French Predominance in Europe: The Financial Crisis of 1924 and the Adoption of the Dawes Plan* (Chapel Hill, 1976), 384.
21. J. Jacobson, 'Strategies of French Foreign Policy', *Journal of Modern History* 55 (1983), 78–95.
22. N. Jordan, 'The Reorientation of French Diplomacy in the mid-1920s: The Role of Jacques Seydoux', *English Historical Review* 117 (2002), 874. In general, P.M.H. Bell, *France and Britain, 1900–1940: Entente and Estrangement* (London, 1996).
23. Jordan, 'The Reorientation of French Diplomacy', *English Historical Review* 117 (2002), 872.
24. Seydoux note of Feb. 1925, ibid., 881.
25. Ibid; P.S. Wandycz, *The Twilight of the French Eastern Alliances: 1926–1936* (Princeton, 1988), 19–258.
26. Jordan, 'The Reorientation of French Diplomacy', *English Historical Review* 117 (2002), 881.
27. See the works by McDougall and Bariéty above.
28. G. Soutou, 'Die deutschen Reparationen und das Seydoux-Projekt 1920–21', *Vierteljahresheft für Zeitgeschichte* 23 (1975), 247. Also M. Trachtenberg, *Reparation in World Politics: France and European Economic Diplomacy* (New York, 1980), 159–60.
29. C. Maier, *Recasting Bourgeois Europe: Stabilisation in France, Germany and Italy in the Decade after World War I* (Princeton, 1975), 411–13; J.F.V. Keiger, 'Raymond Poincaré and the Ruhr Crisis', in R. Boyce (ed.), *French Foreign and Defence Policy, 1918–1940* (London, 1998), 49–70, and idem, *Raymond Poincaré* (Cambridge, 2002).
30. J. Jacobson and and J.T. Walker, 'The Impulse for a Franco-German Entente: The Origins of the Thoiry Conference, 1926', *Journal of Contemporary History* 10 (1975), 170–71.
31. See J. Wright, *Stresemann*, 507; F. Siebert, *Aristide Briand 1862–1932* (Zurich, 1973); Jacques Bariéty, 'Aristide Briand et la sécurité de la France en Europe, 1919–32', in S.A. Schuker (ed.), *Deutschland und Frankreich. Vom Konflikt zur Aussöhnung* (Munich, 2000), 117–34, and idem (ed.), *Aristide Briand, la Société des Nations et l'Europe 1919–1932* (Strasbourg, 2007); A. Elisha, *Aristide Briand, la paix mondiale et l'union européenne* (Louvain, 2003); G. Unger, *Aristide Briand, le ferme conciliateur* (Paris, 2005); W. Roobol, 'Aristide Briand's Plan: The Seed of European Integration', in M. Spiering and M. Wintle (eds), *Ideas of Europe since 1914: The Legacy of the First World War* (Basingstoke, 2002), 32–46.
32. Cited in P.M.R. Stirk, *A History of European Integration since 1914* (London, 1996), 32, and N. Jordan, 'The Reorientation of French Diplomacy', *English Historical Review* 117 (2002), 883.
33. On pro-rapprochement intellectuals and businessmen, particularly on the right, see G. Müller, 'France and Germany after the Great War: Businessmen, Intellectuals and Artists in Nongovernmental European Networks', in J.C.E. Gienow-Hecht and F. Schumacher (eds), *Culture and International History* (Providence, 2003), 97–114.
34. See D. Artaud, *La question des dettes interalliees et la reconstruction de l'Europe, 1917–1929* (Lille, 1978); idem, 'A propos de l'occupation de la Ruhr', *Revue d'histoire moderne et contemporaine* 17 (1970), 1–21; idem, 'Die Hintergründe der Ruhrbesetzung 1923: Das problem der Interallierten Schulden', *Vierteljahreshefte für Zeitgeschichte* 1979, 241–59; and idem, 'La question des dettes interalliées et la reconstruction de l'Europe', *Revue historique* 530 (1979), 375; G. Soutou,

'Problèmes concernant le rétablissement des relations économiques franco-allemandes après la premiere guerre mondiale', *Francia* 2 (1974), 580–96; and idem, 'Die deutschen Reparationen und das Seydoux-Projekt 1920–21', *Vierteljahresheft für Zeitgeschichte* 23 (1975), 237–70.

35. On the Ruhr crisis, see C. Fischer, *The Ruhr Crisis, 1923–1924* (Oxford, 2003).
36. Cooperation and interpenetration in the iron, steel and mining sectors of the Franco-German border region antedated the First World War, as Raymond Poidevin has shown in *Les relations économiques et financières entre la France et l'Allemagne de 1898 à 1914* (Paris, 1969); see also idem (ed.), *Histoire des débuts de la construction européenne* (Louvain, 1986).
37. N. Jordan, 'The Reorientation of French Diplomacy', *English Historical Review* 117 (2002), 885.
38. Ibid., 877–78. On the Quai d'Orsay, from the point of view of an expert on Germany and the League of Nations, see R. Ulrich, 'René Massigli and Germany, 1919–1938', in R. Boyce (ed.), *French Foreign and Defence Policy*, 132–48.
39. Jordan, 'The Reorientation of French Diplomacy', *English Historical Review* 117 (2002), 871.
40. Ibid., 885. On the Quai's economic policies, see J. Bariéty, 'France and the Politics of Steel, from the Treaty of Versailles to the International Steel Entente, 1919–1926'; D. Artaud, 'Reparations and War Debts: The Restoration of French Financial Power, 1919–1929'; and R. Boyce, 'Business as Usual: The Limits of French Economic Diplomacy, 1926–1933', in R. Boyce (ed.), *French Foreign and Defence Policy*, 30–48, 89–131.
41. Seydoux in 1924 and Dec. 1923; Jordan, 'The Reorientation of French Diplomacy', *English Historical Review* 117 (2002), 872.
42. Ibid., 882. The quotation refers to a comment by Seydoux to Edouard Herriot before his meeting in June 1924 with Ramsay MacDonald.
43. A coal and steel community was widely discussed and supported in both the interwar and postwar periods by prominent advocates of Europe unity such as Coudenhove-Kalergi. See Chapter 4.
44. Cited in E. Bussière, 'Premiers schemas européens et économie internationale Durant l'entre-deux-guerres', *Relations internationales* 123 (2005), 62.
45. E. du Réau, 'La France et l'Europe', *Revue d'histoire moderne et contemporaine* 42 (1995), 560; Bussière, 'Schemas européens', 63.
46. In Stirk, *European Integration since 1914*, 35.
47. Ibid.
48. Ibid.
49. Ibid., 35–36.
50. Ibid., 36.
51. Ibid.
52. E. du Réau, 'La France et l'Europe', *Revue d'histoire moderne et contemporaine* 42 (1995), 559.
53. Wright, *Stresemann*, 506; C. Baumgart, *Stresemann und England* (Vienna, 1996).
54. Wright, *Stresemann*, 484. Also, E. Kolb, *Gustav Stresemann* (Munich, 2003); K. Koszyk, *Gustav Stresemann. Der kaisertreue Demokrat* (Cologne, 1989).
55. Wright, *Stresemann*, 484; G. Niedhart, 'Aussenminister Stresemann und die ökonomische Variante deutscher Machtpolitik', in K.H. Pohl (ed.), *Politiker und Burger*, 229–42.
56. Wright, *Stresemann*, 484.
57. P. Krüger, 'European Unity and German Foreign Policy in the 1920s', in P.M.R. Stirk (ed.), *European Unity in Context: The Interwar Period* (London, 1989), 90.
58. Ibid., 96.
59. J. Wright, 'Stresemann and Locarno', *Contemporary European History* 4 (1995), 130.
60. Wright, *Stresemann*, 326–27; G. Arnold, *Gustav Stresemann und die Problematik der deutschen Ostgrenzen* (Frankfurt, 2000); J. Hiden, *The Baltic States and Weimar Ostpolitik* (Cambridge, 2002), 119–70.
61. Wright, *Stresemann*, 508–9. L. Richter, '"Das ausgleichende staatspolitische Moment des zu bildenden Kompromisses". Überlegungen zum politischen Weg Gustav Stresemanns und der deutschen Volkspartei in der Weimarer Republik', and L.E. Jones, 'Stabilisierung von Rechts:

Gustav Stresemann und das Streben nach politischer Stabilität 1923–1929', in K.H. Pohl (ed.), *Politiker und Burger*, 143–93.

62. P. Krüger, 'Das doppelte Dilemma: Die Aussenpolitik der Republik von Weimar zwischen Staatensystem und Innenpolitik', *German Studies Review* 22 (1999), 261.

63. R.P. Grathwol, *Stresemann and the DNVP: Reconciliation or Revenge in German Foreign Policy, 1924–1928* (Kansas, 1980).

64. Wright, *Stresemann*, 510.

65. Krüger, 'Das doppelte Dilemma', *German Studies Review* 22 (1999), 256.

66. J. Jacobson, 'The Conduct of Locarno Diplomacy', *The Review of Politics* 34 (1972), 68. See G. Johnson (ed.), *Locarno Revisited: European Diplomacy, 1920–1929* (London, 2004).

67. Krüger, 'Das doppelte Dilemma', *German Studies Review* 22 (1999), 247–67. Also, H. Ashby Turner, Jr, 'Continuity in German Foreign Policy? The Case of Stresemann', *International History Review* 1 (1979), 509–21; C.M. Kimmich, *Germany and the League of Nations* (Chicago, 1976). On Pan-Europeans' support for the League of Nations in the 1920s, see Chapter 4 of this volume.

68. Stirk, *European Integration since 1914*, 37. W. Lipgens, 'Europäische Einigungsidee 1923–1930 und Briands Europaplan im Urteil der deutschen Akten', *Historische Zeitschrift* 203 (1966), 334–37.

69. Ibid., 324–28, for these countries and those below.

70. Cited ibid., 325.

71. On long-standing Dutch support for economic – more than political – integration, see Chapter 12.

72. Stirk, *European Integration since 1914*, 38.

73. See especially R. Boyce, 'British Capitalism and the Idea of European Unity between the Wars', in Stirk (ed.), *European Unity in Context*, 65–83.

74. Ibid., 79.

75. Ibid., 77.

76. See, for instance, 31 Oct. 1929, ibid., 80.

77. Cited in E. du Réau, 'La France et l'Europe', *Revue d'histoire moderne et contemporaine* 42 (1995), 559.

78. In general, see R. Boyce, *The Great Interwar Crisis and the Collapse of Globalization* (Basingstoke, 2009). On Heinrich Mann's exploration of the 'spirit of Locarno', see Chapter 13.

79. Sir William Tyrrell, Permanent Under-Secretary at the British Foreign Office, on Coudenhove, in Boyce, 'British Capitalism', in Stirk (ed.), *European Unity*, 66.

Chapter 2

EUROPE AND THE FATE OF THE WORLD

Crisis and Integration in the Late 1940s and 1950s

>╥╲╺╦╳

Mark Hewitson

The notion of a more or less continuous crisis between 1917 and 1957 militates against the three principal explanations of European integration, all of which posit – or imply – that there was a fundamental shift in the circumstances of policy making around 1945. The first school of thought, associated with the voluminous and detailed work of Walter Lipgens, contends that federalism became much more significant within the various resistance movements of the Second World War and, subsequently, within the emerging European movements of the late 1940s and within newly constituted postwar political elites.[1] Influential proponents of European integration were able, according to this reading of events, to establish federal or supranational institutions such as the European Coal and Steel Community (1951), Euratom and the European Economic Community (1957) in the changed conditions of the late 1940s and 1950s, making use of the transnational networks of the resistance, the European movements, big business, and Christian Democracy.[2]

To the second school of thought, which has dominated much of the literature on European politics, the grand schemes of federalists – most notably, the supranational designs for the Council of Europe (1949) and the European Political Community, which accompanied the failed project for a European Defence Community (1950–54) – proved unrealizable, necessitating the gradual, functional extension of integration from relatively small economic and administrative – rather than political and constitutional – beginnings. In neo-liberal analyses of this integration, such as that put forward by John Gillingham, it is held that the elimination of 'marketplace distortions in favour of competition' has stimulated growth and resulted in 'closer union' – and will continue to do so, albeit with many 'unintended consequences'.[3] In neo-functionalist accounts, and later institutionalist ones, integration was planned by technocrats and proceeds with a degree of economic and institutional logic, as economies of scale and bureaucratic efficiencies in one sector spill over into another.[4]

The third school of thought, established by the historian Alan Milward and developed by the 'liberal intergovernmentalist' political scientist Andrew Moravcsik, counters the variants of both neo-functionalism and federalism, depicting integration as a series of compromises and ad hoc measures adopted by governments in the name of national interest.[5] To Milward, 'the process of integration was deliberately conceived and developed to preserve the nation-state by supporting a range of new social and economic policies whose very purpose was the resurrection of the nation-state after its collapse between 1929 and 1945'.[6] From this point of view, integration can be understood as the attempt of states to secure their own vital economic and strategic interests after the unprecedented disintegration of institutions and transformation of the states' system before, during and after the Second World War, with surges of activity prompted by French efforts to control Germany; most notably, in 1950 as the United States sought to hasten German rearmament during the Korean War (1950–54), in 1955–56 as the FRG joined NATO, around 1970 at the time of Willy Brandt's *Ostpolitik*, and in 1990–92 after German unification. Here, too, 1945 constitutes a turning point, marking the collapse of the old system and the start of reconstruction, national planning, welfare reform and a bipolar international order.

Such a case, like those of federalists, neo-functionalists and more recent institutionalists, arguably pays too little attention to continuities resulting from a perceived crisis – including a willingness to consider European cooperation because of the supposed eclipse of the continent, the undermining of the nation-state and the fear of war – which extended back to the later stages of the First World War and had characterized the 1920s.[7] As a consequence, it could be contended, decisions for 'Europe' in the late 1940s and 1950s were more precarious and limited than is often supposed, not only because of the opposition of national governments in the throes of reconstruction but also because of the weakness of their position, lacking the means to act effectively or fearing their own unpredictable and divided populations. As in the interwar era, decision makers were confronted by a bewildering cornucopia of ideas about the nature, history and future of the continent, from the conservative revolutionary Ernst Jünger's conviction that Europe could become a 'fatherland' alongside national 'motherlands', to the Catholic poet T.S. Eliot's reaffirmation of the 'unity of European culture', based as it was on Christianity and the legacy of Greece, Rome and Israel.[8] Statesmen such as Konrad Adenauer, Charles de Gaulle, Robert Schuman, Alcide De Gasperi and Jean Monnet appear to have shared at least some of the beliefs articulated by intellectuals, alluding repeatedly to the creation of world powers or blocs, the distinction between 'Europe' and 'Asia', and the crisis of the nation-state and the old European order. This chapter examines decision making in the continuing context of that crisis – and diagnoses of Europe's cultural and political demise – after 1945.[9]

Germany, Europe and the Superpowers

The most salient change in Europe after 1945 concerned the role of the United States, yet it can be contended that U.S. tutelage of European states worked both for and against continental integration. Few contemporaries challenged the assertion of the German Chancellor, Konrad Adenauer, in January 1948 that 'The saving of Europe is only possible via the USA!'[10] The leaders of the defeated powers such as Germany and Italy were perhaps most reluctant to confront or alienate the United States because they were conscious of their weakness, given the partial collapse of their respective states, and they were aware of their reliance on American forces of occupation, given the divisive social and political legacy of dictatorship.[11] Thus, although the presence of U.S. soldiers and civilian authorities caused resentment, with majority support in Germany for denazification and the Nuremberg trials shrinking to the approval of a mere 17 per cent of respondents to polls by 1949, it was seen to be an essential prop by West German political elites.[12] Even Christian proponents of Europe as a 'Third Force', such as Jakob Kaiser, the chairman of the CDU, and socialist advocates such as Carlo Schmid, had by 1947–48, after the Soviet Union's rejection of the Marshall Plan (1947) and blockade of Berlin (1948), come to accept the warnings of Adenauer and Kurt Schumacher about 'Eurasia swallowing Europe', in the words of the SPD leader, already chastened in January 1946 by the conduct of the Soviet Military Authority (SMAD) and its early efforts to force the merger of the KPD and SPD – eventually creating the Socialist Unity Party (SED) in April 1946 – in the eastern zone.[13] With the partition of Germany apparently irreversible except on Soviet terms by 1948, Adenauer was adamant that 'our line is fixed in the field of foreign policy': 'It consists in the first instance of cementing a close relationship with our neighbouring states in the western world, in particular with the United States.'[14] Once the CDU-CSU was in office, after narrowly defeating the SPD by 31 to 29 per cent in the Bundestag election in 1949, Adenauer – whose SPD-inspired nickname of 'Chancellor of the Allies' proved an electoral asset – showed no sign of compromising the Federal Republic's relationship with the United States, which served as the country's main defence against the German Democratic Republic and the USSR.

Likewise, in Italy, policy makers such as Luigi Einaudi, Carlo Sforza and Alcide De Gasperi, who was Prime Minister between December 1944 and June 1953, were cautious and deferential, unwilling to endanger their ties to the United States for the sake of the uncertain benefits of 'Europeanism', despite their federalist rhetoric and their backing of Article 11 of the 1947 constitution: 'Italy consents in the same way as other states to limits of sovereignty which are necessary for the safeguarding of peace and justice amongst nations.'[15] 'For we Italians, it is an historical hour', wrote the Republican Foreign Minister Sforza in 1948: 'Starving, impoverished and having only escaped the abyss of pain and shame, into which fascism threw us, by a hair's breadth, we can regain honour, independence and well-being, if we become heralds of the new order in which the world will now move.'[16] The task for Christian Democrats was to convince a disoriented population and a sceptical left that 'we, like all the other countries of Europe, are no longer independent', as one ambassador put it, meaning that Italy was no more able to move towards Russia than Poland was to enter 'the field of gravity' of the United States, while also lacking 'the power to carry out a policy on the basis of the idea of neutrality'.[17] Many contemporaries were largely ignorant of the United States or harboured anti-American sentiments fostered by the fascist regime, but they had little choice, contended Christian Democrats, but to accept the American international order.[18]

The United Kingdom was the principal champion of the United States in Europe after 1945, but its governments, both Labour (Clement Attlee, 1945–51) and Conservative (Winston Churchill, 1951–55), also proved the least receptive to European integration.[19] Attlee and the Labour Foreign Secretary Ernest Bevin, who dominated the formulation of foreign policy in the absence of a committee for foreign affairs, were closely involved in European politics, pursuing the wartime idea that Britain, with the backing of Europe and the Commonwealth, could be a third world power alongside the United States and the Soviet Union.[20] Sir Orme Sargent, Deputy Under-Secretary of State at the Foreign Office, wrote:

> If we make every move in the realm of high policy contingent on American prior approval, our prospects of being able to give a lead to western Europe will vanish and we shall never attain what must be our primary objective *viz* by close association with our neighbours to create a European group which will enable us to deal on a footing of equality with our two gigantic colleagues, the USA and the USSR.[21]

In common with other Labour ministers, Bevin believed that 'Britain, like the other countries of Western Europe', was 'placed geographically and from the point of view of economic and political theory between these two great continental states', representing neither 'watered-down capitalism' nor 'watered-down communism', but a genuine 'middle way'.[22] To this end, he courted Paris in late 1947 and early 1948 with a view to forming a European customs union on the ground, as he put it to the Foreign Minister Paul Ramadier, so that the British and French Empires could, 'if they acted together, be as powerful as either the Soviet Union or the United States'.[23] 'If some such union could be created, including not only the countries of Western Europe but also their colonial possessions in Africa and the East,' he told the Cabinet on 8 January 1948, 'this would form a *bloc* which, both in population and productive capacity, could stand on an equality with the western hemisphere and Soviet *blocs*.'[24]

Underpinning such aspirations, however, was Bevin's fundamental commitment to the United States, which he had helped to convince not to withdraw from

Europe in 1945–47.[25] British military planners were never in any doubt that U.S. forces were needed to deter and resist the USSR in Europe, prompting the Foreign Office, too, to favour an Atlantic Pact – mooted from early 1948 onwards – and the establishment of NATO in 1949.[26] What was more, the Treasury was always conscious that Britain was what Churchill had called 'the world's greatest debtor', obliging it, in the words of the Chancellor of the Exchequer Hugh Dalton, 'to maintain close economic ties with those countries which were able to supply our needs' – that is, the United States and the Commonwealth – 'in pursuing the aim of closer economic cooperation in Western Europe'.[27] Because of its economic difficulties, the United Kingdom had been forced to merge its zone in Germany with that of the United States and to rely on U.S. intervention in its spheres of interest in the Mediterranean and the Middle East, where 'in a major war the active partnership of the United States would be of supreme importance' and 'alignment of policy with the United States is accordingly essential'.[28] On no account should the U.K. be drawn into Europe, which seemed close to economic collapse, at the expense of its own economic well-being and its relationship with the United States, reiterated a joint paper by Bevin and Sir Stafford Cripps, Chancellor between 1947 and 1950, on 25 January 1949:

> We can ... lay down firmly the principle that, while we must be ready to make temporary sacrifices in our standard of living, and to run some degree of risk in the hope of restoring Western Europe, we must do nothing to damage irretrievably the economic structure of this country. The present attempt to restore sanity and order in the world depends upon the United States and the British Commonwealth and the countries of Western Europe working together. If, however, the attempt to restore Western Europe should fail, this country could still hope to restore its position in cooperation with the rest of the Commonwealth and with the United States. But in these circumstances we could not look for continued United States military, political and economic support if, in the endeavour to re-establish Western Europe, our economic structure had been hopelessly impaired.[29]

In some respects, the United States' role in Europe after 1945 was comparable to that of the interwar era. Although the State Department came to support the idea of a United States of Europe, it proved unable or unwilling to play a leading role in bringing it about.[30] As in the 1920s, the U.S. provided capital to European states, allowing their economies to recover from the war. It is true that Washington had created a much more comprehensive apparatus for free trade and mutual support during the Second World War, setting up the World Bank and the International Monetary Fund and requiring formal commitments at Bretton Woods in 1944, which it consolidated and mitigated through the negotiation of the terms of the Marshall Plan (1947).[31] It is also true, however, that U.S.-style industrial production, productivity, regulation of markets and state intervention had been widely discussed in Europe since the 1920s, attracting both support and opposition. Those who agreed with many of the terms of the new economic order, such as Ludwig Erhard and the 'ordo-liberals' in Germany, could view European organizations, many of which – the Organisation for European Economic Cooperation (OEEC) and the European Payments Union, for instance – had been created by Washington or London, as interim measures on the path to global trade. They remained resistant to the idea of a continental customs union or common market, fearing protectionism and a high external tariff.[32] Those who disagreed, including most Social Democrats and the majority of parties in France, had little option but to work within the American framework and to ensure that any continental customs, currency or industrial union conformed to that framework, given their reliance on $19 billion of Marshall Aid and on American coordination of European security.[33]

The main danger after 1945, it seemed, was not that European states would fail to cooperate, but that the United States would withdraw or pursue its own interests to the detriment of its European partners, as it had done at various points – failing to ratify the Versailles Treaty in 1919 and repatriating capital in 1929 – in the interwar period. Adenauer's fear, as he explained in an interview with Ernst Friedländer just after the Soviet-backed suppression of the workers' uprising in East Germany in June 1953, was that the United States might use Germany as a bargaining counter in a Cold War deal with the Soviet Union, as it had done at the Potsdam conference in 1945, when the country was divided into zones irrespective of German wishes:

> Bismarck spoke of his nightmare of coalitions against Germany. I have my nightmare, too. It is called Potsdam. The danger of a common policy of the Great Powers to the disadvantage of Germany has existed since 1945 and has continued to exist since the founding of the Federal Republic. The foreign policy of the federal government was directed from then onwards at coming out of this danger zone.[34]

Although, of course, the German Chancellor looked to European cooperation as a means of averting the danger of abandonment, his priority remained Germany's relationship with the United States.[35] Thus, when the French Assembly failed to ratify the European Defence Community in 1954, Bonn showed little hesitation in joining NATO in 1955, in spite of Paris's reservations. Other European statesmen seem to have adopted a similar strategy, spending much of their energy cultivating ties with Washington in order to persuade it to remain in Europe and relying on American-backed economic and security structures in the event that supplementary European ones failed to materialize.[36]

Adenauer's foreign policy was founded on the notion that Europe's and the United States' positions had been transformed since the First World War. The Chancellor, born in Imperial Germany and the mayor of Cologne in the 1920s, had adapted to such circumstances and had fashioned the Federal Republic's European policy accordingly, as he conceded in his inaugural address to the first conference of the CDU in October 1950:

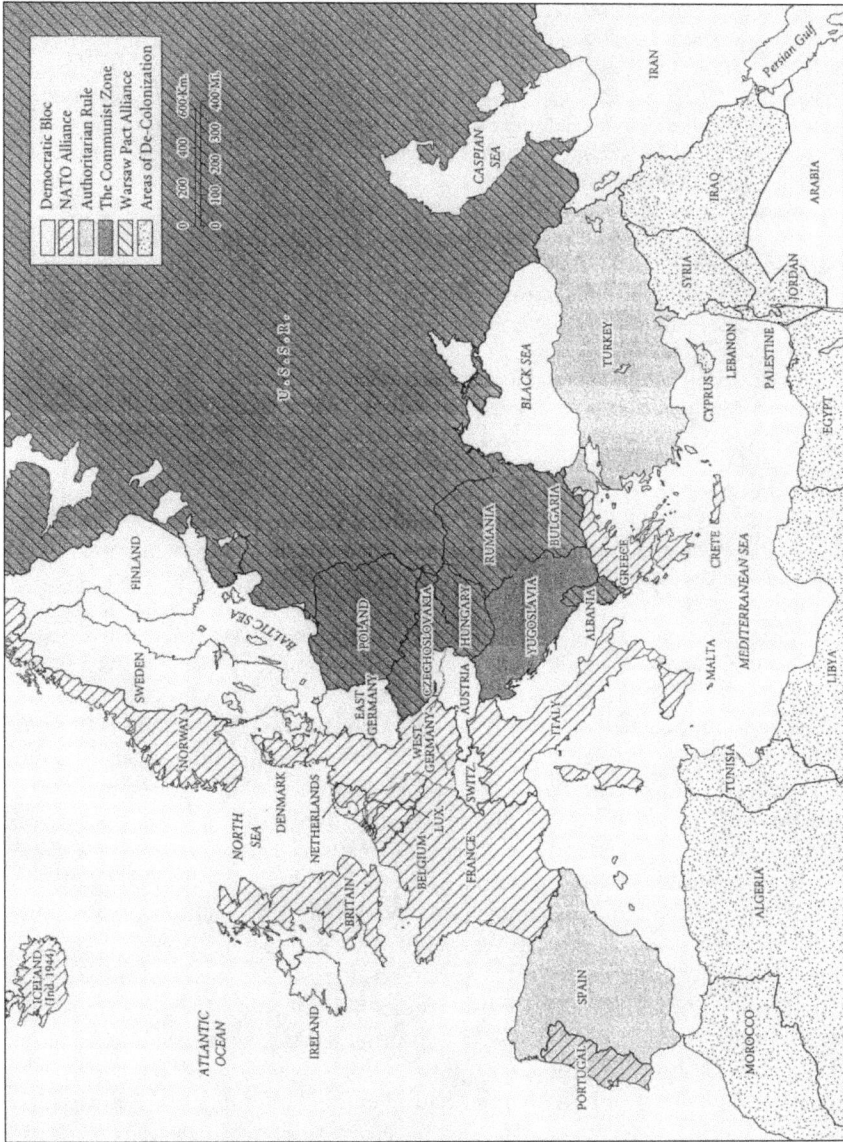

Map 2.1 Europe during the Cold War. Source: Eric Dorn Brose, *A History of Europe in the Twentieth Century* (Oxford, 2005), 293.

Until 1914, the world looked as follows; Germany was the strongest military power, England was the strongest sea power in the world, its fleet was bigger than the two next largest fleets put together. France was an economically and militarily powerful Great Power. The same was true of Italy. As a further, Great Power, Austria-Hungary combined the national forces of the earlier Greater Austria, Hungary and Czechoslovakia, and it bound almost all the Balkan states to Europe. Russia was a Great Power, but it saw itself as part of Europe, belonging to its culture. This politically and economically strong European states' system, which on the whole was in equilibrium, could lead the rest of the world politically and economically, as a consequence of its strength and its balance of power: the United States of North America was a debtor country in 1914 – which is not believed when it is said today. Its military forces were relatively small … Europe decided the fate of the world.

And now? Germany violently split into two parts, politically and economically badly damaged, diplomatically a vacuum. France has not yet been able to recover from the deep wounds which it received in both wars. The same is true of Italy. England has relinquished much of its economic and political influence and has partially lost its world standing, although the diplomacy of its leaders has kept intact, to a considerable extent, its old imperial connections.

Soviet Russia no longer feels a European, but a Bolshevik power … Yet it is in a position to have a decisive influence on the political fate of other European countries because of its expansion into *Mitteleuropa* and by means of its fifth column.

The United States of North America has developed into a world power of the first rank since 1914. One can say, without exaggerating, that no country since the time of the Roman Empire under Emperor Augustus has ever had such power in its hands as the United States does now. It is the strongest military power, the strongest economic power in the world … Whereas Europe since 1914 had a decisive influence on the political and economic workings of the world, it has now fallen into a lame state, which doesn't allow it to intervene decisively in the course of events.[37]

Despite, as a Rhinelander, having a vaguely defined interest in Franco-German reconciliation and European cooperation, Adenauer had become more 'Atlantic' in his definition of priorities as a consequence of the rise of the United States as a world power.[38] At no stage – including his signature of the Elysée Treaty with France in 1963, which incorporated a reaffirmation of support for the United States in its preamble – was the German Chancellor willing to put Europe before America, since he had long recognized the reversal of their positions in the global balance of power. The fact that Washington was prepared to coordinate the continent's security and to prop up its economy after 1945 at times seemed to ease the process of European integration by removing difficult subjects – especially defence – from the negotiating table, yet at other times it made such integration or cooperation seem less necessary or pressing than during the 1920s.

The threat of Communism, which had been evident since 1917 but which seemed to the majority of onlookers to have increased with the victory of the USSR in 1945, was perhaps the overriding impulse behind European leaders' 'Atlanticism'. In Germany, after the effective partition of the western and eastern zones in 1946–49, the menace was most visible, associated with the barbarity of fighting on the Eastern Front during the Second World War, the feared and resented presence of Soviet troops throughout East Germany, the imprisonment of German soldiers in Soviet camps, the increasingly forlorn question of reunification, and a growing sense of insecurity, heightened by Moscow's blockade of Berlin in 1948, its acquisition of the atom bomb in 1949, its suppression of the workers' rising in the German Democratic Republic in 1953 and its replacement by force of the reformist government of Imre Nagy in Hungary in 1956. According to opinion polls, international 'security' remained the dominant political issue in Germany until the 1960s, taking precedence over reunification, which itself was seen by most respondents to be much more important than 'Europe'. On the left, the battle against Communism derived especially from the SPD leadership's experiences of the forced merger of the KPD and SPD in the eastern zone in 1946–47.[39] In the centre and on the right, attitudes to the USSR were strongly ideological, combined with long-standing stereotypes of the 'Slavs' and the 'East' which had been disseminated by right-wing, Christian democratic, liberal and social-democratic intellectuals since the First World War.[40] For Adenauer, the Soviet Union was 'an Asian power', 'a vast power governed by a genius and a way of thinking totally different from our Western European conditions'.[41] 'Asia stands on the Elbe', wrote the future Chancellor in March 1946 to Wilhelm Sollmann, a former Social Democratic deputy who had emigrated to the United States.[42] Although such a fact necessitated 'an economically and spiritually regenerated Western Europe under British and French leadership', which alone could 'check the further advance of this Asian spirit and power', it was accepted amongst CDU and CSU leaders – as Pascual Jordan put it – that 'our security … is guaranteed only by the presence of US troops'.[43] This calculus of power underlay the decision making of the German government between 1949 and the 1960s.

Such calculations should not be confused with the seemingly static analyses of the later Cold War, however. Adenauer's assessment of the Soviet threat and those of his opponents were characterized by an openness which went back to the interwar era. The Chancellor was unusual in opting for the 'West' – primarily the United States, but also Western Europe – so quickly after 1945. On his right, national-minded conservatives such as Heinrich Brüning, the former Chancellor and Centre Party politician, criticized Adenauer for endangering not merely 'the German Reich', but 'the entire nation (*Volk*)': the Federal Republic should not commit itself, recognizing that 'time is working for us' and using 'narrower ties between European states' for 'particular purposes' such as the regaining of economic and political autonomy instead of risking 'an enduring partition of Germany' by adopting 'French' and 'Western' policies, including the founding of the ECSC and the attempt to set up a European parliament.[44] On the Chancellor's left, liberals such as Karl-Georg Fleiderer and Reinhold Maier, together with Paul Sethe, Richard Tüngel and Rudolf Augstein from *Der Spiegel* and *Die Zeit*, also blamed him for entering into Western alliances which prevented reunification and for rejecting Stalin's offer of neutrality for the whole of Germany in 1952.[45] Even Theodor Heuss, the liberal-democratic President of the FRG, distanced himself from

Adenauer's Western policy until 1948, at the earliest, contending that Germany could be a 'bridge' between East and West: 'We, the German people, must not be forced to "opt" either for the East or the West,' he had declared in January 1947, 'though many of our countrymen may, in their hearts, be so inclined, but by ignoring the permanent existence of the areas of German settlement.'[46] The unresolved national question in Germany made it difficult to opt definitively for a French, European or Western system which seemed to prolong partition. In this respect, Adenauer himself, despite discounting the possibility of reunification within an unreliable system of collective – rather than American – security or as a result of a Soviet deal, was unwilling to give up the idea of a successful reconstitution of Germany. Notably, he continued to hope that the USSR might recognize that it could not win against a united and strong West, that it might be overwhelmed by the cost of the arms race, global intervention and the maintenance of its system of satellite states, or that it might become preoccupied by the menace of China in the East, causing it to reduce its commitments in the West.[47] With such apparently shifting points of view, even of the Soviet threat, the German government's commitment to Europe often seemed subordinate either to its relationship with the United States or its longer-term goal of reunification.

Many French policy makers had a similarly shifting view of the USSR and the international order in the late 1940s and early 1950s, which recalled the unpredictable alliances and agreements of the interwar years.[48] Thus, pragmatic economic planners such as Monnet were subject to radical oscillation between practical objectives and nightmarish fears of war and collapse, predicting a nuclear conflagration in 1950 – 'They are going to drop it, the atom bomb, and then …' – even before the outbreak of the Korean War: 'People have latched onto a simple and dangerous aim … The Cold War, the basic aim of which is to make the adversary yield, is the first stage in the preparation of war. This is breeding a rigidity of mind characteristic of fixation on a single goal … We are already at war.'[49] For Monnet, as for other French statesmen, the international system seemed to be characterized by instability after 1945, with earlier hopes – from 1943 – of 'transforming the European epicentre of two world wars into an ensemble pacified by the creation of a "European federation or entity"' by no means certain in the emerging global order.[50] Thus, although 'it was axiomatic' in the late 1940s for the head of the French *Commissariat Général au Plan*, in the opinion of the U.S. Under-Secretary of State George Ball, that 'lasting peace could be achieved only by bringing France and Germany together and exorcising the demons of the past', it was also necessary to work towards 'a real Federation of the West', to include the British dominions and the United States.[51] Without such British participation, Europe would remain a vacuum between the dynamism of communism and U.S. capitalism, Monnet maintained.[52] Yet he found it difficult to escape the logic of the American ambassador in Paris in April 1950 that 'there will be no real European integration without whole-hearted participation by the UK, … the UK will not whole-heartedly participate …, ergo there will be no purely European integration'.[53]

Monnet's contemporaries were likewise uncertain of the relationship between European cooperation and world politics. Many, like de Gaulle in June 1947, wanted France to create a 'Europe' which was in a position 'to meet any possible claim of hegemony and to establish a balance of power between both rival masses which is necessary for the maintenance of peace', but there was little agreement about how to achieve such a goal.[54] De Gaulle's Commissioner for Foreign Affairs during the Second World War, René Massigli, who became the French ambassador in London in August 1944, had envisaged not only a U.S.-led collective security organization, but also a Franco-British alliance and an anti-German Franco-Soviet treaty, which was actually signed in December 1944. Amongst the parties, the Communists, together with the Christian Democratic *Mouvement Républicain Populaire* (MRP) and the Socialists (SFIO) until 1947, were in favour of a Soviet pact, while 'the Gaullists (RPF) and Radicals quickly gave up the idea. Even between the latter parties, however, there was still disagreement about whether a French-led 'European federation' could constitute a third bloc between the superpowers, as the RPF's Jacques Soustelle contended, or whether 'a continental force leaning upon that of the two great powers whose civilization and political ideas are like ours' – namely, that of the United States – was the best that could be hoped for, as the Radical Jean Coutard proposed.[55] As late as 1957, the Socialist premier Guy Mollet was still worried that the USSR might be able to 'blackmail' the Federal Republic of Germany, with the likely election of an SPD government after the death of the ageing Adenauer, into cooperation with Moscow at the expense of Europe, in exchange for 'the mirage of reunification'.[56] In spite of the Cold War, relations between European states remained unstable. The role of the French Empire in European and global politics added a further element of confusion to such debates.[57]

In much of Europe, the movement towards global bipolarity after 1945 continued – as it had been since the First World War – to be complicated by the German question, with many politicians and ministers as mindful of the legacy of the 1930s and the Second World War as they were of the growing antagonism of the superpowers.[58] With the exception of the SFIO, which nonetheless advocated the internationalization of the industry of the Ruhr, majorities in all political parties in France until 1948 seem to have perceived Germany as their principal enemy.[59] Although such continental anxieties, as in the 1920s, eventually pushed many French, German, Belgian and Dutch decision makers to view European cooperation as a means of guarding against a revival of German nationalism, they could easily and rapidly work in the opposite direction. The French could only have confidence in the Marshall Plan, declared Monnet in July 1947, 'if the development of German resources is coupled with safeguards to ensure that they will not, one day, be used again by the Germans to make war'.[60] When Dean Acheson, the U.S. Secretary of State, asked Paris and London to consent to German rearmament at the start of the Korean War in September 1950, the French Foreign Minister Robert Schuman – who was still denigrated by French diplomats 'for having fought in German uniform', as a native of Lorraine, in the First World

War – retorted that 'Germany's malady dates too far back to have been permanently cured'.[61] To Mollet in 1956, 'the risk of a revival of German nationalism' was still 'no myth'.[62] The problem, to which there was a bewildering range of solutions on offer during the late 1940s and early 1950s, was how to control Germany. When Schuman was requested by Acheson to prepare a policy towards Germany for the United States, the U.K. and France in September 1949, 'the bald top of his head went red, as always when he was embarrassed', wrote his chief of staff: 'Back in Paris, hardly a week passed without Schuman pressing me: "What about Germany? What do I have to do to meet the responsibility put upon me?" It became an obsession with him.'[63]

Schuman was confronted by changing conditions and conflicting advice. Initial hopes of a re-agrarianized Germany, along the lines of the Morgenthau Plan, or a loose confederation of individual German states, as in de Gaulle's prediction of 1944 that 'there would no longer be "one" Germany but several', were quickly replaced by a desire in Paris to control the reconstruction of the German economy, state and military, which was being pursued progressively between 1945 and 1950 by the United States, faced with the need to reduce its spending in the Allied zones, to refloat the European economy, to create a strong enough political structure in Germany to resist the Soviet-backed SED regime in the eastern zone, and to allow the transfer of U.S. troops to the war in Korea (1950–54).[64] As after 1924, 'The system of domination of Germany, through the Saar and the Ruhr, could not be maintained forever, but no one wanted to be responsible for the decision to bring it to an end,' wrote Robert Mischlich, a member of Schuman's staff at the Quai d'Orsay.[65] When the Minister of Foreign Affairs had decided on Monnet's limited policy of 'settling the German problem in a … European steel pool in which French and Germans would be equally represented', influential members of the ministry such as the Political Director Maurice Couve de Murville and the Secretary-General Jean Chauvel advised that 'France had to keep a free hand', in Mischlich's words: 'If there were to be a military or economic alliance, it should in no way foreclose France's political freedom, notably to withdraw from any alliance.'[66] French diplomats continued to try to tie the ECSC, after it had been established in 1951–52, to the Council of Europe by insisting – unsuccessfully – on a shared secretariat, and they had nothing to do with the relaunching of European talks which had been proposed by Monnet and the Belgian Minister of Foreign Affairs Paul-Henri Spaak at Messina in 1955, and which led to the founding of the EEC in 1957. Even to figures like Hervé Alphand, who had been Director of Economic Affairs at the Quai d'Orsay after the Second World War, before becoming ambassador to NATO between 1952 and 1954, such economic integration was unlikely on its own to bind the FRG to France, leaving the European Defence Community as 'the last chance to impose on Germany a regime offering guarantees of limiting German militarism'.[67] For his part, de Gaulle, who remained influential in the realm of diplomacy and the military, opposed the EDC in a press conference in February 1953, since it entailed a renunciation of French national interests and 'contains not only equality, but also a route to the hegemony of the Germans', reopening the prospect of 'a Reich'.[68] Adenauer was portrayed in the interview as the 'Chancellor of the Reich' and was accused by implication of harbouring hegemonic designs.[69] In such circumstances, any movement towards European integration, based on Franco-German reconciliation, was neither certain nor separate from policies involving the United States. Formally, the sanction of the U.S. and the U.K., as the other two occupying powers with Allied High Commissions in Germany, was needed for any negotiation involving the FRG to take place at all.

Federation, Confederation and Integration

There were, of course, good reasons for wanting to integrate European economies, military planning and political decision making after the Second World War, yet these were not dissimilar to those of the 1920s.[70] The need to reverse relative economic decline, rebuild legitimate political structures, avoid radicalization at home and abroad, improve relations between continental states, and escape cultural decadence and complacency was widely recognized. 'A number of fervent Europeans', wrote Robert Marjolin, former colleague of Monnet and the Secretary General of the OEEC from 1948 to 1955, 'were quite a strong force during the fifties and early sixties':

> For them, federal Europe was within reach, if the political will were there. Practically speaking, once the first step had been taken in this direction, events would necessarily follow on from one another and inevitably lead to the desired result. This is the gist of the so-called theory of *engrenage* (chain reaction) or the 'spill-over effect'. It is set out in the fullest detail in what may be regarded as the political testament of Walter Hallstein, who, as a close collaborator of Konrad Adenauer, then as President of the EEC Commission from 1958 to 1967, played a large part in the construction of the Common Market.
> The forces which the Europeans had let loose in deciding to create a common market, so Hallstein's thinking went, must inevitably take Europe to economic union, then to political union … Trade policy was an essential part of foreign policy, itself closely bound up with defence policy … Thus, a process that began modestly with the establishment of a customs union and a common agricultural or commercial policy would reach its logical outcome: a European federation, or as others would name it, the United States of Europe.[71]

Such fervent Europeans shared many of the motives of their contemporaries in the late 1940s and 1950s, but they often drew different inferences. Marjolin himself 'did not believe that the concept of nationality could be displaced [by the concept of 'Europe'] within a single generation, or even several generations, merely by creating new institutions', observed the American official George Ball: 'Patriotism had been the coalescing force animating Germany's neighbours to resist her ravaging armies in two world wars, and Britain, in Marjolin's view, was not ready

for Europe. He did not think – as Monnet did – that deeply entrenched habits of
thought could be quickly modified in the pressure chambers of new institutions.'[72]
Marjolin, according to Ball, addressed the same problems as Monnet with similar
intentions, but 'from different angles of attack'.[73] Given the crisis-ridden conditions
of the continent since the First World War, European cooperation was likely to be
modest and reversible.

   The terms of the debate about Europe after 1945 remained confused. Most of
the main protagonists except the British were willing to contemplate giving up
sovereignty in specific spheres, but they disagreed about how much and which
types of power and in which fields of policy making and administrative activity.
Out of office, Winston Churchill, who had earlier been seen as a federalist, was
willing to hand over to European authorities – or 'integrate' – areas of
administration, but not instances of decision making: 'We are ready to play an
active part in all plans for integration on an intergovernmental basis,' he explained
to René Pleven in 1950 on the subject of the EDC, before warning that 'defence
considerations, our Commonwealth connections and the Sterling Area inhibit us
from subordinating ourselves … to any European supranational authority.'[74] As
for the Labour government between 1945 and 1951, a future Conservative
ministry would have to stop 'short of actual membership' of a supranational
organization with the power to make decisions.[75] The Italian government of De
Gasperi, which had put forward the notion of a European Political Community
(EPC) – with a continental constituent assembly to draw up a common constitution
– alongside the European Defence Community, was equally conscious in 1951,
from an opposing point of view close to that of Italian federalists such as Altiero
Spinelli and Luigi Einaudi, that:

> a renunciation of sovereignty, like that foreseen, … could not be put into effect by
> governments or accepted by parliaments without the creation, in response, on the
> federal level, of an organism in which the powers that the National Assemblies were
> giving up could be entrusted and which would have the authority to exercise them
> in the same right as national parliaments … The organism enjoying such powers
> should be, according to the Italian delegation, the European Assembly.[76]

The terms 'federal' and 'federation', however, were ambiguous, usually used in
a very vague, positive sense – as Coudenhove-Kalergi's upholding of both
'federalism' and national 'sovereignty' had demonstrated – or in reaction to a
specific proposal.[77] Thus, when Churchill averred, on returning to office in 1951,
that 'I never thought that Britain or the British Commonwealth should, either
individually or collectively, become an integral part of a European federation, and
have never given the slightest support to the idea', he was referring to the
supranational federation of the ECSC, EDC and EPC.[78] By contrast, when de
Gaulle instructed his commissaires to undertake 'a detailed study of a project for
a federation of western Europe' in October 1943, he had a much more limited
form of economic cooperation in mind, which he later – in March 1944 –
described as a 'form of western grouping that rests principally on an economic

foundation and is as broad as possible'.[79] By August 1949, at the time of the campaign of federalists to turn the Advisory Assembly of the newly founded Council of Europe into a constituent assembly of a future European federation, de Gaulle could be found outlining his plan not for a federation but a confederation – 'unity will initially take the form of a confederation' – in order to highlight the fact that 'each state retains its sovereignty', except for 'those areas which nations will hand over to the community so as to create unity there'.[80] In a similar spirit, de Gaulle's close collaborator, the RPF politician Michel Debré, proposed a 'pact for a union of European states' in early 1950, which – like the General's plan – envisaged the 'giving up of sovereignty of participating states' in specified areas of defence and the economy, but not in other spheres of government.[81] The purpose of terms such as 'confederation' and 'union' was to distinguish between different degrees and levels of decision making, but it was frequently obscured by the participation of Debré, Jacques Chaban-Delmas and other national-minded politicians within organizations such as the *Union Européenne des Fédéralistes*, which continued to call for a European 'federation'. Even within the European networks of Socialists and Christian Democrats, which are rightly seen as one of the principal forums for the propagation and implementation of transnational ideas, there were fundamental disagreements about the nature and desirable extent of 'federation'. 'European planning, much less than national planning,' declared Alexandre Verret, of the *Mouvement pour les Etats-Unis socialistes d'Europe* (MEUSE), in July 1949, 'cannot count on the spontaneous adhesion of the "masses", for Europe is too weak an organic reality, which has not yet blossomed, to make them believe in the same manner as the national idea, with profound echoes in the collective and individual subconscious.'[82] Whether to integrate decision making in the field of defence and what form of political community to create, if any, remained matters of contention.

To federalists such as De Gasperi, a European Political Community was needed in the early 1950s to safeguard the principle of supranationality: 'Either Europe will be established now or it won't be established at all, and that would be a sad day for all countries.'[83] In the event, 'Europe' was not established in the form anticipated by De Gasperi, with the failure to ratify the EDC and EPC. Reform occurred in limited economic spheres, where the need for cooperation had been widely recognized by political elites in the 1920s. French diplomats such as Massigli and ministers like Georges Bidault opposed the proposal for a European Political Community, even after executive power had been vested in the unanimity of a Council of Ministers. The EPC was a 'sprawling monster', which would lead to the loss of France's autonomy in the international order, asserted the Christian Democrat leader Bidault in 1953.[84] The Gaullist Debré was just as emphatic in his rejection of the EDC, at least in retrospect: 'As regards the organisation of Europe as described by the treaty, and as expanded by the complementary project for a Political Community, it implies at this point the disappearance of France ... The federalists are the enemies of the nation-state and want to replace it with Community of Europe. That is what is unacceptable.'[85] Instead, integration

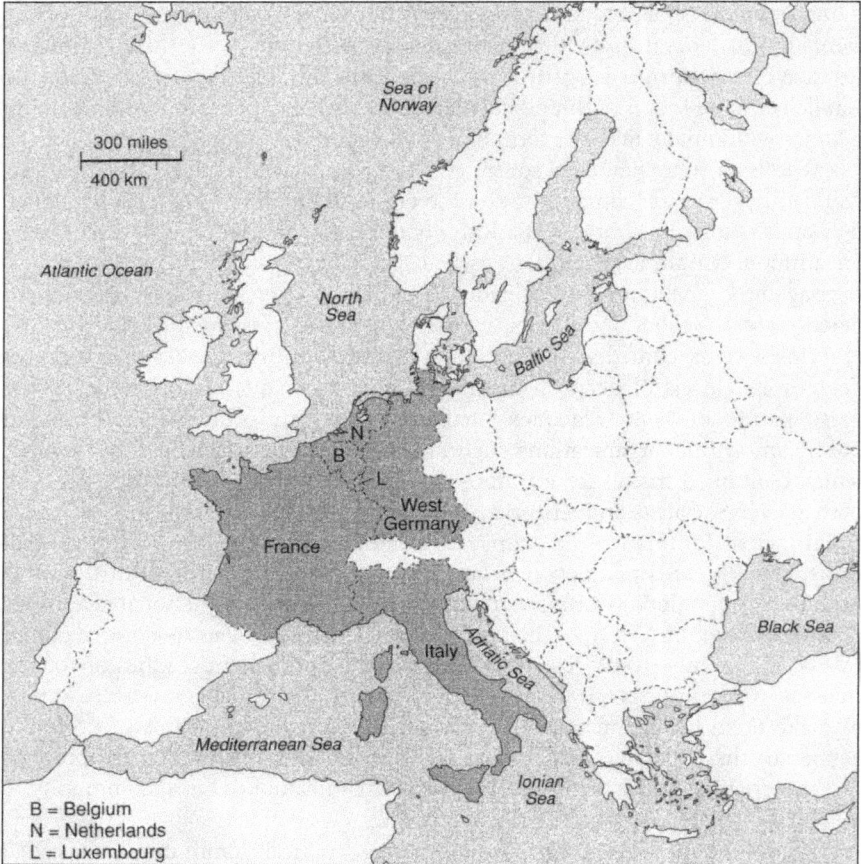

Map 2.2   The European Economic Community in 1957. Source: Alasdair Blair, *The European Union since 1945* (Harlow, 2005), xi.

proceeded through the pooling of coal, iron and steel, with the formation of the ECSC by the Treaty of Paris (1951). The terms and goals of the treaty were limited – in earlier discussions the pro-European Conservative Harold Macmillan had dismissed Monnet's project as 'a plan to have a plan' – and any subsequent 'spillover' into other areas was resisted by individual governments, including those in France.[86] Paul van Zeeland, the Belgian Foreign Minister, was critical of the EDC project precisely because Monnet and other federalists seemed to be 'forcing the pace, apparently in the hope of achieving European unity by the back door, and loading down the European army proposal with a top-heavy superstructure borrowed from the Schuman plan'.[87] When the ratification of the EDC failed, Spaak – van Zeeland's successor – eventually accepted that such failure was 'predictable', resolving with Monnet to return to the more promising task of economic integration: 'Spaak turned up and his first words were,

"Obviously, it's a disaster … Can we do anything in the economic field?" And they were off … Monnet said, "Yes, we must try",' reported André Staercke, the later Belgian permanent representative to NATO.[88] The product of Spaak's and Monnet's deliberations and those of the Dutch Foreign Minister Johan Willem Beyen – the European Economic Community – was carefully circumscribed, like the ECSC, not least because the French government was wary of the free-trading ramifications of a common market. Tariffs, it was agreed, would be reduced gradually in three four-year stages. Initially, the French government only agreed formally to the first stage.[89] 'Europe' for many ministers was a limited and fragile entity until the late 1960s and beyond.

Calls for the revival of 'Europe' after 1945, which was a necessity widely accepted by intellectuals and politicians alike, made the securing of vital national interests, especially on the part of France and the FRG, easier to justify. For postwar French administrations, cooperation with Germany was essential, not simply as a means of addressing the German question and controlling the neighbouring state, but also as a way of regenerating French industry, particularly by giving steel manufacturers in Alsace and Lorraine favourable access to supplies of coke in the Ruhr and Saar. To many ministers, Allied, bilateral or multilateral arrangements, like the International Steel Cartel of the 1920s, would probably have been sufficient, but they were prevented by the insistence of the United States and the U.K. on the rapid reconstruction of the German economy, which entailed the incorporation of the Ruhr and Rhineland in the FRG not their 'internationalization', by France's desire to break up German coal and steel cartels, against the wishes of West German industrialists, and by the German government's determination to reacquire the Saarland, undermining Paris's plans to maintain its separation or keep control of its industry.[90] It was only after the failure of 'traditional' and 'confederal' policies between 1945 and 1949 that the supranational European solution of the European Coal and Steel Community – first outlined by Monnet in a meeting with Spaak, the Belgian Foreign-Minister-in-exile, in 1941 – was actually taken up by the French *Commissaire Général au Plan* and accepted by Schuman and other ministers, permitting the implementation of American-inspired anti-trust clauses in the Treaty of Paris, overcoming a Franco-German impasse over the Saar and reassuring the governments of the Benelux countries, which were anxious that their interests would be overlooked in a bilateral Franco-German treaty.[91] Schuman's declaration of 9 May 1950, which initiated the foundation of the ECSC, did not mention supranationality, and talked instead of an authority 'whose decisions would tie together France and Germany'.[92]

Arguably, the main reason for the existence of an organization like the European Coal and Steel Community, from Paris's point of view, was the perceived decline of the French economy, which had been a matter of discussion since the nineteenth century – heightened in the interwar era – and on which all parties agreed.[93] 'From the very moment when armies are no longer the essence of the nations, it is the ability to cope with life, the capacity for work and production that become at once the essential preconditions for the independence and influence of our

country,' declared de Gaulle in a radio broadcast on 25 May 1945, days after
Germany's capitulation: 'Yesterday there was no national duty that had precedence
over the duty to fight. But today there is none that can take precedence over that
to produce.'[94] Although de Gaulle later bewailed France's exclusive fixation under
the Fourth Republic on 'its standard of living', he continued to emphasize the
theme of decline and to connect it to international influence and power:
'Decadence,' he confided in 1957: 'It is not that we are moving towards it, we are
there, we are rolling in it … France no longer has any national ambition.'[95] The
only way for the French right and centre to improve on what one commentator
– sceptical of policies of *grandeur* – called France's 'folding seat beside the Big
Three' seemed to be to rebuild its economy, maintaining access to raw materials
and markets, increasing its production of capital goods, and avoiding an immediate
and destructive conversion – urged by the United States – to free trade and fully
convertible currencies.[96] Failure to cooperate with Germany, probably – by 1949–
50 – within a European structure, would not be the perpetuation of the status
quo, given Bonn's changing attitudes and Washington's desire to reconstruct and
rearm the FRG, but competition against Germany in an unfavourable world
market. In respect of steel production, Monnet wrote to Schuman on 1 May 1950,
'Germany has already asked to be allowed to increase its output from 10 to 14
million tons', meaning that the myth of Franco-German parity – with French
production standing at 9 million tons – would have been exploded: 'We will
refuse, but the Americans will insist. Finally, we will make reservations and give
way … There is no need to describe the consequences in any detail: German
export dumping; pressure for protection in France; a halt in the freeing of trade;
the revival of prewar cartels; … France back in the rut of limited, protected
production.'[97] In the critical sphere of coal, iron and steel production, which
underpinned both reconstruction and rearmament, France – it was widely agreed
– needed to cooperate with Germany.

Against such a background, with de Gaulle himself conceding to Coudenhove-
Kalergi in 1948 that no one was 'more convinced of the necessity of creating
Europe' – which would mean delegating ' part of [each state's] sovereignty' – than
he was, in order to arrive at a 'regulation of the German question', the slow and
incremental nature of European integration is almost as striking as the
unprecedented establishment of supranational forms of government.[98] On 7 July
1944, Monnet had admitted to Macmillan that Europe's future depended on
Germany and that a United States of Europe was out of the question. Nevertheless,
he was hopeful that European trade and currencies could be coordinated under
the auspices of a strong League of Nations, and he predicted in an interview in
Fortune magazine in August that there would be 'a true yielding of sovereignty' to
'some kind of central union', together with a large European market without
customs barriers, not least to prevent the recrudescence of nationalism, 'which is
the curse of the modern world'.[99] In fact, integration took place more slowly than
Monnet had anticipated. Attempts to set up extensive supranational institutions
within the Council of Europe (1949) and European Defence and Political

Communities (1950–54) failed. To federalists such as Pierre Uri, a professor at the new *Ecole nationale d'administration* and one of the architects of the EEC, the European Coal and Steel Community 'was two things at once', 'a common basis of development' and 'a prototype for general integration', yet the former – as a practical means of developing Western European industry – seemed to have taken precedence over the latter.[100] After the 'defeat' of the EDC, Uri recalled that most members of the High Authority – or supranational executive – of the ECSC agreed that 'we will have to be modest', trying 'to extend the powers of the High Authority' from coal to oil, gas, electricity and transport, since 'it plays a major role in coal, iron ore and steel'.[101] Monnet, too, was cautious, preferring to concentrate on the new industry of nuclear energy – which became the European Atomic Energy Community (Euratom) in 1957 – because it was closely linked to the state and lacked entrenched vested interests: 'We started with Euratom because we didn't dare go to a Common Market.'[102] To Monnet in November 1955, after the matter had been discussed by foreign ministers at Messina in June, a common market, which was a customs union with a common external tariff, also implied 'federal social, monetary and conjuncture policies' to ensure that internal tariffs were removed or retained and other measures such as competition policy were designed which would allow different national markets and industries to coalesce and grow.[103] 'Our ambitions were modest,' Spaak wrote in retrospect: 'So were our hopes. It seemed important to us to advance on solid ground where we had real chances of success, leaving bigger plans till later. Above all, we had to avoid another rebuff.'[104]

In the event, it was the convergence of the German government with those of the Benelux countries which convinced the ministry of the right-wing Radical Edgar Faure that a common market was possible without too much damage to – or resistance from – reluctant sectors of the French economy. On the flight to Messina, the French Minister of Foreign Affairs Antoine Pinay was still expecting to say 'yes to Euratom and no to the Common Market' until Olivier Wormsier, the Director of Economic Relations at the Quai d'Orsay explained that 'it is not quite like that': 'France has already said no to the EDC. It cannot cast an outright veto a second time.'[105] Bonn's position was quite different, with Erhard 'against' Euratom, not least because the United States and Britain enjoyed 'a lead in this field', as Uri accepted.[106] By contrast, 'The German government would agree completely and Erhard would not hold out against' the pursuit of 'both approaches at the same time, Euratom on one hand and a general common market on the other', since the establishment of a European market could be seen as a staging post on the way to the gradual and qualified freeing of global – or, at least, Western – trade favoured by the German Economics Minister.[107]

A similar set of arguments were rehearsed within the Dutch and Belgian governments, where Spaak's own deputy, the Socialist Minister for Commerce and Vice-Minister for Foreign Affairs in Brussels, Victor Larock, had proposed sectoral Free Trade Areas (FTAs), including the U.K., within the OEEC on two separate occasions, in November 1954 and March 1955. In The Hague, too, most ministers were sympathetic to the traditions of free trade, Atlanticism and even neutrality associated with a maritime and imperial power. The Chamber of Commerce in Rotterdam was not alone, recalled Charles Rutten, in the European Directorate of the Dutch Foreign Office in 1956, in fearing that, 'if we get into a customs union with the French, it will be high tariffs, it will be the Continental system all over again. Where Napoleon did not succeed, Mollet will succeed and grass will grow on the quays of Rotterdam.'[108] Beyen, who had moved from the International Monetary Fund to the Foreign Ministry in 1952 as a compromise candidate of the Labour and Catholic parties, was unusual in rejecting 'the general opinion' that a common market 'would only be possible on an intergovernmental basis, and cooperation on a supranational basis only ... for specific sectors'.[109] Earlier, after the collapse of the EDC, he had warned that 'we should not place much hope on further supranational organisation in western Europe' and he had seriously considered the idea of an FTA within the OEEC.[110] By 1955, he was sure that 'the OEEC does not offer the degree of control western European countries need to make sure their economies are not at loggerheads' and that 'sectoral integration does not reinforce the sense of solidarity and unity in Europe to the same degree as general economic integration': 'To strengthen these sentiments, it is vital that a feeling of joint responsibility of the European states for the common welfare should be embodied in an organisation which follows the general interest, with an executive which is answerable not to the national governments but before a supranational parliament.'[111] Spaak, who – although 'scared' – was eventually convinced by Beyen's 'daring' plan, wondered 'if the policy you propose has much chance of success ..., in particular if the French government can accept it'.[112] Shortly afterwards, in May, the Benelux Memorandum, which Beyen and Spaak had drafted, was toned down, removing references to 'treaties', a 'common authority' and 'European Assembly' in favour of further 'studies' in order to determine what was acceptable to Paris and Bonn.[113]

Agreement was possible because the mechanisms of a common market, outlined by the Dutch Foreign Minister, promised to allow the protection of French agriculture and German transfer payments to France's *départements* and *territoires d'outre mer* in return for free access to the markets of the DOMs-TOMs, together with a wider, controlled movement towards freer trade in Europe favoured by Bonn, Brussels, The Hague and Rome. The supranational institutions of the European Economic Community – the European Parliamentary Assembly and the Commission of the EEC – were weaker than those of the ECSC, without a veto and dependent on a council of member states' ministers for the approval of legislation. What was more, they were, as Beyen had spelled out, designed principally to facilitate 'general economic integration'. This aim, it could be held, had long been shared by political leaders in Belgium and the Netherlands, who had signed the Treaty of Ouchy regulating tariffs between the two countries in 1932. It had also enjoyed broad support in France and Germany during the 1920s and early 1930s. Other objectives, such as de Gaulle's initial desire for a French-led, 'European' integration of military command structures or Adenauer's demand for 'equal rights' for the FRG as it sought to regain sovereignty, met with much greater resistance, even though some were eventually realized. Out of office, de Gaulle had summarily dismissed German calls for 'equality' in a radio broadcast of November 1949, despite the fact that he had come to champion a 'direct agreement between the French and German people', resting at first on economic integration and cultural exchange, and later on 'defence and politics'.[114] For his part, Adenauer was 'unable completely to conceal a degree of mistrust' during the negotiation of a European Coal and Steel Community, because 'he could not believe that we were really proposing full equality', recalled Monnet.[115] Mutual mistrust in areas other than the field of economic integration was common and inhibiting, with the chances of reaching agreement correspondingly reduced.

Conclusion

'Europe' was a popular cause and rallying point, founded on a widespread sense of relative decline and perceptions of historical self-destruction, articulated and reiterated by intellectuals in the public sphere. Many contemporaries – perhaps the majority – believed that it was essential for European states to cooperate and to grow in order to avoid eclipse and a lapse back into conflict. By the late 1940s, however, such cooperation – both diplomatic and military – appeared to have been safeguarded by the United States. With the signature of the Bretton Woods agreement and the approval of Marshall Aid, Washington had also helped to reestablish economic cooperation in Europe. Yet, here, European statesmen, even in the U.K., had more reservations about U.S. leadership and saw greater advantages accruing from a regional pooling of resources and the founding of common institutions, which could set, enforce and alter mutually agreeable regulations and restrictions. To advocates of state planning, a social market economy or Keynesian economics, the simultaneous freeing and controlling of trade within a common market proved more attractive than the alternatives of protectionism or U.S.-led laissez faire and currency convertibility. In this context, Franco-German reconciliation and European cooperation made sense in the late 1940s and 1950s, just as it had done in the 1920s. In both cases, they were accompanied and often abetted by appeals to a common European culture, history and 'fate' or 'future'. Crisis at once seemed to have promoted European cooperation and to have made it more precarious. The next chapter investigates how intellectuals helped to interpret and set the terms of such crises.

Notes

1. W. Lipgens, *Europa-Föderationspläne der Widerstandsbewegungen 1940–1945*; idem, 'European Federation in the Political Thought of Resistance Movements during World War II', *Central European History* 1 (1968), 5–19; idem, *A History of European Integration*; idem, *Die Anfänge der europäischen Einigungspolitik 1945–1950*; idem and W. Loth (eds), *Documents on the History*

of European Integration (Berlin, 1985–88), 3 vols.; W. Loth, 'Explaining European Integration', *Journal of European Integration History* 14 (2008), 12–16. For a study of pro-community federalism within French political elites, see C. Parsons, *A Certain Idea of Europe* (Ithaca, New York, 2003).

2. On transnationalism within postwar Christian Democracy, see especially W. Kaiser, *Christian Democracy and the Origins of European Union* (Cambridge, 2007); idem, 'Cooperation of European Catholic Politicians in Exile in Britain and the USA during the Second World War', *Journal of Contemporary History* 35 (2000), 439–65; idem, 'No Second Versailles: Transnational Contacts in the People and Freedom Group and the International Christian Democratic Union, 1936–1945', M. Gehler et al. (eds), *Christdemokratie in Europa im 20 Jahrhundert* (Vienna, 2001); idem and M. Gehler, 'Transnationalism and Early European Integration: The NEI and the Geneva Circle, 1947–1957', *Historical Journal* 44 (2001), 773–98; idem and B. Leucht, 'Informal Politics of Integration: Christian Democratic and Transatlantic Networks in the Creation of the ECSC Core Europe', *Journal of European Integration History* 14 (2008), 35–50.

3. J.R. Gillingham, 'A Theoretical Vacuum: European Integration and Historical Research Today', *Journal of European Integration History* 14 (2008), 32. See also J.R. Gillingham, *European Integration, 1950–2003: Superstate or New Market Economy* (Cambridge, 2003).

4. E.B. Haas, *The Uniting of Europe* (Stanford, 1958), revised edn. in 2004; P.C. Schmitter, 'Ernst B. Haas and the Legacy of Neo-Functionalism', *Journal of European Public Policy* 10 (2005), 255–72; P. Pierson, 'The Path to European Integration: An Historical-Institutionalist Account', in W. Sandholtz and A. Stone Sweet (eds), *European Integration and Supranational Governance* (Oxford, 1998); W. Sandholtz and A. Stone Sweet, 'European Integration and Supranational Governance', *Journal of European Public Policy* 4 (1997), 297–317, and 'European Integration and Supranational Governance Revisited', *Journal of European Public Policy* 6 (1999), 144–54; A.P. Branch and J.C. Ohrgaard, 'Trapped in the Supranational-Intergovernmental Dichotomy', *Journal of European Public Policy* 6 (1999), 123–43; S. Bulmer, '*Politics in Time* Meets the Politics of Time: Historical Institutionalism and the EU Timescape', *Journal of European Public Policy* 14 (2009), 307–24.

5. A.S. Milward, *The European Rescue of the Nation-State*; idem, *The Reconstruction of Western Europe, 1945–51* (London, 1984); idem and V. Sorensen (eds), *The Frontier of National Sovereignty: History and Theory, 1945–1992* (London, 1993); also, B. Bruneteau, 'The Construction of Europe and the Concept of the Nation-State', *Contemporary European History* 9 (2000), 245–60. A. Moravcsik, *The Choice for Europe: Social Purpose and State Power from Messina to Maastricht* (Ithaca, New York, 1998); idem and F. Schimmelfennig, 'Liberal Intergovernmentalism', in A. Wiener and T. Diez (eds), *European Integration Theory* (Oxford, 2009). For a historian's critique of Moravcsik, see M. Pine, 'European Integration: A Meeting Ground for History and Political Science?', *Journal of European Integration History* 14 (2008), 87–104.

6. A.S. Milward, 'Allegiance: The Past and the Future', *Journal of European Integration History* 1 (1995), 11–12.

7. Such oversight even extends to Wilfried Loth's fourfold model, which posits that the preservation of peace, the German question, markets, and power and competitiveness were the main driving forces behind European integration; W. Loth, 'Identity and Statehood in the Process of European Integration', *Journal of European Integration History* 6 (2000), 19–31; idem, 'Der Prozess der europäischen Integration', *Jahrbuch für europäische Geschichte* 1 (2000), 17–30.

8. This was the title of Eliot's lecture in 1946; P.M. Lützeler, *Die Schriftsteller und Europa*, 406–8.

9. For examples of cultural conceptions of Europe after 1945, similar to those of the interwar era, see Lützeler, *Schriftsteller*, 402–41.

10. K. Adenauer to S.J. Vogel, 26 Jan. 1948, in H.-P. Schwarz, 'Adenauer und Europa', *Vierteljahreshefte für Zeitgeschichte* 27 (1979), 482. For Carl Schmitt's long-standing case about the United States as the dominant great power, see Chapter 8 below.

11. On the extent of U.S. involvement in Germany, see A. Schwartz, *America's Germany: John McCloy and the Federal Republic of Germany* (Cambridge, Mass., 1991).

12. Jarausch, *After Hitler*, 55.

13. K. Schumacher, 3–4 Jan. 1946, cited in W. Loth, 'German Conceptions of Europe during the Escalation of the East-West Conflict, 1945–1949', in J. Becker and F. Knipping (eds), *Power in Europe? Great Britain, France, Italy and Germany in a Postwar World, 1945–1950* (Berlin, 1986), 524.

14. K. Adenauer private letter, 27 July 1949, in Schwarz, 'Adenauer und Europa', *Vierteljahreshefte für Zeitgeschichte* 27 (1979), 479–80.

15. E. Di Nolfo, 'Das Problem der europäischen Einigung als ein Aspekt der italienischen Aussenpolitik 1945–1954', *Vierteljahreshefte für Zeitgeschichte* 28 (1980), 151.

16. Ibid., 156. See also M. Miller, 'The Approaches to European Institution-Building of Carlo Sforza, Italian Foreign Minister, 1947–51', in A. Deighton (ed.), *Building Postwar Europe: National Decision-Makers and European Institutions, 1948–1963* (Basingstoke, 1995), 55–69, which emphasizes both the adaptability and the traditionalism of Sforza's approach, rooted in the assumptions of the nineteenth century.

17. Di Nolfo, 'Das Problem', *Vierteljahreshefte für Zeitgeschichte* 28 (1980), 161.

18. See P.P. D'Attore, 'Americanism and Anti-Americanism in Italy', in Stirk and Willis (eds), *Shaping Postwar Europe*, 43–52; J.E. Miller, *The United States and Italy, 1940–1950* (Chapel Hill, 1986). More generally, A. Stephan (ed.), *The Americanization of Europe: Culture, Diplomacy and the Anti-Americanism after 1945* (New York, 2008).

19. J.W. Young, *Britain and European Unity, 1945–1992* (London, 1993), 1–52; W. Kaiser, *Using Europe, Abusing the Europeans: Britain and European Integration, 1945–1963* (Basingstoke, 1997); D. Gowland and A. Turner, *Reluctant Europeans: Britain and European Integration, 1945–1998* (London, 1999), and idem and A. Wright, *Britain and European Integration since 1945* (London, 2009); S. George, *Britain and European Integration since 1945* (Oxford, 1992); N.J. Crowson, *The Conservative Party and European Integration since 1945: At the Heart of Europe?* (London, 2009), 14–44, 71–104.

20. For the case against British isolation in Europe, see N.P. Ludlow, 'Paying the Price of Victory? Postwar Britain and the Ideas of National Independence', in D. Geppert (ed.), *Postwar Challenge*, 259–72.

21. V.R. Rothwell, *Britain and the Cold War, 1941–1947* (London, 1982), 435.

22. *The Times*, 5 Jan. 1948, cited in G. Warner, 'Britain and Europe in 1948: The View from the Cabinet', in Becker and Knipping (eds), *Power in Europe?*, 34.

23. E. Bevin to P. Ramadier, 22 Sept. 1947, ibid., 35.

24. Ibid.

25. On British anxiety about such withdrawal, see Deighton, *The Impossible Peace*; also, W.C. Cromwell, 'The Marshall Plan, Britain and the Cold War', *Review of International Studies* 8 (1982), 233–49.

26. J. Baylis, *The Diplomacy of Pragmatism: Britain and the Formation of NATO, 1942–1949* (Basingstoke, 1993).

27. Cabinet Economic Policy Committee, 7 Nov. 1947, Warner, 'Britain and Europe', in Becker and Knipping (eds), *Power in Europe?*, 36.

28. A paper on 'The Middle East' presented to the Cabinet in April 1949, cited in A. Adamthwaite, 'Britain and the World, 1945–1949: The View from the Foreign Office', ibid., 19.

29. Warner, 'Britain and Europe', ibid., 43.

30. U.S. leaders and officials certainly supported the process at specific points, for instance in putting pressure on Bonn to break up its coal and steel cartels prior to the formation of the ECSC, but they did not seek to bring supranational institutions into being themselves, in contrast to their actions in respect of Bretton Woods, the Marshall Plan, the OEEC, GATT and NATO. Geir Lundestad, *'Empire' by Integration: The United States and European Integration, 1945–1997* (Oxford, 1998) emphasizes U.S. support for integration, but within an 'Atlantic framework', which – at times – took priority and to which Washington devoted most of its energies. See also J.M. Diefendorf et al. (eds), *American Policy and the Reconstruction of West Germany, 1945–1955* (Cambridge, 1993).

31. C. Spagnolo, 'Reinterpreting the Marshall Plan: The Impact of the European Recovery Programme in Britain, France, Western Germany and Italy, 1947–1955', in Geppert (ed.), *Postwar Challenge*, 275–98; M. Hogan, *The Marshall Plan* (Cambridge, 1987); J. Killick, *The United States and European Reconstruction, 1945–1960* (Edinburgh, 1998).

32. S. Lee, 'German Decision-Making Elites and European Integration: German "Europolitik" during the Years of the EEC and Free Trade Area Negotiations', in A. Deighton (ed.), *Building Postwar Europe*, 43–44.

33. See I.M. Wall, *The United States and the Making of Postwar France* (Cambridge, 1991).

34. K. Adenauer to E. Friedländer, 13 June 1953, cited in Schwarz, 'Adenauer und Europa', *Historische Zeitschrift* 27 (1979), 480. Also, G. Schmidt, 'Divided Europe – Divided Germany, 1950–63', *Contemporary European History* 3 (1994), 155–92.

35. D.C. Large, 'Grand Illusions: the United States, the Federal Republic of Germany and the European Defence Community, 1950–1954', in J.M. Diefendorf et al. (eds), *American Policy and the Reconstruction of West Germany*, 375–94; H.E. Volkmann and W. Schwengler (eds), *Die Europäische Verteidigungsgemeinschaft* (Boppard, 1985).

36. T.P. Ireland, *Creating the Entangling Alliance* (Westport, Conn., 1981); F.H. Heller and J.R. Gillingham (eds), *NATO: The Founding of the Atlantic Alliance and the Integration of Europe* (New York, 1992); A. Grosser, *The Western Alliance* (London, 1980); and P. Winand, *Eisenhower, Kennedy and the United States of Europe* (New York, 1993).

37. Schwarz, 'Adenauer und Europa', *Historische Zeitschrift* 27 (1979), 516.

38. According to Andreas Rödder, 'Der Mythos von der frühen Westbindung. Konrad Adenauer und Stresemanns Aussenpolitik', *Vierteljahreshefte für Zeitgeschichte* 41 (1993), 543–73, Adenauer had little knowledge of foreign policy, despite being embroiled in the Ruhr dispute as mayor of Cologne, and he remained opposed to Stresemann's policy of understanding in the West.

39. D. Staritz and A. Sywottek, 'The International Political Situation as Seen by the German *Linksparteien* (SPD, SED and KPD) between 1945 and 1949', in Becker and Knipping (eds), *Power in Europe?*, vol. 1, 213–24.

40. See Chapters 3–8.

41. Cited in M. Overesch, 'Senior West German Politicians and Their Perceptions of the German Situation in Europe, 1945–1949', in Becker and Knipping (eds), *Power in Europe?*, vol. 1, 125.

42. Ibid.

43. Adenauer, ibid.; Jordan cited in W. Becker, 'Views of the Foreign Policy Situation among the CDU Leadership, 1945–57', in Becker and Knipping (eds), *Power in Europe?*, vol. 2, 365–66.

44. Brüning in 1950–51, cited in Schwarz, 'Adenauer und Europa', *Vierteljahreshefte für Zeitgeschichte* 27 (1979), 500–501.

45. Ibid., 502–5.

46. Cited in Overesch, 'Senior West German Politicians', in Becker and Knipping (eds), *Power in Europe?*, vol. 1, 129.

47. Schwarz, 'Adenauer und Europa', *Vierteljahreshefte für Zeitgeschichte* 27 (1979), 512.

48. See, in general, J.W. Young, *France, the Cold War and the Western Alliance* (Leicester, 1990).

49. J. Monnet, mid-April and the start of May, 1950, cited in F. Duchêne, *Jean Monnet: The First Statesman of Interdependence* (New York, 1994), 198.

50. Monnet, 5 Aug. 1943 (Algiers), cited in E. du Réau, 'Integration or Cooperation? Europe and the Future of the Nation-State in France, 1945–1955', in Geppert (ed.), *Postwar Challenge*, 241.

51. Duchêne, *Monnet*, 187–88.

52. Ibid., 188.

53. D. Bruce, 25 Apr. 1950, ibid., 189.

54. De Gaulle, 29 June 1947, in Loth, 'De Gaulle und Europa', *Historische Zeitschrift* 253 (1991), 637.

55. Cited in S. Berstein, 'French Power', in Becker and Knipping (eds), *Power in Europe?*, vol. 1, 180–81.

56. Cited in P. Guillen, 'Europe as a Cure for French Impotence? The Guy Mollet Government and the Negotiation of the Treaties of Rome', in E. Di Nolfo (ed.), *Power in Europe?*, vol. 2, 507.

57. See S. Berstein, 'The Perception of French Power by the Political Forces' and P. Milza, 'Public Opinion and Perception of Power in France at the End of the Fourth Republic', ibid., 333–50, 462–76; M. Newman, 'Léon Blum, French Socialism and European Unity, 1940–1950', *Historical Journal* 4 (1981), 189–200.

58. C. Wurm, *Western Europe and Germany: The Beginnings of European Integration, 1945–1960* (Oxford, 1995); D. Calleo, *The German Problem Reconsidered* (Cambridge, 1978), 161–78; K. Larres (ed.), *Uneasy Allies: British-German Relations and European Integration since 1945* (Oxford, 2000).

59. Berstein, 'French Power', in Becker and Knipping (eds), *Power in Europe?*, vol. 1, 176.

60. Monnet, 22 July 1947, in Duchêne, *Monnet*, 184.

61. Ibid., 206; Réau, 'Integration or Cooperation?', in Geppert (ed.), *Postwar Challenge*, 248.

62. Guillen, 'Europe as a Cure for French Impotence?', in E. Di Nolfo, *Power in Europe?*, vol. 2, 507.

63. Duchêne, *Monnet*, 191.

64. Cited in Loth, 'De Gaulle und Europa', *Historische Zeitschrift* 253 (1991), 631.

65. Duchêne, *Monnet*, 199.

66. Monnet note of 13 Dec. 1948, and Mischlich memoirs, ibid., 206.

67. H. Alphand, 9 Feb. 1953, in G. Bossuat, 'Les hauts fonctionnaires français et le processus d'unité en Europe occidentale d'Alger à Rome, 1943–1958', *Journal of European Integration History* 1 (1995), 101.

68. Loth, 'De Gaulle und Europa', *Historische Zeitschrift* 253 (1991), 645–46. The argument here counters that of Loth, who emphasizes de Gaulle's willingness to consider supranational solutions.

69. Ibid.

70. On continuities in France, see R. Boyer, 'Les bureaux d'études du ministère des Affaires étrangères et l'Europe pendant la Seconde Guerre mondiale', in R. Girault and G. Bossuat (eds), *Europe brisée, Europe retrouvée* (Paris, 1994), 133–52; on Belgium, see G. Duchenne, *Esquisses d'une Europe nouvelle. L'européisme dans la Belgique de l'entre-deux-guerres 1919–1939* (Brussels, 2008), 531–638.

71. R. Marjolin, 'What Type of Europe', in D. Brinkley and C. Hackett (eds), *Jean Monnet: The Path to European Unity* (Basingstoke, 1991), 172–73, extracted from Marjolin's memoirs, published in English in 1989.

72. Ibid., 172.

73. Ibid., 171.

74. Cited in A. Adamthwaite, 'Sir Anthony Eden: Pro- or Anti-European? The Making of Britain's European Policies', in G. Bossuat (ed.), *Inventer l'Europe. Histoire nouvelle des groupes d'influence et des acteurs de l'unitee européenne* (Berne, 2003), 249; J.W. Young, *Britain and European Unity, 1945–1992* (London, 1993), 1–52, and idem, 'Churchill's "No" to Europe', *Historical Journal* 28 (1985), 923–37; C. Lord, '"With but not of": Britain and the Schuman Plan, a Reinterpretation', *Journal of European Integration History* 4 (1998), 23–46.

75. Adamthwaite, 'Eden', in Bossuat (ed.), *Inventer l'Europe*, 249.

76. Memorandum of the Italian delegation at the EDC talks, 9 Oct. 1951, cited in D. Preda, 'De Gasperi, Spinelli et le project de communauté politique et européenne', ibid., 343. See Chapters 15–16 below.

77. See Chapter 4; for Johan Huizinga's loose use of the term, see Chapter 12.

78. Adamthwaite, 'Eden', in Bossuat (ed.), *Inventer l'Europe*, 249. S. Croft, 'British Policy towards Western Europe, 1947–1949: The Best of Possible Worlds?', *International Affairs* 64 (1988), 617–29.

79. Cited in Loth, 'De Gaulle und Europa', *Historische Zeitschrift* 253 (1991), 631.

80. Ibid., 640.

81. Ibid., 641.

82. Cited in G. Bossuat, 'Les euro-socialistes de la SFIO: Réseaux et influences', in idem (ed.), *Inventer l'Europe*, 422.

83. Preda, 'De Gasperi', in Bossuat (ed.), *Inventer l'Europe*, 344.

84. Cited in Réau, 'Integration or Cooperation?', in Geppert (ed.), *Postwar Challenge*, 256. Also, G.H. Sotou, 'Georges Bidault et la construction européenne 1944–1954', *Revue d'histoire diplomatique* 105 (1991), 269–72.

85. Ibid., 257, citing Debré's memoirs, published in 1984. More generally, E. Fursdon, *The European Defence Community* (London, 1980).

86. Eden in Duchêne, *Monnet*, 209; on resistance to federalism, see Bossuat, 'Les hauts fonctionnaires', *Journal of European Integration History* 1 (1995), 100–101; J. Gillingham, *Coal, Steel and the Rebirth of Europe* (Cambridge, 1991), and idem, 'Solving the Ruhr Problem: German Heavy Industry and the Schuman Plan', in K. Schwabe (ed.), *Die Anfänge des Schuman-Plans* (Baden-Baden, 1988), 268–80; A.W. Lovett, 'The United States and the Schuman Plan', *Historical Journal* 39 (1996), 425–55.

87. Duchêne, *Monnet*, 232.

88. Ibid., 262–63.

89. Bossuat, 'Les hauts fonctionnaires', *Journal of European Integration History* 1 (1995), 102–4.

90. On Paris's various attempts and setbacks in the coordination of coal and steel production in the Belgian, French and German borderlands, see F.M.B. Lynch, *France and the International Economy, from Vichy to the Treaty of Rome* (London, 1997); G. Bossuat, *La France, l'aide américaine et la construction européenne 1944–1954* (Paris, 1992); S. Lefèvre, *Les relations économiques franco-allemandes de 1945 à 1955* (Paris, 1998).

91. See Frances Lynch's criticism of Craig Parsons' emphasis of pro-community decision makers in 'France and European Integration: From the Schuman Plan to Economic and Monetary Union', *Contemporary European History* 13 (2004), 117–20. Also, C. Parsons, 'Showing Ideas as Causes: The Origins of the European Union', *International Organization* 56 (2002), 47–84.

92. Cited in G. Trausch, 'Der Schuman-Plan zwischen Mythos und Realität', in R. Hudemann (ed.), *Europa im Blick der Historiker*, 109.

93. S. Berstein, 'French Power', and R. Frank, 'The French Dilemma: Modernisation with Dependence or Independence and Decline', in Becker and Knipping (eds), *Power in Europe?*, vol. 1, 163–84, 263–82.

94. Cited in Frank, ibid., 264.

95. Berstein, 'French Power', in Di Nolfo (ed.), *Power in Europe?*, vol. 2, 335.

96. André Philip, 1–2 Sept. 1946, *Le Populaire*, cited in Berstein, ibid., vol. 1, 166.

97. Cited in Duchêne, *Monnet*, 198.

98. De Gaulle to Coudenhove-Kalergi, 30 Dec. 1948, in Loth, 'De Gaulle und Europa', *Historische Zeitschrift* 253 (1991), 637; on the delegation of sovereignty, de Gaulle to G. Palewski and R. Triboulet, 28 Dec. 1951, ibid., 641.

99. Duchêne, *Monnet*, 187.

100. Ibid., 269.

101. Ibid., 264.

102. Ibid., 270.

103. Ibid.

104. Ibid.

105. Ibid., 281.

106. Ibid., 269.

107. Carl-Friedrich Ophüls, 6 Apr. 1955, cited by Uri, ibid.

108. Ibid., 272. On the antecedents of such a stance, see Chapter 12.

109. Ibid.

110. Ibid.

111. Beyen to Spaak, 4 Apr. 1955, ibid., 273. Also, R.T. Griffith and A. Asbeek Brusse, 'The Dutch Cabinet and the Rome Treaties', in E. Serra (ed.), *Il Rilancio dell'Europa e i trattati di Roma* (Milan, 1989), 461–93; R.T. Griffiths (ed.), *The Netherlands and the Integration of Europe* (Amsterdam, 1990); and W. Mallinson, *From Neutrality to Commitment: Dutch Foreign Policy, NATO and European Integration* (London, 2010).

112. Spaak to Beyen, 7 Apr. 1955, Duchêne, *Monnet*, 274.

113. Ibid., 274, 279.
114. De Gaulle, 14 Nov. 1949, Loth, 'De Gaulle und Europa', *Historische Zeitschrift* 253 (1991), 638.
115. Duchêne, *Monnet*, 207.

Chapter 3

INVENTING EUROPE AND REINVENTING THE NATION-STATE IN A NEW WORLD ORDER

Mark Hewitson

'Europe' might have been a myth, as Simone de Beauvoir claimed, but most policy makers and intellectuals seem to have believed that it was real and that it was under threat, from the final stages of the First World War and the Russian Revolution onwards.[1] This chapter analyses prominent writers' and thinkers' descriptions and evaluations of Europe's predicament, pointing to important continuities which characterized the entire period between 1917 and 1957. As a result of such assessments, political solutions on a European level appeared both desirable and unobjectionable. There was little agreement amongst intellectuals, however, about the extent and political form of any future European project, or about how it could be reconciled with the priorities of reconstructed nation-states.

The Quest for Origins and Identity

The protean and contentious nature of ideas about Europe brings into question the usefulness of any search for origins or enduring and common components. The continent was too complex, as Lucien Febvre indicated, to permit the identification of 'building blocks'.[2] Commentators disagreed about the very foundations of Europe's identity, although few doubted that it existed. In Germany, the terms 'Abendland', 'Mitteleuropa', 'Paneuropa', 'Reich' and 'Grossraum' all subsumed or impinged on the meaning of 'Europe', but they all had different connotations, linked to the domestic disputes of political parties.[3] Was Europe principally a territory or geographical region and, if so, where were its borders?[4]

For Richard von Coudenhove-Kalergi, the founder of the Paneuropa movement, the United Kingdom was not sufficiently European to be included, at least until 1938, whereas for Wilhelm Heile, the head of the *Verband für europäische Verständigung*, Britain was a central part of Europe, on which the future of the continent was likely to depend.[5] Many observers – including Central and Eastern European publicists such as Jerzy Stempowski – were sceptical that geography defined Europe at all, preferring to think of it as a culture or civilization with a shared history.[6] Yet these definitions, too, were marked by ambiguity and contradiction. Europeans in the interwar era, remarked Ortega y Gasset, had seen their fundamental beliefs replaced by doubts under the onslaught of new ideologies and forms of dictatorship, leaving them little sense of the continent's position in the world: 'One part of Europe advocates principles which it considers "new"; the other part tries to defend traditional principles. Now this is the best proof that neither set of principles is in force at the moment, and either they have lost, or have not reached, the status of accepted norms.'[7] After the Second World War, 'each people' in Europe was 'introverted in spite of the visibly gigantic worldwide intercourse' taking place.[8] In the interwar and postwar years, it was hard to distinguish values, ideas, practices or institutions which could unite the continent. Europe after the First World War, went on the Spanish intellectual, had had an 'ignoble vegetative existence …, its muscles flabby for want of exercise, without any plan of the new life', meaning that even a culturally backward event such as the Russian Revolution, which was reminiscent of 1817 rather than 1917, risked attracting Europeans to its cause: 'It is simply a misunderstanding of the European to expect that he can hear unmoved that call to new action when he has no standard of a cause as great to unfurl in opposition.'[9] Many observers repeated 'daily' and 'with moving sanctimony that Western civilisation must be saved', but it was unlikely that such an endeavour would be unifying or worthwhile: its proponents, declared Ortega, 'seem to me like dissectors who tire themselves out trying to resurrect a mummy. Western civilisation has died a beautiful and honourable death. It died alone; its enemies did not kill it.'[10] What, though, was to replace that civilization and to unite the continent?

Most elements of a supposed European identity were contested. The significance and role of antiquity, Christianity, the Enlightenment, science, industrialization and imperialism were all subject to contradictory interpretations. Some authors such as the German playwright Gerhard Hauptmann believed that these traditions had been destroyed by the First World War, turning 'Europe's pride' into 'its shamelessness': 'its most shameless lies are Christianity, love of mankind, the rule of reason, international law, the League of Nations, humanity, culture. Instead of this, they must be called bestiality, hatred of mankind, the rule of unreason, international lawlessness, the persecution of nations, inhumanity and, instead of the word "Kultur", theft, robbery, arson, murder and plunder must stand.'[11] Some observers such as Paul Valéry, who seemed to agree with the German writer in his well-known essay on 'The Crisis of the Spirit' in 1919, in fact continued to presume that European science and technology were superior to those the rest of the world and should not be exported overseas.[12] Yet other intellectuals questioned whether Hauptmann's apparently indisputable grounds for European pride had ever existed. Albert Demangeon, whose *Déclin de l'Europe* (1920) enjoyed a success in France redolent of that of Oswald Spengler's *Untergang des Abendlandes* (1918–22) in Germany, accounted for the continent's decline largely in economic and political terms, as the rest of the world was able to effect a process of 'de-Europeanisation', in much the same way that the editor of *Die Zukunft*, Maximilian Harden, prophesied in 1923 that 'Europe would be the sphere of economically more unified states or it would lose its ascendancy and submit to an honourable calcification'.[13] For his part, Spengler saw Western – or Central and Western European – decline largely in cultural terms, albeit mixed with a determining form of materialism, and he predicted that it was irreversible, as part of the inevitable rise and fall of monadic world cultures.[14] Many commentators continued this tradition after the Second World War, echoing T.S. Eliot's anxiety that 'our entire culture' could 'collapse'.[15] Only a minority, however, placed much hope, like Eliot, in 'our Christian legacy' of morality and its mediation of the 'ancient civilizations' of Greece and Rome.[16] As the British poet Stephen Spender announced to a meeting of European intellectuals – including Karl Jaspers, Georg Lukacs, Georges Bernanos, Denis de Rougement and Julien Benda – in Geneva in 1946, Europe could no longer find its cultural unity in the idea of Europe, since this was characterized by 'nihilism, nationalism, destruction and hatred'.[17] Few found, like Klaus Mann in his posthumously published essay on 'Europe's Search for a New Credo' (1949), cause for celebration in the fact that 'everyone in Europe' was 'tortured and unsettled', ignorant and fearful of what was to come.[18] Despair, nostalgia or utopianism – in the manner of Jean-Paul Sartre's call for 'a united, socialist European Community' in 1949 – were more common responses.[19] As in the years after the First World War, confusion was widespread.

In general, right-wing authors such as Spengler and Hermann von Keyserling tended to stress the continent's cultural collapse to a greater degree, emphasizing the lapsed legacy of Christianity and criticizing the impact of the Enlightenment, science and industrial transformation.[20] Liberal and left-wing observers were often more optimistic about 'rationality' and economic 'progress' and more willing to condemn Christian obscurantism, but there were many exceptions. German commentators across the political spectrum were arguably more suspicious of '*Zivilisation*', or the assimilation of quantifiable methods and material technologies, and they were more receptive to the Romantic irrationality of '*Kultur*' – a proclivity which can even be detected in Max Horkheimer and Theodor Adorno's iconoclastic *Dialektik der Aufklärung* (1944) – than were their French counterparts, who frequently equated 'civilization', humanitarianism, enlightenment and culture.[21] The nationalist right in countries defeated in the First World War was more likely to espouse technology in the name of a new European order and to rail against an old order associated with the Paris peace conferences than was its equivalent in the victorious powers. From a standpoint of formal neutrality in the First and Second World Wars, an observer like Ortega was perhaps especially eclectic but nonetheless indicative in his selection of European attributes, discounting antiquity and downgrading Christianity – 'men have not lived exclusively by faith in God, but … faith in science, in reason' – in his identification of the origins of 'Europe' in the eighth century, as Islam destroyed the civilization of the Mediterranean and the centre of the continent was established in the north by Charlemagne with the emergence of 'Germanism' and the duality of Roman-inspired law and states and Germanic freedom, science and vitality.[22] The confusion caused by such heterogeneity was visible in the mixed response of some contemporaries to the Nazis' exhumation of many of the same tropes, as part of their plan for a 'New Europe' or a 'European confederation'.[23] Although mistaken, John Maynard Keynes's fear in November 1941 that Hitler stood a chance of getting 'his new Europe going properly' hinted at contemporaries' uncertainty about what 'Europe' was or what it stood for.[24]

Europeanism, Nationalism and the State

To many observers, the European project was still obstructed by the tradition and actuality of the state. Was the nation-state compatible with Europeanism? Some, like Benda, denounced nationalism altogether after the Great War, arguing that it had replaced the egotism of the individual with the egotism of the group.[25] The 'treason of the clerks', identified by the French writer in the 1920s, consisted in an 'attachment, more ferocious, conscious and organised than ever, to the *purely temporal*, and contempt for all genuinely ideal and disinterested values', leaving humanity with only two 'religions' – 'Nation' or 'Class'.[26] Accordingly, 'Europe will be above all a moral act, if morality consists in Being ceasing to think of itself under the mode of the real, of the distinct, of the finite, [in order] to think of itself under the mode of the infinite or divine.'[27] This 'passion for reason', intrinsic to Benda's aspirations for Europe, would banish nationalism: 'You will only vanquish nationalist passion by another passion.'[28] Few of Benda's contemporaries imitated such flights of fancy, even if 'Europeanism' extended as far as Pierre Drieu La Rochelle on the far right, with the French fascist maintaining his belief in a 'United States of Europe' from the 1920s, when he put his faith in big business, to the later stages of the Second World War, when he continued to champion Hitlerism as the 'last rampart of some liberty in Europe'.[29] Nationalism, in Drieu's opinion, was one of the 'great doctrinal systems of modern times', along with socialism, but it was 'anti-human' and deterministic, based on notions of soil and climate, and it impeded, at least in the form of the narrow chauvinism of the masses, a necessary transition to a more dynamic and economically successful European federation.[30] Nonetheless, the French writer and journalist continued to conceive of Europe as a collective of nation-states, with nationalism constituting a stage of fascism, which was itself justified – in *With Doriot* (1937) – as a means of bolstering the French state in order to make it unassailable.[31]

Most intellectuals agreed that nation-states and national affiliations were ineluctable. In France after the Second World War, Raymond Aron, who had been a close friend and associate of Jean-Paul Sartre but who was moving towards the centre-right, oscillated between calls for greater European cooperation – both political and economic – and warnings that national obstacles, especially in the U.K. and France, could not be overcome, making a West European federation a 'pure utopia', as he put in *L'Age des empires et l'avenir de la France* (1945).[32] Although he was sure by 1948 that 'only an authority to which states have transferred part of their sovereignty will be capable of substituting the unity of a great economic area for the multiplicity of national economies, each enclosed within its own frontiers, regulations, and monetary and fiscal policy', he continued to doubt 'that ancient nations, intensely conscious of their uniqueness and history and laden with the memory of their secular rivalries, should voluntarily renounce their unconditional sovereignty'.[33] Aron supported the supposedly moderate and limited European Coal and Steel Community in 1950, partly on the grounds that 'Europe cannot afford the luxury of disappointing its peoples and accepting the failure of such an undertaking', but he opposed – in 1954 – the European Defence Community, which had allegedly occasioned 'the greatest ideological and political debate France has known since the Dreyfus Affair', because it implied – or would be seen to imply – 'an abandonment of sovereignty'.[34] For the *Le Figaro* journalist, it was unrealistic to think of a 'European government' akin to a national one.[35] Such an institution could only be a long-term goal not a short-term expectation.

Aron's position was shared by the majority of commentators in other countries, even after the discrediting of extreme – or fascist – nationalism in the Second World War. In Britain, some prominent intellectuals – especially exiles such as Friedrich Hayek and Karl Popper – had come to abhor nationalism as a revival of tribalism, but few saw Europeanism as a plausible alternative.[36] Most continued to assume, like the Oxford philosopher and Russian émigré Isaiah Berlin, that national belonging underpinned citizenship and political participation, taking precedence over other identities and values.[37] In Spain, where authoritarian nationalism persisted under Franco, the principal advocate of Europe, Ortega y Gasset, had contended that the nation – or 'society led by the state' – was not defined by geography, language or culture, but by a vision of the future which it extended to all groups, meaning that it was 'at all times something that comes from and goes forward', and that it was 'always doing something in common: conquering other peoples, founding colonies, aligning itself with other peoples; that is to say that at any moment it is exceeding what appeared to be the basic principle of union, that is, kinship, language, natural boundaries.'[38] Since the Middle Ages, aristocracies, states and nationalities had vied for supremacy, leading in much of Northern and Western Europe to the establishment of powerful, elite-led, more or less democratic nation-states during the third stage of civilization from 1848 onwards, after earlier traditional-mythical and individualistic-rationalistic stages. These 'vertebrate' nation-states – Britain, France and Germany – had created 'that mode of human existence in accordance with which the world has been organised', Ortega had declared in 1929.[39] Spain remained 'invertebrate', since the state had developed too early – in the sixteenth century – and the vernacular traditions of the people had been allowed to weaken the aristocracy, and other elites, permanently. In this context, nationalism was a necessary corrective, to be adopted by all Spanish parties, including the socialists: 'The less developed their respective nations are, the more national socialist parties have to be.'[40] After the imposition of Franco's dictatorship in the Spanish Civil War and the destructive force of national conflicts in the Second World War, it could seem that nationalisms were 'so many blind alleys', which had a 'positive value' in 'periods of consolidation', but which were 'nothing but a mania, a pretext to escape from the necessity of inventing something new', in a Europe where 'everything is more than consolidated'.[41] Yet it was still difficult to discern from Ortega's postwar writings how the existing, 'basically national structure' would 'be replaced by a basically European one'.[42]

The championing of Europeanism and reaction against nationalism went furthest in Germany after 1945, where nationalism had been tarred by the brush of racism under the National Socialists. Academics and publicists, especially resurfacing liberals, criticized Germany under – and prior to – the Nazi dictatorship, emphasizing either the moral failings of an unreflective nationalism, Romanticism and other forms of utopianism – as philosophers such as Karl Jaspers and literary figures such as Thomas Mann were inclined to do – or the institutional shortcomings of Weimar democracy and German liberalism, which became favourite subjects of social scientists such as Karl Dietrich Bracher, whose *Die Auflösung der Weimarer Demokratie* was published in 1955.[43] Their calls, respectively, for reeducation and for a refounding of democracy usually proposed the reconstruction of an acceptable German state, after the unacceptable extremes of the National Socialist regime, and they generally assumed – notwithstanding the early appearance of what Dirk A. Moses has termed 'non-German Germans' on the left – the continuing existence of a German national identity.[44] When the exiled Austrian constitutional lawyer Hans Kelsen, the most prominent legal commentator of the interwar and postwar periods, asserted in 1945 that Germany was no longer a state in international law, since the 'supreme authority' of the Allies contradicted the definition of a state as 'a certain population ... living on a definite territory under an independent government', the majority of political and legal theorists rejected his argument in favour of a continuing tradition of statehood and nationality.[45]

The many points of disagreement amongst academics in the late 1940s and early 1950s about the nature of the state, democracy, political parties and politics, from Carl Schmitt and his followers on the right to Otto Kirchheimer and the Frankfurt School on the left, frequently betrayed uncertainty or scepticism about the national sentiments of significant sections of the German population. Thus, the sociologist Helmut Schelsky opposed Schmittian – and, indeed, Max Horkheimer's – critiques of an apolitical, administered, technocratic society with the argument that such a society created stability in spite of alienation from the modern democratic order on the part of a 'sceptical generation' after 1945.[46] Political abstractions and a rapid transformation of institutions risked a reversion to authoritarianism and nationalism, as had occurred under the Weimar Republic, contended Schelsky, citing the revised edition of Arnold Gehlen's *Der Mensch* (1950) in his support.[47] Likewise, defenders and opponents of different versions of the 'modern democratic state' (Gerhard Leibholz), purportedly based on well-organized political parties and an implied concept of French-inspired direct democracy, and 'traditional, liberal-representative parliamentary democracy' (Ernst Fraenkel), resting on British notions of representation and a strong parliament, were interested in harnessing, educating and controlling a German public that had so recently turned against parties and democracy in the name of a national and racial *Volksgemeinschaft*.[48] The attempt of the liberal journalist and political scientist Dolf Sternberger from the late 1940s onwards to salvage the idea of 'patriotism', as an attachment to laws and *patrie*, explicitly acknowledged the public discrediting of the term 'nationalism' and failed to resolve the problem, which the Heidelberg academic conceded was 'a very remarkable situation', that the Basic Law included as citizens millions of 'Germans' who lived outside the territory of the Federal Republic.[49] The reluctance of many commentators openly to discuss the national question did not mean that it had disappeared in Germany or elsewhere.

The means by which persisting national affiliations were to be reconciled with attachments to 'Europe' were often left undiscussed in the relevant postwar literature, echoing the French publicist Bertrand de Jouvenel's admission in 1930 that 'the reconciliation of nationalism and internationalism, let's be frank, is a fairy tale'.[50] 'The truth is that we have to choose,' he went on: 'If we wish to maintain full and complete sovereignty, a United States of Europe remains a dead letter.'[51] Friedrich Meinecke, the liberal historian and well-known critic of the Nazi dictatorship, had argued in *Die deutsche Katastrophe* (1946) that only those recognizing the 'internal alien domination' of 'a criminal club' of National Socialists would discover 'a solution to the national problem of duty', making 'the era of external, alien domination' of the Allies after 1945 palatable.[52] In other words, Germans who failed to understand that the Allied occupation was a direct consequence of Nazi crimes would not be able to identify and carry out their 'national' responsibilities. Yet Meinecke went on to suggest that National Socialism was not a specifically German phenomenon, but an extension of modern European pathologies resulting – in an echo of Ortega y Gasset and other contemporary thinkers – from the transition to mass society, which had served to simplify notions of national belonging, loyalty and interest and to pervert the dominant nineteenth-century movements of nationalism and socialism. Germany, according to this reading, was not a special case but a European problem.[53] References to 'Europe' here were, in part, designed to relativize and make comprehensible Germans' feelings of guilt and actual culpability for the catastrophe of the Second World War.[54]

Such references were also intended to facilitate the reacquisition of sovereignty, as Adenauer struggled to persuade the Federal Republic's neighbours in the 1950s that West Germany had changed and as the Cold War order in Europe came to depend on the partition and diplomatic weakness of the two German states.[55] The European continent provided an arena, only partially controlled by the two superpowers, in which reconstruction and the regaining of limited independence could be pursued. In the most extreme interpretation, Carl Schmitt's *Der Nomos der Erde* (1950), Europe was seen as a continental bloc, limiting warfare internally and guarding against the escalation of enmity towards its absolute form, as would be the case under the aegis of maritime powers like Britain and the United States.[56] Most authors were much more guarded than Schmitt, doubting that a European bloc could – or should – be restored. The diplomatic historian Ludwig Dehio was typical: the final success of the European international order, the defeat of Nazi Germany, 'cost the system its life, just as the *Reich*, the assailant, paid for its defeat with its existence'.[57] Nevertheless, the past of the European states' system was presented as a series of bids for continental hegemony on the part of individual Great Powers, and its future was left open. Even progressive lawyers such as Ulrich Scheuner and Wilhelm Grewe, who had described limited transfers of sovereign powers to international organizations, balked at applying such principles to the superpowers, which seemed to be engaged in a traditional struggle for power and to have restricted international law, at most, to the regulation of interstate relations.[58]

Despite internationalization, the tradition of the state, it appeared, remained intact after 1945, complicating any transition towards a European sphere or level of government. To an extent, nationalism and racism had undermined the state, challenging the principle of equality before the law and creating 'an anarchic mass of over- and underprivileged individuals', as Hannah Arendt had pointed out in *The Origins of Totalitarianism* (1951).[59] Within National Socialist ideology, the state was subordinate to the movement and party, serving as a guarantor and sponsor of the race rather than as a source of justice or a provider of services, which were deemed to interfere with a legitimate struggle of individuals and groups for supremacy and survival.[60] It is possible, however, that the reaction against radical nationalism and a widespread desire for impartiality and an end to political conflict after the Second World War aided the rebuilding of states – in West Germany, Austria, Italy, France, Belgium, the Netherlands, Denmark and Norway – which had partially collapsed or which had been dismantled. The reestablishment of legal and constitutional states seemed to many onlookers to be the only way to protect the private sphere from the possible recrudescence of 'totalitarian' ideologies and to recreate a public sphere in which genuine political debate could take place. The conditions for a reversion to dictatorship and totalitarianism still appeared to be in place: comprehensive ideologies explaining and promising to replace chaotic conditions retained their appeal (Arendt); the malfunctioning of markets and threat of revolution promoted the reimposition of monopoly capitalism, of which fascism had been an extension (Franz Neumann); the proclivity towards bureaucratization and technocratic rationalization remained unchecked (Friedrich Pollock, Herbert Marcuse); the means of communication had been concentrated and had become more invasive (Adorno, Horkheimer);

and the state had become an impersonal, value-neutral and disposable 'machine', unable to defend itself against seizure and abuse by a single mass party willing to install an 'official ideology' and acquire a monopoly over communication and the military, enforced by a 'system of terroristic police control' (Carl J. Friedrich).[61]

Against such a background, it appeared that the liberal democratic states of the interwar period – the Weimar Republic, the Third Republic, the Italian monarchy – had been too weak and now needed to be strengthened. At the same time, they needed to intervene, becoming planned, welfare or social states, in order to avert the type of social and economic dislocation – and subsequent political radicalization – experienced by citizens during the interwar era. Economic planning and social intervention, even though they threatened to breach some of the barriers between 'state' and 'society' reerected by the *Rechtsstaat*, were believed to be necessary by most observers, including conservative lawyers such as Ernst Forsthoff.[62] This type of intervention, which went alongside the creation of a 'social market economy' in Germany and alongside various forms of Keynesianism and planning elsewhere, gave governments a greater duty of care towards their own citizens and made them at once more energetic and inward-looking, as they grappled with the problems of reconstruction.[63] It was not obvious to observers like Aron how such internal reconstruction, together with different national perspectives and disorienting disputes about executives, parties, parliaments and judicial systems in the context of widespread anxiety about 'totalitarianism', technocracy and radicalism, could be reconciled with a new political structure for Europe, which would not, of necessity, be like those of reemerging nation-states.[64]

Europe, the Nation-State and Global Politics

For the majority of intellectuals, Europe was of secondary importance, frequently eclipsed by domestic affairs and national interests. After the Treaty of Versailles in 1919, Keynes had been appalled by the cynicism of the participants, 'where men played shamelessly, not for Europe, or even England, but their own return to Parliament in the next election', but the worst consequences of the peace, as far as he was concerned, were closer to home: 'No more does he believe ... in the stability of the things he likes. Eton is doomed; the governing classes, perhaps Cambridge too.'[65] In the early 1930s, the historian Arnold Toynbee was certain that the 'catastrophe' which 'Western minds were contemplating' was 'not the destructive impact of any external force but a spontaneous disintegration from within'.[66] Of course, in the defeated and occupied states of mainland Europe after 1945, commentators' insularity was less pronounced than amongst their prewar British counterparts. Nonetheless, most Continental, postwar advocates of 'Europe' continued to prioritize the affairs of their own state. Thus, French intellectuals devoted most of their attention to the consequences of the Liberation and the politics of the Fourth Republic. Inasmuch as they looked beyond metropolitan France, it was to the United States and the USSR at the start of the Cold War, and to French colonies and colonial wars – although even these received relatively little coverage, with Raymond Aron writing only 18 articles on Indochina (out of a total of 162) between 1947 and 1954, Albert Camus only 4, and Georges Bernanos none (out of 78).[67] Aron was unusual in the consistency and intensity of his interest in the European project in the postwar era, partly as a consequence of the time he spent in Germany between 1930 and 1933, yet even he considered Franco-German reconciliation, which he placed at the centre of attempts at European cooperation and integration, in terms of national advantage and necessity:

> Obsessed as we are by our own disparate anxieties, we end up by forgetting the essential: the indispensable effort towards the reconciliation of the two peoples. I know that some of my readers will be surprised and shocked. And yet, if the French and Germans are ever to put an end to a secular conflict which the transformation of the world has turned into an anachronism, could a moment ever be more propitious than this? Will Germany ever be weaker or more amenable (*disponible*) than she is today?
>
> I am certainly not claiming that the Germans have once and for all renounced aggressive nationalism or that they have become good 'democrats'. But what Germany is tomorrow depends partly on what we do. The frank and resolute resumption of humane relations with the Germans is a not unworthy contribution that it is within our power to make to the restoration of the West.[68]

For the dominant coteries of French Marxists, either in the Communist Party or in existentialist circles around Sartre and de Beauvoir, the events of the 1930s, '40s and '50s appeared, in spite of the discomfort occasioned by the discovery of Stalin's purges and gulags, to have confirmed the frailties of the bourgeois order at home and the logic of capitalist imperialism abroad.[69] 'The war and the occupation alone have taught us that values remain nominal and indeed have no value without an economic and political infrastructure to make them participate in existence,' wrote the Marxist philosopher and journalist Maurice Merleau-Ponty in the first issue of *Les Temps modernes* in 1945.[70] 'Europe' was significant mainly as an area of contention for the superpowers and their opposing ideologies, leading left-wing French intellectuals to a detailed and convoluted calculus of American and Soviet criminality. 'I cannot turn my moral values solely against the USSR,' declared Sartre in 1946: 'While it is true that the deportation of several million people is more serious than the lynching of a black man, the lynching of a black man is the result of a situation which has been going on for more than a hundred years.'[71] French colonialism and conflicts on the periphery of Europe were seen to be part of this international ideological struggle, but the focus of French writers – and allegedly that of the targets of their criticism – was usually France itself, which was supposedly subject to the same ideological conflicts as the wider world: it was therefore natural that the bourgeoisie should be 'perfectly indifferent to the 40,000 people killed at Sétif, the 80,000 murdered Madagascans, the famine and the misery in Algeria, the burned-out villages in Indochina, the Greeks dying in the camps, the Spaniards shot by Franco', since such killing was the result of a capitalist system, wrote de Beauvoir in her autobiography, but 'the bourgeoisie was suddenly heart-broken when faced with the misfortunes of the Soviet prisoners'.[72] Despite – and sometimes because of – their internationalism, French Marxists had comparatively little to say about Europe. The European bourgeoisie was in crisis after the Second World War, rejoiced Sartre, having lost its power to the 'non-European' and 'non-bourgeois' giants, the Soviet Union and the United States.[73]

Like Marxists, Catholic intellectuals also appear to have alternated between global and national politics, leaving little room for the regional sphere of Europe. Jacques Maritain's argument that the future would be dominated by Christian-democratic or totalitarian systems, for instance, derived from an adaptation of his earlier horror at the lapse of European civilizations into barbarism in the 1930s (*Ransoming the Times*, 1938) to the new circumstances of the United States' victory in the Second World War, which seemed to have confirmed the vitality of America's Christian-inspired democracy (*Christianity and Democracy*, 1943), and the coming of the Cold War, which had demonstrated the menace of communist totalitarianism and the need for pluralism and moral, socially responsible citizens, rather than the selfish, autonomous individuals promoted by liberalism.[74] Other French Christian-democratic thinkers such as Emmanuel Mounier, whose 'personalism' was close to the 'integral humanism' of Maritain, concentrated more exclusively on domestic politics after 1945, drawing their lessons from the failure of the French bourgeoisie and the fall of France in 1940, after initial cooperation with the Vichy regime and a brief flirtation with the idea of a new conservative or authoritarian European order at the start of the Second World War.[75] 'Europe', as far as it was mentioned at all, was depicted as a purportedly decadent culture – or 'bourgeois Pharisaism', in Maritain's phrase – which had gradually unmasked the 'respectable conventional man' or independent individual of the nineteenth century, through exposure to the theories of Marx, Nietzsche and Freud, to leave a man who 'has lost track of his soul', 'having given up God so as to be self-sufficient'.[76] The continent, contended Maritain during the war, had witnessed the collapse of democracy and 'the twilight of civilisation'.[77] The only way to reinvigorate European culture seemed to be the importation of Christian democracy and, even, capitalism from the United States, but such imports would take place, it was assumed, on a national rather than a European level.

Contemporary intellectuals' oscillation between national priorities and a global struggle of ideologies – with the terms 'earth' and 'globe' being used in the interwar as well as postwar periods – worked against the idea that Europe was a separate, potentially semi-independent, region between the two superpowers. Instead, the continent appeared to be threatened by the incursions of one power and to be protected – in prospect – by the influence and presence of the other. At least until the Soviet intervention in Hungary in 1956, a significant part of the French left remained unapologetic in its support of the USSR, in the spirit of Pierre Courtade's retort to Edgar Morin: 'I was right to be wrong, while you and your kind were wrong to be right.'[78] Another part of the left was more sceptical, with Merleau-

Ponty writing that 'one cannot be anti-communist, one cannot be communist', but they were prepared to excuse or relativize the excesses of Stalinism and to justify the Soviet occupation of Eastern Europe as a defensive shield against capitalism, to the disgust of exiles such as Mircea Eliade, who accused them of giving up the rest of Europe: 'all these countries *are* in Europe, all these peoples belong to the European community'.[79] To French communists, and to others on the left, Eastern Europe had not been given up or excluded as much as the Soviet Union had been included in the affairs of Europe, not least because it still seemed a lesser evil compared to the United States, which – Sartre asserted – had 'gone mad'.[80] The West, contended the French existentialist in the 1950s, had nothing to offer in place of communism.[81]

Much of the centre and right disagreed. To Camus, who had attacked 'progressive' violence in *L'Homme révolté* (1951), it would soon be necessary 'to choose between Russia and America', probably to the advantage of the latter. The former communist and future Gaullist André Malraux, to whom the author was speaking in 1945, replied that the choice was not between Russia and America but 'between Russia and France', for 'when a weak France finds itself confronted by a powerful Russia, I no longer believe a word of what I believed when a powerful France was confronted by a weak Soviet Union. A weak Russia wants popular fronts, a strong Russia wants popular democracies.'[82] When, by the late 1940s, it became evident that the USSR was powerful and wanted to install its own satellite states in Europe, the majority of Gaullist, Christian Democrat and liberal intellectuals had already turned against it. 'Stalin's enterprise is of the same kind as Hitler's,' wrote Aron in 1949: 'Soviet expansion has come to a halt. In no country to the west of the Iron Curtain does the Communist Party still have a serious chance of seizing power either through elections or through a *coup d'état*. And it has been acknowledged, since 1945, that by crossing the line of demarcation, the Red Army would set the world on fire.'[83] Faced with such an enemy, most centrist and right-wing commentators, notwithstanding their continuing complaints, accepted American influence and military assistance. 'This nation ... is more foreign to me than any other,' wrote the Catholic novelist François Mauriac in 1959, before admitting that U.S. culture had already permeated Europe: 'I've never been there ... what is the point? It has done more than just visit us; it has transformed us.'[84] Even to Mauriac, who had called the United States 'this great exterminating nation' after the Suez crisis in 1956, Europe had voluntarily become part of an American-dominated 'West'.[85]

Most commentators perceived Europe's subordination to the United States and the USSR after the Second World War as the latest stage in a long-running crisis. They interpreted the crisis in divergent ways, from Drieu La Rochelle's description of the conflict as a 'war of religions' between incompatible 'Asian' and 'European' cultures to the Nobel-Prize-winning chemist Frédéric Joliot-Curie's championing of a war for communism, of which 'the Party is bound to have a better understanding than each of us'.[86] Some were more pessimistic than others, from the doom-laden pronouncements of Spengler and his followers to the tentative hopes of Croce for 'the birth of a new consciousness, a new [European] nationality' to replace nations and restore 'liberal ideals', or Febvre's championing of Europe as a *'patrie* of freedom', but virtually all were defensive, seeking to protect Europe from a series of internal and external threats.[87] Perceived menaces after 1917 included the recurrence of what Coudenhove-Kalergi referred to as a European 'civil war' akin to the First World War, the decadence of European culture, an increasing population and inadequate territory (Ortega y Gasset), economic collapse (Keynes), the existence of destructive nationalisms and obstructive nation-states, the threat of left-wing revolutions and right-wing coups d'état, the imposition of ideological dystopias and authoritarian or totalitarian dictatorships, invasion or domination by expanding extra-European powers such as the United States and the USSR, the proximity – given the spread of globe-shrinking means of communication – of 'a non-European humanity which has become dangerously closer and easily superior in terms of material force' (Hermann von Keyserling), and the failure of the states' system and international organizations such as the League of Nations, which had not done 'great things', as the left claimed, but which had 'not perished', as the right maintained (Bertrand de Jouvenel).[88] Few of these threats had diminished as a result of the Second World War. Indeed, many observers thought that things had got worse. To Ortega y Gasset, the conflict had confirmed the movement towards state tutelage and mass society, and from 'open' to 'closed nationalism' or *'nationalisme rentré'*, where 'each people would live according to its private style' and 'feels that its way of life clashes with others'.[89] To Keynes, the war was 'a dreadful confirmation of Hobbes's diagnosis of human nature and of what is required to preserve civilisation': 'From one point of view we can regard what is now happening as the final destruction of the optimistic liberalism which Locke inaugurated.'[90] In *L'Homme contre les tyrans* (1944), Aron went even further, predicting the end of the belief in 'progress':

> In the last century, the most popular philosophies of history, and even the consciousness of ordinary people, were dominated by the doctrine of progress, according to which a kind of parallelism or interdependence was said to exist between the accumulation of knowledge, increased mastery over nature, and the moral improvement of humanity. In other words, an indisputable fact – the development of knowledge and technology – was broadened into a naively confident vision of historical development as a whole. The catastrophes of the twentieth century have provoked a complete reversal of attitudes and brought into being a doctrine which is the exact opposite of the doctrine of progress. The same deterministic interpretation has been preserved, whereby the movement which is dragging capitalism to its death and the economy towards a planned regime is held to be irresistible. But instead of linking these transformations with the liberation of man, they are associated with tyranny, wars of conquest and fanaticism … What gives the current pessimism its debilitating poignancy is that it asserts an interdependence between ineluctable necessities and detestable phenomena.[91]

The creation of a European community in such circumstances, if it were possible at all, looked likely to occur for many different – and largely defensive – reasons and to correspond to quite different sets of expectations.

Conclusion: The Meaning of Europe

Few writers doubted that 'Europe' existed, even though they disagreed about its character and purpose. There was broad agreement that European economies would benefit from integration, as subsequent chapters show. The interwar era had witnessed the establishment of increasingly protected markets in Germany, Italy, the USSR and the United States in accordance with the dictates of all-embracing ideologies – save in the case of the United States – and against the advice of the majority of experts.[92] As a consequence, many economists – and other commentators – had called for economic cooperation or integration in the 1920s and 1930s.[93] By 1945, even a 'national planner' such as Keynes, who vigorously opposed Hayek's notion of market-driven distribution and social organization, accepted that European economies needed greater coordination, as he spelled out in an early plan for an International Clearing Bank during the Second World War:

> A view of the post-war world which I find sympathetic and attractive and fruitful of good consequences is that we should encourage *small* political and cultural units, combined into larger, and more or less closely knit, economic units. It would be a fine thing to have thirty or forty capital cities in Europe, each the centre of a self-governing country entirely free from national minorities (who would be dealt with by migrations where necessary) and the seat of a government and parliament and university centre, each with their own pride and glory and their own characteristics and excellent gifts. But it would be ruinous to have thirty or forty entirely independent economic and currency unions.[94]

Not all of Keynes's contemporaries concurred with his preference for a 're-medievalised Europe', an idea which he omitted in later drafts, but most agreed with his economic prescriptions.[95] Ortega y Gasset, for instance, warned in the late 1940s that 'we shall continue with national economies on the defensive, which is the saddest and most dangerous attitude for an economy', unless a European structure could be created.[96] 'Today, production itself, in the forefront of collective life with everything depending on it, is the new form from which could be expected only the politics of grand design,' he went on: 'In these last thirty years, as the need has steadily become more evident, so the numbers have grown of those who advocate supernational institutions matching the gigantic size to which production problems have increased.'[97] Nation-states had not been able since the First World War to find 'a healthy, natural and viable solution to economic problems'.[98] In Ortega's opinion, European economic integration was a commonly shared goal.

Ortega was less confident that his demand for some sort of juridical and political structure for Europe would find support, hinting that many of his contemporaries believed that the 'idea of a European economy' alone would be 'an effective standard', which would regulate its own workings and which would resolve disputes between nation-states.[99] There was, however, a broad commitment amongst intellectuals – and postwar politicians – to human and political rights, pluralism, constitutionalism, political parties, parliaments, liberal democracy, a market or mixed economy and a welfare or social state, which could – in the right circumstances – facilitate political cooperation or limited integration on a European level.[100] The most salient reason for such qualified consensus was opposition to 'totalitarianism' and dictatorship, whether authoritarian, fascist or communist, which extended back into the interwar period. This opposition helped to ensure in Italy that liberal socialists such as Carlo Rosselli (*Liberal Socialism*, 1930) and Gramscian Marxists, reading the *Prison Notebooks* as they were published between 1948 and 1951, remained committed to individual liberties and a democratic path to socialism or communism, joining liberals such as Guido De Ruggiero (*History of European Liberalism*, 1924) and Benedetto Croce, who had revised his formerly Hegelian view of freedom in response to fascism during the 1930s (*History as Thought and Action*, 1938).[101] In Germany, too, despite many individual points of contention, virtually all legal and political theorists had been converted to the necessity of a democratic order, even Carl Schmitt, who conceded in 1963 that his 'concept of the political' in the interwar period had been flawed, since its distinction between friend and foe as the basis of political action had failed to differentiate between 'conventional, real and absolute enemies', permitting an unlimited escalation of political conflict.[102] Pupils of Schmitt such as Werner Weber, in spite of criticism of oligarchical party structures and a call for a strong executive and civil service to fill the 'authority vacuum' of the FRG, claimed that they accepted the need for mass, party democracies.[103] In France, the political debate of intellectuals after 1945 was marked by a division between the communists and existentialists on the left, who – like Merleau-Ponty – were committed in theory to revolution, and 'moderates' in the centre and on the right such as Aron, Mounier, Maritain, Bertrand de Jouvenel, Maurice Duverger and René Capitant, who sought to entrench the four fundamental democratic principles of autonomy, equality, secularism and sovereignty.[104] Aron's attempt to combine bourgeois citizenship, technological efficiency and the right of individuals to choose their own way of life was typical in its negotiation of the potential perils of a technocratic and industrial society and in its renunciation of 'the abstractions of moralism and ideology' and its pursuit of 'the true content of possible choices, limited as they are by reality itself'.[105] In Britain, the main debate was between liberal intellectuals, defending 'negative' liberty (Berlin) and the 'open society' (Popper), advocates of capitalism (Hayek) and proponents of 'social' citizenship and welfare (T.H. Marshall), yet all supported the need for a balanced constitution and a parliamentary democracy.[106] Throughout the continent, the dangers of the European 'crisis', it seemed, had reinforced intellectuals' belief – detectable well before 1945 – in the merits of liberal democracy, social protection and economic cooperation. Whether such cooperation could be achieved on a European level, however, was open to doubt, for the range of answers to the European question in the late 1940s and early 1950s, as in the 1920s, was bewilderingly diverse, as the chapters below demonstrate. To intellectuals and policy makers alike, Europe was definable, valuable and defensible, but its future seemed unpredictable, encouraging many authors to dwell on – and reconstruct – its past.

Notes

1. S. de Beauvoir, *La force des choses* (Paris, 1963), 340.
2. The term comes from H. James, *A German Identity, 1770–1990* (London, 1989). On Febvre, see Chapter 14.
3. V. Conze, *Das Europa der Deutschen* (Munich, 2005), 1.
4. On the relationship between geography, space and 'Europe', see Chapter 8.
5. P.M.R. Stirk, *European Unity in Context: The Interwar Period* (London, 1989), 12. Coudenhove-Kalergi compared the ties between Britain and Europe to the discussion about *Kleindeutschland and Grossdeutschland* in 1848; see Chapter 4.
6. See Chapter 9.
7. Cited in Raley, *Ortega y Gasset*, 141.
8. Ibid.
9. J. Ortega y Gasset, *Revolt of the Masses*, 185–86.
10. In Raley, *Ortega y Gasset*, 175.
11. Gerhard Hauptmann's appeal 'To the Conscience of the World' in 1923, cited in P.M. Lützeler, *Die Schriftsteller und Europa* (Munich, 1992), 287.
12. Ibid., 301–2.
13. Ibid., 279–80. See Chapter 11 below.
14. O. Spengler, *Der Untergang des Abendlandes*, revised edn. (Munich, 1923), 746–83.
15. T.S. Eliot, 'The Unity of European Culture' (1946), in Lützeler, *Die Schriftsteller*, 408.
16. Ibid.
17. Ibid., 410.
18. Ibid., 417.
19. Ibid., 416.
20. On Keyserling, see Chapter 5.
21. M. Horkheimer and T.W. Adorno, *Dialektik der Aufklärung* (Amsterdam, 1947). The work was first published unofficially in 1944.
22. Raley, *Ortega*, 62–76. These views were stated in *Revolt of the Masses* in 1929 and in *Meditation on Europe*, published after the Second World War.
23. Mention of a 'European confederation' was made by Joachim von Ribbentrop, Germany's Foreign Secretary, in March 1943: M. Salewski, 'Europa: Idée und Wirklichkeit in der nationalsozialistischen Weltanschauung und politischen Praxis', in O. Franz (ed.), *Europas Mitte* (Göttingen, 1987), 85–106; P. Krüger, 'Hitlers Europapolitik', in W. Benz, H. Buchheim and H. Mommsen (eds), *Der Nationalsozialismus. Studien zur Ideologie und Herrschaft* (Frankfurt, 1993), 104–32; P.M.R. Stirk, 'Authoritarian and National Socialist Conceptions of Nation, State, and Europe', in idem (ed.), *European Unity in Context: The Interwar Period* (London, 1989), 125–48.
24. J.M. Keynes to 'Sigi' Waley, 11 Nov. 1941, in R. Skidelsky, *John Maynard Keynes* (London, 2000), vol. 3, 197.
25. Nichols, *Treason*, 127. For Benda's discussion of this with Johan Huizinga, see Chapter 12.

26. Benda interview in *Nouvelles littéraires* in 1925, cited in M. Winock, *Le siècle des intellectuelles* (Paris, 1997), 238.
27. Nichols, *Treason*, 128.
28. Ibid., 129.
29. R. Soucy, *Fascist Intellectual: Drieu La Rochelle* (Berkeley, 1979), 93.
30. Ibid., 65–66.
31. Ibid., 176–77.
32. Cited in R. Colquhoun, *Raymond Aron* (London, 1986), vol. 1, 419.
33. Ibid., 420.
34. Ibid., 429, 433.
35. Ibid., 432.
36. J. Gray, *Isaiah Berlin* (London, 1995), 99.
37. Ibid., 98–121.
38. Cited in Raley, *Ortega*, 58.
39. Ortega y Gasset, *Revolt*, 135.
40. Cited in Dobson, *Ortega*, 51.
41. Raley, *Ortega*, 144–45.
42. Ortega, *Meditation on Europe* (1949), ibid., 177.
43. See especially P. O'Brien, *Beyond the Swastika* (London, 1996); also, D.A. Moses, *German Intellectuals and the Nazi Past* (Cambridge, 2007); M. Fulbrook, *German National Identity after the Holocaust* (Cambridge, 1999); J. Herf, *Divided Memory: The Nazi Past in the Two Germanys* (Cambridge, Mass., 1997); K.H. Jarausch, *After Hitler: Recivilizing Germans, 1945–1995* (Oxford, 2007); S. Berger, *The Search for Normality. National Identity and Historical Consciousness in Germany since 1800* (Oxford, 1997); and N. Frei, *Adenauer's Germany and the Nazi Past: The Politics of Amnesty and Integration* (New York, 2002).
44. D.A. Moses, 'The Non-German German and the German German: Dilemmas of Identity after the Holocaust', *New German Critique* 101 (2007), 45–94.
45. H. Kelsen, 'Is a Peace Treaty with Germany Legally Possible and Politically Desirable?', *American Political Science Review* 41 (1947), 1188. See Peter Stirk's excellent study of *Twentieth-Century German Political Thought* (Edinburgh, 2006), 154–55, for commentary on this and many of the points below. Also, J.-W. Müller (ed.), *German Ideologies since 1945: Studies in the Political Thought and Culture of the Bonn Republic* (Basingstoke, 2003), 1–60, 147–60.
46. H. Schelsky, *Die skeptische Generation* (Düsseldorf, 1957).
47. Stirk, *German Political Thought*, 138–39.
48. The quotation comes from Leibholz, a judge and academic. G. Leibholz, 'Der Strukturwandel der modernen Demokratie' (1952), and idem, *Das Wesen der Repräsentation* (Berlin, 1929), and E. Fraenkel, *Der Doppelstaat* (Oxford, 1941), and idem, *Military Occupation and the Rule of Law* (Oxford, 1944). Stirk, *German Political Thought*, 144–46.
49. D. Sternberger, 'Begriff des Vaterlandes' (1947) and 'Das Problem der Loyalität' (1956), ibid., 155–56.
50. B. de Jouvenel, *Vers les Etats-Unis d'Europe* (1930), in J.-L. Chabot, *Aux origines intellectuelles de l'Union européenne* (Grenoble, 2005), 158.
51. Ibid.
52. F. Meinecke, *Die deutsche Katastrophe* (Wiesbaden, 1946), 151–52.
53. See also G. Ritter, *Europa und die deutsche Frage* (Munich, 1948).
54. Meinecke discussed the war, as the main 'catastrophe', more than the Holocaust. His account, and many other accounts which used the passive form, confronted much more uncompromising accusations and analyses of guilt; for example, K. Jaspers, *The Question of German Guilt* (New York, 1947).
55. T. Garton Ash, *In Europe's Name: Germany and the Divided Continent* (London, 1993).
56. See Chapters 7 and 8.
57. L. Dehio, *The Precarious Balance* (London, 1948), cited in Stirk, *German Political Thought*, 156.
58. W. Grewe, 'Die auswärtige Gewalt der Bundesrepublik' (1954), ibid., 157.

59. H. Arendt, *The Origins of Totalitarianism* (New York, 1951), 290.

60. A. Hitler, *Mein Kampf* (Berlin, 1925–26), vol. 1, 280–323; vol. 2, 9–22, 82–91.

61. C.J. Friedrich, 'The Unique Character of Totalitarian Society', in idem (ed.), *Totalitarianism* (New York, 1953); F. Neumann, *Behemoth* (London, 1942), and idem, *The Democratic and the Authoritarian State* (New York, 1957); F. Pollock, *Automation. Materialien zur Beurteilung der ökonomischen und sozialen Folgen* (Frankfurt, 1956); H. Marcuse, *Reason and Revolution* (Oxford, 1941), and idem, *Eros and Civilization* (London, 1956); Horkheimer and Adorno, *Dialektik der Aufklärung*.

62. E. Forsthoff, 'Begriff und Wesen des sozialen Rechtsstaates' (1954), in Stirk, *German Political Thought*, 152–53.

63. A. Nicholls, *Freedom with Responsibility: The Social Market Economy in Germany, 1918–1963* (Oxford, 1994); J.C. van Hook, *Rebuilding Germany: The Creation of the Social Market Economy, 1945–1957* (Cambridge, 2007).

64. Colquhoun, *Aron*, vol. 1, 431–32.

65. J.C. Smuts to a friend, 7 May 1919, in Skidelsky, *Keynes*, vol. 1, 378.

66. Cited in Stirk, *European Unity*, 10.

67. D. Drake, *Intellectuals and Politics in Postwar France* (Basingstoke, 2002), 100.

68. Aron in 1946, cited in Colquhoun, *Aron*, vol. 1, 422.

69. Michel Winock, *Le siècle des intellectuelles*, 487–754, calls the 1940s, '50s and '60s 'les années Sartre'.

70. Cited in A. Rabil, Jr, *Merleau-Ponty: Existentialist of the Social World* (New York, 1967), 90.

71. Ibid., 64–65.

72. Cited ibid., 69.

73. Quoted in M. Poster, *Existential Marxism in Postwar France: From Sartre to Althusser* (Princeton, 1975), 137.

74. M.S. Power, *Jacques Maritain, Christian Democrat, and the Quest for a New Commonwealth* (Lampeter, 1992).

75. Maritain watered down his championing of the common good over individual rights in *Integral Humanism* (1936) as a result of his assessment of the National Socialist dictatorship. On Mounier, see J. Hellmann, *Emmanuel Mounier and the New Catholic Left, 1930–1950* (Toronto, 1981), and R.W. Rauch, Jr, *Politics and Belief in Contemporary France: Emmanuel Mounier and Christian Democracy, 1932–1950* (The Hague, 1972).

76. Maritain, *Scholasticism and Politics* (1927), cited in Power, *Maritain*, 124.

77. This is the title of one of Maritain's books, published in 1943.

78. Cited in T. Judt, *Past Imperfect: French Intellectuals, 1944–1956* (Berkeley, 1992), 290.

79. M. Merleau-Ponty, *Humanisme et terreur* (1947), cited in Rabil, Jr, *Merleau-Ponty*, 94; M. Eliade, 'Examen leprosum' (1952), in Judt, *Past Imperfect*, 280. For a similar argument put forward by Stempowski, see Chapter 9.

80. Ibid., 198.

81. See, for instance, Sartre, 'Le fantôme de Staline', *Les Temps moderne*, 129–31 (1957), 678.

82. Cited in C. Cate, *André Malraux* (London, 1995), 353.

83. Colquhoun, *Aron*, vol. 1, 424.

84. Mauriac in *L'Express*, 29 Aug. 1959, in Judt, *Past Imperfect*, 197.

85. Ibid., 198.

86. Drieu saw the Second World War as a struggle between ideologies, not countries, in his novel *Straw Dogs* (1944). See Soucy, *Fascist Intellectual*, 90–105. On Joliot-Curie, see Drake, *Intellectuals*, 41.

87. B. Croce, *Storia d'Europa nel secolo decimonono* (1932), cited in Chabot, *Origines*, 140–41. On Febvre, see Chapters 11 and 14.

88. R. von Coudenhove-Kalergi, *L'Europe unie* (1938), Ortega y Gasset, *Revolt of the Masses* (1929), J.M. Keynes, *The Economic Consequences of the Peace* (1919), H. von Keyserling, *Das Spektrum Europas* (1928), B. de Jouvenel, *Vers les Etats-Unis d'Europe* (1930), ibid., 221, 139, 157.

89. In Raley, *Ortega*, 144–47.

90. Keynes to S.P. Lamprecht, at the start of the war, in Skidelsky, *Keynes*, vol. 3, 74.
91. Cited in Colquhoun, *Aron*, vol. 1, 273.
92. In the German case, see H. James, *The German Slump* (Oxford, 1986).
93. For France, see A. Shennan, *Rethinking France: Plans for Renewal, 1940–1946* (Oxford, 1989).
94. Cited in Skidelsky, *Keynes*, vol. 3, 218. On 'national planning' and 'market restoration', see A. Gamble, *Hayek* (Cambridge, 1996), 164. On Keynes's gradually softening attitude to capitalism, see A. Fitzgibbons, *Keynes's Vision* (Oxford, 1988), 167–80.
95. Skidelsky, *Keynes*, vol. 3, 218.
96. Ortega, *Meditation on Europe* (1949), in Raley, *Ortega*, 177.
97. Ibid.
98. Ibid.
99. Ibid.
100. See especially M. Conway, 'The Rise and Fall of Western Europe's Democratic Age, 1945–1973', *Contemporary European History* 13 (2004), 67–88. East European critics such as Stempowski contended that such liberal-democratic values were seen to be merely for 'internal use', lacking a claim – typical of the nineteenth century – of 'universality'; see Chapter 9.
101. S.M. Di Scala and S. Mastellane, *European Political Thought, 1815–1989* (Boulder, 1998), 186–88, 197. Also, D.R. Roberts, *Croce and the Uses of Historicism* (Berkeley, 1987), 238–39; N. Bobbio, *Ideological Profile of the Twentieth Century in Italy* (Princeton, 1995).
102. C. Schmitt, Preface to *Der Begriff des Politischen*, new edn. (Berlin, 1963). See Stirk, *German Political Thought*, 135–64, on the democratic basis of political debates in Germany after 1945.
103. Ibid., 143, 150.
104. The reference to 'moderation' comes from N. O'Sullivan, *European Political Thought since 1945* (Basingstoke, 2004), 79–85.
105. Ibid., 83.
106. Ibid., 20–23, 28–35.

Part II

REIMAGINING THE PAST

The period between 1917 and 1957, starting with the birth of the USSR and the American intervention in the First World War and ending with the Treaty of Rome, is of the utmost importance for contextualizing and for understanding the intellectual origins of the European Community. The chapters in this section focus on the era from a critical point of view, considering it a time of 'crisis'; that is, a time when many contemporaries, and especially intellectuals, felt that they were faced with a momentous decision which could not only bring about a radically different future, but which could also signal the end of a glorious or, at least, indefeasible past. At such a time, contemporaries' understanding of what Europe was and what it should be was questioned in a profound way, not only because of the tragedies of the world wars but also because of the rise of external powers like Japan, the Soviet Union and the United States, which appeared to have begun to marginalize the continent. Europe, wrote the German Marxist scholar Karl Löwith, in an essay on 'European Nihilism' during the Second World War, was 'suspended between America and Russia and was forced once again to ask for their economic and political assistance to fight, once again, within its own boundaries'.[1] The continent no longer decided the destiny of the world but was, on the contrary, subject to decisions taken and negotiations conducted by others. This state of affairs forced Europeans to react, seeking an identity for Europe and searching for its 'lost soul'. The idea of a specifically European unity finally became, at least for some, a feasible project. The purpose was not only to avoid another war, but to avoid the destruction of the idea of European unity. Most intellectuals viewed Europe with an ambiguous mixture of pessimism and confidence, believing that an unambiguous decision had to be made about its future. Many, however, yearned above all for the retrieval of Europe's comforting past.

Richard Coudenhove-Kalergi, author of the bestseller *Pan-Europe* (1923), founder of the Pan-European Union (1925) and – with his ally Aristide Briand – arguably the most prominent Europeanist of the interwar era, demonstrated the ambiguity of much advocacy of common European institutions, looking both forwards and backwards, as Anita Prettenthaler-Ziegerhofer demonstrates (Chapter 4).[2] On one level, Coudenhove, who had been born in Tokyo to the

Austrian ambassador and a Japanese mother, had the ability to see the continent from the outside, recognizing the limits of its influence and power. Europe, in his view, was the weakest of the global 'fields of force' as a consequence of the diversity and divisions of its twenty-six states. His call for unity in three stages – political, economic and constitutional – seemed strikingly modern, issuing in a 'United States of Europe' on the model of the United States, with a president, a bi-cameral system of government (a 'House of Peoples' and a 'House of States'), and a constitution guaranteeing the freedom of its citizens.[3] The Czech and, later, French citizen went on to found the European Parliamentary Union in 1947, which successfully lobbied deputies to create a federal Europe at the expense of states' sovereign rights. He welcomed the establishment of the Council of Europe, the ECSC and the EEC, and he continued to champion the enactment of a single European federal constitution. On another level, the Bohemian count, born in 1894, was a representative – albeit an idiosyncratic, pacifist one – of nostalgic, cosmopolitan, aristocratic circles which had lost their former prominence and international points of reference during and after the First World War. Correspondingly, the Pan-European Union aimed to counter both aggressive nationalism, which seemed to have provoked the Great War and the collapse of the old order, and Bolshevism, which appeared to menace what remained of Europe's civilization from the traditional site of barbarity in the East. Coudenhove's switch in the 1930s to a cultural unification of Europe through the 'rescue of the Occident' fitted in with the cultural criticism and regenerative schemes of the right, with which he continued to collaborate until Austria's *Anschluss* with Germany in 1938, when he fled to Switzerland. After the war, which he spent in exile in New York, he continued to strive for the creation of a European 'soul', nation and patriotism, which were tied to his quest for a European constitution. His labelling of the ECSC as the 'Union Charlemagne', resurrecting the medieval imperial union of France and Germany, was in keeping with his earlier aristocratic cosmopolitanism. Despite criticism from advocates of incremental economic integration, Coudenhove continued to prioritize and to link the politics and culture of Europe.

Aristocratic writers such as Coudenhove-Kalergi were well represented in the ranks of Europeanists in the interwar era. Expelled, expropriated or deprived of their remaining privileges, a number of prominent German-speaking noble publicists such as Hermann von Keyserling, Prince Karl Anton Rohan, and Coudenhove himself began to look to Europe in order to reverse or redress some of the most nefarious proclivities of modernity, as they perceived them.[4] According to Dina Gusejnova (Chapter 5), the views of European history and politics displayed by such nobles had three points in common: first, the notion that states and their governments were secondary in international politics to private networks; second, the idea that the nation could only be accepted as a temporary political paradigm, and that a form of supranational identity was needed in Europe; and, third, the recognition that the social foundation of Europe's cultural achievements, which rested on the contribution of prewar aristocratic societies, needed to be reinterpreted because old elites had failed to respond to the pressing problems of their times. Such writers insisted that Europe could be the site of a reinvigoration of politics and culture, drawing on the vital sources of the past, within a new type of Nietzschean 'aristocratic society', open to the most original and strongest willed, and based on former nobles as the supposed guardians of European culture and opponents of the levelling effects of nationalism and mass politics. Analysts of contemporary national institutions in journals such as Rohan's *Europäische Revue* and Coudenhove's *Paneuropa* evoked a perpetual sense of crisis, yet they generally sought solutions in a renewed European past – corporatism, aristocracy, charismatic leadership, high culture – rather than in a radically different future.

Kessler's, Coudenhove's and Keyserling's misgivings about modernity were shared by Rudolf Pannwitz, a representative of the heterogeneous 'Conservative Revolution' in Germany, who contended – like his preceptor Nietzsche – that Europe was undergoing a deep cultural crisis which could only be overcome through the creation of a new society – a 'European imperium' – resting on spiritual regeneration and a revaluation of all values.[5] Unlike many other conservative revolutionaries, contends Jan Vermeiren (Chapter 6), Pannwitz was critical of the German Reich, which he believed had succumbed to hollow materialism and radical nationalism, in common with all the other belligerent states in the First World War. He opposed the left-liberal Friedrich Naumann's conception of *Mitteleuropa* on these grounds, since it was based on the 'small German' nation-state, and he eschewed the total mobilization of the German nation espoused by right-wing revolutionaries such as Ernst Jünger. Instead, he looked back fondly on the multinational Habsburg monarchy and advised Germans to turn away from doomed attempts at political leadership to their traditional role as spiritual leaders of Europe. Germany itself was to be split into three parts – West Germany, Central Germany, and South Germany including Austria – each of which would act as a bridge to neighbouring nations: West Germany to France; Central Germany to Russia, Scandinavia and Britain; and South Germany to South Eastern Europe. Like the works of many of his conservative contemporaries, Pannwitz's treatises contained surprising juxtapositions: he was in favour of a European 'empire of federations' and of supranational institutions, yet he also saw nations, in the 'organic' Herderian sense, as the necessary building blocks of Europe and the creators of its culture; he called for spiritual renewal as the first step towards unity in diversity on the Continent and abhorred the resort to imperialism and the pursuit of power for its own sake, but he argued that only a dictator, following his historical paradigms of Rome and Napoleonic France, could 'tame' the unwieldy elements of Europe; and, although he reviled Soviet Bolshevism and feared attacks from a barbaric 'East', he admired the 'Slavs' and initially took up Czechoslovakia as a worthy polyglot successor of the Habsburg monarchy and a model for European organizations. Pannwitz's anti-modernist, anti-Prussian, anti-communist Europeanism was quite close to that of Catholics in its emphasis on Christianity, the supranational nature of the Holy Roman Empire, and the understanding that Europe was a community of values and culture. However, he was not a Catholic and remained sceptical of religion. Now forgotten, he was heralded as 'one of the greatest German thinkers' by Hofmannsthal, Bahr, Meier-Graefe and Redlich in 1919 and was awarded the Schiller-Gedächtnis prize in 1957.

In many respects, the constitutional lawyer Carl Schmitt was the opposite of Pannwitz as a representative of the Conservative Revolution. The contemporary exegesis of Schmitt's work is marked by the debate about his perspective on how political unity can be achieved in Europe at an international level. In some exegetes' opinion, Schmitt proposes a nationalism which surpasses strictly national borders. According to them, the political model of the German intellectual and publicist was the Holy Roman Empire.[6] Ionut Untea proposes, however, that Schmitt, in his writings before the Second World War, emphasized the medieval model for political unity in the international sphere (Chapter 7). Two of the main reasons for choosing this model were, on the one hand, the fact that Schmitt treasured the medieval idea of a 'charter' (*charte*), as a contract between the sovereign and the 'estates' (communities having a high consciousness of their identity); on the other hand, the medieval model contains a political theology, which he went on to emphasize in *Staat, Bewegung, Volk*, in the form of a theory of a political unity which contained the idea of unity in diversity. The fact that the Holy Roman Empire had maintained such conditions until 1806 suggested to the constitutional lawyer that this form of political unity could be revived in the twentieth century. It rested, above all, on the close relationship of the various parties to territory or 'space', with the start of every great era beginning with the appropriation of land, which came to form the basis of law and a juridical understanding of the world. War, through which land was originally appropriated, and law, by which it was later regulated, were therefore closely related, in Schmitt's opinion. Such relationships were established in Europe well before the advent of the modern state and became characteristic of a European 'great space' (*Grossraum*), within which certain contracts crossed dynastic borders, violence was limited, and enemies were seen to be equal. The reemergence of a European *Grossraum* in the twentieth century, akin to that of the Middle Ages, seemed to offer states a way of escaping a destructive state of nature at the same time as avoiding the illusions of universalism, which attempted to reduce diversity and to remove natural enmities necessary for identity formation and an organic union of the parts with the whole. As a consequence of cultural and territorial contiguity, both of which underpinned politics, 'Europe' as a 'great space' at once helped to maintain and control necessary conflicts.

Both Carl Schmitt, in *Der Nomos der Erde im Völkerrecht des Jus Publicum Europaeum* (1950), and Franz Rosenzweig, a philosopher who wrote *Globus. Studien zur weltgeschichtlichen Raumlehre* in 1917, interpreted the history of Europe by examining the spatial underpinnings of the political system, discerning a movement towards a global order which depended to a significant extent on the relationship between land and sea. To Rosenzweig, a Homeric view of the world as an internal sea with the ocean only on the periphery, which came to be embodied in a Mediterranean civilization, gave way to a Biblical image of the world as terra firma lashed by a surrounding ocean, which paralleled the point of view of the Northern European successors of antiquity, beginning with the empire of Charlemagne in AD 800. In effect, Rome had been the main transition, changing from a sea-borne empire to a land-based one with Julius Caesar's invasion of Gaul, yet the consequences of such a transformation were neither inevitable nor immediate. Enclosed territorial states came to dominate this Western and Northern European order, with France overcoming Spain in the name of king and nation, yet the order was also still a maritime one, with terra firma linked to the Atlantic. Thus, as modern territorial states were forming, Europe was simultaneously exporting its system via the Atlantic to the New World. The triumph of Britain over France demonstrated the powerful logic of this evolving spatial order, as did Germany's decision to attack Britain's 'worldwide empire'. For Rosenzweig, who died in 1929, Europe remained the centre of the globe, with the cultural vitality to enliven 'the senile consciousness of Asia and the juvenile one of America'. To Schmitt, who continued to write for another thirty years after Rosenzweig's death, the place of Europe in the global order seemed less secure, in Vittorio Cotesta's opinion (Chapter 8). Whilst it was true that secular European states had transformed the original relationship between land, appropriation, law and politics into an 'inter-state system of law' or *jus publicum europaeum*, constraining monarchs who were sovereign over their own territories in their dealings with each other, this European order, which had been extended to the rest of the world from the fifteenth century onwards, had been challenged by the United States, which had set up its autonomous 'hemisphere' in the Americas through the nineteenth-century Monroe Doctrine and which now threatened to establish a world hegemony resting on the new foundation of economics. Whereas the older European *jus publicum* was an order, the new global order was chaotic, with little to limit the most powerful states. Europe would not have been able to save itself from the consequences of such chaos – fascism and totalitarianism – had it not been for the intervention of the United States, which viewed itself as the 'true Europe', a democratic successor to the old continent. The pathos of Schmitt's postwar conclusion was difficult to ignore.

Many of the themes explored by Central and Western European counterparts were the subject of the work of Jerzy Stempowski (1894–1969), a prominent liberal Polish essayist and literary critic who contributed in exile after 1945 to the influential Polish political review *Kultura*: the complex relations and interdependencies existing in the 1930s between the West European political powers and Eastern Europe; the political principles that made of Europe a political entity and that gave it its special position and credit among other nations; and the contemporary departure from these principles, leading to a diminution of the continent's cultural and political relevance.[7] After the Second World War, in his essays and various travel journals, Stempowski depicted with bitter elegance the irreversible destruction of Central European multiethnic societies that had come into being after the First World War, and the significance of the political division of the continent. Above all, it was the issue of the long-term cultural consequences of the loss of political power that concerned Stempowski: in a seemingly unemotional way he heralded the growing provincialization of Europe, observing it already in multiple spheres of social life. Lukasz Mikolajewski analyses Stempowski's complex understanding of Europe, comparing his prewar and postwar writings (Chapter 9). He focuses especially on the image of lost 'European greatness', seen from a Central East European perspective, and contrasted in Stempowski's work with the new dependence of Europe on the emergent world powers, the United States and the Soviet Union.

Notes

1. K. Löwith, 'Der europäische Nihilismus. Betrachtungen zur Vorgeschichte des europäischen Krieges', in idem, *Sämtliche Schriften* (Stuttgart, 1983), vol. 2, 475–540.
2. See A. Ziegerhofer-Prettenthaler, *Botschafter Europas. Richard Nikolaus Coudenhove-Kalergi und die Paneuropabewegung in den 20er und 30er Jahren* (Vienna, 2004): V. Conze, *Richard Coudenhove-Kalergi. Umstrittener Visionär Europas* (Zurich, 2004); O. Burgard, *Das gemeinsame Europa – von der politischen Utopie zum außenpolitischen Programm: Meinungsaustausch und Zusammenarbeit proeuropäischer Verbände in Deutschland und Frankreich, 1924–1933* (Frankfurt/Main, 2000).
3. Christian Pernhorst, *Das paneuropäische Verfassungsmodell des Grafen Richard N. Coudenhove-Kalergi* (Baden-Baden, 2008).
4. S. Malinowski, *Vom Adel zum Führer: Sozialer Niedergang und politische Radikalisierung im deutschen Adel zwischen Kaiserreich und NS-Staat* (Berlin, 2003), 198–609; E. Glassheim, *Noble Nationalists: The Transformation of the Bohemian Aristocracy* (London and Cambridge, Mass., 2005), 50–234; K. Urbach (ed.), *European Aristocracies and the Radical Right 1918–1939* (Oxford, 2008).
5. On the 'Conservative Revolution', see J. Herf, *Reactionary Modernism* (Cambridge, 1986); S. Breuer, *Anatomie der konservativen Revolution* (Darmstadt, 1993); idem, *Nationalismus und Faschismus. Frankreich, Italien und Deutschland im Vergleich* (Darmstadt, 2005); K. Sontheimer, *Antidemokratisches Denken in der Weimarer Republik* (Munich, 1978).
6. For instance, J. Bendersky, *Carl Schmitt Theorist for the Reich* (Princeton, 1998). For a recent discussion, see J.-W. Muller, *A Dangerous Mind: Carl Schmitt's Post-War European Thought* (New Haven and London, 2003).
7. Compare with T. Lane and M. Wolanski, *Poland and European Integration: The Ideas and Movements of Polish Exiles in the West, 1939–91* (Basingstoke, 2009), 1–213.

Chapter 4

RICHARD NIKOLAUS COUDENHOVE-KALERGI, FOUNDER OF THE PAN-EUROPEAN UNION, AND THE BIRTH OF A 'NEW' EUROPE

Anita Prettenthaler-Ziegerhofer

> The resuscitation of the pan-European idea is largely identified with Count
> Coudenhove-Kalergi. The form of his theme may be crude, erroneous and
> impractical, but the impulse and the inspiration are true.[1]
> Winston Churchill (1930)

Richard Coudenhove-Kalergi was doubtlessly one of the most colourful figures of the interwar years who dealt with the idea of the unification of the European states. Back then, he formulated his thoughts on a united Europe, which he adhered to consistently, in accordance with the political situation of the time, up to his death in 1972. Thus, he became a 'pioneer thinker' of a united Europe, who never tired of fighting for peace in Europe. Coudenhove's pan-Europeanism went far beyond the Second World War. Temporarily, he put his Pan-European Movement on hold in order to apply himself to the foundation of the European Parliamentary Union (EPU). Therewith, he made an important contribution towards the transformation process of the 'European idea', which he brought from the level of private Europe-architects to the official government level of European states, and thus contributed to the birth of the 'new' Europe.

This chapter focuses, first, on the Pan-European Movement in the interwar period, in order to outline concisely the activities of the European Parliamentary Union later on. The programmes of both movements will then be compared and analysed to demonstrate Coudenhove's contribution to the birth of a 'new' Europe.

Coudenhove-Kalergi and the First World War

Richard Coudenhove-Kalergi was born on 17 November 1894 as the second son of the head of the Austrian Legation in Tokyo, Heinrich Coudenhove-Kalergi and his wife, the Japanese girl Mitsuko Aoyama.[2] In 1896, the family returned to the paternal estate in Bohemian Ronsperg (today's Pobezovice, or Western Bohemian forest), where Richard grew up in an atmosphere of internationalism and cosmopolitanism. This familial environment and above all his aristocratic descent can be seen as the foundations of his later pan-Europeanism. Richard attended the Theresanium Academy in Vienna, which was the Empire's Eton. Afterwards he studied philosophy at the alma mater Rudolfina, where he took his doctorate in 1917. In 1914 he had married Ida Roland, who was a very famous actress at the time. She granted young Richard access to a world of artists, poets and actors, and all at once 'the one and only Roland liberated him from all familial bonds and from the bonds to a conservative milieu from which he had long ago grown apart and whose ideological and political views fundamentally differed from his'.[3] His personal contacts to Thomas and Heinrich Mann also date back to those times.[4] At the outbreak of war, Coudenhove worked as a freelance writer and journalist. Because of his lung disease he was exempt from military service. To him, the pacifist, the awakening of 'the aggressive tendency of nationalism' was the most horrible thing about war and Coudenhove wanted to call a halt to this aggressive nationalism, as he feared that as a result of it there would be 'no more cosmopolitans in Europe'.[5] On the other hand, the outcome of the war meant to Coudenhove that the liberal principle prevailed over the conservative one, that democracy prevailed over autocracy. Because of the First World War, the 'new' could break through. As Europe now received a uniform physiognomy, based on the national state and on democracy, the 'new', namely Pan-Europe, could be realized. Coudenhove's euphoric conclusion was that in order to unify Europe in a pan-European union of free nations it was no longer necessary to overcome political boundaries but psychological ones.[6]

Coudenhove was a declared supporter of Woodrow Wilson's fourteen-point programme for peace and later of the League of Nations. According to him, the League of Nations was the institution that would help to make the 'new' world social democratic, republican and pacifist. In this sense, Coudenhove considered himself as a citizen of the rising League of Nations. Nevertheless, he had to decide upon a citizenship after the Habsburg Monarchy collapsed. Thus, he became Czechoslovakian in 1939 and later a French citizen until his death. Like many of his contemporaries, Coudenhove overestimated the League of Nations in regard to securing peace and overcoming European nationalism. In the end, his disillusion with the lack of success of the world's Areopagus was his motivation to found a peace movement of his own – Pan-Europe. In this way, Pan-Europe was also, to quote Ralph White, 'a reaction of a frustrated Wilsonian, of a frustrated supporter of the League of Nations'.[7]

The Idea of Pan-Europe

The First World War had caused millions of deaths. There were few families who did not bemoan the loss of a war victim. It was a time when the 'Old' had not yet died and the 'New' had not yet been born. It was a time fraught with tension, a time when the doom of Europe was predicted.

Coudenhove, a part of 'yesterday's world' himself, oscillated between the 'world of yesterday' and the 'world of tomorrow', and complained about a backward-thinking public. According to him, contemporaries were always discussing the reasons for the war, instead of agonizing about strategies to prevent future wars. His thoughts constantly revolved around the fear of another war and he did not tire of warning against another catastrophe. In Coudenhove's opinion, the principal reason for Europe's fall was not this common weakness – namely, the likelihood of another war – but the political system. The inspired and convinced, almost obsessed, pacifist was searching for a formula to defuse a tense political climate and to counter apocalyptic prophecies. He was searching for a panacea which at the same time would cure Europe therapeutically and prophylactically of the consequences of war and thus save it from its own downfall.[8] His panacea was called Pan-Europe – the idea that all twenty-six European states as well as the seven small territories and the European colonies could be unified. Its ultimate ambition was the preservation of peace. In this way, 'Pan-Europe' was a political term and served as a dissociation from the geographical term 'Europe'. Pan-Europe should correspond to Pan-America and Pan-Hellenism.[9] A unification of Europe was the order of the day, and Coudenhove named three essential dangers which only such a unification of European states could halt: firstly, the danger of a new war in Europe because of the hereditary enmity between Germany and France; secondly, a terrible economic collapse because of an emerging American economic power; and, thirdly, the danger of Bolshevism.

Coudenhove initiated a new form of 'Europeanism' with Pan-Europe; the 'old' unification idea should now not only be present in the heads of certain Europeans, but put into practice for the first time. After various publications, his famous book on *Pan-Europa* followed in 1923,[10] and thus the 'pan-European propaganda campaign' started. Coudenhove wanted to galvanize the people by publishing *Pan-Europa*. Europe should face the 'European question', which was: 'Can Europe – in its political and economic fragmentation – maintain its peace and independence in the face of the growing extra-European world powers or is it forced to reorganise itself, to become a European commonwealth in order to save its existence?'[11] Coudenhove subsequently modified this European question several times without substantially changing it. 'Is it possible on the small European peninsula,' he asked, 'that 25 states live together in international anarchy without this ending in a horrible political, economic and cultural catastrophe?'[12]

The volume on *Pan-Europa* was a type of history coursebook with the aim of galvanizing the people of Europe in order finally to learn from history. After all, it was Coudenhove's opinion that history would be the *haute école* of politics – in accordance with his attitude that historical events would never recur but were similar to each other, because the same causes had the same effects.[13] In *Pan-Europa*, Coudenhove illustrated the parallels between past and present. For example, he referred to the Russian military dictatorship as Scylla and to the American financial dictatorship as Charybdis. Europe would be faced with a choice between these Homeric monsters or it could choose the alternative – Pan-Europe: 'Europe's fusion into a political and economic administration union'.[14] This was a fusion of all states, from Poland to Portugal, into a commonwealth of nations.[15]

Coudenhove's Europeanism was based on a philosophy in which the world was divided into five planetary fields of force: the American, the British, the Russian, the East Asian, and the European. Whereas four of these fields of force were structured and organized, the European field of force was disjointed, split into national states.[16] This disorganized condition of Europe would lead to further wars and this was the reason why, according to Coudenhove, the European states had to unify to form Pan-Europe.

Although Coudenhove knew about the historical plans for Europe of Pierre Dubois, le Duc de Sully, Jeremy Bentham and the Abbé de Saint-Pierre, Alfred Fried's *Pan-America*[17] influenced him the most; only the latter is quoted in *Pan-Europa*.[18] The book *Pan-America* and the successful operations of the Pan-American Union virtually served Coudenhove as a legitimization for Pan-Europe. Why should the successful American model not also apply to Europe? As the pan-American role model showed, one only had to find a European statesman who could summon a pan-European conference, from which a pan-European movement could arise. Furthermore, a pan-European office had to be set up in Geneva, Vienna or Paris. Here, Coudenhove seized on Fried's statement that if there had been a pan-European office similar to the pan-American office in Washington, the First World War would have never taken place.[19] The principal duties of the headquarters had to be: prevention of war, assistance to the economy, and support for a European civilization. Next to the Pan-American Union, Coudenhove also used the constitutional law of the United States and Switzerland as a role model for his commonwealth of Pan-Europe. However, it was foreign to the nature of the self-proclaimed republican to accomplish a *translatio imperii* in a pan-European sense during the interwar period.[20]

The realization of Pan-Europe was supposed to be accomplished in steps. Thus, one or more European governments would have to summon a pan-European conference in the first instance. According to Coudenhove, Italy and the Little Entente were possible countries for hosting the conference; other options were Switzerland, Spain, the Netherlands, and the Scandinavian countries, as well as Germany and France. The conferences should meet periodically and not discuss territorial questions. However, they should establish committees dealing with questions relating to arbitral jurisdiction, mutual military assistance, disarmament, minorities, traffic, tolls, currency, reparations and culture. In the course of this, a pan-European office would have to be established.[21] In a second step, arbitration and guarantee agreements would have to be concluded between the democratic

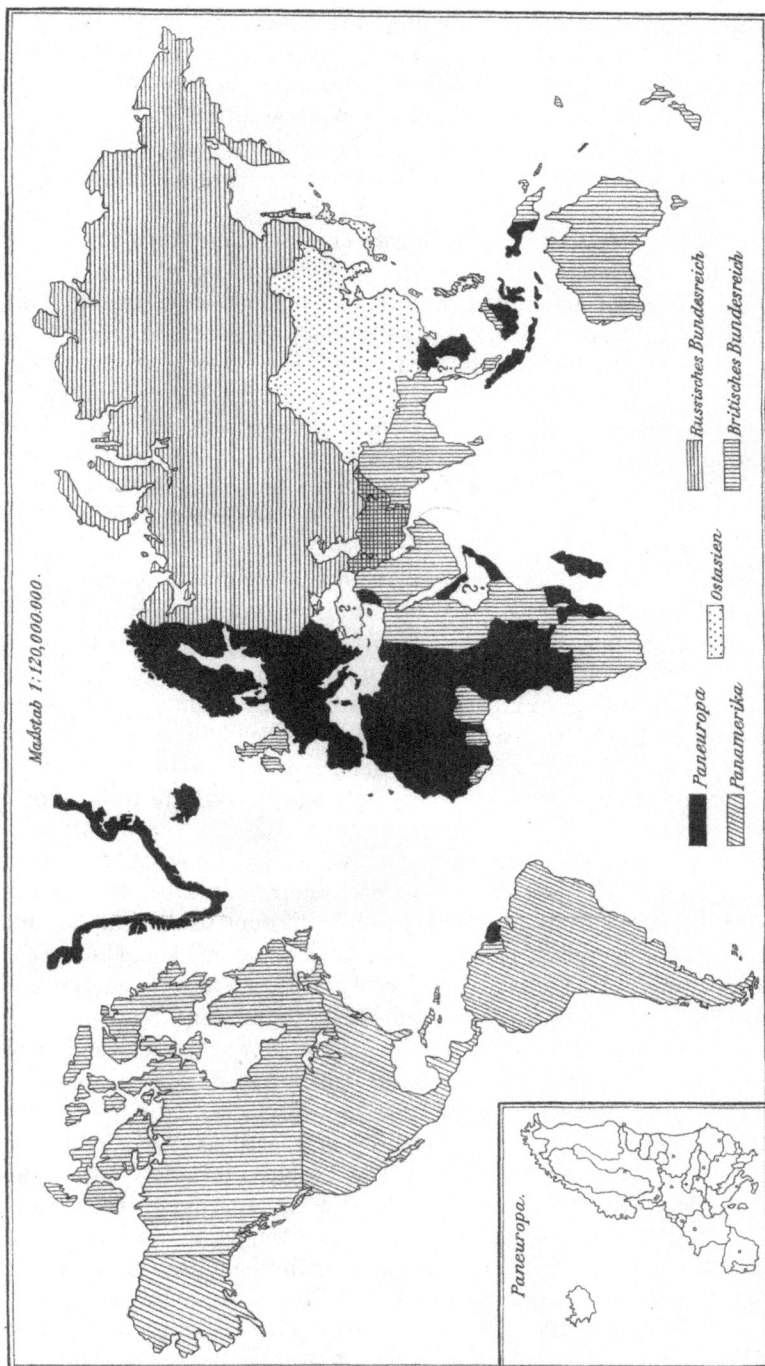

Figure 4.1   Pan-Europe. Source: Richard N. Coudenhove-Kalergi, *Pan-Europa* (Vienna, 1923), Fig. III

states. The arbitration agreement, which Coudenhove saw as a useful protection of the eastern borders and against Russian interference in European affairs, would have to be signed by Britain, too. Unlike the guarantee agreement, this would have implied the eventual interference of Pan-Europe in Asian and Pacific conflicts.[22] The third step was to be the establishment of a pan-European customs union, whereas the dismantling of the European customs borders would have to start immediately.[23]

According to the Count, the 'crowning event of the Pan-European Movement' should be the foundation of the United States of Europe according to the model of the United States of America. The constitution would have to assure the equality of all states and at the same time secure national sovereignties, the freedom of all citizens, and the equality of the different languages (English, however, should function as a lingua franca). In a similar fashion to the U.S. constitution, two houses should represent the legislative branch: a Völkerhaus (House of People), constituted by three hundred parliamentarians, with one parliamentarian representing one million Europeans, and a Staatenhaus (House of States), constituted by representatives of the twenty-six European states.[24] The advantages accruing from this pan-European federal consolidation would be as follows: firstly, protection from an intra-European war; secondly, a neutral position of Europe within world conflicts; thirdly, protection from an invasion of a red or white Russia; fourthly, the possibility of disarmament; and lastly, the ability to compete with U.S. and British, as well as – in the future – East Asian and Russian industry. Coudenhove illustrated the terrible consequences which a failure of the European states to form the Pan-European Union might have: the outbreak of another war, the permanent political and military interference of extra-European powers, a Russian invasion, the inability to compete with Anglo-Saxon industry, bankruptcy and economic enslavement.[25]

Peacekeeping was the most important motivation in the unification of Europe. Here, it was necessary to first settle 'European fraternal strife' between Germany and France. Therefore, Coudenhove requested both countries to tread the path of reconciliation. The end of the path would be Pan-Europe and could be achieved, amongst other things, by uniting German coal and French mineral ores under the umbrella of a Pan-European Coal and Steel Community.[26] It was one of Coudenhove's most important aims to pave the way for this reconciliation, which is why he again and again contributed to the daily discussions of this topic at the time. As far as peacekeeping was concerned, he also attached great importance to a reform of the League of Nations. Yet in 1924, and as late as 1933, Coudenhove, in regard to peacekeeping, referred to the League of Nations, the world's Areopagus, which had started its work in 1920, as 'an outstanding instrument for peace, despite all its deficiencies'.[27] In the end, however, his opinion of the League of Nations was characterized by major disappointments. At least since the outbreak of the Abyssinian War in 1936 and already because of the Soviet Union's accession to the League of Nations in 1934, this world federation had been degraded to a 'club of diplomats'[28] and, according to Coudenhove, had 'lost its soul'.[29] Coudenhove attempted to reform the League of Nations in a way that allowed the United States of America to enter into it.[30] Thus, he wrote a memorandum and directly sent it to the League of Nations. He aimed to substitute the centralized and mechanical organization of the League of Nations by a continental federalism. The feedback was very restrained and, thus, this attempt too was unsuccessful, as was the reconciliation between Germany and France.

The fear of Europe's economic ruin was widespread. Europe was destroyed, Russia was ineligible as a business and trade partner, the Central European economic zone was disrupted because of the First World War, the question concerning reparations payments was unanswered, and the United States inexorably moved towards economic supremacy. These reasons militated in favour of a unification of Europe as a consequence of economic considerations. Coudenhove tried to galvanize the masses by outlining that one had to prioritize unity above partisan interests. In this regard, the United States functioned as a model: their unity had brought unequalled wealth to the country, while the discordance of Europe would lead to a downfall without example. Compared to the United States of America, Coudenhove saw Europe as a dying and weak continent in decline. Here, too, existed only one panacea: the economic consolidation of all continental democracies of Europe, the collaboration of a pan-European customs union with Russia, and the disarmament of the European armies.[31]

Finally, Coudenhove mentioned, in addition to the outbreak of another war and the loss of economic competitiveness, the fear of a Russian invasion as the third reason for the foundation of Pan-Europe. To him, Russia was – in reference to Greek history – Europe's Macedonia. A pan-European defensive alliance could serve as a protection against a Russian invasion and therefore permanently protect Europe from Russia.[32] Nevertheless, Coudenhove constantly alluded to the fact that Russia (and later the Soviet Union) was economically important to Europe and that cooperation was therefore necessary.[33] Coudenhove had rejected Bolshevism all his life; first of all, because he considered it to be the deadly enemy of freedom and, secondly, because he, the idealist, was an opponent of collectivism.[34] To him, Pan-Europe symbolized the spearhead against Bolshevism, which, in his view, was the reason why all democratic parties had to join the Pan-European Movement. Only in such a way could the pan-European federation 'protect European democracy from Bolshevism and reaction'.[35]

One of the most important questions concerning the realization of Pan-Europe was the regularization of the relationship between Great Britain and Pan-Europe. 'The British question was the most difficult and delicate problem of all the complicated problems confronting Pan-Europe,' as Coudenhove put it in 1943.[36] He compared the relationship between Britain and Pan-Europe to the discussion held in St Paul's Church, Frankfurt, in 1848, dealing with the Austrian question and the problem of whether one should agree on a lesser German or greater German solution. The same question was now transferred to the 'European level' and he now asked whether the British Empire should be included in or excluded from Europe.[37] As Coudenhove proceeded on the assumption that the British

Empire was an extra-European empire, he stated that it could not become a part of Pan-Europe. In order to invalidate criticisms, Coudenhove referred to Pan-America, where the leaders had also chosen the lesser American solution by excluding Canada.[38] The establishment of a British-European entente would be the basis for future relations between Britain and Pan-Europe and would therefore dissipate the British fear of pan-European attacks, which the leader of *Pan-Europa* assumed to be significant. Coudenhove's opinion about 'England's' position within Pan-Europe provoked harsh criticism. However, not only Winston Churchill's speech in 1946 but also Great Britain's role within the integration process, starting in 1950, showed that Coudenhove was to be proven right.[39]

As far as his attitude towards Italy was concerned, it has to be mentioned that Coudenhove planned on asking Mussolini to summon the first pan-European conference in 1923, where the Pan-European Union was supposed to be founded.[40] Like many of his contemporaries, the anti-Bolshevist Coudenhove was fascinated by Mussolini, as he considered him to be Lenin's first equal opponent.[41] Therefore, it was hardly surprising that Coudenhove did his utmost to meet the fascist leader. However, the first verifiable personal meeting between them only occurred in May 1933 and probably because Engelbert Dollfuß intervened with Mussolini. Shortly before this meeting and immediately after the Pan-European Congress in Basel in 1932, Mussolini had hosted the fascist Volta Congress in Rome to discuss the fascist future of Europe. Among the participants were, among others, Alfred Rosenberg, Hermann Goering, and Hjalmar Schacht. Coudenhove was absent.[42] During the formative years of the Pan-European Movement, a powerful, anti-European movement had been formed around Asvero Gravelli, editor of the magazine *Anti-Europe*, in Italy:[43] Coudenhove stated that such agitation had stopped after his meeting with Mussolini.[44] In May 1936, the pan-European and the Duce met again; and again Coudenhove tried to convince Mussolini of the necessity of an Italian-French union against Nazi Germany.[45] All efforts to convert the Duce to Pan-Europe were of no avail. They solely document Coudenhove's persistence and, beyond that, also his political misjudgement.

The issue of the colonial properties of European states should also be mentioned here. Coudenhove can be referred to as a follower of a kind of neo-colonialism. From his point of view, European possessions on African territories provided economic opportunities for those states 'that missed out on the distribution of extra-European soil as a consequence of their geographical location and their historic fate'.[46] Furthermore, Coudenhove suggested a transformation of the Sahara into farmland and the eradication of sleeping sickness in Central Africa. Both suggestions corresponded to the consensus of the time and were seen as further tasks of the yet-to-be-united Europe.[47] Thus, the colonies were seen as suppliers of resources important to Europe but also as future habitats for Europeans and therefore gave rise to many geopolitical considerations, such as Hermann Sörgel's plan to drain the Mediterranean Sea.[48]

Coudenhove felt that a unification of European states could be mastered, especially because he held the opinion that the European nations were not communities of blood, but of mind: 'Nations arise from interrelations between gifted peoples and their great men. A genius without his people does not create culture – a people without great men is not a nation.'[49] Moreover, he believed that Europe was connected by Christian religion, European science, art and culture, which were based on a Christian-Hellenic foundation, a common European history, constitutions and laws, and finally, the common arts. According to him, these shared European characteristics constituted the basis for the creation of one European nation; regardless of the 'European confusion of languages'. In order to create a 'European nation' a separation of state and nation, similar to the separation of state and church, had to take place and the constitutive people should be replaced by the free nation within a free state. Coudenhove demanded a national edict of tolerance, a Magna Carta of all European nations; this would entail the 'true protection of minorities', in his opinion.[50] It was Coudenhove's utopian dream that, on the one hand, such an edict of tolerance would erase the meaning of national state borders, while, on the other hand, Europe's economic unification would simultaneously help to close down borders. According to Coudenhove, it was also necessary to develop some sort of European patriotism in addition to national sentiment; a patriotism able to convince all opponents of Pan-Europe: 'By means of written and spoken agitation, the European question shall become the vital question of millions of people; a question discussed by the general public of all people until each and every European is forced to comment on it.'[51]

In order to be able to put this vision into practice, Coudenhove demanded the establishment of a Pan-European Union and appealed to Europe's youth, women, spiritual leaders, and all Europeans, who were full of good intentions. He thought that 'in such a way a final battle for the destiny of Europe would take place between anti-Europeans and pan-Europeans; a battle between past and future, narrowness and reason, barbarity and culture!'[52]

The Pan-European Movement

After the presentation of programmatic principles, Coudenhove started to implement Pan-Europe. Apart from the fact that Prince Karl Anton Rohan founded the European Cultural Association in Vienna almost simultaneously and with the aim of uniting Europe's intellectuals in order to save the Occident, Coudenhove's attempt at implementation has remained original and unique in the history of European concepts.[53] Already at the beginning of 1925, Coudenhove was able to open Pan-Europe's central office at the Viennese Hofburg ('Eagle Staircase'). He was supported by the Austrian government, and Federal Chancellor Ignaz Seipl continued to be honorary president of the Austrian Pan-European Union until his death in 1932. He was followed by chancellors Engelbert Dollfuß and Kurt von Schuschnigg. In the course of time, Pan-European Unions were founded in almost all European capitals in order to foster pan-European patriotism. Pan-Europe was supposed to become a mass movement. At first, Coudenhove used the network of

European aristocracy to garner important supporters for his idea. Baron Louis Rothschild, for instance, helped him to establish important contacts with the banking industry, for example with the Hamburg banker Max Warburg, who generously sponsored the first Pan-European Congress in Vienna.[54] It was also Warburg who recommended Coudenhove to his brothers Felix and Paul in America, who in turn went on to organize Coudenhove's first lecture tour in America.[55] Very soon Coudenhove was in 'pan-European' contact with almost all European government representatives. Tomas Masaryk, president of Czechoslovakia, for instance, put Coudenhove in contact with French government leaders and important French journalists. The German industrialist Robert Bosch was so impressed by Coudenhove that he set up the Pan-Europe Development Fund in Zurich.[56] Although Coudenhove often met with European heads of state and government, their acceptance of Pan-Europe was not automatic. Coudenhove's political contacts had the effect that Pan-Europe was soon stigmatized as an elitist movement, which it stayed until the end. Coudenhove had not been able to make Pan-Europe a mass phenomenon. The pan-European was often criticized because of this and often replied to his critics that he had to win over the politicians first, in order to reach the masses from the top down.

In the execution of his vision, Coudenhove attached great importance to propaganda as a weapon of the pan-European campaign. With this in mind, he organized the first Pan-European Congress with about two thousand participants in Vienna in 1926. Although top-class politicians were conspicuous by their absence or only sent their greetings, the congress had a long-term effect because by 1927, the French politician Aristide Briand had already become honorary president of the Pan-European Movement. The movement gained steam because of this prominent support and Coudenhove knew how to use this support efficiently in terms of public relations. Apart from holding congresses, Coudenhove also used advertising strategies, such as editing a monthly magazine called *Paneuropa*, whose main author was Coudenhove himself. Moreover, he lectured throughout Europe and in the United States, and created a corporate identity by using tiepins, neckties, Pan-Europe cigars, cockades, and so on. All advertising material showed a red cross on a golden sun – the movement's emblem, which symbolized humanness and reason. Further demands, such as the foundation of a pan-European party, a European academy and a European citizenship were not heard because of the political situation at the beginning of the 1930s. The same applied to the demands concerning a European anthem and a Europe Day.

The movement reached its zenith in September 1929. At the same time, the decline of the movement started. At the ninth convention of the League of Nations, Aristide Briand surprised the European public with his proposal for the unification of the European states. Apart from Edouard Herriot, who had already been a supporter of this idea since the late 1920s, Briand was the first European statesman wanting to make the 'European question' a foreign-policy issue. The European heads of state and government present in Geneva engaged Briand to prepare a memorandum on the establishment of the European Union. However, shortly after the convention Briand's fellow campaigner, the German Gustav Stresemann, died, and, in October, the Great Depression began. Thus, the half-hearted programme, a diplomatic masterpiece, was only presented on 17 May 1930. It provided for the political unification of Europe, which was supposed to be organized in a loose structure and strongly linked to the League of Nations.[57] In conclusion, Briand said that it was now for the European governments 'to act in the full consciousness of their responsibility if they did not want to lose the leadership over physical and mental powers to the random initiative of some individuals'.[58] This statement documents the significance Briand admitted to private European organizations, of some of which he was himself honorary president.

Prior to the dispatch of Briand's memorandum, Coudenhove had taken a PR tour to Berlin, Prague and Vienna together with Edouard Herriot, and had published a concept for the constitution of the 'Federal State of Europe' in his magazine *Paneuropa* in April. Before this, he had sent the concept for a federally organized Europe, which included a detailed organizational structure and details concerning rudimentary human rights and a European citizenry, to all European governments indicating that he had conceptualized it as a private person and not as a pan-European. Only the German government responded to the 'constitutional concept'; one government repudiated his utopian plan.[59] On the same day, the second Pan-European Congress met in Berlin to mobilize public opinion in favour of Briand's efforts. In September 1930, the results of the member states were discussed at the meeting of the League of Nations. Soon it became clear that the European members of the League of Nations could not agree on a common consensus: Germany, Britain and Italy strictly opposed the unification of Europe. Briand's memorandum initiated the beginning of the fall of the pan-European idea. Hitler's rise on 30 January 1933 meant the closure of all pan-European offices in Germany, the prohibition of the movement, and the loss of the most important financier of Pan-Europe: German industry.

Now, Coudenhove had to change the aims of Pan-Europe; his central aim was no longer the political unification of Europe, but rather its economic union. This new direction was in part due to the influence of the new Austrian honorary president of Pan-Europe, Engelbert Dollfuß. Dollfuß was a supporter, who also hoped to be able to exploit Pan-Europe and use it against National Socialism. Coudenhove himself described the collaboration with Dollfuß and his successor: during these years, Pan-Europe worked from its Viennese headquarters for a pan-European coalition against Hitler, the aim being to encircle Nazi Germany and isolate it until Hitler had been overthrown and peace reestablished.[60] After the murder of Dollfuß in July 1934, and with the increasing radicalization of European politics, Coudenhove had to change the aims of Pan-Europe again. From this time on, he began to propagate a culturally united Europe with the aim of saving the Occident. On the fateful night of 12/13 March, Coudenhove fled Austria via Italy to Switzerland. From there, he tried to continue Pan-Europe until he finally had to leave Europe for exile in America in 1940. Previously, in 1939, the British Committee of the Pan-European Union had been founded in London, and Alfred

Duff Cooper had become its chairman.[61] At the same time, more and more pan-European sections were continuously closing in continental Europe. The interwar period was characterized by Coudenhove's attempt to propagate the pan-European idea. The question of whether there should be federation (with surrender of sovereignty) or confederation (without surrender of sovereignty) never really arose for him. He probably always argued in support of a federalist Europe with national states retaining their sovereignty. This corresponded to the mainstream view at the time. Only in the course of the Second World War, and later because of the foundation of the European Parliamentary Union, did Coudenhove commit himself. It was then that he added his own constitutional project to the list of constitutional concepts of the resistance fighters, and stuck to it until his death.

Coudenhove and the European Parliamentary Union

Coudenhove was unable to use Pan-Europe as a spearhead against war in his second home of Switzerland, and so he emigrated to New York with his family on 3 August 1940. There he resumed the contacts he had already established in 1926. Murray Butler of the Carnegie Foundation, for instance, helped him to acquire a position at the University of New York, where he did research on the future general peace framework for Europe. Moreover, he tirelessly but unsuccessfully tried to convince the Roosevelt administration of his pan-European idea. In 1943, he even hosted the fifth Pan-European Congress at the University of New York, and Winston Churchill sent his greetings to the participants.[62] At the congress, it was agreed that a draft constitution for the United States of Europe should be elaborated.[63]

Now, Coudenhove clearly had to position himself on the basic issue of union or federation. The term 'union' refers to all kinds of associations of states, including federations, whereas federation is used to describe a special type of union, which to a certain extent directs the policies of the member states with central authority. The question of whether Europe should establish a union or a federation involved the problem of national sovereignty.[64] Because of the current Russian threat, Coudenhove was certain that a united Europe could only be organized as a federation. Moreover, he was certain that only a federation could build an army which was able to fight a possible Russian invasion and to intervene where domestic communists were trying to undermine the democratic system of their states. Coudenhove was of the opinion that only a European federation could protect human rights. The launch of a common European currency was a further economic argument of Coudenhove in favour of a federalist Europe. We already know the two dangers which impelled the foundation of a federalist Europe from 1923: a Russian invasion and economic collapse.

The draft constitution was elaborated by the legal committee of the fifth Pan-European Congress and the research seminar of New York University, and was completed in 1944. Fernando des Los Rios, the former Spanish Minister of

Foreign Affairs and Minister of Justice, was chairman of this legal committee, which consisted of European and American attorneys. The constitution was intended to establish the constitutional fundamentals of the individual member states as well as the personal and social rights of the citizens of every member state. Moreover, under such a constitution, a professional army would have been formed in order to defend the federal territory; its commander-in-chief would have been appointed by the Union and the whole armament industry would have been put under the surveillance of the Union. The idea of establishing a European customs union and a European central bank with the power to launch currencies was also considered. The legislative branch would have been represented by Congress, consisting of a House of Representatives and a House of States. A council consisting of seven members would have formed the executive branch. A Supreme Court consisting of fifteen members, whose decisions would have been passed by a majority, would have represented the judicial branch. The constitution itself would have become effective, when at least ten member states had agreed to it; four out of these ten states would have to have represented a population of at least twenty million people, however. A total or fractional revision would have required a two-thirds majority.

Coudenhove returned to Europe in 1946, where he found some European societies already in existence. Winston Churchill had started off the integration process, which was to begin in 1950, with his speech at the University of Zurich. He also mentioned Coudenhove in this speech, whereupon the pan-European wrote a letter to Churchill telling him that his speech made him the happiest person on earth: 'I can't express how thankful I am for what it [the speech] meant to Europe, the Pan-European Movement and me.'[65] Of further consequence, some private Europe organizations – for example, the Union Européenne des Féderalistes (UEF) and the United European Movement (UEM) – had come into being, momentarily decommissioning Pan-Europe. Coudenhove's European vision was now characterized by the thought that the European idea should no longer be based on private individuals or associations of persons, but on politicians. In this way, he could substantially distance himself from the already existing Europe societies, which he considered children of Pan-Europe, on the one hand, and a danger, on the other. In addition, he gained necessary legitimacy for his movement. His plan was to convert European parliamentarians to the idea so that they could put inter-European pressure on European statesmen. Extra-European pressure was put on them by the Soviet threat anyway. By such means, Coudenhove thought that the European government representatives would be persuaded, as a result, to unite Europe.[66]

As he had already done in the course of establishing the Pan-European Movement,[67] Coudenhove started with a survey among European parliamentarians (except those of states under Soviet influence or those of Germany) with the question: 'Are you in favour of a European Federation within the framework of the U.N?' The answers were very positive, so Coudenhove founded the European Parliamentary Union (EPU) in 1947. For the first time since the Second World

War, 114 West European parliamentarians (among them German parliamentarians) met in neutral Switzerland to discuss the foundation of a United States of Europe. The most important claim of the EPU concerned the elaboration of a European federal constitution for a federalist Europe, including the surrender of sovereignty. It was of great importance to answer the question of how to transform Europe into a federal system. Here, the discussion was raised of whether European governments were prepared to sacrifice national sovereignty on the altar of a European federation. This was also the reason why Coudenhove articulated his idea of establishing a European parliament at the first convention of the EPU in Gstaad in September 1947. The proposed European parliament should not be a constituent assembly, but only a drafting committee of Europe's national parliaments. It should be the voice of the peoples of Europe.

In the meantime, the representatives of the private Europe societies had agreed to hold a joint 'Congress of Europe'. It was finally held under the chairmanship of Winston Churchill between 7 and 10 May 1948 in The Hague. The Congress of Europe, organized by Duncan Sandys, Churchill's son-in-law, aimed to convince Europe's political powers that the European Movement was an actual power supported by the majority of Europe's élite.[68] In its political resolution The Hague Congress formulated the most important measures to be taken for the future Europe, which included the creation of a European Assembly, a European Court, and a catalogue of human rights. A further result was the foundation of an umbrella organization of all Europe societies in late 1948 – the 'European Movement'. Coudenhove did not want to join the private European Movement with his EPU, which he understood as a political and parliamentary movement. Moreover, Coudenhove considered the demands of the Congress of Europe as inadequate. Partly in response to it, the second EPU Congress, held in Interlaken between 1 and 4 September 1949, passed the action plan of Interlaken,[69] which included ten constitutional principles for a European Union.[70] This draft constitution was based on the draft of 1944 and on the 21-page memorandum of the British Labour MP, Ronald Mackay. The preamble of the draft constitution set goals such as the acceptance of the fundamentals and aims of the UN Charter, the conservation of peace, the concentration of all powers on the reconstruction of Europe, the improvement of living standards, human rights, a common defence policy, as well as close economic collaboration between all member states. The sixteen founding states of the OEEC as well as Western Germany and Turkey were to be the members of the union of a 'United States of Europe'. These states had to guarantee the fundamental aims of the UN and of the Declaration of Human Rights. All states that acknowledged the constitution would be free to join the union at any time.

Similar to the draft constitutions of 1930 and 1944, and to the pan-European concept of 1923, the parliament was to consist of a Senate and a Chamber of Deputies, with each member state sending one senator to the Senate. The Chamber of Deputies would be proportionally elected; the stronger a party the more members of parliament would be sent to the Chamber of Deputies.[71] Concerning the areas that were under the responsibility of the federal state, the parliament would have the competence to pass laws. These areas would include: foreign affairs and defence, vital facilities such as communications, health, naturalization of foreign citizens, emigration, immigration, the intrusion of criminals into federal territory, and customs and financial policies. To defend Europe against invasion and civil wars, a heavily motorized European army would have to be established under federal authority. This European army would act autonomously; its bases and airfields would be spread across the whole of Europe. Together with the member states, the federal state would be responsible for the economy, labour and all social issues. Moreover, Coudenhove planned economic unification. The executive branch would be represented by a Federal Council; one of its members would be elected Federal President. The third power, called the 'Administration of Justice', would be executed by a High Court. Its duties would be the construction of the constitution and the compliance with all human rights. As far as the rights of the states were concerned, the subsidiarity principle stated that 'If a state's legislation contradicts federal legislation, federal law takes priority as far as the wordings of both laws are contradictory'; the notion of a constitutive citizenship consisted in 'The citizens of each state [enjoying] the same rights and privileges on the territories of each member state as the citizens of the state itself.' A European federation involved European citizenship. Finally, the principle of equal rights and duties for all member states, with the enactment of the equality of all states within the union, would profoundly affect the future peace treaty with Germany.[72]

The EPU Congress clearly voted for the establishment of a federation. Thus, it went further than the Hague Congress in May 1948, where the French had unwillingly to yield to the demands of the British, who opposed a federally structured Europe. Coudenhove stated that Great Britain so strongly opposed a federation because of sentimental objections; as neither the United Kingdom nor the British Commonwealth had ever had a written constitution, the idea of joining the Continent under a written constitution would not appeal to the British mind.[73] In Coudenhove's opinion, the main reason for the British rejection of federalism was the United Kingdom's role as the head of an intercontinental empire. According to him, membership of a federalist Europe would undermine the role of the British Empire within the Commonwealth of Nations. Yet the Hague Congress, Coudenhove's draft constitution, and the draft constitution of the UEF dating from November 1948 exerted some pressure on the responsible politicians, which led to the foundation of the Council of Europe on 5 May 1949. Although the suggestions of the EPU had not been taken into account when the Council of Europe was founded, Coudenhove welcomed this institution as a child of the EPU. After all, many parliamentarians of the EPU were now parliamentarians of the Council of Europe. In the beginning, Coudenhove held high hopes for the Council of Europe. He even hoped that it would become the germ cell of a European Constituent Assembly. However, when this hope foundered on British resistance, Coudenhove-Kalergi referred to the Council of Europe as a debating club, a club of European nations without any political meaning.[74] To him, the

Council of Europe represented the 'federalist idea's defeat in Strasbourg'.[75] Nevertheless, he judged the European Convention on Human Rights (ECHR) favourably, which, unlike the UN Charter of Human Rights, was legally binding.[76]

Now, Coudenhove became deeply absorbed in the idea of a European federation. For his lifelong commitment to European peace, which he considered as a precondition for world peace, and for his tireless insistence on the foundation of a European Union with a European constitution, Coudenhove became the first to win the International Charlemagne Prize of the City of Aachen in 1950. It was awarded to him on 18 May 1950, a few days after Robert Schuman's speech, in which he had pronounced the amalgamation of the German and the French coal and steel industries. In his official speech Coudenhove welcomed this move and proposed to name the future European Coal and Steel Community (ECCS) the 'Union Charlemagne'. He wanted this name to be understood as a reference to the reformation of the Carolingian Empire on a democratic, federalist, and social basis. According to him, Europe was an entity of the Occident, which had been disrupted by the Treaty of Verdun in 843; this entity had to be reestablished. Thus, the Count became the proponent of the imperial concept, apparently not entirely aware of the negative reactions this naming would cause on the part of the European governments. The glorification of the Middle Ages was completely inappropriate to most proponents of a new Europe.[77] Nonetheless, Coudenhove repeatedly spoke in favour of a continental federation of the Charlemagne union at the fourth EPU Congress in Constance in September 1950. This federation should be built by some kind of a federalist 'core Europe' principally consisting of the six founding states of the later ECSC.[78]

Coudenhove did not tire and risked a last attempt towards a European constitution in May 1951. Relying on the previous draft constitutions, he went some steps further and for the first time demanded the establishment of the supranational principle as well as a two-speed Europe, the acknowledgement of the European Convention on Human Rights, and the introduction of a citizenship status, possibly wanting to impinge upon the ongoing negotiations concerning the ECSC.[79] With the ECSC's foundation, the first law-making supranational organization had been formed. Thus, it was clear that Great Britain would be excluded from further integration measures, as Downing Street ruled out its participation in a supranational organization. Coudenhove succinctly commented that Winston Churchill was not among the leading figures anymore, but Konrad Adenauer, Robert Schuman, Alcide de Gasperi and Paul-Henri Spaak were. In the meantime, the Count had become reconciled with the European Movement and, next to Adenauer, Churchill, de Gasperi, Schuman and Spaak, also became its honorary president. He was the only non-politician to hold this position. Although Coudenhove welcomed the advent of the ECSC, he continued to demand deeper integration in the sense of a constitutional European federation. In spite of the fact that the European Economic Community (EEC, founded in 1957) could not meet his demands, Coudenhove was convinced that it was the realization of the second step of the former pan-European demand: with its foundation 'the Rubicon which separated yesterday's national economic systems from tomorrow's pan-European economic system has been crossed. Its meaning for the unification of Europe promises to become more important than the meaning of the Council of Europe.'[80] According to him, the way was now clear to bring the United States of Europe to fruition.[81]

Conclusion

During the interwar period, Coudenhove planned the unification of European states either as a federal state or as a commonwealth of nations. In the course of this, he was orientated towards the Pan-American Union. The movement's programme was elastic; it adapted to given political and economic events. It was impossible for him to deliver a specific plan for Europe during these suspense-packed and bellicose times. As far as communism, National Socialism, and the membership of Great Britain were concerned, the Pan-European Movement – or, rather, Coudenhove – developed a zero-tolerance policy. As already mentioned, he did not support supranationality or surrender of sovereignty during the interwar period. Consequently, he demanded the amalgamation of the German and the French coal and steel industries as early as 1923. More specifically, he called for the creation of a pan-European public authority for coal and steel; national sovereignties were to be preserved, though. In 1951, this public authority became the first law-making supranational public authority with clearly defined institutions.

The Pan-European Movement survived the Second World War in American exile. The return to Europe caused Coudenhove prematurely to decommission Pan-Europe in order to apply himself to the foundation of the EPU. The EPU's manifesto was more specific and more adjusted to the mainstream than the programme of the Pan-European Movement. Coudenhove might have known the draft constitutions of the European resistance groups, which had already demanded a federalist Europe including surrender of sovereignty, establishment of democracy, constitutionality and human rights during the Second World War.[82] All these demands were propagated by the UEF but also by Coudenhove during the incubation period of European integration from 1945 until 1950. However, Coudenhove, who was very sensitive to and fully recognized the deficits of the plans for Europe, wanted to take a further step and demanded a federalist constitution for a united Europe.

As much as Coudenhove approved of the European integration process, he was very sceptical as to whether a European federation could be established on the basis of this 'continental governmental act'.[83] 'Europe is uniting without the majority of Europeans being ready for it', he wrote in 1953: 'Europe becomes one on the level of parliaments and state chancelleries but not within the hearts of the Europeans.'[84] Thus, Coudenhove became an advocate of the creation of a European identity and state: 'The paradox about the unification of Europe is that it is not supported by a real popular movement.'[85] According to him, the missing link of a European consciousness would only work as long as unification was beneficial; a crisis would lead to disruption, though. Coudenhove far-sightedly predicted that the future of the European Union would only be permanently successful if Europe stopped living only on the administrative level and found its way into the heads and hearts of its citizens. It was Coudenhove's credo that the moment of the creation of the United States of Europe also had to be the moment of the birth of a European soul, European patriotism and one European nation. This prophetic vision went unheard in the economic environment in which the 'new Europe' arose. People sneered at Coudenhove rather than taking him seriously. After 1946, he gave the impression of being a grand seigneur, who had come from a long-forgotten time, was not able to adjust and had not realized that Europe did not need visions anymore but energetic actions. Coudenhove wanted to create 'Europe all at once' and thereby overexerted 'Europe'. Robert Schuman had drawn lessons from all of this and realized that Europe could only be united step by step. Coudenhove, on the contrary, was mentally stuck in the interwar years; Pan-Europe had taken its ideas from European concepts of the past and had now partly become a compilation of all of them.

Without a doubt, one can refer to Coudenhove as an icebreaker when it comes to political unification processes in Europe since the interwar period. After all, he had expressed forward-looking ideas at that time, even without thinking about the surrender of sovereignty. Among other things, his ideas included a customs union, a German–French Coal and Steel Community or a European party. In the interwar era, Pan-Europe seemed like a utopian dream, however. After the Second World War, Coudenhove's plans became more concrete. For instance, he was among the first to demand that a European Constituent Assembly be the cornerstone of a European postwar order.[86] He thought that the time had come to surrender sovereignty to a supranational organization. Even before the foundation of a Common Foreign and Security Policy (CFSP) in 1992 by the Treaty of Maastricht, he had wondered out loud about a common foreign policy as the basis of a European defence policy. He demanded a European constitution and campaigned for a federally united Europe. He was aware of the fact that Great Britain would not become a member of this European federation. After all, he had already got to know the special position of the U.K. during the interwar period.

Richard Coudenhove-Kalergi died on 27 July 1972 in Schruns, Vorarlberg. On 1 August, his mortal remains were conveyed to Gstaad, Switzerland, where he found his final resting place in the vault of an American financier. Today, though, his credo of creating a Europe of hearts is more prevalent than ever.

Notes

Many thanks to René Kallinger for his support of the translation.

1.   Quoted in A. Prettenthaler-Ziegerhofer, *Botschafter Europas. Richard Nikolaus Coudenhove-Kalergi und die Paneuropabewegung in den 20er und 30er Jahren* (Vienna, 2004), 156. These sentences were written by Winston Churchill in the *Saturday Evening Post*, February 1930.

2. Fundamental to the following discussion is A. Prettenthaler-Ziegerhofer, *Botschafter Europas*. See also further pieces of work on Coudenhove, such as the biographical outline by V. Conze, *Richard Coudenhove-Kalergi. Umstrittener Visionär Europas* (Zurich, 2004), and V. Schöberl, *'Es gibt ein großes und herrliches Land, das sich selbst nicht kennt … es heißt Europa'. Die Diskussion um die Paneuropaidee in Deutschland, Frankreich und Großbritannien 1922–1933* (Berlin, 2008); C. Pernhorst, *Das paneuropäische Verfassungsmodell des Grafen Richard N. Coudenhove-Kalergi* (Baden-Baden, 2008); O. Burgard, *Das gemeinsame Europa – von der politischen Utopie zum außenpolitischen Programm: Meinungsaustausch und Zusammenarbeit proeuropäischer Verbände in Deutschland und Frankreich, 1924–1933* (Frankfurt/Main, 2000).

3. R.N. Coudenhove-Kalergi, *Ein Leben für Europa. Meine Lebenserinnerungen* (Cologne/Berlin, 1966), 77.

4. See Chapter 13.

5. R.N. Nikolaus Coudenhove-Kalergi, *Crusade for Pan-Europe. Autobiography of a Man and a Movement* (New York, 1943), 54–55.

6. R.N. Coudenhove-Kalergi, *Pan-Europa* (Vienna, 1923), 109.

7. R. White, 'The Europeanism of Coudenhove-Kalergi', in P.M.R. Stirk, *European Unity in Context: The Interwar Period* (London, 1989), 28.

8. I. Ulrike-Paul, 'Einigung für einen Kontinent von Feinden? R.N. Coudenhove-Kalergis "Paneuropa" und K.A. Rohans "Reich über Nationen" als konkurrierende Europaprojekte der Zwischenkriegszeit', in H. Duchhardt and I. Nemeth (eds), *Der Europa-Gedanke in Ungarn und Deutschland in der Zwischenkriegszeit* (Mainz, 2005), 2.

9. Coudenhove-Kalergi, *Pan-Europa*, 37. These seven territories are the Saar area, Gdansk, Fiume, Monaco, San Marino, Liechtenstein and Andorra (see Figure 1 in *Pan-Europa*).

10. Coudenhove-Kalergi, *Pan-Europa*: already in 1926 this 168-page book had sold 16,000 copies and thus was one of the best-selling books of its time. Moreover, it was translated into almost all languages of the world, excluding Russian and Italian.

11. Coudenhove-Kalergi, *Pan-Europa*, ix.

12. Coudenhove-Kalergi, 'Das Pan-Europäische Manifest', *Pan-Europa*, Eröffnungsnummer (April 1924), 11.

13. Quoted from C. Pernhorst, *Das paneuropäische Verfassungsmodell des Grafen Richard N. Coudenhove-Kalergi*, 43.

14. Coudenhove-Kalergi, *Pan-Europa*, xi.

15. Ibid., 27.

16. Ibid., 23.

17. A.H. Fried, *Pan-Amerika. Entwicklung, Umfang und Bedeutung der zwischenstaatlichen Organisation in Amerika (1810–1910)* (Zurich, 1910).

18. Coudenhove-Kalergi, *Pan-Europa*, 71–75.

19. Ibid., 77; and Fried, *Panamerika*, 291.

20. Coudenhove-Kalergi, 'Monarchie oder Republik?', in *Neue Freie Presse*, 17 Nov. 1922.

21. Coudenhove-Kalergi, *Pan-Europa*, 151–52.

22. Ibid., 152–53.

23. Ibid., 153.

24. Ibid., 153–54.

25. Ibid., 155.

26. Ibid., 127–28.

27. Coudenhove, 'Paneuropa und Völkerbund', *Paneuropa* 6 (1924), 4.

28. 'Abessinische Bilanz', *Paneuropa* (1937), 215.

29. Coudenhove-Kalergi, 'Völkerbund – oder Abendland?' *Paneuropa* (1938), 35.

30. R.N. Coudenhove-Kalergi, 'Weltorganisation und Paneuropa. Memorandum an das Generalsekretariat des Völkerbundes', *Paneuropa* 4 (1925), 14–29. The original can be found in the archives of the League of Nations, ONU Genéve, Box 1566, 1919–1927, Klass. 39, File 45485, World Organization and Pan-Europe – A Memorial of the League of Nations.

31. Coudenhove-Kalergi, *Pan-Europa*, 70.

32. Ibid., 59.
33. Ibid., 63.
34. R. Italiaander, *Richard N. Coudenhove-Kalergi. Begründer der Paneuropa-Bewegung* (Freudenstadt, 1969), 16.
35. Coudenhove-Kalergi, *Pan-Europa*, 162.
36. Coudenhove-Kalergi, *Crusade for Pan-Europe. Autobiography of a Man and a Movement* (New York, 1943), 107; as well as relevant chapters of Schöberl, *'Es gibt ein großes und herrliches Land'*, and Prettenthaler-Ziegerhofer, *Botschafter Europas*, 76–78.
37. Coudenhove-Kalergi, *Pan-Europa*, 41.
38. Coudenhove-Kalergi, *Pan-Europa*, 44.
39. See, for instance, J. Elvert, *Die Europäische Integration* (Darmstadt, 2006); M. Gehler, *Europa. Ideen – Institutionen – Vereinigungen* (Munich, 2005); P. Stirk, *A History of European Integration since 1914*, 119–21; A. Prettenthaler-Ziegerhofer, *Europäische Integrationsgeschichte. Unter besonderer Berücksichtigung der österreichischen Integration*, 2nd edn. (Innsbruck, 2007).
40. R.N. Coudenhove-Kalergi, 'Offener Brief an Benito Mussolini', *Neue Freie Presse*, 21 Feb. 1921.
41. Prettenthaler-Ziegerhofer, *Botschafter Europas*, 386–88.
42. See Chapter 8 below, and Prettenthaler-Ziegerhofer, *Botschafter Europas*, 218–19.
43. Concerning Gravelli compare for instance S. Eleuteri, 'Paneuropa und Antieuropa. Eine Zeitschrift zwischen europäischen Gedankengut und italienischem Faschismus (1929–1943)', a seminar paper at the Ludwig Maximilians University, Munich, 1995.
44. Prettenthaler-Ziegerhofer, *Botschafter Europas*, 398.
45. Ibid., 404.
46. Coudenhove-Kalergi, *Pan-Europa*, 156.
47. Ibid., 157.
48. See W. Voigt, *Atlantropa. Weltbauen am Mittelmeer. Ein Architektentraum der Moderne* (Hamburg, 1998).
49. Coudenhove-Kalergi, *Pan-Europa*, 137.
50. Ibid., 146.
51. Ibid., 167.
52. Ibid.
53. Paul, *Einigung für einen Kontinent von Feinden?*, 21–45, as well as A. Prettenthaler-Ziegerhofer, 'Europa-Utopien, Paneuropa, Kulturbund und die Idee einer paneuropäischen Akademie', in Ita Greenberg's forthcoming edited volume. Fundamental to the discussion on the European League of Nations are G. Müller, *Europäische Gesellschaftsbeziehungen nach dem Ersten Weltkrieg. Das Deutsch-Französische Studienkomitee und der Europäische Kulturbund* (Munich, 2005), and idem, 'Rohan, Karl Anton Prinz', in Caspar von Schrenck-Notzing (ed.), *Lexikon des Konservatismus* (Graz, 1996), 463–65.
54. Prettenthaler-Ziegerhofer, *Botschafter Europas*, 108.
55. Ibid., 128.
56. Ibid., 112.
57. A. Prettenthaler-Ziegerhofer, 'Austria and Aristide Briand's 1930 Memorandum', *Austrian History Yearbook* 29 (1998), 139–59.
58. A. Prettenthaler-Ziegerhofer, 'Aristide Briand und Richard Coudenhove-Kalergi. Zwei Europaprotagonisten und ihre Europa-Entwürfe aus dem Jahr 1930', in A. Bauer and K.H.L. Welker (eds), *Europa und seine Regionen. 2000 Jahre Rechtsgeschichte* (Vienna, 2007), 718.
59. Ibid., 681–733.
60. Coudenhove-Kalergi, *Europe Seeks Unity* (New York, 1948), 17.
61. Ibid., 17–18.
62. A. Prettenthaler-Ziegerhofer, 'Richard Coudenhove-Kalergi', *Deutschsprachige Exilliteratur seit 1933*, 3. *USA*, vol. 4, 15.
63. See C. Pernhorst, *Das paneuropäische Verfassungsmodell*, 124–31; full wording printed on 222–37.
64. Coudenhove-Kalergi, *Europe Seeks Unity*, 26.

65. Cited in M. Posselt, *Richard Nikolaus Coudenhove-Kalergi und die Europäische Parlamentarier-Union. Die parlamentarische Bewegung für eine "Europäische Konstituante" (1946–1952)*, 106.
66. Ibid., 468.
67. 'Paneuropäische Bemühungen um eine deutsch-französische Aussöhnung. Dargestellt anhand einer Rundfrage unter deutschen und französischen Parlamentariern anlässlich der Parlamentswahlen 1928', *Jahrbuch für europäische Geschichte* 4 (2003), 215–42.
68. G. Brunn, *Die Europäische Einigung* (Stuttgart, 2002), 60.
69. Printed in Christian Pernhorst, *Das paneuropäische Verfassungsprojekt*, 238–44.
70. Ibid., 132.
71. Ibid., 239.
72. Coudenhove-Kalergi, *Europe Seeks Unity*, 35.
73. Ibid., 30.
74. Coudenhove-Kalergi, *Weltmacht Europa* (Stuttgart, 1971), 143.
75. M. Posselt, 'Pionier im Kampf um Paneuropa. Die ersten fünf Jahrzehnte der Bewegung', *Paneuropa Österreich* 17 (1992), 16.
76. Coudenhove-Kalergi, *Weltmacht Europa*, 153.
77. This proposal was the reason why, even today, the Pan-Europe plan from interwar period is associated with the imperial concept.
78. C. Pernhorst, *Das paneuropäische Verfassungsprojekt*, 137–40.
79. Ibid., 140–44.
80. Coudenhove-Kalergi, *Eine Idee erobert Europa. Meine Lebenserinnerungen* (Vienna, 1958), 341.
81. Ibid., 342.
82. A. Prettenthaler-Ziegerhofer, '"Die Männer des europäischen Widerstandes werden morgen das neue Europa bauen". Leitbilder für ein vereintes Europa', in J. Elvert and J. Nielsen-Sykora (eds), *Leitbild Europa? Europabilder und ihre Wirkungen in der Neuzeit* (Stuttgart, 2009), 126–38.
83. Coudenhove-Kalergi, *Mutterland* (Zurich, 1953), 10.
84. Ibid., 11.
85. Ibid.
86. M. Posselt, *Richard Nikolaus Coudenhove-Kalergi und die Europäische Parlamentarier-Union*, 468.

Chapter 5

NOBLE CONTINENT?

*German-Speaking Nobles as Theorists of European
Identity in the Interwar Period*

>ⲧⲧ⸱⸱⸱⸱⸱⸱⸱⸱⸱⸱⸱⸱⸱⸱<

Dina Gusejnova

Speaking in the aftermath of the Second World War at Zurich University, Winston
Churchill characterized the preceding decades as a time of 'frightful nationalistic
quarrels, originated by the Teutonic nations'. Europe, this 'noble continent,
comprising on the whole the fairest and the most cultivated regions of the earth,
enjoying a temperate and equable climate, is the home of all the great parent races
of the western world'. It is to 'protect' its heritage for the world, Churchill argued,
using the example of the 'ancient States and Principalities of the Germany of former
days', to which, in his words, 'western civilization' owed much, that Europe had to
unite politically.[1] Churchill's statement deserves attention not only for its rhetoric,
characterized by a deliberate attempt to claim from Hitler his own account of
Europe's racial superiority. It is a curious document also due to its peculiar
genealogy of European heritage, one that contains a positive reference to the
principalities of 'former' Germany, along with a negative evaluation of the 'Teutonic
nations'. The contrast between the 'Teutonic nations' and the 'states and
principalities of the Germany of former days' is so starkly drawn, in fact, that it
appears as if centuries were separating these two phenomena, or, as if they
constituted two entirely unrelated branches in its genealogical tree.[2] But most
German principalities only lost their political autonomy in 1918, together with
Prussia – in Churchill's eyes at least, one of the most 'Teutonic' of all the German
nations. Moreover, German princes have historically been instrumental in shaping
the identity not just of the 'Teutonic nations', but also those of the British: the
monarch to whom Churchill himself was subject was of German origin, even
though the Saxe-Coburg-Gothas had changed their name to the more patriotic

'Windsor' during the first of the 'nationalistic quarrels', in 1917, to avoid confusion with their 'Teutonic' enemies. Was Churchill's rhetorically powerful, yet obfuscating confusion, just an attempt to negate the effects those very Teutonic 'quarrels' had on the construction of a workable political ideology of European identity?

As I will show, the crisis of the nobility as a sociopolitical configuration in Germany and Europe after 1918 meant that 'nobility', German-ness, and the idea of Europe, became deeply intertwined political identities. The concept of a 'European' politics was shaped by specific perspectives, or, as Reinhart Koselleck calls them, 'horizons of experience' and 'expectation'.[3] Churchill's own idea of Europe, like that of other British conservatives such as Leo Amery or Christopher Dawson, reflected the profound influence of German intellectuals of noble descent who became the chief spokesmen for European unification in the interwar period.[4] Count Richard Nicolaus Coudenhove-Kalergi, the founder of the Paneuropa movement and the most prominent noble Europeanist of the interwar period, had spent the last years of the war in exile, a 'Bohemian citizen of the world turned visiting professor of history at New York University', as *Time* magazine described his activities in wartime New York.[5] Other noble theorists of European identity who were based either in Germany or Austria after the First World War included Count Hermann Keyserling, a vitalist philosopher of culture who attained much wider fame both in German-speaking and in international circles, and Prince Karl Anton Rohan. A young follower of Keyserling, Rohan became the editor of the influential literary and political journal *Europäische Revue*. Prince Hubertus zu Löwenstein, Count Ferdinand Czernin, Baron von Waldburg-Zeil, Baron von Rheinbaben, and Otto von Habsburg, claimant to the Habsburg throne, were among the other prominent theorists of 'high' noble descent. Members of the 'lower' nobility – that is, descendants of ennobled subjects of the former German or Austro-Hungarian empires – who engaged in constructions of European identity in their publications included the poet Hugo von Hofmannsthal and the maecenas, diplomat, and dandy, Count Harry Kessler. The idea of a European crisis of values connected with a social crisis permeated the work of noble Europeanists of Christian conservative, liberal and social democratic dispositions. On the Christian conservative side, Friedrich August von der Heydte advocated the need for recreating a Holy Roman Empire for those reasons.[6] All these thinkers had advocated some idea of Europeanist politics in the interwar period, but in the course of the rise of Nazism and the Second World War, their paths split. In Germany and Austria after 1918, nobles saw themselves compelled actively to reclaim a new form of authority as intellectuals. Authors such as Richard Coudenhove-Kalergi, Hermann Keyserling, and Karl-Anton Rohan, who have been described as 'elitist' by contemporaries and by more recent critics, the chapter argues, can also be understood as (self-reflexive) 'aristocratic radicals'.[7] The aim of this study is to reconstruct their perspective on European identity prior to this parting of ways in the later 1930s.

Different political communities and social groups, from families to residents of cities, to religious or ethnic groups, are affected by political upheavals in divergent ways. As Michael Müller rightly remarks, the idea of Europe has frequently been shaped by the geographically peripheral, or otherwise 'marginal' elites.[8] As theorists of Europe, noble writers gave their own biographies a new political significance. Each of their theoretical conceptions of Europe had the image of the new European as its central conceptual feature. Europe for them was not a way of 'conceptualising a continent', as Anthony Pagden has put it, but rather a way of 'conceptualising' themselves in a new socio-political landscape.[9] The diffuse meaning of what is 'European' today thus carries the baggage of these diverse experiences. To understand these different meanings, we need to disentangle how their specific perspectives shaped the way theorists envisioned future politics.

These writers and political thinkers have been remembered individually for different things and in different contexts, which turned some of them into historically exceptional, almost unlikely, cosmopolitans, expiated others of any complicity with ideologies such as fascism, and obscured the very obvious commonality between them: the experience of a crisis of social status in a period of 'democratization', which coincided with constructions of European identity. This shared experience is not only an ideal-typical and retrospective inference of commonality, but was rooted in their networks of sociability, which also substantially overlapped with their networks of publishing houses and journals in which they voiced their theories.

Not all these men – and the theorists of European identity in the interwar period were almost exclusively male – were still being remembered by scholars of European identity in the period after the Second World War. Some of them, like Count Harry Kessler, who died in exile from Nazi Germany in 1937, or Count Hermann Keyserling, who died in 1946, only had a very limited impact on European politics after the Second World War. Others, like the poet and playwright Hugo von Hofmannsthal, are primarily known for other intellectual contributions. Some, such as the Prussian Baron Rheinbaben, became advocates of Nazi visions of Europe and were thus omitted from the history books on European identity. In the remaining group of émigrés from Nazi Europe during the 1940s, Coudenhove-Kalergi, Otto von Habsburg and Prince Löwenstein are probably the best known, yet here again it was only Coudenhove who was, for a time, celebrated as a direct ancestor, or even founding father, of the European Union. Habsburg's restorationist rhetoric made him an unlikely candidate for this role. As the *New York Times* had put it in 1940: 'Few among all these hundreds of thousands of young men who have in these past 500 years crossed the Atlantic seeking to amend their shattered fortunes have seemed engaged on such a forlorn hope as Otto von Habsburg.'[10] Upon his return to Europe after the war, Habsburg's alliance with Franco's Spain through the 'Centre Européen d'Information et Documentation', a stronghold of European conservatism, made him an unsuitable candidate for the political construction of democratic Europe, whose educational institutions also shaped the historiographical analysis of Europe's political and intellectual identity.[11] The most lasting influence of noble perspectives on Europeanist ideology after the Second World War was that of the predominantly Christian *and* non-Fascist constructions of Europe, expounded by thinkers such as Fürst Löwenstein, and the oecumenical-technocratic conception of Paneuropa-man Coudenhove-Kalergi, whose earlier flirtations with Mussolini's fascism, however, had been conveniently forgotten by the 1990s.

Starting from the transformation of these former units of political organization in the German Empire, to the abolition of all forms of nobility in both Germany and Austria, the significance of the abolition of the old nobility in Germany and Austria on the political imagination of this period has been underestimated. The year 1918 was a turning point that started a new controversy in German political and intellectual circles concerning the status of the historical nobility.[12] In this discourse, German-speaking nobles as theorists of Europe understood the period not only as a Spenglerian 'decline of the West', but particularly as a decline of the status and values of the old nobility which they saw as the agent of Europe's cultural production in former days. With the idea of Europe, they reinvented the feudal cosmopolitanism of the historical nobility by endorsing a new and positive concept of Europe. The more existential experience of the crisis of the nobility for nobles gave them specific discursive weapons that allowed them to turn part of the debate concerning the nobility into a debate about the future of Europe.

The views of European history and politics displayed by nobles in interwar public discourses had three points in common. First, the idea that states and their governments were secondary in international politics to private networks; second, the idea that the nation could only be accepted as a temporary political paradigm, and that a form of supranational identity was needed in Europe; finally, the acknowledgement that the social foundations of European cultural excellence, which rested on the contribution of aristocratic societies, needed to be reinterpreted, because the old elites failed to respond to the pressing problems of their times. In their accounts, 1918 appeared as a historic caesura. Nobles utilized the emerging structures of liberal internationalism, represented in the League of Nations, but did so with the aim of a post-national European community; they insisted on government by social likeness rather than party politics. They attributed to a new nobility the role not just of a privileged elite, but of one whose very task is to link family history with public history, to be the guardians of European heritage. Nobles became 'idea-mongers' linking very different traditions of imagining Europe together. To explain their political views, we need to understand better the social change that occurred in Germany and Austria and affected circles of intellectuals in particular ways.

Nobles and the Crisis of 1918

'German Princes and Nobility Rush Funds to Neutral Lands', the Geneva correspondent for the *New York Times* cited a Swiss banker in October 1918. 'A large proportion of the depositors' bringing their money from Germany and

Austria,' the journalist remarked, 'belong to the princely families, posing under assumed names.'[13] Between 1917 and 1920, not just Germany and Austria, but most of Eastern and Central Europe witnessed an extraordinary number of sociopolitical changes involving political demands to abolish the nobility. These not only enforced the abdication of the Habsburg, Romanov, and Hohenzollern emperors in the wake of the First World War, but also brought about the abolition of noble titles and the expropriation of other noble families. The process did not leave many 'neutral lands' for nobles.

The geopolitical and social transformations in Europe after the First World War had a particular impact on nobles associated with German culture; that is, members of families who had historically been loyal to the Hohenzollern or the Habsburg family. 'German' nobles in this sense occupied elite positions in the German, Austro-Hungarian, and Russian empires. In 1919, the new republican parliaments of Germany and Austria decreed the abolition of the nobility.[14] The new government of Austria passed a law concerning the 'abolition [*Aufhebung*] of the nobility, its external privileges and titles awarded as a sign of distinction associated with civil service, profession, or a scientific or artistic capacity'. After 1919, nobles were to become 'German Austrian citizens', equal before the law in all respects.[15] The German Constitutional Assembly ratified the abolition of the nobility as §181 and §109 of the Weimar Constitution, giving this event primary political importance.[16] Those nobles who had organized themselves in noble corporations such as the Deutsche Adelsgenossenschaft (DAG) in the late German Empire, were now explicitly discouraged from party political participation. Following a first law of June 1920 'concerning the abolition of the privileges of the nobility and the dissolution of their estates' passed by the German government, in 1929 German President Gustav Stresemann demanded that membership in the DAG was unacceptable for members of the Reichstag, the cabinet as well as the army, spurring a flood of protests in noble circles.[17] Many members of the DAG, already a conservative organization with clear anti-Semitic influences prior to 1933, moved further to the right and found themselves in the ranks of the Nazi Party a decade later.[18]

Outside Germany, the crisis of the nobility in the period from 1919 until the occupation by Nazi Germany affected nobles of a German cultural background beyond the boundaries of what in 1918 became the German and the Austrian republics. German noble families of old lineage such as the Teutonic knights that had served a number of changing polities from the Swedish and Lithuanian kingdoms to the German and Russian empires, and branches of other European noble families that historically had been loyal to the Austrian Habsburgs, formed the core of the political elite in regions formerly belonging to the Russian, Austro-Hungarian and German empires, which had now formed new nation-states. This was especially pronounced in the Baltic region, where the Keyserlings formed part of the feudal elite, and in Bohemia, where Coudenhove-Kalergi was based. After 1918–20, in the new Baltic nation-states and in Czechoslovakia, such families no longer epitomized a functional political elite. The high proportion of nobles from these regions among the aristocratic writers whose subject was the idea of Europe was deeply entangled with this geopolitical and social transformation.

In the new nation-states of Eastern and Central Europe, other varieties of abolishing the nobility 'in the name of the nation' emerged in the early 1920s. There, nobles were considered to be 'foreign' elements who were also historical enemies of nations in the making. Thus in Czechoslovakia, the new governments required the confiscation of property on the grounds of nobles' foreign background, and only in the second place as a betrayal of other social groups or the nation. Politicians like the representative of the Czech National Democratic Party, Bohumil Němec, argued that 'nationally foreign ... and rapacious noble families' had been causing harm to the Czech nation throughout history.[19] His, ironically, Slavic surname, which means 'German', in fact gives some linguistic evidence to the case that the arguments for a policy of ethnic purity in this region were deeply flawed given the historically mixed populations in these areas. What mattered with regard to nobles was that they were both foreign and formed part of the Habsburg imperial elite. In Czechoslovakia, the imperial nobility backed by the ancient power of the Habsburgs in the region, became but an ethnic German minority, which the new governments viewed on a par with other Germans like the Sudeten Germans.[20] Following this line of argument, large noble estates were partially nationalized. In Estonia and the other new Baltic nation-states, a similar process occurred. In both cases, German nobles obtained the citizenship of the new states, but were effectively barred from any political participation, or from exercising their traditional feudal privileges like holding courts (as in the case of the Baltic knights).

The abolition of the nobility in these postimperial peripheries was therefore entangled with a reconceptualization of notions of nobility and aristocracy, ethnicity and social status, and minority and majority in political debates. Nobles like the elder brother of the Europeanist Karl Anton Rohan, Prince Alain Rohan, not only became 'lords' by profession, as new documents attested, but also now belonged to a German minority in a Czechoslovakian nation-state. In such regions, this was above all a crisis of the German nobility, not because noble families like the Keyserlings or the Coudenhoves were German (they were only partially of German descent), but because they were now 'perceived' as German. In response, while many high noble families from Bohemia sought to restore their authority through identification with forms of German nationalism, allying with the Sudeten Germans and seeking unity between Germany and Austria, there were also many nobles who, especially in the early 1920s, sought direct protection from the League of Nations under its 'ethnic minorities' act. Only when the league showed its incapacity to enact its vision did these groups move closer to the German nationalists.

Consecutive governments in Germany, Austria, and other Central European states after 1918 gave different answers to the question 'What is noble?' at different points in the interwar period. In this light, it seems fairly difficult to give a tight description of the nature of the 'crisis of the nobility' in the period from 1918 to 1920. To use Max Weber's analysis, depending on the region and the family, some nobles still constituted a feudal estate whose power rested as much on their material superiority as on other forms of authority. For example, Alain Rohan, the head of the Rohan family of exiles from revolutionary France who had lived under Habsburg protection in Bohemia since the nineteenth century, retained his estate at Sychrov, Czechoslovakia, after 1919. Here, as diaries and archives of other noblemen like Friedrich Thun attest, nobles maintained their old lifestyle of the high nobility of the Habsburg Empire, continuing at least into the late 1930s. By contrast, in Germany, princes such as Grand Duke Ernst Herzog of Hesse-Darmstadt, lost their power as feudal sovereigns in 1919, or their income from feudal estates. Such was also the case for the Baltic nobility whose estates were expropriated by the new national governments of Estonia and Lithuania. Yet in other cases, nobles, who in economic respects were members of the upper bourgeois class, did not suffer financial losses in 1918, but rather, were hit by the international economic crisis of 1929.

As far as the perception of noble identity and values in Nazi ideology was concerned, nobility played an ambivalent role. The Nazi government partially reinstated some noble privileges after 1935, and indeed managed to create attractive positions in power for nobles such as Gottfried von Bismarck or the von Hessen family, while also maintaining its image as a revolutionary and socialist party.[21] Thus, in keeping with republican legislation, under the Nazis, noble titles continued to be seen as part of the family name. Nobles were mere 'members of families with a noble name', although the regime itself opened up more exclusive opportunities for nobles than the Weimar Republic.[22] Nobles were 'recruited' for active collaboration with the regime in connection with the conquest of Eastern Europe. Following the Hitler–Stalin pact of 1939, Hitler's 'chief ideologue' for Eastern colonization, Alfred Rosenberg, invited nobles from the Baltic region to lead the colonization of parts of Poland and Ukraine and to employ their knowledge of agricultural organization since 'feudal' times for a new economic exploitation of the region, using forced Polish labour. For this purpose, the Nazis even briefly reinstated the Teutonic order, the medieval knighthood which established the legal stronghold of German aristocrats in the Baltic region, which were abolished by the nationalist governments of Estonia and Lithuania.

Ideologically, the Nazi vision of Europe drew much from the symbolic historical imagination of the European nobility. The Nazi foreign propaganda journal *Signal*, for instance, edited by former co-editor of the *Europäische Revue*, Max Clauss, in 1944 supplied a 'genealogical tree' of the generic Aryan family with its journal.

The map shows to what extent the ideological exploitation of noble identity by the Nazis parted ways from its original. Like genealogical trees of noble families, this tree contains elements of heraldry along with the image of a tree, yet it remains abstract in its attempt to link the 'geographical', European, identity of the Nazi regime to the non-concrete, 'universal' family on the top of the tree, while differentiating the 'evil' branches of the tree in negative heraldic and geographically detached form. By contrast, traditional genealogies of noble families that emerged in the early modern period but became particularly fashionable in the historicist nineteenth century, emphasized the concretes of one particular family whose story

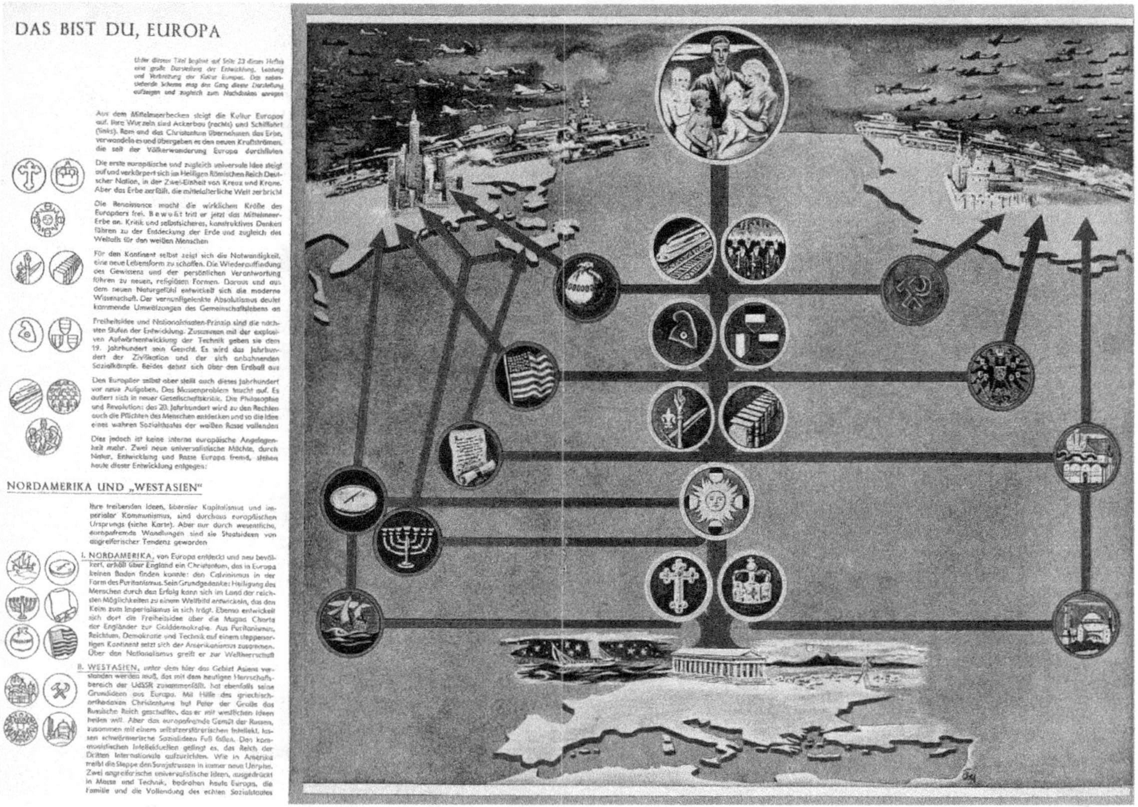

DAS BIST DU, EUROPA

Unter diesem Titel beginnt auf Seite 23 dieses Heftes eine große Darstellung der Entwicklung, Leistung und Verbreitung der Kultur Europas. Das nebenstehende Schema mag den Gang dieser Darstellung aufzeigen und zugleich zum Nachdenken anregen

Aus dem Mittelmeerbecken steigt die Kultur Europas auf. Ihre Wurzeln sind Ackerbau (rechts) und Schiffahrt (links). Rom und das Christentum übernehmen das Erbe, verwandeln es und übergeben es den neuen Kraftströmen, die seit der Völkerwanderung Europa durchfluten

Die erste europäische und zugleich universale Idee steigt auf und verkörpert sich im Heiligen Römischen Reich Deutscher Nation, in der Zwei-Einheit von Kreuz und Krone. Aber das Erbe zerfällt, die mittelalterliche Welt zerbricht

Die Renaissance macht die wirklichen Kräfte des Europäers frei. B e w u ß t tritt er jetzt das Mittelmeer-Erbe an. Kritik und selbstsicheres, konstruktives Denken führen zu der Entdeckung der Erde und zugleich des Weltalls für den weißen Menschen

Für den Kontinent selbst zeigt sich die Notwendigkeit, eine neue Lebensform zu schaffen. Die Wiederauffindung des Gewissens und der persönlichen Verantwortung führen zu neuen, religiösen Formen. Daraus und aus dem neuen Naturgefühl entwickelt sich die moderne Wissenschaft. Der vernunftgelenkte Absolutismus deutet kommende Umwälzungen des Gemeinschaftslebens an

Freiheitsidee und Nationalstaaten-Prinzip sind die nächsten Stufen der Entwicklung. Zusammen mit der explosiven Aufwärtsentwicklung der Technik geben sie dem 19. Jahrhundert sein Gesicht. Es wird das Jahrhundert der Zivilisation und der sich anbahnenden Sozialkämpfe. Beides dehnt sich über den Erdball aus

Den Europäer selbst aber stellt auch dieses Jahrhundert vor neue Aufgaben. Das Massenproblem taucht auf. Es äußert sich in neuer Gesellschaftskritik. Die Philosophie und Revolution: das 20. Jahrhundert wird zu den Rechten auch die Pflichten des Menschen entdecken und so die Idee eines wahren Sozialstaates der weißen Rasse vollenden

Dies jedoch ist keine interne europäische Angelegenheit mehr. Zwei neue universalistische Mächte, durch Natur, Entwicklung und Rasse Europa fremd, stehen heute dieser Entwicklung entgegen:

NORDAMERIKA UND „WESTASIEN"

Ihre treibenden Ideen, liberaler Kapitalismus und imperialer Kommunismus, sind durchaus europäischen Ursprungs (siehe Karte). Aber nur durch wesentliche, europafremde Wandlungen sind sie Staatsideen von angreiferischer Tendenz geworden

I. NORDAMERIKA, von Europa entdeckt und neu bevölkert, erhält über England ein Christentum, das in Europa keinen Boden finden konnte: den Calvinismus in der Form des Puritanismus. Sein Grundgedanke: Heiligung des Menschen durch den Erfolg kann sich im Land der reichsten Möglichkeiten zu einem Weltbild entwickeln, das den Keim zum Imperialismus in sich trägt. Ebenso entwickelt sich dort die Freiheitsidee über die Magna Charta der Engländer zur Golddemokratie. Aus Puritanismus, Reichtum, Demokratie und Technik auf einem steppenartigen Kontinent setzt sich der Amerikanismus zusammen. Über den Nationalismus greift er zur Weltherrschaft

II. WESTASIEN, unter dem hier das Gebiet Asiens verstanden werden muß, das mit dem heutigen Herrschaftsbereich der UdSSR zusammenfällt, hat ebenfalls seine Grundideen aus Europa. Mit Hilfe des griechisch-orthodoxen Christentums hat Peter der Große das Russische Reich geschaffen, das er mit westlichen Ideen heilen will. Aber das europafremde Gemüt der Russen, zusammen mit einem selbstzerstörerischen Intellekt, lassen schwärmerische Sozialideen Fuß fassen. Den kommunistischen Intellektuellen gelingt es, das Reich der Dritten Internationale aufzurichten. Wie in Amerika treibt die Steppe den Sowjetrussen in immer neue Utopien. Zwei angreiferische universalistische Ideen, ausgedrückt in Masse und Technik, bedrohen heute Europa, die Familie und die Vollendung des echten Sozialstaates

Figure 5.1 Europe's cultural and historical development. Source: Hans Dollinger (ed.), *Facsimile Querschnitt durch Signal* (Munich, 1969), 180–1. The original is from *Signal*, Nr. 11, 1944.

was being told, and reserved heraldic images to that family only. To the extent that the coat of arms was a symbol, it was a symbol of a family, rather than an entire ethnic group, as for the Nazis. Conversely, in terms of political practice, the initial promise by Rosenberg to the old Baltic nobles that in colonizing the East, they would also restore the ancient knighthoods, was soon being broken. As early as 1941, these knighthoods were again abolished and replaced by the Nazis' own neo-medieval Gau structures, while German nobles were not returned to their original territories in the Baltic but were forced to colonize Southern Poland instead.[23] Thus, by 1942, while nobles continued occupying some high ranks in the army and administration of Nazi Germany, there was also an increasing propensity to resist Hitler among noble-dominated social networks such as the Kreisau and the Stauffenberg circle. This rising proportion of nobles in resistance circles towards the end of the Nazi empire, by contrast to the early resisters of mostly working-class background, has led to the postwar image of 'the nobility' at large being resistant to Nazism, one that has only recently been qualified.

The events of 1917–20 were not only a socioeconomic crisis of the nobility, but also an intellectual one: the very idea of the removal of the nobility as de-aristocratization and democratization surfaced simultaneously in different successor states to the Habsburg, Hohenzollern and Romanov empires that disintegrated during the First World War. The discourse concerning the future of the nobility continued in these states throughout the interwar period. It is in this respect that the abolition of the nobility contributed to the discourse of Europeanism in a particular way. By analysing the meaning of 'Europe' for nobles, the chapter proposes in some sense a narrower focus than previous studies of interwar Europeanism; but in another sense, it hopes to open up new comparative perspectives on interwar political thought and social history by referring to the abolition of the nobility as a pivotal moment in the history of Europeanist discourses.

Nobles and Interwar Ideas of Europe

Nobles found themselves in opposition to the neo-Jacobin politics of nation building that dominated the politics of the early Weimar and Austrian republics, which entailed a search for a national community defined by ethnic and social homogeneity. Recent scholars have identified the circles that formed the archipelagic landscape of intellectual life in Germany and Austria by looking at groups of authors that published in similar journals or shared similar circles of sociability.[24] When we look at some of the more prominent authors publishing works on the idea of Europe during the interwar years in Germany and Austria, the high number of nobles in this group catches the eye. For members of the nobility, after 1918 the idea of Europe provided above all the chance to contribute to a restructuring of the political landscape in which they could maintain their social status. In order to do so, many resorted to radically utopian ideas and entirely new paradigms of thought. Historical imagination was a constitutive part of noble self-understanding. Today, in fact, its specific memory remains one of the main identifying criteria for noble identity, as anthropological comparisons between noble and 'bourgeois' interviewees have shown. Nobles tend to remember several generations more than other social groups.[25] What is important for nobles as political thinkers in this regard is the fact that nobles often tend to consider themselves in some sense personally connected with the diplomatic and territorial history of several states. By contrast, after 1918, nobles in Central and Eastern Europe had to choose new forms of political identity. This historical imagination placed personal claims on what often was the history of the entire European continent, which nobles traditionally represented with the paradigm of family lineage.[26]

The abolition of the nobility affected nobles' political imagination in ways that contradicted the politics of *tabula rasa* of the new republican governments of Germany and Austria. By far the greatest number of nobles identified with conservative, particularly with Christian, positions. Parties such as the Catholic 'Zentrum' in Germany, or the Austrian People's Party, journals such as *Abendland* and *Hochland*, owned by the Waldburg-Zeil family, provided points of identification for many nobles who looked either to a restoration of noble privilege, or the formation of a neo-medieval corporatist society in which the nobility would obtain its own place.[27] The Catholic church with its 'transnational matrix of power based on formal rationality and hierarchical leadership' was one point of orientation for these nobles disenchanted with modern democratization; the other was the model of the Holy Roman Empire as a heterogeneous state in which the nobility proved to be a guarantor of the legal and economic organization of a large territory with conflicting confessions.[28]

Precisely given the importance of Catholic identity for South West German and for Austrian nobles, monarchism was not the most natural response to the crisis of 1918. Among Protestant nobles, monarchism – in Austria, particularly salient – or its replacement with cult-leader figures in Germany, such as Hindenburg, who obtained much support from nobles in 1925, was a more prominent response. Nobles from the peripheries of the former empires in particular, such as the prominent Ledebur, Schwarzenberg or Thun families in Bohemia, tended to advocate the unity of Germany and Austria following the model of the failed 1848 project, but with a restoration of the nobility, rather than the nation-state principle, in force. However, despite these shifts in noble circles towards conservative, corporatist or Caesarist visions of future politics, some, though not all, of which blended well into the emerging Nazi ideology, there was also a small yet significant number of nobles who became interested in the alternative projects of European unification. Among these, the social democratic, the liberal and the fascist are the most significant.

Many Baltic and Bohemian German nobles who had lost their estates and became journalists published 'geopolitical' commentaries and books reflecting on the past and future of Europe. Some of them became 'nostalgic' political 'agnostics', while others turned the nostalgic reminiscence of a past age itself into a form of political criticism of the present.[29] For instance, the Bohemian Count Ferdinand

Czernin, the son of the Austro-Hungarian ambassador to Britain during the First World War, became a journalist and wrote histories and critiques of the problems of the old Empire, as well as critical commentaries on ongoing political affairs regarding Central Europe.[30] Others decided to pursue an academic career that they had previously undertaken as a freelance pastime. For instance, the philosopher of biology, Jakob von Uexküll, embarked on an academic career after 1918.[31] The Baltic German novelist Otto von Taube published books reflecting on the political and biographical crisis of 1918.[32]

Intellectuals of noble status espoused the role of the politically engaged intellectual with more zeal after the First World War. Before the 'upheavals' around the year 1918, nobles were more directly related to the 'political' dimension of society, be it in virtue of holding some 'feudal powers' or simply in virtue of the public visibility of the noble name in political culture and history. After 1918, aristocratic writers turned into more explicit political theorists because this background had changed. Nobles themselves explained why authors like the Austrian Europeanist Prince Karl Anton Rohan chose to publish their works in Berlin rather than in Vienna, by pointing out that in Vienna 'there is no Prince Rohan any more, only Karl Anton Rohan'.[33]

As Coudenhove-Kalergi put it, in the interwar period, 'the only [true] Europeans were the writers', mentioning authors like Heinrich Mann or Maximilian Harden.[34] Such authors published in multiple journals, their texts appeared in different forms and translations in a diversity of journals discussing geographical and cultural identity. Nobles who redefined their very nobility through being writers but in doing so also communicated their noble heritage to larger publics were prominent among the Europeanists.[35] Each of these circles had overlapping 'members', even though some of the main editors of these journals were openly critical of each other, as in the case of Coudenhove and Rohan.[36]

One of the unifying features of the group of nobles under consideration here was to seek out a future community in which their social status could be recreated.[37] In this socio-literary sphere, nobles of varying degrees of nobility occupied a distinctive niche in theorizing Europe. The fact that such authors continued to be perceived as 'former' nobles created a special position within the circles of German and Austrian elites to which they belonged, comprised of intellectuals of different social backgrounds. After 1918, journals and publishing houses became important meeting grounds for like-minded intellectuals. In these contexts, theorists of formerly noble status had a distinctive voice.

The Case of Hermann Keyserling: European Renewal and the Aristocratic Sage

In his lifetime, Count Hermann Keyserling (1880–1946) enjoyed the status of a 'social celebrity', philosopher and public sage. Keyserling descended from the Teutonic knights (*Ritteradel*) which had settled in the Baltic region in the twelfth century, and from Russian nobility. As the author of a number of works on European identity, he was also an influential theorist of the idea of Europe. His works combined critiques of contemporary Europe with the prophecy of a future supranational European state: first in the orientalist *Travel Diary of a Philosopher* (1918), then in his book *Europe* (*Das Spektrum Europas*) (1928); and finally, in his *South American Meditations* (1932).[38] As an intellectual, his biggest source of fame was his much acclaimed *Travel Diary of a Philosopher*, which introduced travel as an existential experience and a form of cultural criticism to a European readership in the aftermath of the First World War.[39] Keyserling undertook a comparative analysis of the links between high society and cultural excellence with regard to Chinese, Latin American and European cultures, indicating the need for a future aristocracy.

Following his return from his first trip around the world, Keyserling's life had taken a sharp turn. 'Between 1918 and 1920, centuries have passed', Keyserling later summed up the changes of this period.[40] After the peace of Brest Litovsk of 1918, when the Republic of Estonia (Eesti) was founded, part of Keyserling's province of Livonia was incorporated into it, and Keyserling changed his citizenship from being a Russian subject to becoming an Estonian citizen.[41] With the Estonian government's Land Reform Act of 10 October 1919, land ownership by the Baltic German families, who had owed up to 58 per cent of Estonian land, was abolished.[42] This radical change in his personal circumstances opened up a new career for Keyserling: he became a public intellectual and turned this into a profession of its own, making some of his living from royalties, while marrying into the Bismarck family. In this capacity, Keyserling founded the School of Wisdom, an academy whose goal was to train future leaders who were culturally rooted, yet also had an identity as Europeans open for dialogue with other, non-European, cultures. What was crucial about aristocracy in general, he thought, was not blood, but the public belief in the fact that it was a superior caste. Whilst criticizing European culture for its petty nationalism and lack of men of large stature, he sought to infuse those he educated at the school with the knowledge of other cultures in which a hierarchical order existed. His work constitutes the most poignant synthesis of noble perspectives on Europe's future, seen both from within and from without European history itself.

As another noble Europeanist based in Germany, Count Harry Kessler, recalled in 1918, Keyserling's political programme demanded 'a rapprochement from above between the nations as a parallel activity to the International of the proletariat'. As Keyserling told Kessler, 'in questions of foreign policy we cannot be left-wing enough' and have to become the 'model socialist state: then with our population of 70 million we would necessarily acquire a leading position in Europe'. In terms of the question of nationalities, Keyserling argued, we should follow 'the Otto Bauerian principle', an idea Keyserling communicated to the Foreign Ministry, implying that politicians should reconcile themselves to the fact that the national idea was at present a progressive unifying force, but that it should be abandoned as soon as the times were ripe for more progressive forms of political identity.[43]

Keyserling wrote along similar lines in publications on Germany's future in 1919.[44] He strongly believed that great culture and politics were only attainable for a society with a strong aristocratic principle. Conservatives dubbed him the 'red Count', while liberals and socialists called him a conservative aristocrat.[45]

Some of his own students had reservations about his project of European renewal for precisely this reason. One of them, Rom Landau, later recalled that 'the old but powerless aristocracy', whose representatives were among his students, 'disapproved of Keyserling's advanced ideas, and called him a 'Socialist'.

> What kept them attracted to the *School* was that Keyserling seemed to be creating a new aristocracy: a new caste in which their own ancient traditions would be invigorated by his spiritual reform. For the old nobility there must have been something very satisfactory in the promise of a new aristocratic order, essentially German, which was likely to carry its influence far beyond the frontiers of a diminished fatherland.[46]

The importance of the aristocratic sages in the creation of a supranational Europe made up the second important characteristic of his political thought. At Keyserling's Darmstadt School conferences, the notion of the leader was discussed in many facets, including an understanding of the leader as a hero,[47] an aristocrat and a cleric of the Islamic kind, following very much the Carlylean history of hero worship.[48]

Keyserling's belief in the decline of the European order was founded on his social and political critique of various aspects of contemporary European politics. His cultural critique of Europe viewed in juxtaposition with oriental and South American culture informed his vision of Europe's future in similar ways. Ever since his *Travel Diary of a Philosopher*, Keyserling wrote about European identity 'from without', epitomizing an eccentrist view of the Occident which was often compared with Spengler's cultural criticism. 'Spengler and Keyserling have turned toward the Orient for destruction and salvation of the Occident', one reviewer remarked in 1928.[49] In China and India, Keyserling was received by intellectuals who, like him, theorized on 'continental identities' and cultural morphologies.[50]

Among the most important influences on his work was the Academy at Santiniketan (today known as Visva-Bharati University), founded in 1921 by the Bengali writer and poet Rabindranath Tagore on the location of his father's *ashram*. Keyserling first met Tagore, twelve years his senior, during the Indian part of his world tour, in 1912, when he stayed at Tagore's house in Calcutta, then again in London in 1913, and soon after the foundation of the Darmstadt School, in 1921, he invited Tagore on a lecture tour of Germany. Both men had taken up similar roles, even though Tagore's fame surpassed that of Keyserling by far after the former won a Nobel Prize in 1913. Both were of noble origin but also critical of the ossification of nobility; both were in some sense nationalists but at the same time considered their mission to be reaching humanity at large, and therefore travelled the world to give public lectures and, not least, receive financial backing for their educational institutions; both also took some inspiration from another Count, Leo Tolstoy, whose revolutionary peasant communities in Russia also inspired movements in South Africa. Moreover, like Keyserling, Tagore had been impressed by Victoria Ocampo's cosmopolitan cultural patronage in Argentina, where he too stayed as an honorary guest.[51]

Inspired by Tagore, Keyserling positioned himself as bridging East and West. His intention was to turn the position of Europe between the two into an advantage, and criticize the old aristocratic system without rejecting it entirely.[52] Even though he shared some premises with other elitist educational programmes of the period, Keyserling's orientalist school differed markedly from the neo-classical background of other contemporaries. For instance, the classicist Werner Jaeger decried in 1925 that while 'in Beijing Rabindranath Tagore proclaims the reawakening of Asia's soul to the gathered crowd of yellow-skinned students, we, tired from the World War and the crisis of culture, are staring at the fashionable theory of the decline of the West'.[53] Keyserling's school proposed an entirely different use of the comparative shift in cultural criticism by bringing Tagore to a gathering of the Darmstadt crowds and selected participants of his school at the princely palace.

The political goals of Keyserling's school were threefold: to assess the present situation of European politics as a decline into anarchy and mass culture, a period of radical and socialist ideas which had to be accepted; to emphasize the importance of aristocratic and intellectual leadership in overcoming this process of decline; and to learn from other cultures in preparing for a future transformation at the hands of aristocratic sages. In this sense, the school constituted a sharp break from its humanist foundations, which rested on the superiority of Western civilization's Greek roots. It was not just a break from humanism, but above all a radically different project from that of bourgeois intellectuals. After the over-democratized state it was in now, Keyserling concluded, the future belonged to a 'supranational European idea', which would overcome the extreme democracy of America, and Russian Bolshevism.[54] His Baltic experience showed him that the princely attitude of being rooted to a region and simultaneously standing 'above nations', pointed to the future of European regeneration.[55]

Rom Landau, recalling Tagore's visit in 1921, hosted by the former Grand Duke of Hesse Ernst Ludwig, gave a sense of the appeal of the poet:

> After tea we went into the neighbouring fields, and grouped ourselves on the slope of a hill, on the top of which stood Keyserling and Tagore ... The Indian poet was wearing long silk robes, and the wind played with his white hair and his long beard. He began to recite some of his poems in English. Though the majority of the listeners hardly understood more than a few words – it was only a few years after the war, and the knowledge of English was still very limited – the flush on their cheeks showed that the presence of the poet from the East represented to them the climax of the whole week. There was music in Tagore's voice, and it was a pleasure to listen to the Eastern melody in the words. The hill and the fields, the poet, the Grand Duke and the many royal and imperial princes, Keyserling and all the philosophers and philistines were bathed in the glow of the evening sun.[56]

Keyserling's own intentions of learning from Tagore for the purpose of a European renewal had hit a nerve among his postwar audiences.[57] Keyserling was particularly interested in proving that different cultures have always been associated with aristocracies. In his book reviews of 'oriental' cultural critics, therefore, he reserved critical positions, such as the views of Tagore himself, to footnotes, in which he commented on Tagore's remark that Indian culture had been shaped by the Kshattryas, not the Brahmins, merely as 'interesting'.[58] With regard to the more radical movement of Mahatma Gandhi, he expressly described him as a 'reactionary', because in 'sympathising with the false progressivism of modernisation he denied Indian culture'.[59]

Another interest of Keyserling's in comparing his contemporary 'postwar' Europe with other cultures, was his desire to relativize the impression cultivated by many Germans that Germany had been mistreated the most by the postwar political settlements. Other countries, Keyserling argued, had suffered an even more catastrophic decline, drawing attention to Turkey. Nonetheless, as he put it, it was due to this imperial decline that countries like Turkey or Germany would be able to recreate a new European order, as the Turkish intellectual Halidé Edib wrote in a book which she sent to Keyserling with a dedication.[60]

Keyserling espoused a form of neo-aristocratic internationalism that was attractive to a number of nobles in his position. He argued that a new aristocracy would be necessary in order to give shape and cohesion to a new political structure of the future, which would no doubt be 'supranational'. Only a reformed aristocracy could offer such a structure.[61] In this new state of the future, the 'idea of quality' would be absolutely central, for even now, alongside processes of internationalization, 'an aristocratic order' was in the making. Yet the path of socialist transformation, which, according to Keyserling, was necessary before this stage was reached, was rejected by many of his readers. Keyserling, like Coudenhove, not only had a distinctly non-racialist view of the ideal nobleman, but also accepted certain features of modern civilization, such as fascism and socialism, with a degree of fatalism, as transitory stages towards a different order. Keyserling believed that the European 'knight' of the future would return as a 'sage'. Nietzsche was a central source of inspiration for this idea.[62] There was thus in his eyes no contradiction between espousing socialist radicalism, succumbing in a fatalist sense to the Nazi revolt, and being a neo-aristocratic theorist of Europe.

As Prince Karl Anton Rohan wrote in his book *Europe*, first published in 1923, the old 'nobility' now had 'to transform the old values in a conservative way, according to its tradition, using the new impulses of the revolution'. Unlike the class struggle that motivates the Bolshevik conception of the revolution, he thought, the goal of this one was the creation of a 'unified Europe' instead of an 'ideological brotherhood of mankind'.[63] Count Keyserling, in his correspondence with Rohan, engaged in theorizing the new status of the nobility further. He described to him that he was also, 'under conditions of utmost secrecy', working on a 'vision for all the peoples of Europe'.[64] Keyserling had already sent Rohan a letter 'concerning the nobility' for Rohan's private circle of 'friends' studying the 'problem of nobility' under his 'guidance', and he was supposed to contribute a chapter on 'Germany's Task in the World' to a forthcoming publication on *Germany and France* to be edited by the Prince.[65] In the proposal for an edited book on *Germany and France*, Rohan lined up not only well-known historians and legal theorists like the German nationalist historian Hermann Oncken and the constitutional theorist Carl Schmitt, but also now forgotten German and French authors who fall into the suggested category of 'aristocratic writers'. They included names such as Wladimir d'Ormesson, Alfred Fabre-Luce, Henry de Montherlant and Knight Heinrich von Srbik. Keyserling, in turn, also used Rohan's network of relatives and acquaintances among the German-speaking Habsburg nobles in Bohemia to promote his own work. In this connection, he approached Rohan's elder brother Prince Alain, as well as members of the oldest Austro-Bohemian noble families like Count Erwein Nostitz, Count Karl Waldstein, Count Feri Kinsky, Countess Ida Schwarzenberg, Count Coudenhove, Senator Count Eugen Ledebur and other, exclusively noble, families that he wanted to win over as 'donors' for his own project of a 'School of Wisdom' for the creation of future European leaders.[66]

Keyserling's work shows particularly poignantly the extent to which those belonging to the historical nobility combined the consciousness of belonging to an 'aristocracy' with the emphasis of generational, patrilineal descent from a family that claimed as its property a particular territory, and to which other social groups owed a specific form of 'fidelity'.[67] Instead of reconciling themselves with the new state forms, or seeking to resist them entirely, some nobles envisioned a new European order to replace the old regime, and treated the politics of the present as a political intermezzo – what Nietzsche called *'entr'acte* politics' (*Zwischenaktspolitik*).[68] While, broadly speaking, this was a shared perception of the present as a caesura before a new future European politics among intellectuals of different social backgrounds, for nobles, the crisis of noble status as a symbol of the decline of 'old Europe' gave the crisis conundrum of 'World War I' a particular connotation.[69]

Noble Perspectives on Europe: Crisis, the Need for Aristocracy, and the Critique of Bourgeois Values

The reinterpretation of a strong politics of the future in conjunction with a revision of what constituted the nobility was an expression of noble authors' belonging to a generation of Nietzscheans. The theoretical impulses all three thinkers – Keyserling, Rohan and Coudenhove – derived from Nietzsche as a critical 'historian' of the nobility, as a philologist of the meaning of 'what is noble' and, as his Danish contemporary Georg Brandes put it, as an 'aristocratic radical' demanding that culture be agonistic, provided the most important intellectual foundations for twentieth-century German nobles as political theorists. If Nietzsche had only invented his status of a Polish nobleman for himself, there were 'actual', albeit now 'former', nobles who thought of themselves as particularly suitable to lead the process of an intellectual 'revaluation of values'. Nietzsche's project of a genealogy of morality as a preparation for a revaluation of values proved highly attractive to noble intellectuals, who saw the philosopher's work as a foundation for their own reinvention of their status.[70]

Noble Europeanists interpreted Nietzsche's notorious 'good Europeanism' as a politics of the future whose continuity with the past would be provided by a new form of 'aristocratic society'.[71] Importantly, in their reception of Nietzsche, noble Europeanists differed markedly from the later Nazi readings of his thought.[72] For, unlike Nazi attempts at radically equating nobility and racial purity, they believed that future 'good Europeans' would continue to have an 'aristocratic' 'pathos of distance' within the new society. Nietzsche in *Beyond Good and Evil* distinguished between two forms of 'unification' process of Europe. One, which he evaluated negatively, was the 'democratic movement' that caused the process of 'assimilation of the Europeans'. The outcome was a 'supranational', 'nomadic' kind of human being, whose main skill was 'adaptation'.[73] One could describe the interpretations of Nietzsche adopted by the three German-speaking aristocratic writers as a demand for a new European order with an aristocratic hegemony.

In their capacity as intellectuals, noble writers offered a particular interpretation of the European crisis as a crisis of noble values, and their pessimism about Europe's future combined scepticism about liberal democracies with a particular concern for the loss of social hierarchy. In keeping with this, the supranationalism that informed their political views was the perspective of an elite that could coexist comfortably with lower social strata holding nationalist or other kinds of political beliefs. Finally, nobles engaged in critiques of bourgeois values from a radically different perspective than Marxists, of course, yet they drew a remarkable amount from Marxist literature.

Historians so far have viewed interwar Europeanism as an 'elitist' or 'neo-aristocratic' discourse associated both with 'noble' and with 'bourgeois' thinkers.[74] Europeanism has also been discussed as one of several interwar conceptualizations of the 'new human type'.[75] Scholars have rightly associated this 'elitist' discourse about politics with the 'noble-bourgeois' segment of German and Austrian society. But in order to understand the specific character of interwar Europeanism more fully, the biographical experience of its authors needs to be reconstructed not only in terms of individual authors, but also in terms of their belonging to groups with particular 'horizons' of experience, as is the case with nobles. Authors like Coudenhove, Rohan and Keyserling were not only part of a general transformation of the intellectual sphere after the First World War, but they occupied a particular position in this sphere.[76] Historians of political concepts such as the 'nation' have frequently explained their changing meanings by referring to key historical events in which these terms were negotiated afresh. In the case of the modern concepts of the 'nation' or 'democracy', such a key event is obviously the French Revolution.[77] For nobles, the twentieth-century déjà-vu Jacobinism of most governments in Central and Eastern Europe was a phenomenon of comparative impact on their political imagination: thereafter, Europeanism was a response to this Neo-Jacobinism not only in terms of being a supranational discourse, but also in terms of being the language of an old elite whose status was under threat.

Disclosing their views on Europe's future in political journals and even in works of fiction offered intellectuals of noble origin a stage on which to reinvent themselves not only in the eyes of other nobles, but also among the German and Austrian intellectual elite at large. Their in many ways forward-looking ideas of European identity, the cosmopolitan comparative analysis of other cultures which they undertook in this context, and in some cases, even the willingness expressed by nobles such as Harry Kessler to welcome liberal democratic and socialist forms of European political power, should not obscure the fact that interwar Europeanism was also shrouded in a defensive attempt at preserving the cultural community of a lost imperial world.

Notes

1. W. Churchill. *Europe Unite: Speeches 1947 and 1948* (London, 1950), esp. 'A Speech at Zurich University', 19 Sept. 1946, 197–202, and at the Albert Hall on 14 May 1947, 194–97. On Churchill's connections with Coudenhove-Kalergi, see Leo Amery papers, Churchill Archives Centre, Cambridge.
2. On the construction of the British view of the 'two Germanies' in which Prussia represents the reactionary and militaristic one, see C. Clark, *Iron Kingdom. The Rise and Downfall of Prussia 1600–1947* (London, 2007), 670ff. Conversely, the revised view of Prussia emerges here with a pointer towards the European Union.
3. Here, Reinhart Koselleck introduced a helpful distinction when the 'space of experience' forces to change one's 'horizon of expectations', in R. Koselleck, *Vergangene Zukunft. Zur Semantik geschichtlicher Zeiten*, (Frankfurt/Main, 1988), 349–76. However, the problem with these categories is that they abstract from the fact that societies are structured into different fragmented groups of perception whose 'horizons' on one and the same thing can be radically different.
4. W. Churchill, 'United States of Europe', *Saturday Evening Post*, 16 Feb. 1930; C. Dawson, *The Modem Dilemma: The Problem of European Unity* (London, 1932).
5. NN, 'One Europe', *Time Magazine*, 26 Mar. 1945.
6. M. Gehler, W. Kaiser, H. Wohnout (eds), *Christdemokratie in Europa im 20. Jahrhundert* (Vienna, Cologne and Weimar, 2001). W. Kaiser, *Christian Democracy and the Origins of European Union* (Cambridge, 2007).
7. B. Detwiler, *Nietzsche and the Politics of Aristocratic Radicalism* (Chicago, 1990).
8. See M. Müller, 'In cerca dell'Europa: realtà e rappresentazioni di un continente', *Contemporanea* 1 (1999), 81–87.
9. On this characterization of the political idea of Europe, see A. Pagden, 'Europe: Conceptualizing a Continent', in Pagden (ed.), *The Idea of Europe: From Antiquity to the European Union* (Cambridge, 2002), 33–54.
10. P.J. Philip, 'A Habsburg Seeks His Fortune Here. Followers of Archduke Otto Seek to Re-establish Old System in Europe', *New York Times*, 3 Mar. 1940.
11. H. Brugmans, *Europe: Dream, Adventure, Reality* (Brussels, 1987).
12. H. von Kalm, *Das Preussische Heroldsamt, 1855–1920: Adelsbehörde und Adelsrecht in der Preussischen Verfassungsentwicklung* (Berlin, 1994); L. Cecil, 'The Creation of Nobles in Prussia, 1871–1918', *American Historical Review* 3 (1970), 757–95.

13. NN, 'German Princes and Nobility Rush Funds to Neutral Lands', *The New York Times*, 22 Oct. 1918.

14. For Austria, see H. Stekl, *Adel und Bürgertum in der Habsburgermonarchie, 18. bis 20. Jahrhundert* (Vienna and Munich, 2004), 104–6; for Germany, see E. Conze, *Von deutschem Adel. Die Grafen von Bernstorff im zwanzigsten Jahrhundert* (Stuttgart, 2000), 242–44.

15. As the Austrian constitution stated: 'der Adel, seine äußeren Ehrenvorzüge, sowie bloß zur Auszeichnung verliehene, mit einer amtlichen Stellung, dem Beruf oder einer wissenschaftlichen oder künstlerischen Befähigung nicht im Zusammenhange stehenden Titel und Würden und die damit verbundenen Ehrenvorzüge deutschösterreichischer Staatsbürger' aufgehoben. Der Gebrauch von Adelsbezeichnungen, Titeln und Würden wurde unter Strafe gestellt (Adelsaufhebungsgesetz StGBl. Nr. 211, Vollzugsanweisung am 18. Apr. 1919, StGBl. 237). The Austrian constitution of 1920 noted in Article 7: 'Alle Bundesbürger sind vor dem Gesetz gleich. Vorrechte der Geburt, des Geschlechtes, des Standes, der Klasse und des Bekenntnisses sind ausgeschlossen.' In Czechoslovakia and Poland, similar legislation was passed in 1918 and 1921 respectively. In Russia, the nobility was abolished in November 1917.

16. On the abolition of titles in the Weimar Republic, see B. Raschauer, *Namensrecht. Eine systematische Darstellung des geltenden österreichischen und des geltenden deutschen Rechts* (Vienna and New York, 1978).

17. On the Nazi reevaluation of nobility, see Bundesarchiv, R R 43 II 1554–55. 'Adel (1925–38)', as above. Letter of 18 September 1929, E. Piper, *Alfred Rosenberg. Hitlers Chefideologe* (Munich, 2007).

18. S. Malinowski, *Vom Adel zum Führer: Sozialer Niedergang und politische Radikalisierung im deutschen Adel zwischen Kaiserreich und NS-Staat* (Berlin, 2003).

19. E. Glassheim, *Noble Nationalists. The Transformation of the Bohemian Aristocracy* (London and Cambridge, Mass., 2005), 65.

20. By contrast to later historians, contemporaries were very interested in investigating the impact of the abolition of the nobility on Central and East European politics and society. For a sample of this, see V. Alton Moody, 'Reform Before Post-War European Constituent Assemblies', *Agricultural History* 7 (1933), 81–95; L.E. Textor, *Land Reform in Czechoslovakiania* (London, 1923).

21. BA, 'Adel' 1925–38.

22. BA, R 43 II 1554–55, p. 80. Berlin, 14 July 1933. Justice Minister Gürtner to Hitler, 2.

23. On the ideology of German expansion to the East, see Piper, *Rosenberg*; E. Mühle (ed.), *Germany and the European East in the Twentieth Century* (Oxford, 2003).

24. For a good example of the intellectual history of social circles, see R. Faber and C. Holste (eds), *Kreise – Gruppen – Bünde. Zur Soziologie moderner Intellektuellenassoziation* (Würzburg, 2000). This method has been particularly developed by historians of the political right. See, for instance, M. Grunewald, U. Puschner and H.M. Bock, *Le milieu intellectuel conservateur en Allemagne, sa presse et ses réseaux (1890–1960)* (Bern, 2003).

25. B. Le Wita, *Mémoire familiale et mémoire généalogique dans quelques familles de la bourgeoisie parisienne* (Paris, 1983); see also S. Chuikina, *Dvoryanskaja pamyat': "byvšie" v sovetskom gorode (Leningrad, 1920 – 30-e gody) / Aristocratic Memory: The "Former People" in a Soviet Town* (Sankt-Peterburg: Izdat. Evropejskogo Univ.), 185. It should be added, however, that firstly, in modern society, nobles form part of the bourgeoisie, which Le Wita does not indicate. Secondly, there are also other sub-groups within the 'bourgeoisie' whose historical family memory extends much further. Jews are the most obvious example in this regard.

26. On the paradigm of the genealogical tree, see K. Heck, 'Das Fundament der Machtbehauptung. Die Ahnentafel als genealogische Grundstruktur der Neuzeit', in S. Weigel (ed.), *Genealogie und Genetik* (Berlin, 2002).

27. V. Conze, *Das Europa der Deutschen. Ideen von Europa in Deutschland zwischen Reichstradition und Westorientierung (1920–1970)* (Munich, 2005).

28. J.W. Boyer, 'Catholics, Christians and the Challenges of Democracy: The Heritage of the Nineteenth Century', in W. Kaiser and H. Wohnout (eds), *Christdemokratie in Europa im 20. Jahrhundert Political Catholicism* (Vienna, Cologne and Weimar, 2001), 22.

29. L. Höbelt, 'Nostalgic Agnostics: Austrian Aristocrats and Politics, 1918–1938', in K. Urbach (ed.), *European Aristocracies and the Radical Right 1918–1939* (Oxford, 2008).

30. F. Czernin, 'A Common United Nations Policy-Now!', *Annals of the American Academy of Political and Social Science* 228 (1943), 11–15.

31. J. von Uexküll, *Umwelt und Innenwelt der Tiere* (Berlin, 1921); J. von Uexküll and D. L. Mackinnon, *Theoretical Biology* (New York, 1926).

32. O. von Taube, *Baltischer Adel. Drei Novellen* (Oldenburg, 1932), 3. See also O. von Taube, 'Der baltische Adel', *Süddeutsche Monatshefte* (thematic issue 'Deutscher Adel'), xxiii: v (Munich, 1926), 396–402.

33. K.A. Rohan, *Umbruch der Zeit, 1923–1930* (Berlin, 1930), introduction by Freiherr Rochus von Rheinbaben, 9.

34. R.N. Coudenhove-Kalergi, *Ein Leben für Europa. Meine Lebenserinnerungen* (Berlin and Cologne, 1966), 121.

35. Keyserling to Rohan, 18 July 1924. 'Mein lieber Rohan, Obgleich es meinen Grundsätzen u. Gepflogenheiten widerspricht, autorisiere ich Sie, in Rücksicht auf Ihr Verständnis für meine Ziele, meinen Namen schon jetzt auf die Mitarbeiterliste der europäischen Revue zu setzen.' In Hermann Keyserling Archive, Darmstadt, Universitäts- und Landesbibliothek, Handschriften- und Musikabteilung, Hermann-Keyserling-Nachlass (HKN), R-3 172.0. Coudenhove-Kalergi's *Paneuropa* was launched in 1924, Keyserling's two journals, *Der Leuchter and Der Weg zur Vollendung*, earlier, in 1920 and 1919 respectively, and *Die Deutsche Nation*, co-edited by Kessler with members of the November Club, an association of diplomats who had been critics of the politics of the late Wilhelmine Empire in 1919. Keyserling also backed the foundation of Prince Karl Anton Rohan's *Europäische Revue*, which was first published in 1925 (Vienna and Berlin, 1925–1943).

36. On the international spectrum, Coudenhove's *Paneuropa*, Kessler's *Die Deutsche Nation* (co-edited jointly with five other editors), Keyserling's *Der Leuchter* and Rohan's *Europäische Revue* can be compared with José Ortega y Gasset's *Revista del Occidente*, Victoria Ocampo's *Sur*, Romain Rolland's *Europe Nouvelle* or the British journal *New Republic*. *Paneuropa*, the *Europäische Revue*, and *Der Leuchter* were associated with a network of intellectuals and industrialists who were involved either in Coudenhove's Paneuropa movement, or in Rohan's 'Coopération intellectuelle internationale', an association organizing international conferences which emerged in the shadow of the League of Nations. See also K. Brockhausen, *Europa 1914 und 1924. Bild und Gegenbild* (Vienna, 1924); P. Drieu de la Rochelle, *L'Europe contre les patries* (Paris, 1931); and F. Delaisi, *Les Deux Europes* (Paris, 1929). In his 1929 book *Les Deux Europes*, Delaisi described the division of Europe in two halves, 'Europe A' and 'Europe B'. The former consisted of the wealthy and industrialized countries in Western Europe, the latter of the newly founded states of Eastern Europe with a mainly agricultural economy. See also F. Théry, *Construire l'Europe dans les Années Vingt: L'Action de l'Union Paneuropéenne sur la Scène Franco-Allemande, 1924–1932* (Geneva, 1998).

37. G. Müller, '"Europa" als Konzept adlig-bürgerlicher Elitendiskurse', in H. Reif (ed.), *Adel und Bürgertum in Deutschland II. Entwicklungslinien und Wendepunkte im 20. Jahrhundert* (Berlin, 2001), 235–69.

38. H. Keyserling, *Das Spektrum Europas* (Heidelberg, 1928); idem, *Südamerikanische Meditationen* (Stuttgart and Berlin, 1932); idem, *Das Reisetagebuch eines Philosophen* (Darmstadt, 1930), 2 vols.

39. On Keyserling as an orientalist, see V. Ganeshan, *Das Indienbild deutscher Dichter um 1900: Dauthendey, Bonsels, Mauthner, Gjellerup, Hermann Keyserling und Stefan Zweig: ein Kapitel deutsch-indischer Geistesbeziehungen im frühen 20. Jahrhundert* (Bonn, 1975); S. Marchand, 'German Orientalism and the Decline of the West', *Proceedings of the American Philosophical Society* 145 (2001), 465–73.

40. Keyserling, *Spektrum*, 369–70. On the opinions of Baltic nobles on the first revolution of 1905, see Frhr.v. Sass, 'Die Sozialdemokratie und der baltische Adel', *Deutsches Adelsblatt* xxiv (1906), 113; and H. v. Wedel, 'Die Zerstörung der Schlösser und Gutshöfe des deutschen Adels in den russischen Ostseeprovinzen', in *Deutsches Adelsblatt* xxiv (1906), 160–61.

41. Estonia was only accepted de iure by Russia and the Entente powers between 1920 and 1922, i.e. it was not yet recognized as a fully fledged state at the Paris peace conference of 1919. See J. Hiden and M. Housden, *Neighbours or Enemies? Germans, the Baltic and Beyond* (Amsterdam, 2008); J. Hiden and P. Salmon, *The Baltic Nations and Europe: Estonia, Latvia and Lithuania in the Twentieth Century* (London, 1994); C. Mothander, *Barone, Bauern und Bolschewiken in Estland* (Weißenhorn, 2005).

42. On the history of the Baltic–German relations, see F. Anton and L. Luks (eds), *Deutschland, Russland und das Baltikum. Beiträge zu einer Geschichte wechselvoller Beziehungen. Festschrift zum 85. Geburtstag von Peter Krupnikow* (Vienna, Weimar and Cologne, 2005); A. Bues, *Zones of Fracture in Modern Europe: The Baltic Countries, the Balkans, and Northern Italy* (Wiesbaden, 2005); W. Kaschuba and T. Darieva (eds), *Representations on the Margins of Europe: Politics and Identities in the Baltic and South Caucasian States* (Frankfurt/Main, 2007); H.–E. Volkmann, *Die deutsche Baltikumspolitik zwischen Brest-Litovsk und Compiègne: ein Beitrag zur 'Kriegszieldiskussion'* (Cologne, 1970); H.N. von Pistolekors, *Livlands Kampf um Deutschtum und Kultur: Eine Übersicht aller bedeutungsvollen Ereignisse aus der Geschichte des alten Ordensgebietes Livland* (Berlin, 1918).

43. R. Kamzelak and U. Ott (eds), *Harry Graf Kessler. Das Tagebuch 1880–1937* (Stuttgart, 2004). Hermann Graf Keyserling, *Deutschlands wahre politische Mission* (Darmstadt, 1919).

44. H. Keyserling, *Was uns not tut; was ich will* (Darmstadt, 1919); S. Marchand, 'German Orientalism and the Decline of the West', *Proceedings of the American Philosophical Society* 145 (2001), 465–73.

45. On Keyserling's elitism, see 'Rainbow Folk', in *Time*, 23 Jan. 1928, reports on Keyserling's lecture for members of the Lion's Club, the New York Rotarians. On Keyserling as an irrationalist, see G. Lukács, *Die Zerstörung der Vernunft* (Berlin, 1984), 367. See also R. Kuehnemund, 'German Prophets of Doom and Hope', *Journal of the History of Ideas* 3 (1942), 443–57. For the perception of Keyserling as a 'Red Count', see R. Landau, *God is My Adventure: A Book on Modern Mystics, Masters and Teachers* (London, 1935).

46. Landau, *God*, 33.

47. W. Deubel, 3 July 1921, 'Tagung der Gesellschaft für freie Philosophie', *Frankfurter Nachrichten und Intelligenz Blatt*, 11 Oct. 1922, HKN.

48. R. Landau, *God*, 25.

49. See NN, Review of Paul Morand, *The Living Buddha* (New York, 1928), 'East is East', in *Time*, 14 May 1928.

50. Review of Keyserling in 'Wedlock', in *Time*, 29 Nov. 1926. For Keyserling's book reviews of other authors, see A. Keyserling (ed.), *Das Erbe der Schule der Weisheit. Unveröffentlichte Essays und Buchbesprechungen 1920–1946. Aus dem Mitteilungsblatt der Schule der Weisheit "Der Weg zur Vollendung"* (Vienna, 1981). See also H. Keyserling, 'Spengler und Wir' (1923).

51. However, Tagore was far more critical of the Indian caste system than Keyserling was of the European aristocracy.

52. Neither Spengler nor the leader of the anthroposophic movement, Rudolf Steiner, nor Stefan George, Landau argued, had 'gained such a spectacular success as Count Hermann Keyserling'. 'Keyserling's fame spread over the spiritual horizon of Germany overnight, and this fame was due to his origins and to his looks at least as much as to his uncommon philosophical attitude. People compared his narrow eyes and high cheekbones with those of Ghenghis Khan, and they talked of him as though he were an Eastern autocrat' (Landau, *God*, 25).

53. W. Jaeger, *Humanistische Reden* (Berlin, 1960), 104.

54. Keyserling, *Spektrum*, 194.

55. On marriage between the Balts and non-German princes, see also O. von Taube, 'Russische und litauische Fürsten an der Düna zur Zeit der deutschen Eroberung Livlands' (12. und 13. Jahrhundert), *Jahrbücher für Kultur und Geschichte der Slawen* (1935), 3–4.

56. Landau, *God*, 36–37.

57. H. Keyserling, *Politik, Wirtschaft, Weisheit* (Darmstadt, 1922). Review of Hu-ming Ku, *Vox clamantis* (Leipzig, 1921), 24, in *Der Weg zur Vollendung* (1921), 2.

58. Review of Tagore's 'Vision of Indian History', in *The Visva-Bharati Quarterly* (Calcutta, 210 Cornwallis Street), review in *Der Weg zur Vollendung* (1923), 6.

59. Keyserling, Book Review section of *Der Weg zur Vollendung* (1921), 2.

60. Keyserling's review of Halidé Edib, *Turkey faces West* (New Haven and London, 1930), in *Der Weg zur Vollendung* (1931), 19.

61. Keyserling, 'Eine Vision der kommenden Weltordnung', 5 Jan. 1925, p. 5, HKN, *Deutsche Allgemeine Zeitung* (1 Jan. 1925).

62. H. Keyserling, 'Der Sozialismus als allgemeine Lebensbasis', *Neue Europäische Zeitung für Staat, Kultur, Wirtschaft*, 26 Nov. 1918.

63. Cited from Müller, '"Europa" als Konzept adlig-bürgerlicher Elitendiskurse', 251.

64. Keyserling to Karl Anton Rohan, 14 July 1927, in Darmstadt, Universitäts- und Landesbibliothek, Handschriften- und Musikabteilung, Hermann-Keyserling-Nachlass (HKN), Correspondence, R-3 172.01.

65. As it transpires from the letter sent by Rohan to Keyserling on 9 Dec. 1926, in HKN, Correspondence, R-3 172.01. Rohan wrote: 'Ihren beiligenden Brief in Sachen des Adels darf ich Sie bitten, so gütig sein zu wollen und mir umgehend korrigiert hierher zurückzuschicken, da ich ihn einem Rundschreiben von mir an meine Freunde beilegen möchte, die seit etwa 1 1/2 Jahren unter meiner Führung das Adelsproblem studieren.' Rohan to Keyserling, 16 Aug. 1927, in HKN, Correspondence, R-3 172.01. When, in the end, Rohan failed to carry through this edition, he apologized to Keyserling for not writing sooner. He was in fact out of reach due to 'a small tour of the Bohemian castles, visiting acquaintances and relatives'. Rohan to Keyserling, 1 Mar. 1923.

66. See Keyserling to Rohan, 1 Mar. 1923, in HKN, Correspondence, R-3 172.01. See Appendix 4b.

67. Nobles' commonality of 'consciousness' insofar as it can be reconstructed from personal and published sources was not the idea of belonging to the same 'class', but rather the nature of their status whose privileges not only consisted in various forms of 'capital', to speak with Pierre Bourdieu, but also in a particular historical imagination. On a reading of 'visibility' as a form of 'symbolic capital' in Bourdieu's sense, see M. de Saint Martin, *Anciennes et nouvelles aristocraties, de 1880 à nos jours* (Paris, 2007), esp. Postface by P. Bourdieu, 'La noblesse: capital social et capital symbolique', 385–99.

68. F. Nietzsche, *Beyond Good and Evil. Prelude to a Philosophy of the Future*, Rolf-Peter Horstmann and Judith Norman (eds), (Cambridge, 2002), section 256, p. 148.

69. H. von Kalm, *Das Preussische Heroldsamt, 1855–1920: Adelsbehörde und Adelsrecht in der Preussischen Verfassungsentwicklung* (Berlin, 1994); L. Cecil, 'The Creation of Nobles in Prussia, 1871–1918', *American Historical Review* 3 (1970), 757–95.

70. Nietzsche, *Beyond Good and Evil*, section 9, 'What is noble?', 151–53.

71. Ibid., 151.

72. See Alfred Baeumler's introduction, in Friedrich Nietzsche, *Jenseits von Gut und Böse. Zur Genealogie der Moral* (Stuttgart, 1940).

73. Nietzsche, *Beyond Good and Evil*, section 242, pp. 133–35.

74. For these paradigms, see, respectively, W. Struve, *Elites Against Democracy. Leadership Ideals in Bourgeois Political Thought in Germany, 1890–1933* (Princeton, 1973); G. Müller, '"Europa" als Konzept adlig-bürgerlicher Elitendiskurse'; and, most recently, A. Gerstner, *Neuer Adel: Aristokratische Elitekonzeptionen zwischen Jahrhundertwende und Nationalsozialismus* (Darmstadt, 2008).

75. See A. Gerstner, B. Könczöl and J. Nentwig (eds), *Der neue Mensch. Utopien, Leitbilder und Reformkonzepte zwischen den Weltkriegen* (Frankfurt/Main, 2006); G. Müller, '"Europa" als Konzept adlig-bürgerlicher Elitendiskurse'; A. Gerstner, *Neuer Adel*.

76. On this view, see H. von Nostitz, *Aus dem alten Europa* (Leipzig, 1924). F. Czernin von und zu Chudenitz, *Europe, Going Going Gone: A Sketch Book Trying to Give a Rough Explanation of Europe*,

Its Politics, and Its State of Mind, for the Benefit Mainly of Anglo-Saxons, Politicians, and Other Folk with Uncomplicated Minds (London, 1939), published with drawings by Bohemian nobleman Count Eugen Ledebur.

77.   On the status of this historical narrative in political ideologies, see F. Fehér, *The Frozen Revolution: An Essay on Jacobinism* (Cambridge and Paris, 1987).

Chapter 6

IMPERIUM EUROPAEUM

Rudolf Pannwitz and the German Idea of Europe

>⌒⌒⌒<

Jan Vermeiren

The writer Rudolf Pannwitz (1881–1969) was once hailed as 'one of the greatest German thinkers; a poet, a philosopher, a universal genius who has given the world immortal ideas'.[1] An early recipient of the prestigious Schiller Memorial Prize (1957) and thus preceding Max Frisch, Ernst Jünger, and Christa Wolf, he is known today only to a handful of literary academics and historians of philosophy.[2] This subsequent neglect may be due to the scope and complexity of Pannwitz's work which spans an impressive amount of (partly unpublished) poems, epics and dramatic pieces, as well as pedagogical treatises and cultural-historical essays: a mixture of philosophy, poetry and educational utopianism, relating art and political analysis, metaphysics and historiography. What is more, Pannwitz's intricate writing style that emanated from his early association with the elitist Stefan George circle makes his texts a peculiar challenge to the reader and probably explains the limited circulation of his publications. Yet Pannwitz never wrote for the tastes or interests of the wider public. Rather, his intended audience and correspondents comprised high-ranking intellectuals and politicians such as Hugo von Hofmannsthal, Thomas Mann, Tomáš Garrigue Masaryk and Count Richard Coudenhove-Kalergi, who were supposed to help overcome the ostensibly depraved state of European society, morals and culture. A devout follower of Friedrich Nietzsche and a representative of the German 'Conservative Revolution', Pannwitz shared the civilizational critique of many of his contemporaries. However, he stands out due to his Europeanism, promoting the abolition of the German nation-state, a rapprochement with the Central European Slavs, and the establishment of an 'Imperium Europaeum' as a remedy for the decadence and materialism of his time. Pannwitz's aesthetic fundamentalism and Nietzschean attitudes clearly set his vision apart from other prominent conceptions of European unity in early twentieth-century Germany. His Europe was not to be established by the deepening and dissemination of Catholicism (the 'Abendland' idea), through Pan-German hegemony in Central Europe ('Mitteleuropa'), or via a transnational pro-European movement ('Paneuropa'). According to Pannwitz, it was up to the moral and spiritual regeneration of the individual, the thoughts and actions of the youthful and open-minded *Übermensch*, to create a common Europe – and the philosopher obviously considered himself as such.[3] Pannwitz accepted no criticism whatsoever and declared himself a prophet and saviour who lived in 'complete martyrdom' for the benefit of humankind: 'My work gives the world not less but something different from what Christ gave'.[4] With this attitude, he predictably remained a marginal thinker in his time. His ideas were often unrealistic and pretentious, and his eccentric personality, elitist gestures, and hubris ultimately prevented Pannwitz from playing a greater role in European intellectual life. However, as one of the most prolific and difficult German-speaking essayists who engaged with the idea and future of Europe during the forty years' crisis, this Prussian-born poet and writer undoubtedly deserves more attention than he has yet received.

'The Holy Shrine of the German Spirit': The Nietzsche Legacy

Friedrich Nietzsche's impact on German cultural and intellectual thought can hardly be overstated.[5] For Pannwitz, the philosopher epitomized 'the highest idea of the German name, the holy shrine of the German spirit', and 'the creator of our new life'.[6] It is questionable whether Pannwitz can indeed be described as Nietzsche's 'most faithful disciple' but he clearly was at pains to portray himself as the only legitimate interpreter and finisher of the great thinker or, as he put it, 'the present ruler of the immortal dynasty of Nietzsche'.[7] Like his idol, Pannwitz did not worry much about bourgeois morals or expectations. Notorious for his peculiar behaviour and megalomania, he led an unconventional way of life, and was almost always dependent on friends and admirers, from whom he expected absolute worship and financial assistance.[8] This lifestyle often made it difficult to sustain the writer's large family (including a devoted private secretary and several lovers complete with their children) who followed him on his moves through Germany and Austria until he settled down on the Dalmatian island Koločep in 1921 before relocating to the Ticino in 1948. Pannwitz was obviously attracted by sites of multiculturalism and shared Nietzsche's preference for secluded, unspoiled locations and southern climes to his German home country.

More important, of course, is the philosopher's influence on Pannwitz's work. For Nietzsche, art was more 'than an entertaining irrelevance'; it was 'the supreme task and the truly metaphysical activity of this life'.[9] The notion that art had an almost religious function, a didactic and moral purpose; that writers could reform society and reenchant the world, has belonged to the fundamental beliefs of cultural critics since Rousseau and Schiller, and was widespread amongst German-speaking neo-Romantics and 'aesthetic fundamentalists'.[10] Pannwitz held similar views. He was convinced of his vocation to be the educator and redeemer of the German people, herald of a new age and a fresh spirit that would lead humankind from the confusion and degeneration of modern life to a new and superior cultural order.[11] The thinker wanted his individual publications to be read and understood as part of a greater, holistic project whose universal-anthropological aim and purpose he once summarized as 'the overcoming of modernity, a synthesis of great cultures, a classical European culture, and a new classical man'.[12] Like Nietzsche, Pannwitz was striving for the new, all-embracing and life-affirming man who would triumph over the fragmentation of the self: 'the crystalline individual representative of the cosmos'.[13] His deep commitment to European unity has to be seen against this background.

Having studied, inter alia, German literature, philosophy and classical philology in Marburg and Berlin, Pannwitz first worked as a teacher before fully concentrating on writing. His early publications – some poems, a collection of tragedies, and several pieces on pedagogy and church architecture – went largely unnoticed. However, Pannwitz's wartime book *Die Krisis der europäischen Kultur* (The Crisis of European Culture), written after his emigration to Austria in 1915, attracted more attention and interest amongst contemporaries.[14] To be sure, the writer was not an outspoken anti-war protester like Hermann Hesse, Heinrich Mann or Alfred H. Fried. He agreed with Nietzsche's opinion that war was 'indispensable' to gain new energy and rejuvenate society, and that 'culture' could 'in no way do without passions, vices and acts of wickedness'.[15] Indeed, Pannwitz similarly described war as 'the eternal father of all things', 'a great primordial matter': '[a] certain degree of disintegration must be reached; rebirth can only be found on the border of death'.[16] He thus seemed to follow the large majority of German intellectuals and academics, such as Ernst Troeltsch, Gerhart Hauptmann and Georg Simmel, who embraced the global conflict as a purifying event that would lead to the moral and cultural regeneration of the German nation by bringing an end to party strife, class struggle and materialism.[17] But whereas these authors regarded such a societal mindset as a short-term aberration, a result of the Westernization of the German being, Pannwitz insisted that the whole of Europe was undergoing a profound cultural crisis and that all warring states, including Germany, had neglected or forgotten the great traditions and models of ancient times and the Renaissance. Instead, they had taken up the wrong and superficial values of industrial-capitalist society, such as scientific positivism, empty consumerism and extreme nationalism. Pannwitz shared Nietzsche's criticism of the apparently artificial, shallow and pretentious German nation-state, the 'destroyer' of genuine Germanness, and regretted that in place of great ideas and creative will 'one's own being – *Volk* and fatherland – had become the sole driving force and aim' of unified Germany.[18] In contrast to the Austro-German writer Robert Musil, for instance, who celebrated the return to the nation and the overcoming of 'the ideal of the European beyond state and *Volk*', Pannwitz lamented the 'collapse of Europe' and the 'hopeless shedding of the last drop of blood for heroism and hysteria', emphasizing that 'the love of life and of humanity's greatness' should take priority over the 'love of one's fatherland'.[19] He thus refrained from juxtaposing Western *Zivilisation* and German *Kultur*, the ideas of 1789 and those of 1914. Rather than denigrating the members of the Entente he devoted large sections of his book to an intensive discussion of French and Anglo-American culture from Rabelais and Shakespeare to Baudelaire, Carlyle and Whitman, stating for instance that prejudiced accusations of 'French cultural flatness' were just 'absurd [*lächerlich*]'.[20]

Considering Germany's depraved condition, and echoing Nietzsche's famous caution that great victories could lead to 'the defeat, if not the extirpation, of the German spirit for the benefit of the "German Reich"', Pannwitz was certain that the way to cultural and spiritual rebirth lay not in the German wartime community or ultimate military triumph, but elsewhere – a new society would have to be based on a revaluation of all values and the absorption of Asian wisdom: the ideas of Confucius, Laozi and Buddha.[21] As he was to expound more clearly the following year, a new, more united, free-spirited Europe, the 'Imperium Europaeum', was the answer to the questions of the day, the counter-model to the decadence and fragmentation of capitalist, alienated civilization. However, given the war-induced hyper-nationalism in Germany, where the great majority of political and intellectual opinion leaders campaigned for a peace of victory and German political hegemony in Europe, the *Krisis der europäischen Kultur* was largely ignored. In war-weary Austria-Hungary, in contrast, it received strong and positive reactions.

'Europe in Miniature': The Austrian Idea in the First World War

The critic Hermann Bahr and the novelist Stefan Zweig were among a number of Austrian commentators who reviewed the *Krisis der europäischen Kultur* favourably.[22] The dramatist and essayist Hugo von Hofmannsthal also showed himself deeply impressed by Pannwitz, sharing the philosopher's cultural diagnosis and admiration of Asian society and thought. Like fellow Austrian intellectuals, Hofmannsthal held the opinion that the multinational Habsburg Empire had a world-historical vocation, demonstrating how to overcome the negative nationalism which had set the continent alight. To Bahr, it was not a peoples' prison but the first great attempt or scheme 'of an organisation of nations in freedom, an order of diversity in unity'.[23] On this view, Austria-Hungary guaranteed peace and stability in Central Europe, which would fall prey to Balkanization if the realm were ever to stop existing. According to Count Alfons Mensdorff-Pouilly, a prominent member of the Austrian Upper House, the Dual Monarchy was an 'empire of peace' and the 'most modern and ... most democratic state entity in the world'.[24]

A large majority of Germany's political and cultural elite, however, had a different conception of the Habsburg ally. Even though its German-speaking population accounted for merely half of the population, Austria was widely perceived as 'a second Germany', a German outpost and bulwark in South-Eastern Europe. From this perspective, the Danube Empire did not exist in order to secure a fruitful cultural interaction or exchange of ideas but to contain the Western Slavs and employ them as 'auxiliary people'. The liberal politician and publicist Friedrich Naumann did not fully disagree with such notions. Indeed, his highly influential vision of a Central European union between Berlin and Vienna (Mitteleuropa) only partly offered a moderate alternative to the uncompromising imperialism of Germany's national Right. It did not imply the principle of equality or joint decision making. Furthermore, in spite of many references to the Holy Roman Empire and Greater German traditions, the Prusso-German nation-state remained Naumann's starting and focal point. He ultimately shared the widespread belief in Germany's organizational and civilizational superiority: only the adoption of its business spirit, characterized by orderliness, discipline and high productivity, could guarantee prosperity and progress in Mitteleuropa.[25]

It was this emphasis on Prusso-German attainments and the misapprehension of the Habsburg concept of the state which led to Pannwitz's critique in his book *Deutschland und Europa* (Germany and Europe), written in early 1918. Inspired by Austrianists such as Hofmannsthal and Bahr, Pannwitz here favourably compared the apparently traditionalist, peace-loving Danube Monarchy to militaristic and materialistic Germany, a parvenu which was supposedly characterized by 'naked pragmatism' and the lack of a genuine 'German idea' as envisaged and embodied by Goethe, Wilhelm von Humboldt and Hölderlin.[26] In his view, the German Reich could learn from the neighbouring empire, which stood for the possible reconciliation of national interests and exemplified Europe's problems on a smaller scale: 'Austria is not just the core of Europe; it is also Europe in miniature'.[27] As he put it elsewhere: 'Austria is the prototype of Europe, not national or international, but supranational', the 'first embodiment of the European idea'.[28]

More generally, Pannwitz was convinced of the necessary and inevitable evolution from the nation-state to greater entities or empires, which would in fact be a mere return to an older but superior form of political organization. As he declared in *Die Krisis der europäischen Kultur*, 'a Europe without an empire' was 'impossible'; it was the 'precondition for world peace'.[29] The fall of the Roman Empire, the philosopher maintained, had been 'a more terrible tragedy for Europe than anything before or after'.[30] Unfortunately, Napoleon's attempt to unify and consolidate the continent had failed, which led to the fateful age of the nation-state and the more recent decline of Europe. In *Deutschland und Europa*, Pannwitz expanded on his imperial idea. For the future, he envisioned a loose 'Imperium Europaeum' – 'an empire of federations [*Gesamtreich aus föderierten Reichen*]' – which would be based on a flexible German-Austrian association, and cooperation or joint 'world-leadership' with Great Britain.[31] It would resume and combine the different traditions and historical experiences of ancient Rome, its medieval successor, and the Napoleonic period. Pannwitz understood these empires as manifestations of the same idea, an organic synthesis of different nationalities and mentalities, a bridge between the past and the present, not so much rooted in politico-pragmatic considerations as in spiritual and cultural principles. He consequently opposed Naumann and other 'Mitteleuropa' advocates for trying to organize the new Europe 'like a co-op [*Konsumverein*]'.[32] Instead, it could only come about as the result of a gradual process, a comprehensive change of mind: 'The way to Europe does not lead through the establishment of a European confederation or federation, possibly with a centre of power and mechanisation, but via the dissemination and realisation of the European idea.'[33]

A third point of criticism of Naumann concerned the ostensible lack of understanding of the nationality question. According to Pannwitz, Austria's task was not to Germanize or centralize the realm but to 'demonstrate greater comprehension, support and gratefulness' towards the Slavs, whom he deemed to be 'the people of the future' and (in association with the Germans) 'the last European hope'.[34] Influenced by Herder's Slavophilism and probably also by Nietzsche's admiration for Dostoevsky, the philosopher advocated a Slavo-German synthesis, based on an initial rapprochement with the Czechs as the most advanced and leading representatives of the Austro-Slavs – truly an exceptional point of view during the heyday of German-Czech antagonism. In late 1917, he travelled to Prague to meet prominent intellectuals, and subsequently published a series of journal articles on Czech cultural history, reprinted after the war under the title *Der Geist der Tschechen* (The Spirit of the Czechs).[35] Pannwitz was fascinated by Bohemia, which he regarded as the real centre of Europe, a mediator between East and West, and asserted that the Czechs, as a young, dynamic and creative nation, had not yet fallen prey to modernism or aggressive nationalism. Following the breakup of the Dual Monarchy and the establishment of a number of new states in Central and Eastern Europe, he advised the Germans to give up their power-political rivalry with the Czechs and to acknowledge the latter's leading role in this part of the continent. The philosopher intensified relations with Czech intellectuals and got in contact with President Masaryk and Foreign Minister Beneš, who provided him with a small grant to fund his move to Dalmatia and employed him as a contributor to the newly established *Prager Presse*, which was supposed to promote the ethnic German minority's integration into Czechoslovakia. This collaboration, however, was soon brought to an end because of political and financial disagreements: Pannwitz had increasingly criticized Prague's pro-Western foreign policy course, which in his view impeded the consolidation of Central Europe and better relations between Germans and Slavs.[36]

The 'Religion of the Soul': Nations and Nationalism in the New Europe

After 1918, Pannwitz continued to campaign for a new Europe in various essays for leading literary and political journals such as the *Neue Rundschau* and *Der Neue Merkur*.[37] In 1919, he published his *Europäisches Zeitgedicht* (European Poem of the Times), a rare and peculiar discussion of the European problem in poetic form. Europe is described as 'hope, future, creation', and 'the world's salvation [*Du leibst der welt heiltum*]'.[38] In its current state, however, it appears in chaotic decline and in need of spiritual renewal: 'In place of freedom: commotion / in place of state: tribe [*Geblüt*] ... / in place of order: coercion / in place of power: temper.'[39] One year later, Pannwitz brought out a small but notable pamphlet, which was simply entitled *Europa* and has somewhat exaggeratedly been termed a 'forerunner of Graf Coudenhove Calergi's [*sic*] Paneuropa'.[40] Reiterating his demand for national self-reflection and self-mastery, for restoration and moderation, the philosopher asserted that a new understanding of the national idea and the national interest was the precondition for unity and solidarity in Europe:

> The nations must deepen the national idea ... instead of throwing it as dirt into each other's faces. Nationalism must not remain mass politics but be transformed into a religion of the soul. The nations shall regenerate themselves ... so that they cannot be absorbed by one another but only merge into a chorus. However, the nation which requires the nation-state as its patron is not worthy of protection ... Truly, the combination of nationalism and mass politics brings the quickest death to the holy ethnic community [*Volkstums*].[41]

Pannwitz obviously adhered to a Herderian, romantic idea of the nation as an organic entity with spiritual qualities, as an 'un-political' being. He clearly distinguished between 'good' and 'bad' nationalism, a deep feeling and understanding of a nation's history, traditions and 'mission', on the one hand, and aggressive nationalism, nationalism as *Massenpolitik* and as a vulgar expression of the will to power, on the other. To him, nations per se were not a threat to Europe but represented its necessary constituents, its core and binding element. It was only once they became the driving force and major concern of state politics that they would constitute a danger to the European spirit and lead to a 'war of all against all'.[42] The writer consequently backed supranationalism as a political principle, holding that internationalism (in the sense of interstate cooperation) was too 'powerless' and could even lead to 'destruction and dissolution' – one of the reasons why he had criticized U.S. President Wilson's wartime proposals and rejected the Versailles Peace Settlement. Not 'world coalitions and global trade but only a compact empire, a geographical, historical and economic continuum' could guarantee some stability.[43] A superior, federal political authority and some loss of sovereignty would only curtail states' power but not threaten national individualities.

The distinction between politics and spirit, state and culture was a common feature of German political and intellectual thought in the early twentieth century.[44] Politics was often associated with the West, with party quarrels and a lack of principles. Whereas the Western European nations were ostensibly motivated by an ignorant self-interest and a desire for political hegemony, the Germans were characterized by metaphysical depth and a receptive cosmopolitanism, predestined to play a special and leading role in Europe and the world – a widespread notion that went back to the late eighteenth century. As Thomas Mann put it in his famous *Betrachtungen eines Unpolitischen* (Reflections of a Nonpolitical Man) of 1918: 'Yes, we are, we were, we remain the schoolmasters, the philosophers, the theosophists, the religious teachers of Europe and the whole world. This is our genius, our ideal national unity, honour and mission … We are and remain a cosmopolitan, world-historical people in a privileged sense.'[45] Like many other German wartime writers and academics, Mann was convinced that the Germans would think and act beyond the German national interest, that they were more tolerant and fair minded in their treatment of other nationalities than France or Britain, and that only a German victory could bring long-lasting peace and stability to Europe. Pannwitz, too, advanced ideas of German 'culturalism', universalism, and spiritual leadership. In his view, the Germans were preordained to establish a European synthesis: 'A European spirit, a European human type, a European race, a European empire is to be created. Only those in the centre can do that.'[46] However, whereas Mann and other intellectuals ultimately meant to justify German political supremacy in postwar Europe, Pannwitz drew a very different, and much more radical, conclusion: the abolition of the unitary nation-state.

Already during the war, the philosopher had suggested that the Germans give up politics and concentrate on reinventing or rediscovering German national culture, which they had allegedly lost in the early nineteenth century as a result of the striving for a sovereign nation-state and imperialist power politics. As he stated in *Europa*, a nation-state would always 'enslave the spirit of the nation' and 'spoil [*massiert materialisiert*] all values'.[47] Pannwitz was convinced that the German spirit and the German Reich 'could never coexist in harmony [*zu einer wirklichen Schmelzung gelangt*]' and that the German nation-state, which he depicted once again as driven by 'envy, greed, anxiety, listlessness, and delight in destruction', had obliterated and replaced the nation's traditional, cultural supranationalism, its vocation as 'midwife and foster mother of future mankind'.[48] A German Reich would always represent 'massism, something inorganic, an imperialistic Socialism, a Central European America and Russia, a Greater Prussia'.[49]

Pannwitz consequently opposed German–Austrian unification in a Greater Germany (the *Anschluss*), certain that it would only lead to attempts to establish German hegemony in Europe, cripple German creativity, and estrange Germany's neighbours, in particular the Slavs.[50] In his *Europa* book, the thinker clarified his preferred solution to the German and European problem, a scheme that was very unlikely to be accepted by many contemporaries. Germany was to be divided into three parts: West Germany, South Germany including Austria (but without Vienna, which was to be internationalized), and Central Germany. Each part was supposed to serve as a linking element to the bordering nations; in this form, Germany could take up again its medieval mission and real task, which was not to rule over Europe but to mediate between East and West, North and South, thus bringing long-standing peace to the continent. Pannwitz particularly promoted German–French reconciliation, considering both states 'the supreme powers of the Continent, the ancestral forces of the second Europe, the Christian Europe of

Charlemagne': 'They will be the creators of the third and lasting Europe.'[51] Britain, on the other hand, apparently thought of as an associate rather than an integral member of Europe, was to consolidate its empire in order to guarantee the continent's independence and standing in the world. Without significant colonies in Asia Minor or Africa, Pannwitz held, Europe would become 'a pawn in the hands of non-European world imperialisms and possibly their battlefield'.[52] Russia was, at least in the long term, considered indispensable as a bulwark and ally in the inescapable war against Japan – 'the America of the East, but incomparably more dangerous'.[53]

Despite his disappointment in the Czechoslovak government, Pannwitz retained a certain admiration for the Slavs. His attitude, however, seemed more ambivalent, oscillating between a fascination for their 'dark' and mysterious culture and revulsion against untamed nationalism. The philosopher in fact lamented that, following their national-political independence, the Slavs had rushed to modernize and politicize their societies, thus spoiling their irreplaceable energies and ruining their authentic culture. They would now embrace a violent and 'flaming nationalism' and suppress ethnic minorities: 'The Germans, in contrast, are the only godly [*gottgeborne*] people of this age who under the right leaders ... can already today overcome all nationalism.'[54] Again, Pannwitz underlined Germany's special role in Europe. Given their central position between the established West and the emerging East – not just geographically, but also mentally and spiritually – the Germans were essential to the construction of the new Europe. They were pioneers and teachers of a selfless supranationalism as its core principle: 'The task of the German and his spirit is not to dominate the world militarily and politically but, by cross-stitching threads and inventing patterns, to become the master weaver of an unfrayable pan-European world carpet.'[55]

'Paneuropa', 'Mitteleuropa', and the Conservative Revolution of Europe

According to Pannwitz, Germany's spiritual leadership in Europe necessitated self-restraint and a fundamental reorientation, 'the renunciation of all external power and the exclusive focus on inner rebirth'.[56] Instead of thinking in terms of power-political and economic rivalries the Germans would have to depoliticize themselves. Principally, it was up to the youth to carry out this transformation, ultimately facilitating the establishment of the 'Imperium Europaeum'. Indeed, the opening sentence of his *Europa* book reads: 'Thou, O spiritual German youth, youth of vitality and not of age, art designated to create the European man as the heir to the Christian, and the European empire as the successor to the Imperium Romanum.'[57] Defeated and unsettled, they would be able to dispense with all restricting conventions and to concentrate fully on moral and spiritual renewal. Several of Pannwitz's postwar works contain guidelines and suggestions for Germany's new generation, most notably his *Deutsche Lehre* (German Doctrine) of 1919, which was a catechism in the declamatory and instructive style of Nietzsche's *Zarathustra*, and advised readers to reflect on themselves and find their way back to a genuine Germanness, to an organic and unspoilt sense of community.[58] By honouring the German cultural heritage, respecting ancient traditions, and learning from the Orient, Germany's youth could vanquish the decadent spirit of the time and, as Pannwitz had already stated in *Deutschland und Europa*, overcome 'shallow' and divisive ideological slogans such as 'mankind, world peace, freedom, democracy, capitalism, Socialism, parliamentarianism, nationalism, militarism, imperialism', thus returning to totality, to a European whole.[59]

As the 'unforgiving enemy and relentless destroyer of all the lies and deception of modern ideas and ideals and what is nowadays called *Weltanschauung*', Pannwitz rejected the Western tenets of egalitarianism, rationalism, and contractualism, hoping to restore a premodern world order, rooted in traditions and hierarchy.[60] As he put it in the *Zeitgedicht*: 'State without social ranks [*Stände*] is violence and chaos / World without master and servant vulgar and despicable'.[61] The writer imagined a social and economic order based on self-governing smaller communities which exchanged goods and services on a local level (barter economy) and were disinterested in global trade, high finance, or work migration. All citizens were supposed to be actively involved and participate in the corporative polity, a practice which he regarded as genuinely democratic in contrast to the 'monstrous nonsense' of party politics and parliamentary representation, leading to his criticism of the Weimar Constitution as 'worthless and bloodless'.[62] The actual management of state, society and culture, however, was to be a matter of a qualified minority, a select few. As a 'prophet for prophets', Pannwitz in fact spoke to those who were independent, radical, and creative enough to build the new Europe: 'You will be warriors, discoverers, guardians, founders, workers, agencies: you will be architects of the earth, which is more than being a world ruler.'[63] These representatives of a new mankind, of the refined and holistic *Übermensch*, were expected to renounce empty slogans and romantic enthusiasm. Their task was not to compose programmes and resolutions, or to form organizations and parties, but to build organic work groups: 'Authentic individuals must get in touch and talk to each other … But no alliances! Instead, occasional connections … No associations, no events, no meeting places, no common sites, no cultural festivals – no bar-room politics and no *Wartburgfest!*'[64]

With his anti-modernism, social organicism, and scepticism towards parliamentary democracy and Western liberalism, Pannwitz shared the fundamental beliefs of the Conservative Revolution.[65] His postwar work was discussed by Alfred Döblin, Stefan Zweig, Count Hermann Keyserling and Theodor Däubler, but it appears that his wider ideas proved particularly popular in right-wing circles: *Der Stahlhelm*, *Der Vormarsch*, and other like-minded periodicals published favourable reviews by Ludwig Gurlitt, Friedrich Lange and Leopold Ziegler. Interestingly, even though Pannwitz and the Austrian aristocrat Karl Anton Rohan seem to have ignored each other's work, their visions of a new Europe showed many parallels.[66] Both held Nietzsche in the highest regard, considered nations an essential and natural element in the organization of society, and promoted an outspoken elitism and cult of youth. Their ideas also corresponded closely to the Catholic notion of an 'Abendland': there was a common stress on the spiritual and cultural foundations of Europe, on the Christian and supranational heritage of the Holy Roman Empire, and Germany's mission as guardian and defender of the West. Rohan and Pannwitz equally expressed resentment towards the modern nation-state and related international concepts such as the League of Nations, and objected to any abstract, technocratic, or centralizing solution to the European question.[67]

However, the differences between Rohan's right-wing Europeanism and Pannwitz's thought are striking, in particular with reference to the proposed methods of interaction and communication, their stance towards Paneuropa and Mitteleuropa, and their views on National Socialism. In contrast to the Catholic aristocrat, Pannwitz retained a strong religious scepticism, aiming for an all-inclusive *Menschheitsreligion*, a new spiritual belief rather than embracing a particular confession. His Europe clearly had a transcendental quality, but it was not a God-sent gift or otherwise based on faith in God. Both Rohan and Pannwitz adhered to a distinct political and social Romanticism, arguing that the new Europe was a matter for an exclusive caste of outstanding individuals but not a task for the masses. Rohan, however, developed substantial organizational activity with the *Europäische Kulturbund* and the publication of the *Europäische Revue*, a high-flying cultural and political journal. Even though the Austrian did not have a clear political agenda and primarily intended to facilitate cultural exchange between Europe's intellectual elites, he thus followed a similar strategy as Count Richard Coudenhove-Kalergi, the leader of the Paneuropa movement. Indeed, despite repeatedly speaking of a 'nobility of the mind' (*Geistesadel*) who would build Paneuropa, Coudenhove-Kalergi ultimately believed that it could only be realized through political action and campaigning, through the active work of a political mass movement, a party-like transnational organization. One only needs to think of the Pan-European Union with its several thousand members, the numerous Pan-European gatherings (congresses), and the well-known and influential *Paneuropa* journal, which – combined together – turned the scheme into the most prominent conception of European integration in the interwar period. Pannwitz, in contrast, did not want to have anything to do with parties or public manifestations. He attempted to disseminate his ideas through publications, occasional lectures, and the exchange of letters or meetings with like-minded individuals, amongst them the writers and poets Alfred Mombert, Hermann Hesse, Gerhart Hauptmann and Gertrud Kantorowicz, the philosophers Martin Buber and Edmund Husserl, the historian Kurt Breysig, the sociologist Georg Simmel, and the psychiatrist Carl Gustav Jung. Remarkably, Pannwitz almost never seems to have tried to get in touch with non-German intellectuals – the Dutch writer Albert Verwey and some Czech thinkers were but exceptions.

Altogether, the philosopher demonstrated a more positive attitude towards Paneuropa than Rohan. Both understood Europe primarily as a community of culture and values, and wanted to safeguard the diversity of European life against

concepts of a European superstate. Yet whereas Rohan and his followers openly
attacked Coudenhove-Kalergi, Pannwitz never publicly condemned Paneuropa.
He had initially embraced the idea, holding that the formation of the 'United
States of Europe' was necessary in order to preserve peace and independence as
preconditions for European reconstruction and the cultivation of a 'Pan-European-
classical culture'.[68] As he wrote in a letter to Coudenhove-Kalergi: 'I hope you
understand ... that you do not feel different from myself, that we are striving for
similar if not the same ideals and are fighting the same fight.'[69] Sharing Heinrich
Mann's disappointment that Paneuropa had become 'the opportunistic aim of
business people and power politicians', and insisting that the conversion of the
Europeans and the formation of a common spirit would have to come before the
political and economic unification of the continent, Pannwitz, however, kept his
distance.[70] Still, the writer termed it the 'most noble-minded of all modern
possibilities', thus clearly disagreeing with Rohan's hostile disparagement of the
scheme and growing preference for an economic Mitteleuropa.[71] Indeed, the
aristocrat increasingly associated himself with leading industrialists and bankers,
who supported his movement financially, and promoted a Central European
union based on a German–Austrian partnership. For Pannwitz, in contrast,
Mitteleuropa represented an arbitrary and ideological creation, a scheme of
German political and economic hegemony in Europe. He had anticipated an
extended and overpowering Prussia-Germany as a result of Naumann's project,
and maintained this scepticism after 1918 when the concept became increasingly
coupled with an expansionist Reich myth and German ethnic nationalism.[72]

'Nationalist Pharisaism' and Cultural Primitivism: Pannwitz and the Totalitarian Ideologies of the Interwar Period

Rohan and Pannwitz represented two strands of the highly heterogeneous
Conservative Revolution. Like Ernst Jünger, Wilhelm Stapel and Carl Schmitt, the
Austrian adopted *völkisch* rhetoric and publicly supported National Socialism,
probably expecting from it 'a spiritual renewal of life in its entirety, a reconciliation
of social antagonisms and a deliverance of Western *Dasein* from the dangers of
Communism', as the philosopher Martin Heidegger tried to explain his own
stance after the war.[73] Pannwitz, in contrast, took a similar standpoint to George
or Hofmannsthal, who despised Hitler's primitivism and terroristic violence. To be
sure, he initially opined that Europe needed an 'enlightened dictatorship', to use
Thomas Mann's words.[74] As mentioned above, for Pannwitz it was the task of a
youthful avant-garde to prepare society for the new Europe and to serve as an
intellectual aristocracy in the 'Imperium Europaeum'. Its actual establishment,
however, would have to be carried out by a single authority, a new Caesar: 'Europe
will not attain peace before a dictator tames [*gewältigt*] it.'[75] Or as he had declared
in his wartime book on Germany and Europe: 'A European state can ... only be
founded by a Napoleon.'[76] Pannwitz shared Nietzsche's praise of the French

statesman, holding that it had always been war heroes and glorious victors who had established stable peace after a period of conflict, and that 'the freedom of mankind and society can in fact only be realised by an imperator who has emerged from chaos'.[77] However, he never supported Hitler. Not unlike many contemporaries, including Coudenhove-Kalergi, Gottfried Benn and Alfred Weber, the thinker instead admired (at least temporarily) Benito Mussolini as a man of culture and art, a reformer of the world, and restorer of the Imperium Romanum.[78]

In late 1931, the same year he was elected to the Prussian Academy of Arts, Pannwitz published *Die deutsche Idee Europa* (The German Idea of Europe), which analysed contemporary affairs and giving relatively specific guidelines for the following few months, which he deemed crucial for the future of Europe. Starting with a harsh critique of German politics since 1870, which had resulted in a fateful alienation from France and Britain, Pannwitz promoted international reconciliation along the lines of Aristide Briand and Gustav Stresemann: 'The historic moment has come when Germany must integrate into Europe.'[79] He disapproved of the project of a German-Austrian customs union and Greater German tendencies, asserting that this would thwart supranational integration, alarm Germany's neighbours, and prompt a Pan-Slav movement, thus leading to 'Europe's breakdown'.[80] The thinker once again pondered the idea of a constitutional transformation and division of the nation-state, but ultimately discarded the scheme of a confederation of Northern Germany and a Southern, German-Austrian entity as impractical.

In his book, Pannwitz also warned against the danger of the National Socialist movement which he interpreted as a coalition or combination of lower-middle-class protestors, traditional nationalists, and younger war veterans: 'What they share is a tendency against France, the rejection of Russian Bolshevism, anti-Socialism, anti-Semitism, *völkisch* presumption, and an interest in atypical economic conceptions.'[81] He particularly attacked Nazism for adhering to a false idea of national rebirth: 'It is irresponsible to link a process of national regeneration … to unreasonable demands for other parts of the world, attesting to nationalist Pharisaism … It is not acceptable to connect religious pathos with the ordinary patriotic hypocrisy of the heart.'[82] Related to this was the rejection of a 'total mobilization' of the German nation, the combination of *Volksgemeinschaft* and modernity, as propagated by the new nationalists or 'reactionary modernists' such as Oswald Spengler and Ernst Jünger. Pannwitz in fact differed substantially from Spengler's pessimistic historical determinism and belief that the future belonged to pragmatic and heroic men of action who would devote themselves to 'technology instead of poetry, the navy instead of painting, politics instead of epistemology'.[83] In Pannwitz's view, Germany should not become a vanguard of a new, energetic culture of imperialism and militarism, but ought to retire from political and economic competition to renew and distil its heritage.

In the ideological struggle between fascism and communism, Pannwitz chose neither side. He condemned both political extremisms as threats to Europe's freedom, and propagated the integration of the continent's non-dictatorial states into an organic political and economic union (in association with the British Empire). As has been seen, his main criticism of National Socialism did not concern Hitler's anti-liberal or anti-democratic propensities but rather his intrinsic cultural primitivism, collectivism and expansionism. This standpoint led Pannwitz to reject communism, too, quite in contrast to many left-wing intellectuals such as Heinrich Mann, Bertolt Brecht, Kurt Tucholsky and Ludwig Renn. Indeed, more than previous publications, *Die deutsche Idee Europa* displayed an unambiguous anti-communism, describing the Soviet Union as a nihilistic, brutal, primitive, and chaotic state of 'enemies of culture', as 'hell on earth'.[84] In this context there emerged a fundamental, though still somewhat inconspicuous change in Pannwitz's thought: the transition to a pro-American position. The philosopher regarded the firm and united stance of France, Britain and Germany as necessary but not sufficient for the struggle against the communist threat. The protection of the continent would also require the moral and power-political assistance of Washington in a world union of capitalist great powers. This implied a new or different conception of socioeconomic relations, and it appears that Pannwitz's anti-modernism and critique of capitalism became less pronounced than before. On the other hand, the new partnership between Europe and the United States was but a marriage of convenience between two rather different systems; an organic and largely autarkic economic order and the establishment of 'a new kind of corporate state' was still considered best for Europe.[85]

In early 1933, Pannwitz refused to sign a pledge of loyalty to the Nazi regime and subsequently lost his pension from the Prussian Academy of Arts, thus sharing the same fate as Ricarda Huch, Käthe Kollwitz, Max Liebermann and the Mann brothers.[86] During the next decade or so he focused on issues other than the European idea, publishing, for example, a book on sexual hygiene, several drawings, a study of Nietzsche, and anthropological-philosophical works.[87] For a while, the thinker continued to write for German periodicals such as the *Frankfurter Zeitung* and the *Literarische Welt*, but apart from one or two early exceptions where he criticized cultural assimilationism and the *Gleichschaltung* of German public life, these essays were largely unpolitical.[88] In 1936, Pannwitz translated Verwey's poem *De Dichter en het Derde Rijk* (The Poet and the Third Reich), which emphasized that Hitler's regime had not come to match the ideal of many poets who had imagined and called for a spiritual Third or Fourth Reich, an empire of liberty and tolerance.[89] Fearing the consequences for his German-based wife and friends, Pannwitz, however, released the translation anonymously. It was only in his unpublished works and letters that he commented openly on political developments in Nazi Germany and Europe, discussing, for instance, Austria's and Czechoslovakia's role and calling for a firm association or agreement between Great Britain and France to contain Hitler. In one aphorism, he described Hitler as 'the mass in person', and elsewhere he summarized his shattered belief in German cultural superiority and spiritual leadership, declaring resignedly: 'The unity of the German people: concentration camps and sterilisation; *Führer*, masses, and spies.'[90]

Conclusion

After 1945, the concept of European unity developed from a largely cultural but ineffective idea into a successful project of political and economic integration. Notions of cultural superiority, spiritual leadership, and moral regeneration were replaced by institutional pragmatism, while the divided continent was subordinated to ideological and geostrategic competition between two non-European superpowers. The Europeanists of the interwar period and the representatives of the resistance movements played an insignificant role in the postwar integration process, which did not evolve according to idealistic blueprints or visions of a federal Europe but was driven by economic considerations and national security interests. For Pannwitz, this development did not lead to despair or disillusionment. To him, the postwar division of Europe merely confirmed what he had pointed out as early as 1931: the need to unite and defend the West against the advancement of 'the Communist East'. The philosopher soon took up his public engagement again and in several speeches, essays and books identified Western Europe with Europe proper, arguing that it would have to unify, to associate with the United States, and to rearm quickly to withstand the dangers from the East. Defeatism or a policy of understanding with the communists would lead to a catastrophe; only a policy of strength and deterrence could maintain peace on the continent. On many points, Pannwitz agreed with the FRG's conservative government under Konrad Adenauer, similarly prioritizing Western integration over German reunification and embracing a policy of German–French reconciliation. He did not, however, refrain from criticism, disapproving of French nationalism and obstinacy, and British reluctance to participate in the integration project. As a result, he feared, Western Europe would be too disunited and fail to fulfil its political and historic vocation. Its unification would be a long process, necessitating determination and a new ethos, a post-materialistic *homo europaeus* with a comprehensive understanding of Europe's task and heritage.[91]

Obviously, despite a more realistic stance, Pannwitz maintained the fundamental tenets of his European idea. The thinker did not propose a political programme or a well-conceived utopia; he did not found a political party or organize European congresses. Europe to him could not be established by a single act; it was a dynamic and open process, a matter of self-restraint and self-reflection, a distant vision of a way out of the hopeless present, preventing humankind from sinking into absent-mindedness, from losing its identity. It was thus not an agglomeration of coexisting nations which compete for political and commercial hegemony, nor a means to enhance production, power, or centralization; nor a matter of treaties, free trade, or party-political favouritism ultimately leading to rootless mediocrity – above all it was a spiritual and intellectual principle, a transcendental idea. As he put it in one of his last publications: 'Europe must act in the awareness of its common tasks and transcend state-political borders. In this, the spirit is more important than the treaty and the constitution.'[92] Even after 1945, Pannwitz gave priority to the spiritual dimension and cultural foundations of Europe, to national-cultural diversity and intellectual exchange over political pragmatism and economic expediency as binding elements of a peaceful, animated and self-confident common Europe – perhaps this is why he deserves to be re-read today.

Notes

1. 'Aufruf zur Pannwitz-Spende' (1919), signed amongst others by Hugo von Hofmannsthal, Hermann Bahr, Julius Meier-Gräfe, and Josef Redlich, in G. Schuster (ed.), *Hugo von Hofmannsthal – Rudolf Pannwitz. Briefwechsel 1907–1926* (Frankfurt/M., 1993), facsimile between 456–57.
2. E. Jaeckle, *Rudolf Pannwitz. Eine Darstellung seines Weltbildes* (Hamburg, 1937); idem (ed.), *Rudolf Pannwitz – Eine Auswahl aus seinem Werk* (Wiesbaden, 1983); idem, 'Rudolf Pannwitz – Eine Einführung', in Schuster (ed.), *Hofmannsthal – Pannwitz*, 647–99; H. Wolffheim, *Rudolf Pannwitz. Einleitung in sein dichterisches Werk* (Wiesbaden, 1961); U. Rukser, *Über den Denker Rudolf Pannwitz* (Meisenheim am Glan, 1970); A. Guth, *Rudolf Pannwitz. Un européen, penseur et poète allemand en quête de la totalité, 1881–1969* (Paris, 1973); G. Rovagnati (ed.), *"der geist ist der könig der elemente"*. *Der Dichter und Philosoph Rudolf Pannwitz* (Overath, 2006); A. Gambo, *Mondo disponibile e mondo prodotto. Rudolf Pannwitz filosofo* (Milan, 2007).
3. On Pannwitz's idea of Europe, see Guth, *Rudolf Pannwitz*, 157–321; J. Nurdin, 'Rudolf Pannwitz (1881–1969) et la rédemption de l'Europe', in D. Minary (ed.), *Expansions, ruptures et continuités de l'idée européenne*, 3 vols (Paris, 1993–97), III (1997), 189–99; E. Franzini, 'Pannwitz und die Idee Europa', in Rovagnati (ed.), *"der geist ist der könig der elemente"*, 15–32; L.V. Szabó, '"Die Zukunft festgründen". Der "Übereuropäer" Rudolf Pannwitz', *Kritische Ausgabe* 17 (2009), 37–40. Summaries can be found in E. Jaeckle, *Die Idee Europa* (Berlin, 1988), 345–62, and P.M. Lützeler, *Die Schriftsteller und Europa. Von der Romantik bis zur Gegenwart* (Munich, 1992), 255–61, 264–67, 357–60, 428–32. Most of these texts fail to contextualize Pannwitz historically.
4. Pannwitz to Hofmannsthal, Mondsee in Oberösterreich, 18 November 1920, in Schuster (ed.), *Hofmannsthal – Pannwitz*, 557–65 (560).
5. R.F. Krummel, *Nietzsche und der deutsche Geist. Ausbreitung und Wirkung des Nietzscheschen Werkes im deutschen Sprachraum*, 4 vols (Berlin, 1974–2006); S.E. Aschheim, *The Nietzsche Legacy in Germany, 1890–1990* (Berkeley, Calif., 1992); R. Furness, *Zarathustra's Children: A Study of a Lost Generation of German Writers* (Rochester, New York, 2000).
6. R. Pannwitz, *Einführung in Nietzsche* (Munich, 1920), 1; idem, *Dionysische Tragödien* (Nuremberg, 1913) [unpaginated].
7. L. Weltmann, 'Eminent European: An Approach to the Work of Rudolf Pannwitz', *German Life and Letters* IX/4 (July 1956), 306–12 (307); Pannwitz, *Einführung in Nietzsche*, 45. See also H.-J. Koch, 'Die Nietzsche-Rezeption durch Rudolf Pannwitz. Eine kritische Kosmologie', *Nietzsche-Studien* 26 (1997), 441–67; L.V. Szabó, 'Der Kampf gegen den europäischen Nihilismus. Der Nietzsche-Verehrer Rudolf Pannwitz', *Pro Philosophia* 17–18 (1999), 121–36; Furness, *Zarathustra's Children*, 17–47.
8. See, for instance, his *Aufruf an Einen. Zur rechtzeitigen Ermöglichung eines Lebenswerkes* (Nuremberg, 1919).
9. F. Nietzsche, *The Birth of Tragedy*, trans. by S. Whiteside (London, 1993), 13.
10. See S. Breuer, *Ästhetischer Fundamentalismus. Stefan George und der deutsche Antimodernismus* (Darmstadt, 1995).
11. See, for instance, Pannwitz's essay 'Der Dichter', *Die Welt im Wort*, 19 October 1933, 3, and his poem 'Der Dichter. Albert Verwey zum siebzigsten Geburtstag' (1935), in idem, *Wasser wird sich ballen. Gesammelte Gedichte* (Stuttgart, 1963), 59–60.
12. Idem, 'Mein Werk und was es will', *Geisteskultur und Volksbildung*, March/April 1921, 63–71 (71).
13. Idem, *Einführung in Nietzsche*, 9.

14. See also G. Streim, 'Deutscher Geist und europäische Kultur. Die "europäische Idee" in der Kriegspublizistik von Rudolf Borchardt, Hugo von Hofmannsthal und Rudolf Pannwitz', *Germanisch-romanische Monatsschrift*, N.F. 46 (1996), 174–97.

15. F. Nietzsche, *Human, All Too Human: A Book for Free Spirits*, trans. by R.J. Hollingdale (Cambridge, 1996), 176.

16. R. Pannwitz, *Die Krisis der europäischen Kultur* (Nuremberg, 1917), 49, 64.

17. On German war ideology, see K. Flasch, *Die geistige Mobilmachung. Die deutschen Intellektuellen und der Erste Weltkrieg. Ein Versuch* (Berlin, 2000); J. Verhey, *The Spirit of 1914: Militarism, Myth and Mobilization in Germany* (Cambridge, 2000); S. Bruendel, *Volksgemeinschaft oder Volksstaat? Die "Ideen von 1914" und die Neuordnung Deutschlands im Ersten Weltkrieg* (Berlin, 2003); P. Hoeres, *Krieg der Philosophen. Die deutsche und britische Philosophie im Ersten Weltkrieg* (Paderborn, 2004).

18. Pannwitz, *Die Krisis der europäischen Kultur*, 32.

19. R. Musil, 'Europäertum, Krieg, Deutschtum' (1914), in idem, *Gesammelte Werke*, 9 vols, ed. by A. Frisé (Reinbek, 1978), VIII: *Essays und Reden*, 1020–22 (1020); Pannwitz, *Die Krisis der europäischen Kultur*, 33, 76, 3.

20. Pannwitz, *Die Krisis der europäischen Kultur*, 67.

21. F. Nietzsche, *Untimely Meditations*, trans. by R.J. Hollingdale (Cambridge, 1997), 3.

22. A comprehensive bibliography of studies and articles about Pannwitz can be found in Guth, *Pannwitz*, 767–80.

23. H. Bahr, 'Deutschland und Österreich', *Neue Rundschau*, April 1916, 826–35 (829).

24. A. Graf Mensdorff-Pouilly, 'Völkerreich-Friedensreich', *Süddeutsche Monatshefte*, May 1917, 227–32 (227).

25. On Naumann and the 'Mitteleuropa' idea see, with further references, R.G. Plaschka et al. (eds), *Mitteleuropa-Konzeptionen in der ersten Hälfte des 20. Jahrhunderts* (Vienna, 1995), and H.-H. Brandt, 'Von Bruck zu Naumann. "Mitteleuropa" in der Zeit der Paulskirche und des Ersten Weltkrieges', in M. Gehler (ed.), *Ungleiche Partner? Österreich und Deutschland in ihrer gegenseitigen Wahrnehmung. Historische Analysen und Vergleiche aus dem 19. und 20. Jahrhundert* (Stuttgart, 1996), 315–52.

26. R. Pannwitz, *Deutschland und Europa. Grundriss einer deutsch-europäischen Politik* (Nuremberg, 1918), 62, 67. On the following see also M.-O. Thirouin-Déverchère, 'L'idée d'Europe de Rudolf Pannwitz: l'Autriche et la Bohême comme modèles culturels européens' (unpublished doctoral thesis, Université de Grenoble, 1997).

27. Pannwitz, *Deutschland und Europa*, 53.

28. Idem, *Der Geist der Tschechen* (Vienna, 1919), 32–33.

29. Idem, *Die Krisis der europäischen Kultur*, 4, 49.

30. Ibid., 75.

31. Idem, *Deutschland und Europa*, 30, 37.

32. Idem to Hofmannsthal, Fürberg, 30 October 1917, in Schuster (ed.), *Hofmannsthal – Pannwitz*, 144–48 (145).

33. Idem, *Deutschland und Europa*, 23.

34. Ibid., 59, 55; idem, *Die Krisis der europäischen Kultur*, 202.

35. Idem, *Geist der Tschechen*. See also M.-O. Thirouin-Déverchère, '"Die Zukunft fordert ein agonales Ideal". Rudolf Pannwitz' *Der Geist der Tschechen* von 1919', *Halbasien* 2 (1992), 16–23.

36. M.-O. Thirouin (ed.), *Briefwechsel Rudolf Pannwitz, Otokar Fischer, Paul Eisner* (Stuttgart, 2002).

37. See e.g. his 'Europäische Politik, nicht Weltpolitik', *Der Neue Merkur*, October 1919, 297–307; and 'Internationale und Europäertum', *Neue Rundschau*, May 1922, 449–70.

38. R. Pannwitz, *Europäisches Zeitgedicht* (Nuremberg, 1919), 11–12.

39. Ibid., 28.

40. Weltmann, 'Eminent European', 307.

41. R. Pannwitz, *Europa* (Munich, 1920), 12.

42. Ibid.

43. Idem, 'Internationale und Europäertum', 460, 454.

44. W. Lepenies, *Kultur und Politik. Deutsche Geschichten* (Munich, 2006).
45. T. Mann, *Betrachtungen eines Unpolitischen* (Frankfurt/M., 1983), 242–43.
46. Pannwitz, *Europa*, 10.
47. Ibid., 11.
48. Idem, 'Die Bedeutung des deutschen Geistes für die europäische Kultur', *Der Neue Merkur*, January 1920, 551–59 (551) and *Europäisches Zeitgedicht*, 19, 24.
49. Idem, *Europa*, 13.
50. Idem, 'Aufruf an die Besten Deutschösterreichs (Spätherbst 1918)', in idem, *Geist der Tschechen*, 160–68.
51. Idem, *Europa*, 3.
52. Idem, 'Internationale und Europäertum', 455.
53. Idem, 'Europäische Politik, nicht Weltpolitik', 303.
54. Idem, *Europa*, 14.
55. Idem, 'Die Bedeutung des deutschen Geistes', 559. See also idem, 'Anteil des Geistes', *Der Neue Merkur*, May 1919, 73–86.
56. Idem, 'Internationale und Europäertum', 461.
57. Idem, *Europa*, 1.
58. Idem, *Die deutsche Lehre* (Nuremberg, 1919). Extracts were published as separate pamphlets, such as *An die Jugend. Von falscher und rechter Jugend* (Nuremberg, 1919), and *An die deutschen Krieger* (Nuremberg, 1919).
59. Idem, *Deutschland und Europa*, 7.
60. Idem, 'Mein Werk und was es will', 65.
61. Idem, *Europäisches Zeitgedicht*, 31.
62. Idem, 'Internationale und Europäertum', 457; 'Die Bedeutung des deutschen Geistes', 558.
63. Idem, *Einführung in Nietzsche*, 4 and *Europa*, 20.
64. R. Pannwitz, 'Anteil des Geistes', 85. See also his 'Paneuropa und die Jugend', *Paneuropa* 11/12 (1926), 9–16.
65. S. Breuer, *Anatomie der konservativen Revolution*, 2nd rev. edn. (Darmstadt, 1995); R. Woods, *The Conservative Revolution in the Weimar Republic* (Basingstoke, 1996); M. Travers, *Critics of Modernity: The Literature of the Conservative Revolution in Germany, 1890–1933* (New York, 2001).
66. On Rohan and the *Europäische Kulturbund*, see G. Müller, *Europäische Gesellschaftsbeziehungen nach dem Ersten Weltkrieg. Das Deutsch-Französische Studienkomitee und der Europäische Kulturbund* (Munich, 2005).
67. See on these and other prominent ideas of Europe in interwar Germany, R. Faber, *Abendland. Ein politischer Kampfbegriff*, 2nd edn. (Berlin, 2002), and V. Conze, *Das Europa der Deutschen. Ideen von Europa in Deutschland zwischen Reichstradition und Westorientierung (1920–1970)* (Munich, 2005).
68. Pannwitz's answer to Coudenhove-Kalergi's survey in *Paneuropa* 2/1–3 (1925), 56–57.
69. Letter of 30 April 1922, quoted from K. Orluc, 'A Wilhelmine Legacy? Coudenhove-Kalergi's Pan-Europe and the Crisis of European Modernity, 1922–1932', in G. Eley and J. Retallack (eds), *Wilhelminism and Its Legacies: German Modernities, Imperialism, and the Meaning of Reform, 1890–1930* (Oxford, 2003), 219–34 (232, fn. 29).
70. H. Mann, 'Paneuropa, Traum und Wirklichkeit' (1927), in idem, *Sieben Jahre. Chronik der Gedanken und Vorgänge. Essays* (Frankfurt/M., 1994), 347–48 (347).
71. Pannwitz, 'Pan-Europa', *Der Neue Merkur*, October 1924, 78–80 (80).
72. On the 'Mitteleuropa' idea after 1918, see J. Elvert, *Mitteleuropa! Deutsche Pläne zur europäischen Neuordnung (1918–1945)* (Stuttgart, 1999).
73. Heidegger to Marcuse, 20 January 1948, in R. Wolin (ed.), *The Heidegger Controversy: A Critical Reader* (Cambridge, Mass., 1993), 162–63 (162).
74. T. Mann, 'Pariser Rechenschaft' (1926), in idem, *Gesammelte Werke*, vol. 11: *Reden und Aufsätze 3* (Frankfurt/M. 1990), 9–97 (26).
75. Pannwitz, *Die deutsche Lehre*, 111.
76. Idem, *Deutschland und Europa*, 30.

77. Idem, *Krisis der europäischen Kultur*, 6.
78. See his retrospective remarks in his letter to O. Fischer, 10 July 1934, in Thirouin (ed.), *Briefwechsel*, 218–22.
79. R. Pannwitz, *Die deutsche Idee Europa* (Munich, 1931), 1.
80. Ibid., 31.
81. Ibid., 34.
82. Ibid., 33–34.
83. O. Spengler, *Der Untergang des Abendlandes*, 6th edn. (Munich, 1920), 57.
84. Pannwitz, *Die deutsche Idee Europa*, 22, 50.
85. Ibid., 47.
86. On Pannwitz after 1933 see, apart from Guth's major study, E. Jaeckle, *Rudolf Pannwitz und Albert Verwey im Briefwechsel* (Zurich, 1976), 92–102.
87. R. Pannwitz, *Der Ursprung und das Wesen der Geschlechter und der geschlechtlichen Fortpflanzung* (Munich, 1936); *Zeichnungen* (n.p., 1936); *Weg des Menschen* (Nuremberg, 1942); *Nietzsche und die Verwandlung des Menschen* (Amsterdam, 1943).
88. See e.g. his 'Volk, Staat und Künstler', *Literarische Welt*, 28 April 1933, 1–2.
89. The German translation is reprinted in Jaeckle, *Rudolf Pannwitz und Albert Verwey*, 117–21.
90. Unpublished aphorisms, quoted from Guth, 231.
91. See in particular the following publications: *Das Weltalter und die Politik* (Zurich, 1948); *Der Friede* (Nuremberg, 1950); *Der Nihilismus und die werdende Welt. Aufsätze und Vorträge* (Nuremberg, 1951); *Beiträge zu einer europäischen Kultur* (Nuremberg, 1954); *Aufgaben Europas* (Bremen, 1956); *Das Werk des Menschen* (Stuttgart, 1968).
92. Idem, *Aufgaben Europas*, 17.

Chapter 7

NEW MIDDLE AGES OR NEW MODERNITY?

Carl Schmitt's Interwar Perspective on Political Unity in Europe

><rr>~<rr>

Ionut Untea

At a conference in Kiel held two weeks after the Third Reich had annexed what remained of the territory of Czechoslovakia (after the establishment of the Protectorate of Bohemia and Moravia on 15 March 1939) and four months before the beginning of the Second World War, Carl Schmitt proposed a vision of the world order in which the international system of national states would be replaced by a system of political relations between 'greater spaces' (*Großräume*).[1] Although this was not an attempt by Schmitt to regain the favours of the National Socialist Party which he had lost in 1936, his notion of *Großraum* captured the attention not only of academic circles but also of Germany's domestic and foreign policy makers – not to mention the foreign press, which saw him as 'the key man' behind Hitler's expansionary projects.[2] Yet Schmitt was soon to be criticized again by Nazi ideologists once they realized that his *Großraum* was quite different from their own *Lebensraum* and 'Mitteleuropa'.[3]

Joseph Berdersky has established that Schmitt went on lecturing and writing about his new concept until 1943 without so much as a passing reference to Nazi criticisms or tailoring it to the official ideology.[4] How could one explain then the introduction of such a concept exactly at a time when there were pressures for an ideological understanding of it? Why did Schmitt choose to come out of his 'internal exile'[5] and take the risk of proposing a political concept that could easily be misinterpreted and, contrary to its original purpose, used in support of the *Führer*'s expansionist ambitions? One of the central points of this chapter will be to focus on an aspect already observed by some contemporary scholars[6] but insufficiently explored in the direction of finding some deeper roots of his conception of political unity in the internal and international sphere: his admiration for the political unity of the Holy Roman Empire in the Middle Ages. I will show that Schmitt's belief that a new type of political unity, both in internal and in international contexts, was urgently needed did not result from the situation created by the Nazi regime but rather from his appreciation of the merits of the medieval 'Respublica Christiana' and of the Holy Roman Empire. As will be shown, according to Carl Schmitt the political unity of the early medieval German Reich was based especially on the fact that the communities that composed it were administrative rather than political entities. The early medieval model of political unity helped Schmitt to launch in 1933, in *State, Movement, People*, a theory of a new type of state, having a triadic structure, inside which administrative units should not have the power of political decision.

During the Weimar period and at the beginning of the 1930s, Schmitt's initial project was only meant as a theoretical contribution to the consolidation of the German state's political unity; yet the definition which he gave in 1928 of the German nation – as the entire German-speaking population beyond the borders of the actual Weimar Republic – led him later to develop his position presented in 1933 and to propose a new theory of *Großraum*, this time as a necessary stage in the accomplishment of his idealized German nation's political destiny.

The Medieval 'Estates', 'Autarkic Entities' and the 'Monstrosity' of the Political Unity of the 'German Reich'

In 1928 and again in 1950, Carl Schmitt argued that from the thirteenth century onwards the unity of Respublica Christiana – that is, the international law applying within medieval Europe[7] – started to weaken. In *The Nomos of the Earth*, published in 1950, he explained that this was due to the emergence of a number of 'autarkic entities' within the Christian European order.[8] Schmitt had previously argued in *Constitutional Theory* (1928) that it was the 'estate associations' which endangered political unity. The question discussed in this chapter is whether the two expressions, 'autarkic entities' and 'estate associations', have the same meaning. Although they appear to do so, comparing them provides a better understanding of Schmitt's intention in his 1928 thesis on Germany's political unity. *The Nomos of the Earth* provides an important key to establish the specific meaning of the phrase 'autarkic entities': the couple *potestas-auctoritas*. Schmitt says that *potestas* – which he also refers to as *imperium* – was usually considered to be the prerogative of the emperor whereas *auctoritas* – or sometimes *sacerdotium* – was that of the pope. Drawing on the work of historian John Neville Figgis, Schmitt emphasizes that the coexistence of *potestas* and *auctoritas* had no negative effect on the general unity of the Christian Empire because 'the medieval West and Central European unity of *imperium* and *sacerdotium* was never a centralized accumulation of power in the hands of one person' and also because 'the antitheses of emperor and pope were not absolute, but rather *diversi ordines* [diverse orders], in which the order of the *Respublica Christiana* resided'.[9] Moreover, medieval unity was not threatened even in cases where the emperor claimed *auctoritas* or the pope *potestas*.[10] It was only with the emergence in the thirteenth century of 'political units' that started claiming independence both from *auctoritas* (restricting it to 'purely spiritual matters') and *potestas* (in a legal withdrawal from the *imperium*) that 'the medieval Christian order began to dissolve'.[11] Consequently, the 'autarkic entities' are none other than these 'political units' that proclaimed their independence. Schmitt mentions that some French and Italian cities of the Holy Roman Empire took the name '*civitates superiorum non recognoscentes*' (commonwealths not recognizing a superior).[12] Yet he takes the view that there are three reasons why their proclamations did not make such 'autarkic entities' actually independent: firstly, the German king retained his imperial title despite all the attempts by the French and Spanish kings to be recognized as *imperator*; secondly, the German emperor's *potestas* remained effective, as was demonstrated by his settling of disputes in the Italian *civitates superiorum non recognoscentes* and by his fighting against tyrants in the fourteenth century; and thirdly, the pope retained his *de facto auctoritas* in issuing mandates for new crusades and missions and for spreading Christianity in new territories. Because *potestas* and *auctoritas* continued to operate, the medieval Respublica Christiana remained a 'spatial order' where essential traditional distinctions were valid, such as between 'various types of wars' and between 'the soil of Christian princes and peoples vis-à-vis that of non-Christian countries'. Schmitt concludes that 'only a completely different spatial order ended medieval international law in Europe. It arose with the centralized, spatially self-contained, continental European state that faced emperor and pope, as well as other, similarly organized, neighbouring states.'[13]

As will be seen below, Schmitt's analysis of the end of the medieval order in *The Nomos of the Earth* is globally similar to that which he had presented in 1928, the main difference being that in *Constitutional Theory* the emergence of political units is described as an evolutionary process, based on the case of the Holy Roman Empire. In the chapter entitled 'Historical Overview of the Origins of the Modern European Constitutions', Schmitt's premise is that '[t]he political situation of the late medieval period (from the thirteenth until the sixteenth century) is often designated as the "state of estates"'.[14] This must be understood as a statement on the political situation not just of the Holy Roman Empire but of medieval Europe as a whole. This is confirmed by the fact that Schmitt dedicates the first three parts of the chapter to looking at how medieval institutions and ideas evolved 'into modern state institutions' successively in England, the Holy Roman Empire and the rest of the European continent; that is, Spain, France and the German territorial states. He points out that even in the eighteenth century the Holy Roman Empire (designated by Schmitt as 'the German Reich') 'remained only a heterogeneous composite of still developing political formations and fragments'.[15] As already noted, this coincides with the view later expressed in *The Nomos of the Earth* that the emergence of the modern state was the key factor in the dissolution of the Respublica Christiana.

A notable difference between Schmitt's analyses of 1928 and 1950 lies in his discussion of the formation of 'estate associations' in the Holy Roman Empire. Schmitt's central point in the above-mentioned chapter is that there is no direct link between the modern constitutions and the medieval contracts by which estates either pledged to limit their power or on the contrary tried to increase it through the promise of legal privileges. The only indirect connection is that both medieval contracts and modern constitutions established limitations in principle on the power of the sovereign. It might seem at first that Carl Schmitt implicitly refers to the category of *civitates superiorum non recognoscentes*, in view of their attempt to curb the emperor's power. On closer examination, however, it becomes apparent that '*civitates superiorum non recognoscentes*' only refers to 'political unities' such as Prussia, Bavaria, Württemberg and Saxony, which are explicitly mentioned by Schmitt in the second part of the chapter.[16] The first part is mainly concerned with the limitations that some estates attempted to impose on their princes, who in fact were themselves subject to the German emperor's authority. Schmitt gives some examples of 'estate associations' ('higher aristocracy, gentry, spiritual authorities, the urban bourgeoisie') and argues that contracts between estates or between an estate and its prince (or foreign princes) came to exist because 'the traditional military constitution based on fealty had dissolved, and vassals became mostly independent'.[17] Actually the reduced political significance he confers on the estate associations may be seen from his argument that estates were not the representatives of the whole population of a territory:

> When in the Magna Carta certain rights for protection against the misuse of royal authority are guaranteed to every "free man" (freeman), that is entirely different from a modern declaration of human and civil rights. The "free man" was at that time only the baron, who alone counted as homo liber or just as homo … Historically, therefore, the Magna Carta is only the agreement of the feudal aristocracy with their feudal master, to whom the aristocracy renew their oath of fealty in exchange for guaranteed rights.[18]

This suggests that the 'estate associations' are different not only from the 'autarkic entities' which Schmitt refers to in his work of 1950 but also from the 'political unities' discussed in *Constitutional Theory*. However, the chapter 'Historical Overview of the Origins of the Modern European Constitutions' establishes a close connection between the terms 'estate associations' and 'political unities'. In the first part of the chapter, Schmitt gives a detailed analysis of the historical emergence of the estate associations, yet at the beginning of the second part he merely mentions the emergence of the political units or of the states within the Holy Roman Empire: '*Moreover*, new political unities, states like Prussia, Bavaria, Württemberg, Saxony, formed in the territories of the Reich.'[19] The introduction of the term 'new political unities' immediately after the discussion of the emergence of the medieval estates strongly suggests that the new German states were formed in the same way as the German estates. Without further discussion, Schmitt is able to conclude: '*As a whole*, the Reich in the eighteenth century remained only a heterogeneous *composite of still developing* political formations and fragments. Hegel best formulated this circumstance in his youthful writing on 'The German Constitution' (1802): "The German state structure is nothing other than the sum of the rights that the individual parts took from the whole."'[20] In this conclusion, 'individual parts' refers both to the estates and to the 'new political unities' within the 'German Reich'. Having thus superposed the meanings of 'estate' and 'state', Schmitt is able to describe the political situation of the Holy Roman Empire of the late medieval and modern period as a 'peculiar conglomerate' in which – unlike in most European states – 'medieval conditions were preserved until the end of the Reich in 1806'.[21]

In order to offer a more precise characterization of this 'conglomerate', Schmitt argues that it is neither a '*mixture* of state forms (specifically, limited monarchy and aristocracy)' nor a '*system* of states, that is, a federal formation', but, as Samuel von Pufendorf had said of the Holy Roman Empire, 'an abnormality' or 'a monstrosity'.[22] Agreeing with Pufendorf's analysis, he claims that the 'monstrosity' of the 'German Reich' lies in the fact that 'the Kaiser cannot burden the estates with anything against their will, but these estates can certainly obtain every advantage for themselves at the expense of the Reich and can anchor them in "fundamental laws"'.[23]

At least some imperial estates appear in the second part of the chapter as representatives of the new developing political formations, but in fact Schmitt had argued in the first part of the chapter that the estates are in no way the political representatives of the entire population. Therefore the limitations imposed by the estates on the Kaiser's sovereignty appear not only to be illegitimate but also to endanger the political unity of the empire. As an example of this, Schmitt cites the demise of General Albrecht von Wallenstein in 1634, caused by Kaiser Ferdinand II who, under the influence of the estates, put an end to Wallenstein's call for religious tolerance, which 'would have been the prerequisite of Germany's state unification'. Schmitt points out that Wallenstein's death 'eliminated the last possibility of creating out of the German Reich a unity that *existed* politically on a *national* level'.[24] In Schmitt's opinion, the estates were responsible for breaking the political unity which the German 'nation' had achieved by the middle of the Thirty Years' War.

By deliberately applying the adjective 'national' not only to the German-speaking populations of the early modern Holy Roman Empire but also of the modern German states and developing political formations, Carl Schmitt reveals his ideal of a return to medieval German unity. In establishing a direct connection between the medieval contracts between estates and princes and the formation of the new political units, Schmitt intends to show that the formation of the new German states was the result not of the people asserting their political identity but of the ambitions of some social classes which did not politically represent the people. Moreover, because the emperor trusted the estates, he failed to fulfil the political unity that already existed at the level of the German nation. In other words, the Kaiser failed to remain the true representative of the entire German nation because he chose to rely on the estates rather than to listen to its will. This view already introduces Schmitt's later position in *State, Movement, People*, published in 1933, where he tried to provide a 'triadic' scheme for a new form of a state. As we will see, this scheme was produced mainly in order to overcome the past failures (in particular to prevent the apparition of new forms of estates which could interpose between the nation and the representative government), but also to regain and preserve what he considered most precious: the early medieval unity of the German nation.

State, Movement, People: The Project of a New Type of State

The most obvious obstacle Carl Schmitt was facing in his attempt to give an important place in contemporary political theory to the restoration of the German nation's idealized former unity was that the two heads of the medieval Respublica Christiana had lost their influence. As already noted, the emperor had ceased to be the true representative of the nation, having betrayed it by following the interests of the estates; as for the pope, his authority hardly got a passing reference in *Constitutional Theory*.[25] When, in *The Nomos of the Earth*, Schmitt revisited the issue of papal authority, his views bore the mark of the evolution of his political thinking between the wars. For instance he describes the opposition between the pope and the emperor as only relative because the sharing of supreme political influence meant that they were 'two orders ... of one and the same unity ... *two diversi ordines*'.[26] The notion of orders and the idea that their opposition was also a source of complementarity between them are both present in Schmitt's earlier work *State, Movement, People* published in 1933. In it he emphasized that the three orders forming the new type of state which he advocated must not be thought of as being in absolute opposition. *Staat* (administration) was the 'politically static part', *Bewegung* (movement) was 'the dynamic political element', and *Volk* was 'the apolitical side, growing under the protection and in the shade of the political decisions'.[27] But neither pope nor emperor were included in these three orders. This indicates that Schmitt saw a relatively irreversible process of evolution in political forms leading from the empire to the 'centralized, spatially self-contained' modern state.

In *Constitutional Theory*, Schmitt remarked that in continental European states, such as Spain, France and the German territorial states, royal absolutism led to the evolution of the modern state, whereas the Holy Roman Empire was kept in its late-medieval conditions by the German Emperor until 1806.[28] The absence, in 1928, of arguments concerning any role of papal *auctoritas* in the preservation of the German Empire until the nineteenth century shows that, according to Schmitt, the late medieval situation in the empire had been maintained only due to the German Kaiser's factual but ever diminished *potestas*. In other words, only one source of authority remained in the Holy Roman Empire. This was a precarious situation, which ended with the abdication of Francis II, an event which was the consequence of the fact that the Kaiser alone could secure neither *potestas* nor *auctoritas* over the princes and estates, who kept trying to limit his influence and gain new rights. In *Constitutional Theory*, Schmitt criticizes the imperial estates for having used every election of a new Kaiser from the late medieval period onwards as an opportunity to reassert and expand their privileges.[29] According to Schmitt, the preservation of the Kaiser's domination until the early nineteenth century, instead of playing a positive role, tended to weaken the political unity of the German nation. The Kaiser only perpetuated a situation originating in the thirteenth century where certain groups which lacked political representation were gaining ever-increasing power. From this point of view Schmitt admits that, as a new political form, the modern state had 'a grand function: the overcoming of the legitimacy of the (feudal and estate-based) *status quo* at that time'.[30] So, in 1928, he recognized the importance of the evolution from a decadent medieval political form to a modern one.

Why, then, had Schmitt started criticizing the modern state even before 1928? It appears that he thought that, like the Holy Roman Empire of the Middle Ages, the state in its modern form had several flaws – one at least in common with the medieval political form, others new ones. In *State, Movement, People*, Schmitt criticizes a state of affairs – originating in the late medieval period – which the modern state tended to perpetuate: political life remained dominated by organizations which, although deprived of political representation, sought to further their interests through political means.[31] Moreover, as George Schwab notes, Schmitt had written ten years earlier, in 1923, that 'the nature of political parties changed profoundly'.[32] In Schmitt's words, 'smaller and smaller committees of parties or party coalitions decided behind closed doors the fate of millions of people'.[33] In the 1926 edition of *Die geistesgeschichtliche Lage des heutigen Parlamentarismus* he wrote that 'political parties, no longer concerning themselves with discussion, now appear as social or economic power groups facing each other, calculating ... the interests and power possibilities and [then] deciding ... on compromises and coalitions'.[34] In short, the situation in the modern state was approximately the same as in the medieval political system: on the one hand private associations were gaining power by influencing the political process in their favour, on the other hand public associations – for example, political parties – set up to represent the nation were increasingly looking like the private ones, in that their political decisions ignored the interests of 'millions of people'.

In 1933, Schmitt noted that in the political system of the Weimar Republic there were many cases of the same person holding private and public positions, with members of the Parliament confusing public and private interests. With irony he called the Weimar Republic 'the Reich of unlimited compatibilities' (*Das Reich der grenzenlosen Kompatibilitäten*).[35] His use of the term 'Reich' in the context of his criticism of the political power gained by private organizations could be an allusion to the decadent situation of the Holy Roman Empire, where political decisions favoured the interests of certain estates which did not represent the German nation.

In fact, the perpetuation of a late medieval factor in the dissolution of the political unity of the nation was possible because of the modern state system's fundamental binary opposition between the government and the people or between the state and the individual.[36] According to Schmitt, such an opposition remains inadequate in the twentieth century, where the reality of political and social life was still dominated by politically very powerful non-state or supranational organizations. Schmitt argues that Chapter 2 of the Weimar Constitution, in spite of trying to take into account the reality of the social life, led to a chaotic mixture of the public and the private, of the state and the non-state, and of the political and the non-political in the Weimar Republic.[37]

Because he saw both medieval and modern political forms as having major deficiencies, Schmitt began in the early 1930s to project a new type of state system, based, on the one hand, on the medieval idea of a political unity shared by different orders and, on the other hand, on a 'triadic' structure, seen as a necessary tool to understand the complexity of the contemporary state's social and political life.[38] As will be seen below, the early medieval model plays a major role in Schmitt's theoretical project, although it was modified by him. For instance, we have seen that Schmitt believed that in the medieval period before the thirteenth century the general unity of Respublica Christiana was assured by the two orders, one of *potestas* (the emperor), the other of *auctoritas* (the papacy). With the thirteenth century, however, major changes appear in the traditional way of conceiving medieval unity, as more and more estate organizations aspired to political power. In other words, the period that began with the thirteenth century had shown that the dual structure of the medieval Respublica Christiana was not able to deal with a new political reality, the consequence being the diminution and, finally, the elimination of both the emperor and the papacy as the central actors in maintaining the unity of the European international system. The modern state placed in the centre of political preoccupations the efforts for a unity at the national level, instead of traditional international unity, because the state was a 'centralized, spatially self-contained' political unit.[39] But because it had eliminated the medieval idea of 'diverse orders' and proposed a new dualism (state–individual), the national liberal state still proved unable to impede the fulfilment of the political ambitions of social groups based on private interest and it failed, under the influence of these types of organizations, as the German Kaiser had done, to serve the will of the 'millions of people' that formed a nation.

Because in Schmitt's perspective both these historical political forms had failed to preserve political unity at both a European level (in the case of Respublica Christiana) and a national level (in the case of the modern state in general, and in the case of the Weimar Republic in particular), Schmitt offers in *Staat, Bewegung, Volk* (1933) a project of a new type of state where national political unity could be attained and preserved.

In *Constitutional Theory* (1928), the term 'nation' is defined in the chapter 'Origin of the Constitution' as 'a people brought to political consciousness and capable of acting'.[40] The detailed discussion on the French revolution creates the impression that Schmitt believes that this revolution was the first event in history when a people became 'a nation'. But in fact on the previous page Schmitt had stated that in 1634 the demise of Wallenstein 'eliminated the last possibility of creating out of the German Reich a unity that *existed* politically on a *national* level'.[41] This means that, according to Schmitt, even during the Thirty Years' War, the German-speaking population of the Holy Roman Empire and outside it were already politically aware of its identity. This awareness appears in the context of the ever-weakening power and authority of the emperor and the pope respectively. In the chapter 'The Basic Rights of Constitutional Theory' Schmitt writes that in the sixteenth century the medieval theory of the 'political universal' maintained by the two heads of the Respublica Christiana 'became impossible' because 'the sovereignty of the numerous states formed then was recognized and the world had obviously now made a transition into the condition of a political universe that was pluralistic'.[42] Within the framework of the pluralistic political universe which formed in the sixteenth century, the pope's *auctoritas* was still limited to 'purely spiritual matters', as it had been from the thirteenth century onwards.[43] Religion remained an important factor in social and political life, regarded in some states as a national matter and in others as a private one.[44] The aspect to be retained is that religion, at least from the time when the sovereignty of the political units became obvious, kept its authority. This was because, even where religion was seen as a private matter, in comparison with it 'everything else … can derive its value only as a means of assistance to every absolute value'.[45] But here the *auctoritas* was no longer a prerogative of the papacy, rather – depending on the policy of each modern sovereign state – either the prerogative of the nation (because in some sovereign states 'religious life cannot be a private affair') or of the individual (because in other states the individual 'is the bearer of an absolute value and remains with this value in his private sphere').[46] The reluctance of Emperor Ferdinand II to uphold a policy of religious toleration during the Thirty Years' War negated the possibility of 'creating out of the German Reich a unity that existed politically on a national level'.[47] The distance between the Kaiser's *potestas* and the nation's commitment to its political unity shows that already in 1928 Carl Schmitt believed that the new historical holder of *auctoritas* was the nation.

This idea appears more clearly if one considers that, in Schmitt's view, the centre of the pope's medieval *auctoritas* was the maintaining of universal unity in Europe.[48] The main difference between papal *auctoritas* and the new national *auctoritas* (in the case of the German nation) was the fact that, during the Thirty Years' War, the German nation expressed itself politically by choosing a unity no longer based on religious uniformity, but primarily on national uniformity and secondarily on religious tolerance. Schmitt first presented his conception of this national uniformity (named 'homogeneity') in *The Crisis of Parliamentary Democracy* (1923).[49] I quote a passage from *Legality and Legitimacy* (1932) in order to show its central characteristic: 'One must assume that, by virtue of being a part of the same people, all those similarly situated would in essence will the same thing.'[50]

Because it remained hard to understand how belonging to a people would make him have the same political will as the other members of the same people, Schmitt tried to give to this rather ideal 'homogeneity' the characteristics that could present it as an effective and credible concept in the political theory of his time. On account of the new type of state he proposed in *State, Movement, People*, as the unity of three orders that supported the political unity of the nation, Schmitt makes an important step in the theoretical explanation of his concept: the *Movement* (*Bewegung*), being the dynamic element in the state, penetrates the other two orders and it is at the same time a *State* (*Staat* in the sense of 'administration') and *People* (*Volk*) because it recruits its members from all the social layers of a people. In this way Schmitt explains theoretically why, in the new type of state, there can be no divide between *potestas* and *auctoritas*: *Movement* (the leading order of a state) is in essence identical with *People*, as the members of the *Movement* are the elite in every social layer of society.[51] As will be seen below, in 1934 he further defined these layers of society as being themselves 'concrete orders'.

Further Theoretical Developments in the 1930s, and Schmitt's Aspiration to Apply the Medieval Model to the Sphere of International Relations

The concept of 'concrete order' was proposed by Carl Schmitt in the 1930s[52] and its use remains in harmony with his criticism of the rise to power of the medieval estates or their modern counterparts. In 1934 he argued that concrete-order thinking had provided the basis for regulating interpersonal relations in medieval society until Roman law became dominant in the fifteenth century. According to George Schwab, Schmitt held the view that, despite its general replacement by *Corpus Juris Civilis* in the fifteenth century, concrete-order thinking never entirely vanished in Germany, although it had been further undermined by nineteenth-century juristic positivism.[53] This is consistent with my interpretation that Schmitt wanted some elements of the early medieval period to be included in the new form of state which he proposed. In *Über die drei Arten des rechtswissenschaftlichen Denkens* (1934) he argues that contemporary political theory ought to give greater attention to the notion of *Nomos Basileus* than to the 'rule of law'. Whereas the rule of law destroys the concrete order and can be used as a political tool against the sovereign (being the principle used by so-called constitutions to limit sovereign power), *Nomos Basileus* presupposes the existence of a concrete order and community directly subordinated to the sovereign.[54] Instead of trying to gain political power for themselves, the estates should have continued to abide by the rules of the concrete orders that formed naturally in the early Middle Ages. George Schwab sums up Schmitt's conception of the concrete orders as follows:

> Underneath the sovereign the people are organized in a series of concrete orders reflecting essentially professional groupings.[55] Representatives of these orders meet

in a kind of parliament – not a liberal one – which is at the service of the sovereign, but, simultaneously, the sovereign assures its existence. The citizen of the state realizes himself within the confines of a particular concrete order.[56]

The importance that Schmitt attempted to give to the notion of medieval orders in his political theory partly explains his criticism of the Hobbesian conception of the state in *The Leviathan in the State Theory of Thomas Hobbes* (1938): 'this covenant does not accord with medieval conceptions of an existing commonwealth forged by God and of a pre-existent natural order ... This covenant is conceived in an entirely individualistic manner. All ties and groupings have been dissolved.'[57] The consequence of the establishment of an absolute beginning of politics and society in Hobbes's thought is the elimination of any pre-existent value and 'truth'. According to Schmitt, the modern state, being 'technically neutral', cannot distinguish between right and wrong, true and false, just and unjust, because 'the absorption of other kinds of standards and values into juristic argumentation would only create new conflict and new insecurity'. Schmitt goes on to compare the 'technically neutral state' with the 'medieval community': 'In a medieval community, the feudal, or estate "right to resist" an unlawful ruler is self-understood. The vassal (or the estate) may invoke here divine right just as much as the feudal lord or ruler has the authority to do.'[58] From the wider context of this quotation the term 'community' appears to have three important meanings. First, it refers to the coexistence of the 'feudal' lord and his vassals on the same land; because of this, 'community' means 'administration' of the land and of the legal relations between the inhabitants and their landlords. The second meaning is given by the idea that 'the right to resist' is 'self-understood' both for the landlord and his vassals: here 'community' means 'community of values' not formed through a state mechanism but natural or pre-existent to the political order. A third meaning is suggested in the text by terms like 'unlawful' and 'authority': an allusion to the couple *potestas-auctoritas*. The first term reminds us of the *de facto potestas* reserved only to the emperor to overthrow a tyrant, even when the cities were *superiorum nonrecognoscentes*; by the second term Schmitt may be referring to *auctoritas* which, as in 1928 and 1933, no longer comes from the pope, but from the commonality of values.

The use of the term 'community' with these three meanings in *The Leviathan in the State Theory of Thomas Hobbes* owes nothing to chance: several scholars agree that the period when it was written, the late 1930s, was a decisive stage in the development of Schmitt's thought, the moment when 'he turned his attention primarily to international affairs. He claimed that with the end of the state, a particular European interstate law, or what Schmitt called the *ius publicum Europaeum*, had also ended.'[59] Beginning in 1939 he proposed a new international system based on a plurality of 'Greater Spaces' or *Großräume*, each with its specific internal and concrete political order.[60] In the article 'Völkerrechtliche Großraumordnung mit Interventionsverbot für raumfremde Mähte; Ein Beitrag zum Reichsbegriff im Völkerrecht', presented at a conference in Kiel in 1939 and published in 1941, Schmitt asserted that the concept of *Großraum* 'like our new concepts of state (*Staat*) and people (*Volk*)' were more appropriate to express the international political situation at the beginning of the Second World War.[61] This shows that he had the aspiration to propose *Großraum*, together with its medieval-like orders, as a central concept in international political theory.

Schmitt's project of an international law system was influenced by a conception that originally was conceived to help to secure a political unity only at national level. The source of his growing interest for the theory of international relations rests on the fact that for him the nation also referred to the German-speaking population beyond the borders of the Weimar Republic. As already shown, his particular understanding of the term 'nation' pre-dated Nazi ideology rather than resulting from it. Schmitt's hope that national socialism would fulfil his dream of a return to neo-medieval unity may explain his early enrolment in the party. At the beginning of the Second World War he was still animated by the ideal of a national homogeneity in a given *Großraum*, which determined his view that the return of the German-speaking population from Estonia and Lithuania in 1939, and from Bessarabia and Volhynia, were a direct consequence of the 'political reorganization in the East',[62] namely the formation of the Soviet *Großraum*.

Carl Schmitt's interwar conception of national political unity in Europe in general and of *Großraum* in particular remained, however, only at a schematic level. In 'Völkerrechtliche Großraumordnung' he declared that the term '*Großraum*' was only a necessary bridge between the old and new conceptions of space. He also said that he was convinced that, as political theory evolved, more appropriate terms would replace that which he was proposing as a provisional step.[63] After the war he incorporated some aspects of his incipient theory of *Großraum* into *The Nomos of the Earth* but, because he was facing an international situation he had not previously expected, his conception of the political unity of the different *Großräume* within Europe remained ambiguous.

Notes

1. J.-W. Müller, *A Dangerous Mind: Carl Schmitt's Post-War European Thought* (New Haven and London, 2003), 43; H. Meier, *The Lesson of Carl Schmitt; Four Chapters on the Distinction between Political Theology and Political Philosophy*, trans. M. Brainard (Chicago and London, 1998), 168.
2. J. Bendersky, *Carl Schmitt Theorist for the Reich* (Princeton, 1998), 258.
3. Ibid., 251–52, 260–61; C.L. Connery, 'Ideologies of Land and Sea: Alfred Thayer Mahan, Carl Schmitt, and the Shaping of Global Myth Elements', *Boundary 2*, 28 (2001), 187–89.
4. Bendersky, *Carl Schmitt Theorist*, 261.
5. Müller, *A Dangerous Mind*, 51.
6. Ibid., 45; G. Schwab, *The Challenge of the Exception: An Introduction to the Political Ideas of Carl Schmitt between 1921 and 1936* (Berlin, 1970), 121; A. De Benoist, *Carl Schmitt actuel: guerre 'juste', terrorisme, état d'urgence, 'Nomos de la terre'* (Paris, 2007), 146.
7. C. Schmitt, *The Nomos of the Earth in the International Law of the Jus Publicum Europaeum*, trans. G.L. Ulmen (New York, 2003), 58.
8. Ibid., 64.

9. Ibid., 61.
10. Ibid., 61.
11. Ibid., 65.
12. Ibid., 65.
13. Ibid., 65–66.
14. C. Schmitt, *Constitutional Theory*, trans. J. Seitzer (Durham, 2008), 97.
15. Ibid., 99.
16. Ibid., 99.
17. Ibid., 97.
18. Ibid., 98–99.
19. Ibid., 99 (emphasis added).
20. Ibid., 99 (emphasis added).
21. Ibid., 99.
22. Ibid., 99 (author's emphasis).
23. Ibid., 100.
24. Ibid., 100 (emphasis added).
25. The term *auctoritas* related to the pope appears only in a footnote to chapter 8. Ibid., 459.
26. Schmitt, *The Nomos*, 113 (author's emphasis).
27. C. Schmitt, *State, Movement, People: The Triadic Structure of the Political Unity; The Question of Legality*, trans. S. Draghici (Corvallis, 2001), 11–12.
28. Schmitt, *Constitutional Theory*, 99–100.
29. Ibid., 100.
30. Ibid., 101.
31. Schmitt, *State, Movement, People*, 25–26.
32. Schwab, *The Challenge*, 68.
33. C. Schmitt, *Die geistesgeschichtliche Lage des heutigen Parlamentarismus* (Munich, 1923), 39; quoted in G. Schwab, *The Challenge*, 68.
34. Ibid., 11.
35. C. Schmitt, *Staat, Bewegung, Volk, Die Dreigliederung der politischen Einheit* (Hamburg, 1933), 27.
36. Schmitt, *State, Movement, People*, 17, 28.
37. Ibid., 28–29.
38. Ibid., 11.
39. Schmitt, *The Nomos*, 65–66.
40. Schmitt, *Constitutional Theory*, 101.
41. Ibid., 100 (emphasis added).
42. Ibid., 198.
43. Schmitt, *The Nomos*, 65.
44. Schmitt, *Constitutional Theory*, 198.
45. Ibid., 198.
46. Ibid., 198.
47. Ibid., 100.
48. In addition to the arguments already shown in the previous and present chapters that sustain the centrality of the idea of universal political unity of the pope's *auctoritas*, I mention the passage in *Nomos of the Earth* (1950) where Schmitt presents the pope as limiting the use of weapons between Christian political units inside Europe: Schmitt, *The Nomos*, 58.
49. See E. Balibar, 'Le Hobbes de Schmitt, le Schmitt de Hobbes', in C. Schmitt, *Le Léviathan dans la doctrine de l'Etat de Thomas Hobbes; Sens et échec d'un symbole politique*, trans. D. Trierweiler (Paris, 2002), 17.
50. C. Schmitt, *Legality and Legitimacy*, trans. J. Zeitzer (Durham and London, 2004), 28.
51. Schmitt, *State, Movement, People*, 11–12.
52. See Schwab, *The Challenge*, 115.
53. C. Schmitt, 'Nationalsozialistisches Rechtsdenken', *Deutsches Recht* 10 (1934), 226. Cited in Schwab, *The Challenge*, 121.

54. C. Schmitt, *Über die drei Arten des rechtswissenschaftlichen Denkens* (Hamburg, 1934), 15–16.
55. It should be understood that, according to Schwab, Carl Schmitt's concrete orders do not reflect exclusively the professional groupings, because Schwab also indicates that the family, a concrete but natural order, was given as an example by Schmitt. In his introduction to *On the Three Types of Juristic Thought*, Joseph Bendersky also indicates that the components of a 'concrete order' include cultural foundations besides traditional institutions. See Schwab, *The Challenge*, 122; J. Bendersky, 'Introduction: The Three Types of Juristic Thought in German Historical and Intellectual Context', in C. Schmitt, *On the Three Types of Juristic Thought* (Westport, 2004), 2.
56. Schwab, *The Challenge*, 145.
57. C. Schmitt, *The Leviathan in the State Theory of Thomas Hobbes: Meaning and Failure of a Political Symbol*, trans. G. Schwab and E. Hilfstein (Westport and London, 1996), 33.
58. Ibid., 45–46.
59. Müller, *Dangerous Mind*, 41. See also E. Kennedy, *Constitutional Failure: Carl Schmitt in Weimar* (Durham and London, 2004), 26; J. Hummel, *L'irréductible réalité du politique* (Paris, 2005), 96–97.
60. Meier, *The Lesson*, 168.
61. C. Schmitt, 'Völkerrechtliche Großraumordnung mit Interventionsverbot für raumfremde Mähte: Ein Beitrag zum Reichsbegriff im Völkerrecht', in C. Schmitt, *Staat, Großraum, Nomos: Arbeiten aus den Jahren 1916 bis 1969* (Berlin, 1995), 305.
62. Ibid., 295.
63. Ibid., 315.

Chapter 8

ROSENZWEIG, SCHMITT AND THE CONCEPT OF EUROPE

>━━◟◞━━◟

Vittorio Cotesta

Political Systems and their Spatial Order

Before discussing the concept of Europe in Franz Rosenzweig's *Globus. Studien zur weltgeschichtlichen Raumlehre* and Carl Schmitt's *Der Nomos der Erde im Völkerrecht des Jus Publicum Europaeum*, it might be opportune to explain why we are proposing to compare these two authors. There is no known personal relationship between the two. Rosenzweig died in 1929, already in intellectual decline due to illness; Schmitt, thanks to the publication of his *Verfassunglehre* in 1928, acquired a position of great cultural prestige in German philosophical and political circles. Nowhere does Schmitt quote Rosenzweig in his works. Above all, he seems to be unaware of *Der Stern der Erlösung*, published for the first time in 1921. There are other reasons which might explain this: Rosenzweig attempted to build his philosophical perspective within his Jewish perspective; Schmitt, on the contrary, stood firm in his own political Catholicism. The theologies of the two authors, then, stem from different backgrounds and have different aims.

Consequently, comparing such different philosophers might seem misguided. Nonetheless, there are important theoretical reasons which justify a parallel reading of their works. First of all, *Globus* and *Der Nomos der Erde* present a strong paradigmatic unity. In short, they both attempt to interpret the history of Europe by focusing on the spatial order of the political system. For both authors, the history of Europe is, in fact, the history of its spatial order. More precisely, Rosenzweig and Schmitt's interpretations of the history of Europe are narratives of the process of destructuring a spatial configuration and the restructuring of the parts into a new whole. The space within which such processes take place will no longer be the same. Each cycle of destructuring and restructuring will produce a space which only partially coincides with the previous configuration.[1]

To use space as the basis for interpreting and narrating history is far from being an innovation in the history of Western culture. Herodotus, Ptolemy, Montesquieu, Hegel, Tocqueville are just a few among the many who started their histories from the orography of a given territory.[2] Nonetheless, with regard to Rosenzweig and Schmitt, this paradigm, combined with other analytical dimensions (the political order for Rosenzweig and the political-juridical order for Schmitt), offers a noteworthy contribution to the understanding of Europe's history.

There is a further striking convergence between the two authors. Both consider the sea as the constitutive element of European culture and the basis of its supremacy over the other civilizations. Such a reading might already be found in Montesquieu and, above all, in Hegel. In the comparison between Europe, on the one hand, and India and China, on the other, Montesquieu highlights the role of the environment in the formation of political systems. The vast desert lands favour despotism, while a territory divided into many small states and bordered on all sides by the sea creates monarchical regimes such as those found in Europe. In Hegel's writings, the role of the sea is even greater:

> For Asia the sea is meaningless … In Europe the relationship with the sea is precisely what is important … A European state can be great only in connection with the sea. To be sure, the sea separates lands but unites people. Seafaring – that going out of oneself – is the entirely distinctive feature lacking in the Asian way of life.[3]

In different ways, such a Hegelian view operates both within *Globus* and within *Der Nomos der Erde*, yet this may be grasped only through an in-depth analysis of the two works.

Franz Rosenzweig's *Globus*

The subtitle of *Globus*, 'A universal-historical theory of the state', suggests the designing of a great theory; in point of fact, the text is a collection of scattered thoughts formulated in extremely hostile conditions, during the Great War, while Rosenzweig was an officer in the Balkans. They are thoughts on the development of history moved by the desire to outline a project for the postwar period, when the Great Powers would be forced to sit around the peace table and find a solution to the problem of world government.

Globus is divided into two parts, *Ecumene* and *Thalatta*, which are, as Rosenzweig himself claims, complementary to one another.[4] We shall start with the second essay, *Thalatta*, in an attempt to understand the global dynamics depicted by Rosenzweig, and then turn to *Ecumene*, where we shall examine the historical development of the different ideas of Europe. In the former, the relationship between land and sea was crucial: 'The act of tracing boundaries depicts the history of one single land. But land itself, right from the start, has had its own boundaries. All around, everywhere, the sea lashes its coasts. Two or three great islands: this is how dry land finds itself in the middle of the sea.' Different images of the earth and of its boundaries come to mind; furthermore, a discrepancy emerges from these images: 'The political and the geographical images of the world do not overlap'.[5] Political consciousness and the shape of the world change. This was obviously true at the time Rosenzweig was writing, but it is still so today.[6]

Two great images of the world have opposed one another throughout history: the Homeric and the biblical. The first one represents the world 'as a great internal sea surrounded by an oceanic hairline'.[7] However, the most ancient image comes from the Bible and refers to the:

> image of the world of the great Eastern empires ... In the latter world-image there is no sea boiling at its centre, but only *terra firma* stemming from it; *terra firma* on which rise and fall great empires, on which northern storms and tempests, produced by the Nordic people, discharge themselves and on which are discharged the thundering hurricanes generated by the tensions among powers. All the surrounding sea, which lashes the coasts of this compact mass of *terra firma* is the ocean of an indefinite immensity.[8]

Sea and earth are the two principles on which the images of the world are created and on which civilizations are built.[9]

The collocation of sea and earth clearly becomes strategic. Rosenzweig sees in Alexander the Great the embodying of the maritime principle, with Caesar embodying the opposing idea, namely the search for land and the creation of a terrestrial empire. 'The impetus of Alexander the Great drove the Hellenes deep into the *terra firma* ... but the road through the infinite "planes" of Ectabana is outstretched towards a single aim: towards the sea; ... it is the Ocean itself, which up until then had only been an obscure "out", which he wanted to disclose to the Greek world.'[10] 'Beyond the boundaries of the closed sea, ... the Greek sea must stretch to infinity.'[11]

Rome, states Rosenzweig, becomes the maritime-coastal empire foreseen by the Greeks. At the acme of this project, the man of destiny, Caesar, changes direction and, for the first time, Rome turns to the conquest of land, the land of the Gauls: 'The conquest of Gaul by Caesar has become the foundation of all ensuing European history.'[12] With him a 'new Atlantic-European history' is born and, while the Mediterranean history of Europe comes to an end,[13] Caesar takes the empire to the endless northern ocean. Had he not been killed before his time, Caesar would have turned towards Eastern Europe and founded a great 'continental' empire.[14]

The geopolitical configuration created by Caesar represents a turning point. From then on the history of Europe becomes a history in which different actors and different principles of organization confront one another. Yet contrary to what it may seem, this path is far from linear. For a long time in fact it seemed that the

Mediterranean design of the empire would last – since the North, by now pacified, no longer threatened the Mediterranean. It was not until Christmas of the year 800 that the new principle was at work. If Charlemagne was able to establish, for a while, the synthesis between old and new, after him a hitherto unknown conflict animated the history of Europe: 'It was the tension between "Paris" and "Rome", between king and emperor, between nation and *oecumene*, between Atlantic and Mediterranean which was the vital source of the medieval world', and not their unification, which for a moment had become real in the person of Charlemagne.[15]

If with Charlemagne there had been temporary pacification among the old competing elements – the North and the European Mediterranean – new actors now arrive on the scene and, with them, another principle of spatial organization: the nation and the king. According to Rosenzweig, at this moment a conflict between two ideas or concepts of Europe arises; from now onwards the Europe of nations and kings will confront the cosmopolitan Europe ('oecumenic') of the emperor. While the first phases of the duel within Europe are being played out between king and emperor, another conflict is born east of Europe between Rome and Mecca: 'When the Turks received the empire from the hands of the Arabs and the Caliph came to the throne of the Rome of the East, this fight, the fight between Mecca and Rome, had already been decided. Mecca had won; and the transfer of the caliphate to Byzantium proved it.'[16]

Yet this challenge opens a new scenario: while Islam shifts its own centre of gravity to the Mediterranean, 'Christianity sails towards new seas'. The year 1492 opens a new phase in the history of the world, one in which 'the entire ocean starts to turn itself into a single sea'.[17] In the new 'global' theatre, three great protagonists play important roles, while the others are but second leading actors of the 'global Atlantic struggle':[18] first of all Spain, which had had the great merit of 'financing Columbus'; second, France, which, having consolidated itself as a nation, had become the engine of the formation of modern statehood; and finally, Great Britain, the most Atlantic of them all. Their first great clash is still one between a king and an emperor, a state and the empire. Charles V, the last emperor, in the end loses the battle with France and from then onwards the 'imperial' sceptre slowly gives way to the 'national' principle. The core of the conflict is played out in the Low Countries, which, after the defeat of Spain, gain momentum and become the centre of political and economic innovation. Nonetheless, when France believes it has imposed its hegemony, then its strongest enemy appears: Great Britain. The latter, having partly lost its American territory (the colonies out of which the United States were born), continues, on the one hand, to limit French power in Europe and, on the other, to build its own world empire.

There is one further point to highlight which also clarifies the scenario in France. The construction of the modern European state takes place from above: kings 'build' their people. In the first phase of modernity, when the creation of the state is still in train, the predominant dimension is the external one. As soon as this dimension is consolidated, it then becomes necessary to manage internal conflicts. France, which had solved its external problem, takes care of this issue before others do. According to Rosenzweig, the European states become 'saturated'. They must integrate new classes and new ranks within the state under pain of rebellions and revolutions. In the end, and not only because it was a 'terrestrial' power as Rosenzweig and Carl Schmitt argue, France loses its conflict with England because, from the seventeenth century onwards, internal problems find no solution; class hegemony and class balance do not last long – contrary to what happens in England, thanks to the compromise between the nobility and bourgeoisie.

Now that even the great ocean has become a sea, Great Britain can build its own empire. At the centre of this completely new construction is Africa, which becomes the new land of conquest and the basis for the construction of the network of roads necessary for the empire. Thus, the struggle over Africa becomes the cause of the First World War. 'The 1914 Great War is for the domination of Africa ... for the most ancient continent and at once the youngest, for the continent which confines with all the seas of world-history, and therefore a war for the dominion of the world.'[19] Meanwhile, another new actor has appeared on the global scene: Germany, which is also striving to create a worldwide empire. In effect, argues Rosenzweig, if one focuses on Africa and the African issue, then one can also understand why Germany attacks 'the British worldwide empire'. In its attempt to construct its own empire, Germany necessarily clashes with the existing worldwide empire. The First World War, then, is, on the one hand, a European civil war and, on the other, a war for hegemony over the world. In this clash, as Rosenzweig fears, the role of the United States of America becomes more and more significant,[20] announcing the passage of worldwide hegemony to the West – a consideration which constitutes the core of Carl Schmitt's own work.

Rosenzweig understands that a new scenario has come into being: a global scene with a centre and a periphery. He also understands that the actors at the periphery, Japan and America, 'seem to forget that they also have a "back" and that they could "turn". If they did indeed do so, the two future enemies would find themselves face to face. But they don't.' 'Politics,' Rosenzweig continues, 'certainly works for the first time with an entirely complete planisphere, but on the flat surface ... only a single world and a single sea exist, whose areas are in communication, but this world still has a centre and peripheries ... the earth in reality is not yet a sphere.' We are confronted by a separation of the world's geographical and political shape. We are nonetheless at a crucial point: a geopolitical world has been constructed, though it still lacks a government. At this stage, Rosenzweig sees a new and central role for Europe: to enliven the 'new world':

> Europe raises its head, turning to Africa from the ancient and common worldwide sea, surely the central point of the world, towards which its own extremities look. But there still are 'extremities': a world that is more ancient than Europe – that therefore was not born out of it – and a younger one – which pretends to be older: the senile conscience of Asia and the juvenile one of America.[21]

The task of enlivening the 'new world' does not seem to be justified on the grounds of the previous analysis. In fact, quite the opposite seems to be true. European nations which fight for worldwide dominion are neither one nor the other Europe – they are rather its partial and conflicting expressions. Depending on which prevails, a specific Europe will come into being. In a way, throughout the text, Rosenzweig applies his own specific understanding of 'Europe', referring simply to its geographical meaning and always by playing on the difference between spatial and geopolitical form.

Now, without warning, Europe is once again assigned the role of 'centre of the world', just when the intervention of other countries (Japan and America) in its own internal affairs should announce to everybody, including Rosenzweig, the end of a long historical phase. Rosenzweig's conclusions, then, foreshadow the creation of a new world in which all peoples can live, nourished by the spiritual force of Europe: 'The waters around the three coasts of Africa are already foaming and merging into a single sea. But the dry part of the world is not yet included in one single sphere. Humanity does not dwell in a single house. Europe is not yet the world's spirit.'[22]

Schmitt's Conception of Europe

The 'nomos', according to Carl Schmitt, is 'the first measure of all subsequent measures', the 'first land-appropriation understood as the first partition and classification of space, the primeval division and distribution' of the earth.[23] As the effective order of a space, in antiquity the 'nomos' stands for the cultivated land or that which, thanks to subdivision and repartition, can be cultivated.[24]

Against juridical normativism, represented at its best in German legal culture by Hans Kelsen, Schmitt turns the primeval occupation of soil into the foundation of legal order. From this angle, Schmitt's work is first and foremost a monumental attempt to re-create a logical and actual hierarchy in the relationship between politics and law, between acts of appropriation and property rights. In his perspective, right does not establish possession and property; on the contrary, it is the act of appropriation which founds both – possession and property. 'In any case, land-appropriation, both internally and externally, is the primary legal title that underlines all subsequent law. Territorial law and territorial succession, militia and the national guard presuppose land-appropriation. Land-appropriation also precedes the distinction between private and public law.'[25] In other words, the actual spatial configuration is the foundation of law – and not the contrary. Today, this principle would be expressed by stating that discovery and occupation are the foundation of legal order.[26] The history of international law 'hitherto known', argues Schmitt, 'is a history of land-appropriations. In given epochs, *sea-appropriations* also became part of this history, and then the nomos of the earth rests on a particular *relation* between *terra firma* and free sea.'[27] Remarkably, today, another spatial evolution is possible. In the first evolution, the juridical order has enclosed the sea; in the second it may well concern even aerial space.[28] This revolution implies a change of the dimensions of sovereignty – to earth and sea is now added space – a new means of power and of communication but, above all, a change in the contents of the effectiveness of power. 'By such a token,' says Schmitt, 'a new phase of human knowledge of space and order begins.'

A temporal division is necessary: pre-global orders, global orders and, it may be hypothesized, once aerial space is included, post-global orders. 'All pre-global orders were essentially *terrestrial*, even if they included sea powers and *thalassocracies*. The originally terrestrial world was transformed in the age of geographical discoveries, when the earth for the first time was understood and measured by the global consciousness of European peoples.' 'Thus was born,' Schmitt continues, 'the first *nomos* of the earth', here understood as the whole globe and not as a surface separated by the sea.[29] With this conception of the nomos of the earth – an actual and primeval act of appropriation of space and of ensuing division – and with the sketching of the historical sequence of its different configurations, we can try to retrace in Schmitt's arguments his personal ideas of Europe.[30]

The first European legal order is the 'Respublica Christiana'. Its spatial division establishes that 'the territory of non Christian and pagan people is the land of Christian mission and can be assigned through papal charge to a Christian king'; that 'the continuity between the Roman and Byzantine empires ... in practice affected only the Balkans and the East'; that 'the soil of Islamic empires was considered to be enemy territory that could be conquered and annexed through the Crusades'; and that 'the land of the kings and people of Europe was divided according to the land law of the time, among princely houses and crowns, churches, cloisters and sponsors, lords of the land, castles, marches, cities, *communitates* and *universitates* of various kind'.[31]

An important corollary of such a division is the idea of 'just war'. According to this perspective, only the war waged on a papal mandate and to conquer enemy territories or territories occupied by enemies (re-conquest) can be seen as 'just'. This specific understanding of the concept of 'just war' stems from the actual order of the Respublica Christiana. As is well known, the pillars of this order are twofold: the *imperium* and the *sacerdotium* respectively embodied by the emperor and the pope. This empire has a tie with Rome that is represented by the continuity of Roman localization based on faith in Christianity. The tie with Rome is considered a criterion of legitimacy so that, according to Schmitt, 'the history of the Middle Ages is the history ... of a war for Rome, and not a history against Rome'.[32] In other words, the conflict among the different kings or emperors, or among real or imaginary powers, favours the person or the power which can claim a relationship (made up of an 'actual spatial localization') with Rome and above all, with its mission as formulated by the Church fathers and their medieval followers. The empire designates '[t]he historical power which is capable of holding back the advent of the Antichrist and the end of the current eon'.[33] The empire is 'a braking power', the 'kat-echon'. Only the fight 'against the overwhelming power of evil' can legitimate the 'Imperium Romanum' and its

Christian prosecution.[34] Therefore, any proposed order must be inscribed in this mission of avoiding or, at worst, of delaying the coming of the reign of evil.

The appropriation of enemies' lands or the re-conquest of lands under their control is part of such a messianic plan. This aspect of the legitimacy of political power also implies a precise hierarchy between the various 'ordines' of the Respublica Christiana, between the pope and the emperor. *'Auctoritas'* belongs to the pope while *'potestas'* belongs to the emperor – even though each one seeks to increase his influence in the other's domain. This system worked for a long time, up until a new principle of legitimacy of power was introduced. The system lasted so long that even the dominion over the new world, at a time when legitimacy was already based on discovery and conquest, was legitimated with the idea of a mission, with the conversion of the pagan American people. The European Respublica Christiana, fearing the possibility of the advent of the antichrist and the victory of evil, tries to avoid or even only delay the advent of the kingdom of evil; its legal order is conceived so as to achieve this historical mission.

From a more practical perspective, all this implies the attempt, by the Respublica Christiana, to regain Jerusalem[35] and to try to regain the Iberian peninsula. Its formal dawning is belated, while its actual ending comes quite soon, when the unity of the various 'ordines' is shattered and when political power starts seeking legitimacy within itself and no longer in a mission against the powers of evil. The new political power calls for a 'completely different spatial order ... it [is] the centralized, spatially self-contained, continental European state that faced the pope and the emperor, as well as other, similarly organized neighbouring states. Unlimited free space for overseas land-appropriations was open to all such states.'[36] The military strength and the cultural capacity proven by the discovery and in the conquest are the new legal titles on which the legitimacy of power is built. The juridical order born out of this revolution presupposes in fact the first spatial revolution; that is, the discovery of the New World and its occupation by European powers. As Rosenzweig argues, precisely at the time when the Islamic world seizes the other Rome (Byzantium), the Christian world, with the discovery of America, reunites the world, creating the conditions of a global order.

The unification of the world prefigured by Christopher Columbus's discovery of America is juxtaposed with other political and cultural revolutions. For our purposes, of particular relevance is the process of secularization, which requires political authority to seek sources different from the medieval ones; furthermore, its legitimacy is no longer justified by religious orders but by a class of jurists at the service of kings, dukes, princes and, more generally speaking, of any power seeking its independence from the two universal medieval powers of the papacy and the empire. The new founding arguments of legitimacy leave out any religious content or mission. The 'sovereign' is such only if he is 'sovereign' over a given territory. Once more, Schmitt uses the spatial configuration as an analytical unity. The fact that sovereignty is such only over a territory implies that there is no other power towards which one is responsible. In fact, argues Schmitt, the state is only 'modern' because, for the first time in Europe, this political-spatial configuration is born without superior powers and independent from all neighbours: 'the concept of statehood is not therefore universal, valid for any age and for any people; it is rather an actual historical phenomenon related to a specific age'.[37] When this principle is generalized, then the European system of modern states comes into being. This system generates a masterpiece of European history: the 'jus publicum europaeum'.

Such European public law, argues Schmitt, is essentially a 'law among states, among European sovereigns; this European core determined the nomos of the rest of the earth'.[38] 'European-continental international law' stemmed from the need to regulate relations among the emergent powers of Europe: the system of the sovereign states. At the same time, since the action of these states, during the sixteenth century and in the ensuing centuries, unfolds upon the earth in its entirety, the validity of the jus publicum europaeum was extended to the entire globe. The first global order was born in Europe.

The jus publicum europaeum is, in the first instance, a web of norms by means of which different spatial ambits are identified – the mainland and the 'free' sea; for each of these a specific norm is then conceived. Relationships among the states, in Europe, are based on 'civil' laws, while on the 'free' sea they are based on competition and maritime war. There are many implications of this global order. Between the European and the other peoples a series of hierarchical relationships are established. Other peoples' lands can be conquered and occupied. The right over 'free' territories derives from the ability to occupy them. It has been discussed at length, says Schmitt, whether 'free' seas were res nullius (of nobody) or res omnium (of everybody): 'To discover – reperire, invenire, then découvrir – previously unknown seas, islands and lands (in the sense of unknown to Christian monarchs): this is the only legal title that remains to the European international law after the medieval order has disintegrated.'[39] In turn, this implied conquest and, more precisely, occupation: 'Discoveries are made without the permission of the discovered. Their [the discoverers'] legal title consists therefore in a superior legitimacy. Only those who, on a spiritual and historical plane, are so superior as to apprehend the discovered by superior knowledge and consciousness.'[40] None of the discoverer states, in fact, ever intended to derive its own right of 'succession' from the indigenous people. Each has, instead, asserted its own 'original acquisition'.[41]

It could be concluded, on this delicate point of the relationships between European and non-European people, that: (a) normally, only Europeans are considered to be civilized; (b) the European peoples, the discoverers, the conquerors and the colonizers, are 'superior' to others; and (c) for both these reasons, any act of conquest (discovery or occupation) is legitimate. The jus publicum europaeum as a global order – of free sea and of terra firma – contains the idea of a triumphant Europe. In fact, its history starts with the geographical unification of the world through the discovery of America by Christopher Columbus, and ends with the Great War.

A Lost Europe

While Rosenzweig still looks at the United States of America through Hegel's eyes, seeing America as a 'young' 'continent' and as the land of the future, Schmitt believes, on the contrary, that America has already reached its status of great world power and is now preparing to take the place of Europe as a hegemonic world power. Schmitt uses a series of arguments to support his thesis. The first is that, in the division of the world into two hemispheres, the Monroe doctrine has been used to legitimate two trajectories of American policy. On the one hand, if there are two hemispheres, each power is hegemonic within its own hemisphere. This ensures the autonomy of the United States of America and avoids any European interference. A corollary of this form of legitimacy is the possibility that the United States becomes the hegemonic power within its own hemisphere. Independence from Europe and hegemony in the western hemisphere: this is the sense of the policy adopted by the United States in the nineteenth century. At the end of the century, nonetheless, something changes. Once hegemonic only within its own hemisphere, the USA begins a global policy. Schmitt notes that the USA, for the entire nineteenth century, has oscillated between 'beautiful isolationism' and a world policy justified by a cosmopolitan and universalistic vision of history. At the end of the past century, also because of divisions among the European nations and due to their impotence, the USA starts to insinuate itself in the thread of European relations which are less and less regulated by the *jus publicum europaeum*. This new policy is based on the great global transformation taking place in those years. Economics, increasingly more important than politics as the engine of international relations, gradually shifts from the Atlantic to the Pacific; political hegemony passes into the hands of those who are on the waves of change. European states fight among each other for hegemony over a world which is falling out of their hands. The Great War – and in this, Schmitt's diagnosis converges with Rosenzweig's – marks the change of the historical scenario from a European to a global one.

Yet there is an important difference between the viewpoints of the two authors, related, obviously, to the fact that Schmitt has had another thirty years to write his diagnosis. If Rosenzweig believed that Europe could enliven the world, moving in between the 'senile conscience' of China and the 'juvenile conscience' of America, Schmitt has seen, with the Second World War, the definitive passage of world hegemony to the West. In this phase, Europe is still aggressive and yet substantially passive, resigned and under tutelage. Importantly, this is not about a change of actor on the same stage. Schmitt has an acute awareness of the transformation that has taken place. The engine of the world, on which Europe's hegemony had been built, no longer works. The politics of the European nation-states which had created the *jus publicum europaeum* is in crisis because now a different engine is propelling world history. Now economy commands politics; the contrary is no longer true.

According to Schmitt, this may easily be seen in the new world order. The Eurocentric global order was an 'order'; the global order which has taken its place is a 'chaos'. The European order had limited wars for a very long time; the new order is neither capable of preventing nor of limiting wars. Out of the conflict between the old and the new global order, stems the image of an unjust, cruel Europe, mean towards its own sons, while America claims to be the 'true Europe', established under the 'aegis of law and of freedom', generous toward the sons of Europe who, from the old continent, travel to the new world.[42] In the hegemonic passage towards the West a crisis of identity is also implied. Europe loses itself, its values and its soul, which, instead, seem to live once again in the American democracy.

At the time, argues Schmitt, the transition is not complete, but clear signs are already perceptible. After the Second World War, totalitarian and fascist Europe is judged by the victorious powers. Among the latter are France, Great Britain and the Soviet Union, which are European powers – an element which might allow us to believe that world hegemony, if not entirely, is at least still partly in European hands. Nonetheless, it is clear that without the United States, democratic Europe would hardly have defeated its internal enemy, animated by the devil of ethnic and racial superiority. In this sense, the importance of the effective ruins deriving from the fulfilment of the history of European hegemony is enormous. The fact of not being able to look completely within oneself, scared of falling into the abyss, has become a nodal point in the construction of the identity of Europe in the second half of the twentieth century. Constitutional patriotism (Jürgen Habermas) looks at the future and tries to overcome the past. The new makers of Europe start from the ruins, from the moral and material destruction caused by the appalling clash between two enormous wills to power: the British global empire, on the one hand, and, on the other, the German empire, animated, in its final phase, by a racial and racist conception of humanity. Now, at the beginning of the third millennium, even the youngest 'Europe', the Europe of the United States of America, seems to have established its own hegemonic path over the world. A global scenario with various actors seems to be arising, and all seem to want to play an equally important role. Yet this presupposes that each one of them, Westerners first of all, have the courage to look into the mirror of their 'soul' and find good reasons for living together, as brothers, since 'amid the four seas, all are brothers' (Confucius, XII, 5).

Notes

1. This model is used by Anthony Giddens in his interpretation of modernity. See A. Giddens, *The Consequences of Modernity* (Cambridge, 1990).
2. G. Simmel, *Soziologie* (Leipzig, 1908), rigorously applies this epistemological principle starting from its spatial systems. See G. Simmel, ibid., chap. IX: *Der Raum und die räumlichen Ordnungen der Gesellschaft*.
3. G.W.F. Hegel, *Vorlesungen über die Philosophie der Geschichte* (Frankfurt, 1997), 103.
4. F. Rosenzweig, *Globus* (Casale Monferrato, 2007), 131, written in 1917.
5. Rosenzweig, *Globus*, 83.

6. The Chinese philosopher Zhang Tingyang, in his philosophy of 'tianxia' (all that which is under the sun), starts precisely from this assumption in order to offer (a) his analysis of 'mundus qua mundus' and (b) his proposal for a global government. The world is still merely a geographical expression; it also needs to be given a political shape. Therefore, Rosenzweig's vision is prophetical and strikingly up to date.
7. Rosenzweig, *Globus*, 84.
8. Ibid.
9. The comparison between West and East, here merely outlined, is integrated in *Der Stern der Erlösung* (Frankfurt, 1988), first published in 1921, with a fundamental reference to the idea of God: in the Asian world (within which, now, besides the Chinese and the Indians, are also included the Greeks) God rules over the world; in the Christian, Jewish and Muslim world, on the contrary, God creates the world (*Der Stern*, 124).
10. Rosenzweig, *Globus*, 86–87.
11. Ibid., 87.
12. Ibid., 89.
13. It should be noted that these rapid descriptions by Rosenzweig on the history of Europe have a real historical basis. For a description of the passage of civilization from the East to the Mediterranean, and from there to most of northern Europe, see C. Ponting, *World History: A New Perspective* (London, 2001).
14. Rosenzweig, *Globus*, 90–91.
15. Ibid., 93.
16. Ibid.
17. Ibid., 95.
18. Ibid., 100.
19. Ibid., 108.
20. Ibid., 120, 110–11.
21. Ibid., 111.
22. Ibid., 112.
23. C. Schmitt, *Der Nomos der Erde* (Berlin, 1997), 54.
24. A comparison between Chapter 1, 'Law as Unity of Order and Localization of *Der Nomos der Erde*' by Schmitt, and the Introduction of Rosenzweig's *Ecumene* shows amazing analogies in the way they conceive of the relationship between order and localization. In Rosenzweig the elements used by Schmitt to describe the nexus of juridical order and localization are also expressed in synthesis. There are also similar references to the sea as an undifferentiated unity and a sterile place, since the work of man is not retained – contrary to the land.
25. Schmitt, *Nomos*, 24.
26. Ibid., 52.
27. Ibid., 28; italics in the text.
28. On the possibility of a second spatial revolution in Schmitt, see V. Cotesta, *Sociologia del mondo globale* (Rome, 2004).
29. Schmitt, *Nomos*, 28; italics in the text.
30. On the basis of his reconstruction of the concept of 'nomos', Schmitt analyses ancient worlds; but he is more interested in understanding the potential conditions of the modern European juridical order.
31. Schmitt, *Nomos*, 41–42.
32. Ibid., 42–43.
33. Ibid., 43.
34. Ibid., 44.
35. On the conflict between Christians and Muslims for Jerusalem and for the other Rome (Byzantium), see also Rosenzweig, *Globus*, 93–94.
36. Schmitt, *Nomos*, 52.
37. Ibid., 142.

38.   Ibid. Italics in the text.
39.   Ibid., 149.
40.   Ibid., 150.
41.   Ibid., 157.
42.   Ibid., 382.

Chapter 9

FROM CENTRE TO PROVINCE

Changing Images of Europe in the
Writings of Jerzy Stempowski

>⟊⟋⟋⟋⟍⟍⟍<

Łukasz Mikołajewski

In this chapter, I shall present and analyse the changing reflections on Europe that can be found in the writings of Jerzy Stempowski, the Polish essayist, literary critic and political exile, who resided in Switzerland after the Second World War. From 1947 until his death in 1969, Stempowski was one of the key contributors to *Kultura*, the influential Polish political and literary periodical published on the outskirts of Paris by a group of Poles opposing the existence of communist regimes in Eastern Europe. Alongside other prominent exiled writers who contributed to *Kultura*, such as Czesław Miłosz and Witold Gombrowicz, Stempowski played an important role in the literary section of the monthly publication. Moreover, for many years he was involved in the process of shaping the political profile and orientation of *Kultura*, especially the ideas advanced by the periodical in the sphere of international relations, including its famed 'Eastern policy', consisting in the strong support given to Ukrainian, Lithuanian and Belarusian democratic movements and a critical reassessment of the previous relations of Poland with its neighbours.[1]

As is visible in the multiple texts written by Stempowski for *Kultura*, the issue of Europe and its contemporary situation was among the most important, recurrent themes for the Polish writer, if not the central one. However, it suffices to look into his debut from 1924, a travel account from the Netherlands and inflation-stricken Germany,[2] to realize that already in his texts from the interwar period the ongoing political changes in Europe were the focus of his attention. The aim of the chapter is to examine how the ideas of Europe appearing in Stempowski's writings changed over a longer period of time. I will represent the continuities and differences that can be traced in Stempowski's works, taking into consideration both the interwar period and the years of his exile.

Reconstructing the evolution of Stempowski's reflection on Europe, one needs to take into account not only the ideas put forth in his texts, but also the various literary genres and different literary images used by him to write about Europe. The metaphorical aspects of literary works tend to be more suggestive and memorable to readers than the author's explicit statements or direct political interventions. I will take this into account, treating the metaphors used in his texts not solely as a general background for his political ideas, but as an essential part of what needs to be presented and put into historical context. But before we turn to the analysis of his texts, more biographical context is needed.

Who Was Stempowski in the Interwar Period?

Born in 1893, Stempowski belonged to a rather limited, elite circle of Warsaw liberal intellectuals who in the interwar period aimed to promote their liberal-democratic and socialist ideals in the new-born Polish Republic. This private 'society' was a small yet influential section of the Polish intelligentsia, a social group that in this period was in large part composed of Poles of noble descent, occasionally still owning big family estates in different parts of the territories of the old Polish-Lithuanian Commonwealth, and who despite their often liberal democratic or even socialist political ideas maintained many of the eighteenth- and nineteenth-century traditions characteristic of nobility. Many of these intellectuals thus grew up on their families' estates and received their education through private tuition, to a large extent still based on the old canon: learning Greek and Latin, and studying classical history. From an early age, they lived in a multilingual environment, speaking Polish and French at home, outside the domestic circle in Russian, reading in English or German, and, depending on the language of the population living in the vicinity of the estate, often speaking Lithuanian, Belarusian or Ukrainian with their neighbours. Another important element of these traditions was, if the family's finances permitted, to continue and complete their education by studying at universities abroad – being sent by their parents to the big cities and capitals in the West, or to Petersburg in the East. Lastly, a characteristic elite feature shared by this social group was a certain ideal of dilettantism combined with high political aspirations: instead of becoming professionals, many of these people wanted to be politicians, artists and scholars at the same time.

Stempowski's father, Stanisław, had his estates in Podolia in Ukraine. Before 1918, he was a socialist and press editor, interned several times by the tsarist government; during the period of the Great War he supported the Ukrainian struggles for independence (he even became a minister in the Ukrainian People's government of Semen Petlura). Later, in the independent Polish Republic, he created the Polish masonic lodge, and throughout the first half of the twentieth century he remained one of the key figures in Warsaw's liberal society of intellectuals.

Stempowski junior shared many of his father's political opinions, interests and social contacts. Keeping with tradition, after having passed his final exams (*matura*, or the equivalent of the baccalaureate) in Odessa and Nemirov, young Stempowski was sent to study abroad: he spent the years of the First World War studying at various universities in Germany and Switzerland. After this he did an internship in the new Polish Ministry of Foreign Affairs, where, following his father's political involvement, he was mainly dealing with the new republic's Eastern policies. Having left the Ministry in the early 1920s, Stempowski started working as a political press correspondent in Paris, Berlin and Geneva; his interest was mainly the functioning of the League of Nations. In 1926, he came back to Poland to support the military coup organized by Józef Piłsudski, and took a post in the prime minister's office. He was involved in the ongoing political conflicts for three successive years. In 1929, Stempowski distanced himself from the politics of the ruling camp and focused on writing and publishing book reviews, political articles and essays. He lived in Warsaw until September 1939 when he fled occupied Poland.[3]

Stempowski's Cultural and Political Mapping of Europe in the 1930s

Reading the articles published by Stempowski in the interwar period, one sees that he used to appear on the pages of the Polish liberal and socialist press not only as a quite prolific book reviewer, but occasionally also as a political analyst. What strikes the reader today in his political analyses written throughout the 1930s is the sombre tone of the conclusions he offered about the future. When, in May 1933, in a Warsaw weekly he published an analysis accounting for the recent Nazi takeover and anti-Semitic incidents in Germany, the editors of the weekly provided a note, in which they asserted that the author was 'one of the biggest experts on the political life in Germany', but stated that his 'final conclusions seem to us too pessimistic'.[4] A similar awareness of the collapse of the political system in Europe is clearly visible in his analyses of the international situation on the continent, published in early 1936, and in July 1939.[5] In those texts, Stempowski's reflections on Europe seem to be defined by two interconnected but distinct types of mapping. One is the division of Europe into 'West' and 'East'; the second was the idea that Europe is one political unity, existing not on a fixed geographical territory, but rather as a political space subject to changes, potential enlargements and shrinkages – as a comity of nations sharing certain ethical and economic concepts.

'Already in the eighteenth century Europe was too meagre a territory to contain multiple foundations of power or social regimes', Stempowski wrote in 1936. 'Today, the need for political unity in Europe is stronger than ever before. It is induced primarily by the economic life of this part of the world and its exchange mechanisms based on credit. Credit relations are only possible among nations whose citizens have the same idea about cheques.'[6] Analysing the political situation, Stempowski pictured the transformations in Soviet Russia and Germany as signs of these countries' 'secessions' from the European system. He interpreted these splits in externalist terms, seeing them as products of the mistakes made by European politicians, who due to their unimaginative politics radicalized and enforced the separation of those countries.

It was Russia that first broke away from Europe, 'reducing the potential for economic exchange by a sixth'. Aware of the rising political terror in Soviet Russia,[7] Stempowski hardly ever justified why he treated the Soviet Union as a non-European state; in numerous instances he underlined, however, that despite its tsarist despotism pre-revolutionary Russia was an integral part of the European political system. His perception of the German case was similar. Stempowski saw the spread of radical nationalism as an outcome of bad policies taken by the West European powers towards the Weimar Republic. In 1933, he wrote that the West European politicians favoured coping with German nationalists rather than social democrats. For this reason, he commented bitterly:

> the Hindenburg-Hitler-Hugenberg regime is not a pure German-bred product. Trying to understand it, we arrive at a conclusion that it is, at least partly, a shared creation of Europe, produced with the expectation that it would please Europe, or rather this part of European opinion that had the biggest influence on the shape of this sad world in which he happens to live.[8]

By 'this part of the European opinion', Stempowski clearly meant Western Europe, and more precisely Britain and France. Writing about the 'West' and the 'East' of the continent, Stempowski followed the mapping of Europe that started to take shape in Poland (and in other parts of Europe)[9] over the course of the eighteenth century, and which as a concept of the 'West' came into use in the Polish language in the early nineteenth century. In this period, Poles looked for the support of the West European empires in their political struggles against the empires that had partitioned the Polish-Lithuanian Commonwealth: Russia, Prussia and the Habsburg Empire.[10] It was against the backdrop of the political and economic differences occurring between these three East European empires and the Western 'great powers' that the division into West and East acquired primary importance for Poles in their thinking about Europe. These differences made them perceive Britain, and especially France, as the true Europe – the model part of the continent, the imagined touchstone for 'Europeanness', and a badly needed political ally. Much of political life in the interwar East European national republics created at Versailles rested on such a cultural and political Occidentalism. However, Stempowski already estimated bitterly in 1939 that France's political influences in Europe had receded to the Maginot line.[11]

Western Europe:
From 'Central Laboratory' to 'Central Museum'

The evolution of the image of Western Europe that we find in Stempowski's interwar writings could be roughly summed up as a story of initial idealization of the West leading to a gradual embitterment and a final disappointment with it. This is well expressed by the two metaphors that he started to use already in the essays from the 1930s: what once used to be 'the central laboratory of critical thought' with the advent of the Great War began to turn into 'the central museum'.[12]

At the basis of the image of the West as 'the central laboratory' lay Stempowski's firm conviction that for at least the last two centuries, since the Enlightenment, Western Europe had been 'the source of all the social, intellectual, artistic, and also technical innovations', the centre from which all the important ideas had come to Eastern Europe and which had shaped the ideals of those who yearned for change. In short, the greatness of the West, according to Stempowski, was to be seen in the political acumen displayed by the Western powers' governments, in the innovative political ideas born in the West, formulated in such a way that they gained universal appeal, and in their humanitarian principles. The combination of political power with innovative ideas went hand in hand with the cultural authority that the West had in the world, whereby its cultural resonance, for example, made artists from all over peregrinate to Paris. It was there, in 'the West' – and to be more precise, in the continental capital of the West, Paris – that 'things happened' and occurred for the first time. Thus, for East Europeans, the West stood – to use another metaphor coined by Stempowski – as the 'Land's End of the future'.

According to Stempowski, this idealized and potent image, deeply rooted in the culture of the Polish intelligentsia, started to shatter with the advent of the Great War. The war for continental hegemony that led to unprecedented bloodshed was a clear sign that the credit of trust given by East Europeans to the West European powers and its politics had been grossly overestimated. The many spheres of authority of the Western powers were thus seriously undermined. For young Stempowski, what was especially scandalous was the support given to the mass slaughter by many West European intellectuals. Praising the war, they supported modern nationalist politics with, as Stempowski called it, its 'morality of a besieged city' – an ideology of constant mobilization in a struggle for the survival of the nation, imagined to be encircled by enemies. Instead of being universalist, these intellectuals wanted to prove themselves to be socially useful to their national audiences.[13]

According to Stempowski, in 1917–1918 the governments of the Western powers, especially France and Britain, lacked the political sense or ability to devise the innovations for which they had been so admired in the East; this was manifest in their highly inconsistent policies towards revolutionized Russia, in their excessive burdening of postwar Germany with reparations and military restrictions, and in the fact that the nationalist principle (the main cause of the recently ended war) was unwittingly transmitted eastward in the design of postwar Europe projected in

Versailles. The disaster of the Great War, and its unsatisfactory global outcomes in the following years, caused the voters of the West to become increasingly disinterested in general European and, more widely, international matters. Instead of trying to maintain their alleged universalism and humanitarianism, they became more relativist and focused on the political issues solely concerning their own nation-states, ignoring the fact that events happening elsewhere would also eventually affect them. In 1936, Stempowski wrote thus in an accusatory tone: 'The western voters believe that the parliamentary system is best for them but they will just as easily concede that for the Germans the national-socialist system might be better, for the Italians – the fascist, and for the Russians – the soviet.'[14]

The failed politics of statesmen and the general lack of support for universalist political ideas, and especially humanitarianism, resulted in a slow degradation of the global position of West European artistic and cultural centres. Thus Stempowski commented on the declining attraction of Paris as the modernist capital of art. Describing the successive waves of artists who had left the city, he judged that Paris would soon become like Rome, a town of famous museums rather than a vibrant centre of living art.[15] He noted a similar process as well in the sphere of language – the cultural attraction of French had already, by the 1930s, seemed to Stempowski to be steadily declining.

Did, then, all these multiple aspects of the general disappointment with the West lead to a revision of the idealized image of the West in the texts of Stempowski? Only to some extent – even if he recognized that East European Occidentalism had been grossly exaggerated and devoid of realism, Stempowski never ceased to maintain that for a long period of time Western Europe had been the political and cultural centre of the world, promoting many important innovations. Moreover, in opposition to the East European empires, which were seen as expansive and deriving their power from conquest, the power of 'the West' seemed to rely largely on respect and wealth – the imperialist and colonial aspect of their contemporary authority was largely ignored and underplayed. For Stempowski, what really used to be once 'the central laboratory' was in the process of slowly being degraded into 'the central museum' – a place where liberal-conservative ideals were kept for internal use, but no new universal ideas produced, promoted or consistently supported abroad; a place visited with interest by the people coming from new centres of political power and cultural influence, based on new, not necessarily European traditions, for example from 'totalist' Soviet Moscow.

Eastern Europe: From a Province to 'Intermarium'

In Stempowski's writings we can observe a different evolution in his thinking about the East of Europe. In the 1920s and the early 1930s, he seemed to treat this region rather dismissively as a poor province of Western Europe, lagging behind the Western societies, to a large extent deprived of its multiple achievements. The idealized picture of the West, sustained by its political, cultural and scientific achievements, had a strong influence on the perception of one's own native lands. In a particularly vivid fragment of an essay from 1933, Stempowski went as far as to describe his part of Europe as a land of mental clichés, 'cultural borderlands', where everything had been automatically imported from the centres in the West:

> A huge part of our most common judgements, tastes and gestures was born in the flame of the struggle for new ways of living, understanding and feeling. However, in this fight [for novelty] we took no part. We received ready-made formulas and recipes, which we accepted without discussion, but nor with any great conviction. This is the reason why in our lands we observe this strange simultaneous coexistence of most different tastes and styles: gothic and renaissance, classical and romantic, academic and modernist, this is why we have here such a peculiar mixture of seemingly contradictory opinions. The opinions are devoid of the force of conviction, because they are detached from their original social functions.[16]

While in the West, ideas were formed and made clear in social and political conflict, here, in the Eastern lands, they were often transmitted unwittingly and superficially; their realizations – based on the politicians' neglect of a different social background – often seemed clumsy and crude, close to caricature.

In this vein Stempowski perceived and opposed the spread of nationalism in the East European republics created in Versailles. He considered the Eastern territories to be particularly unfit for the realization of the nation-state principle – in this part of Europe the ethnic borders were always in a state of flux, and thus the application of the nationalist principle would lead unavoidably to damaging conflicts; this would be the case with the new Polish Republic where ethnic minorities equalled 30 per cent. Together with liberals and socialists from the circle of his father, Stempowski was in opposition to the political camp of Polish National Democracy, its modern vision of a homogenous nation-state and anti-Semitism. In a text from 1942 he described manifestations of nationalist sentiments observed at interwar Polish universities as something 'in a very bad taste, vulgar, good only for uncouth parvenus'.[17] This political antagonism was so strong that in 1926 Stempowski and his circle even supported the military coup organized by Józef Piłsudski. However, the logic of Piłsudski's authoritarian regime pushed the ruling camp of military men into embracing increasingly centralist and nationalistic politics. Most critical of the development of the political situation in Poland, as well as in other increasingly authoritarian Central and East European countries, Stempowski already in 1936 wrote about the political split in Europe, between its liberal-conservative Western part and the 'totalist' East (lands from Germany to the Soviet Union), predicting that most probably it would take a couple of decades to bring the two parts back together.[18]

After 1936, as Stempowski's pessimism about the future of Europe grew, a considerable change could be observed in the way he described the lands of Eastern Europe. The very same cultural traits that once used to be for him pejorative signs of the provinciality of Eastern Europe, of it being a 'borderland' distant from political and cultural centres, now seemed to gain value.

This became even clearer during and after the Second World War. Writing his essays in exile in Switzerland, already in the early 1940s, Stempowski was aware of the irreversible social disasters, mass murders, ethnic cleansing, and forced deportations happening in Eastern Europe. The provinces of Eastern Europe started to appear in his texts as the lost ideal of 'the Dniester Valley' or 'Intermarium' [Międzymorze]: the vast territory of unstable borders (once Polish or Ottoman, Habsburg or Russian) lying in between the three seas – the Black Sea, the Adriatic and the Baltic. In 1942, in one of his autobiographical essays, Stempowski recalled these lands as 'one great chessboard of peoples, full of islands, enclaves and the strangest combinations of mixed population'.[19] East European societies were amalgams of different social groups of various nationalities, speaking different languages (and dialects), having different religions, communities and pasts, and also representing various hierarchies of values and professions. According to Stempowski, the term 'nationality' before the first decades of the twentieth century used to have another meaning in Eastern Europe. Nationality was not treated so much as a sort of 'racial *fatum*, inherited by each newborn baby', but as a thing subject to change, sometimes even a question of personal choice. Various processes of interpenetration between Poles, Jews, Russians, Ukrainians, Germans, and so on, took place, making the ethnic picture more and more complex:

> All the different nationalities and languages, with their multiple variations, were to some extent fluid. Sons of Poles sometimes became Ukrainians, sons of Germans and Frenchmen – Poles. In Odessa incredible things used to happen: Greeks came to be Russians, Poles were seen to enter *Soiuz russkogo naroda* [the Union of the Russian People]. Even stranger combinations were created out of mixed marriages. My father used to say: If a Polish man marries a Russian woman, their children will be Ukrainians or Lithuanians.[20]

Stempowski stressed the novelty and foreignness of aggressive nationalistic ideologies seeking to simplify or even erase all the historical complexities existing in Eastern Europe.

This new image of the lost 'Intermarium', the land rich with cultural and historical complexities, can be viewed as a cultural transposition of an earlier federalist concept advanced by Polish socialists, with whom Stempowski's circle was associated. During the First World War they projected the creation of a broader East European federacy, unifying most of the lands between the Adriatic, the Baltic and the Black Sea. The borders of member states of the federacy would roughly cover the ethnic divisions in the region, but they would not seek to become homogeneous states of 'one nation, one religion, one language', as was explicit in the policy of National Democracy. This federal project, often named *idea jagiellónska* (the Jagiellonian idea) referred to the Polish-Lithuanian Commonwealth that existed from the sixteenth century until the state's partition in the eighteenth, and which was based on the earlier Jogaila dynastical union between Poland and Lithuania. Unsurprisingly, the idea did not meet with much enthusiasm from the side of the other national movements that had found themselves included in Piłsudski's project, especially the Lithuanians. The legacy of the old Polish-Lithuanian Republic, with Polish imperial traditions inherent in it, was too evident. Still, it had a considerable resonance in the politics of the region, until the end of the Polish-Soviet War in 1920–1921, and its final discredit in the treaty signed in Riga, in which Poles divided with the Soviets the lands of Ukraine and Belarus, abandoning their military allies from Ukraine and Belarus, the two most important member nations of the projected federation.

Much later, Stempowski wrote sceptically about the Polish political federalist ideas advanced by Polish socialists in the interwar period: he compared them to a magical formula that helped to sweep away all the true difficulties related to the presence of so many Ukrainians, Belarusians and Lithuanians in the eastern parts of the Polish Republic. 'As we know, magical formulas work only when uttered precisely, without any mistake in pronunciation of the words, without even a single letter skipped. And nobody remembered the text well, nobody was even aware of its length.'[21] To speak about federalism was not enough – one would also need to have an idea of how to make it possible and acceptable for the different sides, and one would need to be ready for compromises and their consequences.

The somewhat nostalgic image of 'Intermarium', the land of cultural and historical diversity destroyed by the wave of nationalisms, the Nazi and Soviet occupations and population transfers, led to a reevaluation of the eastern part of the continent in Stempowski's reflection on Europe. Yet it did not mean that he stopped considering it a political periphery. In his opinion, it was precisely because of its provinciality, its dependency on foreign political centres, and the incapacity to change one's own situation or to cooperate politically, that the region of 'Intermarium' was so helpless and politically ineffective. In 1947, soon after the war, in one of his articles Stempowski gave a brief account of the political inability of interwar East-Central Europe – a term appearing only rarely in Stempowski's essays that he probably used to differentiate the region of the interwar republics from the new, communist 'Eastern Europe' of the Cold War:

> Its population was bigger than a hundred million, it was thus theoretically in the same category as the population of the United States, the Soviet Union and the British Commonwealth. However, this population was very poor, divided into many sovereign backwaters, lacking political skill and devoid of any sense of solidarity. This is why it was first drawn into war, against its own will and its interests, why it suffered the greatest victims, and why, eventually, muted like a flock of sheep, it became the object of trade between the great powers.[22]

Writing about Europe after the Second World War

Stempowski's opinions on Europe did not change much in the postwar period. The main theme and political diagnosis remained the same. Residing in exile in Switzerland, and banned from publishing in Poland, with the exception of one small cycle of essays in French,[23] Stempowski wrote almost all of his works for *Kultura*.

We can roughly divide his postwar texts on Europe into two groups. The first group would be the multiple travel journals, mainly from his many trips to postwar Germany – for example from a journey through Western occupation zones made as early as 1945[24] – but also from Austria, Italy and the Netherlands. In his early postwar travelogues Stempowski concentrated on picturing the depth of the crisis of Western Europe, divided by multiple borders and trade barriers, unsure about its future and afraid of the Soviets, having to confront its new role as a field of contest between the two superpowers. After 1951, the tone of the travelogues changed slightly. Noticing the quick tempo of changes, Stempowski wrote about the economic and political reconstruction of Western Europe, and especially West Germany. Still, despite promising political processes like the first steps toward European integration, or the economic boom, Stempowski's perception of postwar Europe did not change: it was a politically truncated land, divided by the iron curtain and strongly dependent on political decisions made elsewhere.[25]

The second group of his postwar works on Europe comprises essays in which, by applying elaborate new metaphors and literary riddles, Stempowski offered several literary accounts of the recent history of Eastern and Western Europe's political degradation. In some of them he referred to classical analogies, comparing for example the two world wars to the Peloponnesian War, and rereading the work of Thucydides in this modern context.[26] In others, instead of the metaphor of 'central museum', he started to invent new metaphors of European degradation. What was new in them was the fact that Stempowski started to refer to prewar Eastern Europe as a point of reference for Western Europe. In 1954, for example, he published the essay entitled 'Rubis d'Orient', in which provocatively and ironically he wrote that Western Europe found itself in a situation similar to Romania. With a certain *Schadenfreude* Stempowski suggested that, from now on, Western Europe, too, would need to adapt to foreign invasions, such as had been experienced by the Romanian people for many centuries.[27] Using such comparison as a literary paradox, Stempowski switched the usual source and target domain of comparisons made between Western and Eastern Europe.

I will present in this section only two major issues among the multiple topics present in Stempowski's postwar works: one aspect of his observations noted in the travel journals, namely the image of the United States and the Americans as Europe's 'other', and one literary metaphor used by him in his essays.

In his interwar political texts, Stempowski only occasionally referred to the United States, writing about the great crisis or their inflexible war debt policies towards Europe. Even if he wrote then about Northern America as being the most industrialized area in the world, he seems to have treated it still as a wealthy but distant periphery of the European 'West'.[28] This changed during the Second World War. In his travelogue from Germany and Austria in 1945, the Americans suddenly appear as representatives of a foreign power, depicted with much disdain as the new governors of Western Europe. Stempowski criticizes the U.S. policies in the occupied zones of Germany, writing about the ignorance of American the military (visible in their way of editing propaganda press for Germans) and their growing indifference to the multiple problems encountered by Europeans – shown especially towards the hundreds of thousands of displaced persons who had been trying to avoid deportation to the Soviet-dominated regimes.[29]

In his early travelogues from Germany, Stempowski underlined many times that the Americans, whose role was now to decide on the crucial issues for Europe, would treat Western Europe as a strategic zone of influence, solving its problems by use of simple pragmatic means, often going against old traditions of the continent, and of its particular regions. In this vein, he viewed the restrictive border policy in postwar Western Europe as an example of a 'non-European' Anglo-Saxon tradition of designating arbitrary frontiers between subject countries. According to Stempowski, the Americans wanted to administer 'Europe' as a whole, ignoring and wiping away the diversity of its particular regions. He accused them as well of a 'barbarous' lack of the sense of history (which they were supposed to share with Nazi Germans and the Soviets), particularly manifest in their decision to bomb historical districts of German cities.

This negative and rather resentful image of the Americans (and along with them the suddenly 'un-European' British) was to a large extent a reaction to the agreements made by the three powers in Yalta, constituting for Stempowski, as for most Poles at that time, a forced partition of the continent by the two new emergent world powers. His anti-Americanism, thus, had slightly different origins and different intellectual consequences from those manifested in those years by many West European intellectuals.[30] The popularity of communism among his West European counterparts, often leading to marginalization of non-communist exiles, was therefore interpreted by Stempowski, an exile himself, to be yet one more sign of European provincialization: a degradation of a sense of political reality, and the orientation of a periphery towards distant and idealized political centres (like Moscow or Beijing).

The theme of Europe, with its Western part becoming a 'museum' instead of a 'central laboratory', returns frequently in the postwar essays written by Stempowski and in the many different literary figures used by him, but here I will refer to only one particularly vivid and radical literary metaphor he used in a late essay from 1964 ('Esej berdyczowski').

In this text Stempowski recalled his juvenile voyage to Berdichev made with his father in 1909. Berdichev was a town in the Ukraine, and in the old Polish tradition and proverbs, the name appeared as a synonym for a deep provincial centre, in the middle of nowhere. Stempowski described the peaceful, slow life of Berdichev, its merchants and other inhabitants, with their peculiar old-fashioned habits, their delayed and somewhat fuzzy understanding of events happening far away, and their lack of political orientation and realism. He stressed that the Berdichev that he had seen then, with its Polish-Jewish-Ukrainian population and diverse ways of living, had practically ceased to exist. The image of Berdichev, as it was in 1909, was presented by Stempowski as a model for the situation of the whole of Europe:

> Only thirty-five years later, when on a terrace of a Genevan café I read the first detailed report from the conference in Yalta, I suddenly saw before my eyes the local gathering of noblemen at the front of Schafnagel's shop in Berdichev. In the frame of the American-Russian peace treaty, greatly diminished territorially, Europe had been degraded to the role of province. Busy with their prosperity, like the Berdichev Sarmatians used to be with their grain-selling and bills of exchange, the Europeans can do nothing now that could change the order of things arranged at Yalta. Some look at this situation with disbelief, or even indignation. The wiser advice is not to become exasperated; to withstand it patiently, and wait. Even the conversations of the Europeans have started to resemble the talks that I once had heard in Berdichev. News from the places where the decisions are made arrives belatedly, in distorted versions, not unlike the stories of Hejbowicz from his travels to Petersburg.[31]

The parallel drawn between the East European provincial town, its twentieth-century history, and Western Europe with its political degradation, served in the essay as a sort of memento and evoked, once more, the crucial issues for Stempowski of political dependency, the relation between a centre and a province, and finally the cultural and political consequences of being a periphery. We can see in this metaphor an interesting mixture of political analysis, the bitter resentment of an East Central European exile towards Western Europe, and finally a disguised catastrophist image of the possible future of Europe.

Concluding Remarks

I would like to conclude this chapter only by briefly pointing to three groups of questions that, I hope, my reconstruction of Stempowski's changing images of Europe has made more visible, as well as demanding a further critical and historical reflection. The first is a general historical problem of political power as the ability to influence a course of events, and of the consequences – political, intellectual or cultural – of losing this power, analysed in the case of twentieth-century Europe. In Stempowski's writings, we can see how this problem was approached by a Polish liberal who rejected both modern nationalism and communism. His East Central European perspective strengthened the perception of Europe as a complex system of political interdependencies that could contribute to the spread of civil liberties and economic cooperation, or of political terror and ambitions of conquest. At the same time, this perspective also had its limitations. First of all, it was undoubtedly Eurocentric – even if Stempowski strongly criticized imperial tendencies displayed by the political centres existing in Eastern Europe, he virtually ignored the colonial side of the West European empires.

The second issue leads us to the way centres and provinces are represented in Stempowski's writings. It seems to me that we encounter in his texts an interesting and rather unresolved tension between a strong conviction that only a powerful centre can lead a successful, inventive and clear-sighted politics (while a province is almost always politically impotent and unskilled, even if culturally rich and diverse) and, on the other hand, a persistent rejection of centralist ideologies such as modern nationalism.

The final historical remark addresses the issue of the changing attitudes of the Polish intelligentsia towards Western Europe, and Europe in general. The works by Stempowski can be read as an example of a cultural change in the way Polish intellectuals related Eastern Europe to Western Europe. For many of them, it was the West of Europe that provided most of the concepts and images to speak about, and to understand the East. It seems that in Stempowski's texts we encounter an example of an interesting change, a case of inversion and a reinvention of the relation between the two regions of Europe. Due to tragic historical circumstances, old Eastern Europe became in his writings an ironic and bitter imaginary model for the whole of Europe and its future. At the same time, the images and understanding of Eastern Europe and its past became in his texts more refined, reformulated in such a way that they were no longer defined only by Eastern Europe's deprivation of the 'normality' or 'modernity' existing in the West.

Notes

1. For an account of the political influence of *Kultura* in postwar international relations in Eastern Europe, see: T. Snyder, *The Reconstruction of Nations. Poland, Ukraine, Lithuania, Belarus, 1569–1999* (New Haven and London, 2003), 217–31; for a history of the political ideas advanced by *Kultura*, see the monograph written by J. Korek, *Paradoksy paryskiej 'Kultury'. Style i tradycje myślenia politycznego* (Lublin, 2000).
2. J. Stempowski, 'Pielgrzym' [Pilgrim] in J. Stempowski, *Od Berdyczowa do Lafitów* (Wołowiec, 2001), 29–52.
3. For more information on Stempowski's biography, consult A.S. Kowalczyk, *Nieśpieszny przechodzień i paradoksy: rzecz o Jerzym Stempowskim* (Wrocław, 1997).
4. Orosius (J. Stempowski), 'Starając się zrozumieć … Hitler i Europa' (Trying to understand … Hitler and Europe), *Epoka*, 19 (1933), 3. All the quotes from Stempowski's texts given in the chapter are my translations, except when noted.
5. J. Stempowski, 'Zachód w 1935', *Wiadomości Literackie* 8 (1936), 3; J. Stempowski, 'Europa w 1938–1939', in J. Stempowski, *Od Berdyczowa do Rzymu* (Paris, 1971), 71–89.
6. Stempowski, 'Zachód w 1935', 3, translated by B. Stefańska and Ł. Mikołajewski.
7. A lot of information on the perception of the Soviet Union in the political and social circle of Jerzy Stempowski can be found in the monograph on Henryk Józewski, the governor of Polish Volhynia from 1926–1938: T. Snyder, *Sketches From a Secret War. A Polish Artist's Mission to Liberate Soviet Ukraine* (New Haven, Conn. and London, 2006).
8. Orosius, 'Starając się zrozumieć … Hitler i Europa', 6.
9. L. Wolff, *Inventing Eastern Europe. The Map of Civilization on the Mind of the Enlightenment* (Stanford, 1994).

10. J. Jedlicki, 'Les Mirages de l'Occident', in Ch. Delsol, M. Masłowski and J. Nowicki, *Mythes et symboles politiques en Europe centrale* (Paris, 2002), 613–14.
11. Stempowski, 'Europa w 1938–1939', 71.
12. Stempowski, 'Zachód w 1935', 8. Quotes in the paragraph below are also taken from this article.
13. See his review of E.M. Remarque's *All Quiet on the Western Front*, 'Żołnierz niemiecki jako moralista' [German Soldier as a Moralist], printed in 1929 in *Wiadomości Literackie*, and reprinted in J. Stempowski, *Szkice literackie* (Warsaw, 2001), vol. 1, 35.
14. Stempowski, 'Zachód w 1935', 8.
15. Ibid.
16. 'Znaczna część najbardziej przyjętych u nas ocen, gustów i gestów wyszła z ognia walki o nowe sposoby życia, rozumienia, odczuwania. W walkach tych nie braliśmy jednak żadnego udziału. Otrzymaliśmy gotowe formuły i recepty, które przejęliśmy bez dyskusji, ale i bez wielkiego przekonania. Stąd pochodzi u nas dziwne współżycie równocześnie różnych gustów i stylów, gotyckich i renesansowych, klasycznych i romantycznych, akademickich i modernistycznych, dziwne pomieszanie na pozór wykluczających się nawzajem opinii. Opiniom tym brak siły przekonania. Są one oderwane od swych pierwotnych funkcji społecznych.'; J. Stempowski, 'Sceptycyzm w twórczości Wacława Berenta' [Skepticism in the works of Wacław Berent], Stempowski, *Szkice literackie*, vol. 1, 205.
17. J. Stempowski, 'W dolinie Dniestru' [In the Dniester Valley], in J. Stempowski, *W dolinie Dniestru. Listy o Ukrainie* (Warsaw, 1993), 16.
18. Stempowski, 'Zachód w 1935', 8.
19. Stempowski, 'W dolinie Dniestru. Listy o Ukrainie', 10.
20. 'Wszystkie te odcienie narodowości i języków znajdowały się nadto w stanie częściowo płynnym. Synowie Polaków stawali się nieraz Ukraińcami, synowie Niemców i Francuzów – Polakami. W Odessie działy się rzeczy niezwykłe: Grecy stawali się Rosjanami, widziano Polaków wstępujących do Sojuza Russkawo Naroda. Jeszcze dziwniejsze kombinacje powstawały z małżeństw mieszanych. – Jeśli Polak żeni się z Rosjanką – mawiał mój ojciec – dzieci ich są zwykle Ukraińcami lub Litwinami.' Stempowski, *W dolinie Dniestru. Listy o Ukrainie*, 11.
21. 'Moi rówieśnicy, ilekroć dochodzili do wniosku, że na naszych kresach źle się dzieje, zaczynali mówić o idei jagiellońskiej. Była to magiczna formuła pozwalająca pokonać wszystkie trudności wynikające z obecności na obszarze Rzplitej tylu Ukraińców, Białorusinów i Litwinów. Formuły magiczne, działają jednak, jak wiadomo, tylko wówczas, gdy wymawiane są dokładnie, bez przeinaczenia jednego słowa, bez opuszczenia jednej litery. Nikt zaś nie pamiętał dobrze jej tekstu, ani nie zdawał sobie nawet sprawy z jego rozciągłości.' P. Hostowiec (J. Stempowski), 'Idea jagiellońska', *Kultura* 11 (1956), 34. On this see also P. Hostowiec (J. Stempowski), 'Notatnik nieśpiesznego przechodnia' [Notes of an Unhurried Wanderer], *Kultura* 7–8 (1962), 29–36. Stempowski wrote there: 'Jagiellonian words have magical power only to those who pronounce them: others remain unimpressed. Already since the times of Khmelnytsky, the Ukrainians and the Belarusians have associated them only with serfdom.' [Jagiellońskie słówka mają bowiem siłę magiczną tylko dla tych, którzy je wymawiają: na innych nie robią wrażenia. Dla Ukraińców i Białorusinów, już od czasów Chmielnickiego, jagiellończyzna kojarzyła się tylko z pańszczyzną.]
22. 'Ludność jej przekraczała sto milionów, znajdowała się więc zatem w tej samej kategorii co ludność Stanów Zjednoczonych, Unii Sowieckiej i Commonwealth Brytyjskiego. Ludność ta była jednak bardzo uboga, podzielona na suwerenne zaścianki, politycznie niewyszkolona i pozbawiona jakiegokolwiek poczucia solidarności. Dlatego też – wbrew jej woli i interesom – została wciągnięta w wojnę, poniosła najcięższe ofiary i, pozbawiona głosu, stała się, niby stado owiec, przedmiotem handlu między wielkimi mocarstwami.' P. Hostowiec (J. Stempowski.), 'Z powodu sytuacji demograficznej Francji', *Kultura* 2–3 (1947), 187.
23. G. Stempowski, *La terre bernoise* (Geneva, 1954).
24. P. Hostowiec (J. Stempowski), *Dziennik podróży do Austrii i Niemiec* (Rome, 1946). The text was published also in an Italian translation: P. Hostowiec (J. Stempowski), *Il Calvario continua … Diario di un viaggio in Austria e Germania*, trans. C. Verdiani (Rome, 1947).

25. The full anthology of Stempowski's travelogues is Stempowski, *Od Berdyczowa do Lafitów*.

26. P. Hostowiec (J. Stempowski), 'Czytając Tukidydesa', *Kultura* 5 (1957), 7–18, reprinted in J. Stempowski, *Eseje dla Kassandry* (Gdańsk, 2005).

27. P. Hostowiec (J. Stempowski), 'Rubis d'Orient', *Kultura* 5 (1954), 3–13, reprinted in Stempowski, *Eseje dla Kassandry*, 167–76. For the French translation, see J. Stempowski, *Essais pour Cassandre*, trans. K. Bourneuf and A. Ciesielska (Paris, 1991).

28. However, in the previous years we can find in his texts minor references to the books on America and its relation to Europe, written in the period of the First World War by the anti-fascist Italian historian Guglielmo Ferrero; J. Grahit (J. Stempowski), 'Guglielmo Ferrero', *Nowa Polska* 6 (1942), 482–87.

29. In 1945 Stempowski learned about two cases of handing over the East European political refugees to the communists: the actions in the refugee camps in Spittal and Kempten. In those camps several thousand Slovenian and Ukrainian refugees, who had tried to escape from the new Soviet zone of power, were 'returned' by the Allies to the communist authorities and then executed. About the events in 1945 in Spittal, see: J. Corsellis; M. Ferrar, *Slovenia 1945. Memories of Death and Survival after World War II* (London and New York, 2006); about Kempten: Y. Boshyk, 'Repatriation and Resistance: Ukrainian Refugees and Displaced Persons in Occupied Germany and Austria, 1945–1948', in A.C. Bramwell (ed.), *Refugees in the Age of Total War* (Oxford, 1988), 198–218.

30. On this, see the chapter on the French intellectuals' anti-Americanism in T. Judt, *Past Imperfect. French Intellectuals, 1944–1956* (Berkeley, 1992).

31. 'Dopiero w 35 lat później, gdy na tarasie genewskiej kawiarni przeczytałem pierwszą obszerniejszą relację z konferencji jałtańskiej, zgromadzenie szlachciców przed sklepem Szafnagla stanęło mi przed oczami jak żywe. W ramach amerykańsko-rosyjskiego pokoju okrojona Europa zeszła do rzędu prowincji. Zajęci swą prosperity, jak berdyczowscy Sarmaci sprzedażą zboża i płatnością weksli, Europejczycy nie mogą dokonać niczego, co by mogło zmienić ustalony w Jałcie porządek rzeczy. Niektórzy patrzą z niedowierzaniem lub nawet wzburzeniem na nową sytuację. Mądrzejsi radzą nie szarpać się, znosić, czekać. Nawet rozmowy Europejczyków zbliżyły się do berdyczowskich wzorów. Wiadomości z miejsc, gdzie zapadają decyzje, przychodzą w późnych i zniekształconych wersjach, podobnych do relacji Hejbowicza z podróży do Petersburga.', Stempowski, *Od Berdyczowa do Lafitów*, 24–25.

Part III

MAKING SENSE OF THE PRESENT

During the first half of the twentieth century, Europe experienced two world wars, both begun on the Continent, the Great Depression, the Holocaust, and the onset of the Cold War. Despite such catastrophic events, pride in a specifically European civilization remained remarkably resilient, reemerging quickly in representations and personifications of the continent. As Michael Wintle's investigation of cartoons, paintings, monuments and statues reveals (Chapter 10), 'Europe' throughout the period between 1917 and 1957 was normally represented as a self-confident, richly decorated female figure, comparable to incarnations of liberty and justice, or 'Europa' in the legend of the 'Rape of Europa', as a young woman is carried off by a bull towards an uncertain but promising and, possibly, heroic future. In the interwar era, many such depictions rested on a sense of cultural and, even, racial superiority, reinforced by the continuing existence of the world empires of Britain, France, Belgium, the Netherlands, Portugal and Spain. This confidence was replaced by despondency in the late 1940s and 1950s as decolonization took place, but it was partially eclipsed by new hopes for Europe associated with economic recovery and consumerism. Some tropes, such as the defence of the continent against communism in the East, were more or less continuous, established in the 1920s and '30s, used by the National Socialist regime in its vision of a 'New Order' for Europe during the Second World War, and kept in place during the Cold War. Eurocentrism can thus be understood as a response to enduring sets of conditions, which continued to delimit and define the continent in the early twentieth century. It can also be seen as an anthropologically inescapable set of biases and self-centred points of view. Most of all, however, it bore witness, perhaps, to the restless sense of experimentation and criticism which had been visible in European universities, public spheres, economies and states since at least the eighteenth century. Notwithstanding the disasters of the first half of the twentieth century, many Europeans retained a belief in a perpetual present.

Contemporaries' confidence in Europe seemed to be embodied in the new cultural organizations of the 1920s and 1930s. Europe remained the main concern of the League of Nations. Despite its international role, the League was largely designed to safeguard the treaties of Versailles and Paris in 1919–20. Its principal cultural organization, the Institut de Coopération Intellectuelle (IICI), was even more pronouncedly Eurocentric, mounting projects such as 'The Future of the European Spirit' (1933) and 'Towards a New Humanism' (1936), which focused almost exclusively on the continent. Although it included members from outside Europe, most of its membership consisted of prominent continental intellectuals such as Johan Huizinga and Paul Valéry. The main impulse for a cultural branch of the League of Nations came from France, initiated by Léon Bourgeois, the President of the French Senate, who also became the President of the League itself in 1920. The International Institute of Intellectual Cooperation was based in Paris, like its successor UNESCO in the postwar period, and its first director was Julien Luchaire, the French General Inspector of Public Education. Notwithstanding the diversity of views represented within its membership, the premises of the IICI remained relatively uncontroversial; namely, that Europe was in need, above all, of cultural and moral regeneration and that its existing national cultures could be reconciled with a wider European civilization promoted by France, as the birthplace of a universal European culture and of human rights. The terms 'universal' and 'European culture' were generally equated. As the first Congress of Popular Arts organized by the IICI in Prague in 1928 evinced, even the Romantic notion of a 'Volksgeist' was acceptable, combined with modern comparative human and social sciences. As Annamaria Ducci shows (Chapter 11), the emphasis of the various projects, including those of the Office International des Musées, was on communication rather than exclusivity and conservation, and on national diversity within an overarching European culture. Consciousness of a common European culture was seen by most intellectuals to be a prerequisite of political cooperation and peaceful coexistence.

The unwillingness of many intellectuals to repudiate their European inheritance was illustrated by Johan Huizinga, who was Rector of the University of Leiden and the most famous historian in the Netherlands.[1] As a member of the International Institute of Intellectual Cooperation from 1935 onwards, which existed under the auspices of the League of Nations and whose members became virtual intellectual ambassadors for their countries, he argued – in line with the majority of his counterparts – for the regeneration of a specifically 'European spirit' and a reaffirmation of morality as preconditions of political cooperation. Like his fellow IICI member Julien Benda, with whom he had entered into a public dispute in 1933, Huizinga denied that intellectuals should assume a political role – an opinion which he abandoned only after the German invasion of the Netherlands in 1940. He disagreed with Benda, as Anne-Isabelle Richard demonstrates (Chapter 12), that nationalism and patriotism were the same thing and that nations had to give up powers to European organizations. What was needed in Europe, he contended, was not political and economic cooperation at the expense of nation-states, since a patriotic attachment to one's own country was natural and usually benign, but the development of international law and mutually accepted legal limitations on the excesses of aggressive, extreme and self-interested governments. The political threats – fascism, communism, technocracy, moral decline, 'heroism' – faced by a European spirit would soon disappear, making the radical nationalism of 1933 appear 'absurd'. Overall, Huizinga's position was similar to that of the Dutch government, which had been protected by neutrality from the worst effects of the First World War and which continued to champion free trade, independent states, international law, and the League of Nations. After the Second World War had proved these defences ineffective against the predations of an extreme and belligerent neighbour, Huizinga came to favour political federation, admitting the failure of his earlier call for moral regeneration: his conversion was moderate, however, predicated on the voluntary and pragmatic cooperation of independent states for limited ends.[2] The Dutch historian showed how cultural criticism, which characterized *In the Shadows of Tomorrow* (1935), could serve as a moderate affirmation of the status quo, on the one hand, and could be reconciled with political and economic coordination and reform in Europe, on the other.

The German intellectual and novelist Heinrich Mann was more sceptical than Huizinga, preferring a power-political rapprochement between Germany and France to the voluntary constraints of international law, but he was also more utopian, proclaiming the idea of a united, democratic Europe as the only means to prevent a future war. Ernest Schonfield (Chapter 13) uses Mann's political essays and speeches of the Weimar Republic, most of which have never been translated before into English, to demonstrate that the author had already provided a utopian fictional model of grass-roots European democracy as early as 1909, in his novel *Die kleine Stadt* (The Small Town).[3] The focus of Mann's political campaign throughout the 1920s and early 1930s, however, was his attempt to promote Franco-German understanding, which he regarded as the precondition for a united Europe. Thus, during the crisis of 1923 in which French troops occupied the Ruhr, Mann wrote a series of essays attacking nationalist sentiment and arguing that the ones who had the most to gain from a rise in nationalism were French and German industrialists and weapons manufacturers. The essays conclude with an open letter to Stresemann, urging him to drop the policy of passive resistance and to come to an agreement with Poincaré. In this letter, Mann describes economic unity between France and Germany as the only way for Europe to maintain its independence against the threat of other rising global powers. In the late twenties, Mann gave numerous speeches in France and Germany promoting peaceful economic cooperation between the two nations, based on their close historical links and shared cultural references. The chapter concludes with an analysis of Mann's last great essay of the Weimar Republic, 'Das Bekenntnis zum Übernationalen' (Confession of Supranationalism) (1932), in which he asserts that the threat of war can only be averted by supranational proceedings designed to create a united Europe.

Unlike his diagnosis of Europe's condition, Mann's supranational prognoses were not widely shared. The French historian Lucien Febvre stood in the same progressive tradition as Mann but reached very different conclusions.[4] 'Is Europe an out-of-date concept or is it a necessity for the progress of the world?' asked the founder of the Annales school. Far from being a circumstantial question, Febvre actually posed the problem of the identity and the destiny of Europe in such terms while presenting his history course at the Collège de France for the academic year 1944/45, which started a few days after the liberation of Paris by the Allies. The twenty-five lectures, which were related to a project already hatched in 1925, resembled an ethics course more than a history one. In fact, the course was not – nor did Febvre want it to be – an ordered, positive history of Europe; on the contrary, his plan was meant to be something much more ambitious, dealing with the concept of Europe as such, purging it of the myths and falsifications which, he argued, had been the main cause of Europe's destruction. In order to do so, suggests Vittorio Dini (Chapter 14), Febvre envisaged examining the idea of Europe through the lens of those categories which, up until that point, had directed him in his research and which made up his conceptual framework of 'civilization'. Giving his lectures while the old continent was still struggling for its freedom, Febvre could clearly see that the concept of Europe called to mind a dramatically defeated ideal rather than a civilization of free men belonging to the same democratic and Enlightenment tradition of Western culture. What the war had demolished needed to be rebuilt; it was imperative to restore the notion of Europe as the 'patria' of freedom. Never had so many words been spent on the unity of Europe, Febvre remarked bitterly, as by the Nazis, whose voices were the least European. To be itself, Europe had to be the land of free nations on the model of France, which epitomized the unity of the Mediterranean and Northern elements, blending them together to form the essence of Europe's cultural unity. As for the continent's political unity, argued Febvre, this was but a delusion and a delirium behind which was concealed the folly of universal dominance. Febvre ardently believed that, in order to retain its moral unity, Europe had to be politically divided, preserving the natural building blocks of the nation-states. Febvre's pioneering course was highly controversial at the time – and, in a way, is even more so now. The most striking element is that Febvre rejected the need to unite Europe politically and to maintain the cultural independence of its nations. The French historian feared, as an ardent European, that the aim of political unity risked undermining Europe's true essence as the 'land' of freedom. Europe's 'essentially' divided political identity was a necessary support of an existing European 'civilization'. As a consequence, Febvre stood in opposition to the various schemes put forward by European federalists.

Notes

1. C. Strupp, *Johan Huizinga. Geschichtswissenschaft als Kulturgeschichte* (Göttingen, 2000).
2. For a comparison with government – and other – thinking, see R.T. Griffiths (ed.), *The Netherlands and the Integration of Europe* (Amsterdam, 1990), and W. Mallinson, *From Neutrality to Commitment: Dutch Foreign Policy, NATO and European Integration* (London, 2010).

3. P. Gay, *Weimar Culture* (London, 1968); H. Koopmann, *Thomas Mann – Heinrich Mann. Die ungleichen Brüder* (Munich, 2005); R. Wittig, *Die Versuchung der Macht. Essayistik und Publizistik Heinrich Manns im französischen Exil* (Berne, 1976); D. Gross, 'Heinrich Mann and the Politics of Reaction', *Journal of Contemporary European History* 8 (1973), 125–45.

4. A. Burguière, *The Annales School: An Intellectual History* (Ithaca, 2009); P. Burke, *The French Historical Revolution: The Annales School, 1929–1989* (Stanford, 1990).

Chapter 10

VISUALIZING EUROPE FROM 1900 TO THE 1950s

Identity on the Move

>✂

Michael Wintle

In studying the history of the idea of Europe, it rapidly becomes apparent that people's ideas about what Europe should or does consist of have changed over time, and indeed are still changing. It is possible to provide a legal definition of the European Union, or the Council of Europe, or similar formally constituted institutions, but there is no objective or fixed definition of 'Europe'; rather it differs radically according to the temporal and spatial location of the commentator. Charlemagne's Europe was very different from Tony Blair's, F.D. Roosevelt's or Genghis Khan's. This chapter is concerned with documenting the changes which took place during the early twentieth century in the views that Europeans held about Europe. Those changes were triggered by a series of world-shattering events: the First World War was obviously of crucial importance for Europe's self-image, but there were several others which will be considered here.[1] These notions of Europe were to do with the values Europe represented, its civilization, its identity, and the ways in which Europeans identified with their continent; sometimes they involved schemes about how Europe should be organized in a political, diplomatic or economic sense.

The particular kind of evidence selected here for illuminating these ideas of Europe asks what people have thought Europe 'looks like'. It consists of visual images such as drawings, engravings, paintings, cartoons, maps and architectural decoration.[2] There was a time when historians were reluctant to employ visual material in their evidence arsenal; it was too subjective, difficult and impressionistic to be relied upon, especially when compared with the written word. But over the last generation there has been a general movement towards embracing visual evidence alongside the written and spoken texts as a valuable addition to the information available to historians for testing their hypotheses. For example, maps are now often used to help analyse power relations, for a map has a message, whether it is brash or discreet, and is in many ways an ideal medium for cultural assertion about identity, territory and power.[3] In other disciplines, such as the history of art and cultural studies, the interest shown in recent decades in 'visual culture' points in precisely the same direction. There is an increasing recognition that many of the images which surround us in our daily lives are charged with meaning, and as a whole can be highly active in the social process. Images can be of considerable and even crucial importance as historical evidence.

There is little point, and there would be manifold methodological dangers, in using visual images in isolation: they must be corroborated with each other, and used in combination with written texts. Source or text criticism is the essential exercise in utilizing this material, as it is in any branch of historical research. In the early twentieth century, images of Europe and the other continents could and often did manifest cultural and geopolitical aspirations. In addition to the simple propaganda value of some of them, there was a discourse involved: knowledge was selected and encoded into the images, representing ideology and political or cultural aspirations. If we can use visual images to get behind a *mentalité*, or as a way of approaching or thinking about Europe, then we may well advance our understanding of the manner in ways which the other sources cannot always offer. Such images of Europe are not simply a reflection of the status quo at any one time, but can also, through public opinion and reception, have an impact on the practical situation, much in the way that news media perform in a dynamic exchange between 'image maker' and 'audience'. Here we shall pinpoint some of those interchanges in the course of the first fifty years of the twentieth century.

A Tradition of Representing Europe

By the end of the nineteenth century there was an established tradition of portraying the world in pictures with Europe as the first and greatest continent. It began in the Renaissance and continued throughout the early modern period into the Enlightenment, right up to the age of New Imperialism. The main methods of depicting Europe visually, apart from on maps, were twofold. The first was personification as a gracious lady, usually crowned and luxuriously gowned, full of sophistication of every kind, covered in the regalia which showed her to be queen over the other continents and of the world as a whole. Her attributes were nobility, learning, might, the arts, warfare, goodness, the true Christian religion, and industry. She could be shown alone, or with the other continents (usually four in total, sometimes supplemented by Australasia or Oceania), which allowed the artist to show off the direct contrast between all-powerful Europe and the other, less well-endowed parts of the world, ranging from the exoticism of Asia to the primitivism of America and Australia.

There are many examples available. One which dates from 1884, at the peak of Europe's imperially inflated ideas of its own grandeur at the end of the nineteenth century, but which reveals the pedigree of the notion of a continental hierarchy of civilizations, is shown in Figure 10.1.[4] It features one of the famous 'guild houses' on the Grand Place in Brussels, which date from the medieval period and have been much restored ever since. This one is called 'The Fox' (*In den Vos*), and was home to the drapers' or haberdashers' guild. The date on the building is 1699; Saint Nicholas, the patron saint, appears at the top. However, the statues on the first storey on the front elevation date from 1884, and are by Julien Dillens, who was commissioned to replace earlier similar sculptures of the continents. They are, from left to right, Africa, Europe, Justice (blindfolded, with sword and scales), Asia and America. The four continents have accoutrements and emblems which go back to the sixteenth century and had been universally used in continually updated versions since that time; the rules of how to portray them were laid down in guide books for artists and decorators, the most famous of which was first published by Cesare Ripa in 1593.[5] Their dress, accompanying objects, animals and bearing laid down a pecking order which was instantly recognizable; here we have a version by Dillens which uses conventions of the sixteenth century, placed on an important building in a major public space in Europe in 1699, and recommissioned with approval by the civic authorities in 1884. Africa is stereotypically negroid, carries a great club and a tortoiseshell shield on her arm, has a top-knot, and wears golden

Figure 10.1 Statues of the continents, Grand Place, Brussels, 1699/1884

earrings and a gold bracelet, plus an anklet which is not gold, but probably a manacle indicating slavery. And this is no 'mere' decoration: it is chilling to think that the statues were placed here in the very year, 1884, of the Berlin Conference which regulated the Scramble for Africa and legitimized the appalling regime which King Leopold II of Belgium was to inflict on his huge fiefdom in the Congo. Europe is finely drawn, in flowing robes, and bears a great cornucopia showing her natural wealth and prosperity, but most importantly she wears a golden crown, which has some Habsburg allusions, but whose principal meaning is that Europe is the senior continent, and so Queen of the World. On the other side (to our right) of the central Justice figure is Asia: she carries her principal identifying symbol of a censer or incense burner (straight from Ripa); here she is clearly in Ottoman mode, with the horsetail associated with command of the janissary armies; she wears a turban with a great Islamic crescent at the front, golden earrings, and is shown with stereotypically 'Asiatic' features.

The other time-honoured method of projecting the idea of the continent of Europe in art was through the medium of the legend of Europa and the Bull, or the Rape of Europa. Certainly not all renderings of that immensely popular subject around 1900 made reference to the continent which shared a name with the abducted demi-goddess, but many did. As the bull swims off with the damsel Europa on his back, Europe the continent can be represented by the maiden herself, or by the bull, or by the ensemble. By the nineteenth century the violence of the scene had dissipated, at least when it was meant to represent the continent, but the signification was still very much in use, for example at the Albert Memorial in London, completed in 1876. At the south-west of the site, the Europe group is made up of five noble young women grouped around a huge standing bull, sculpted by Patrick MacDowell. Europe herself is mounted on the bull; she has a crown, and is holding an orb and sceptre. Around her are France, Britain, Italy and Germany, also personified. Both these traditions of representing Europe had pedigrees lasting many centuries, and were instantly recognizable to all those with even a smattering of classical education, for example in cartoons in the popular press.

The early twentieth century, the subject of this essay, was to experience great fluctuations in the assertiveness of the European self-image, and indeed would see the self-definition of 'Europeanness' called into doubt and questioned, as a result of a string of disastrous events with their attendant mass slaughter and misery. Much of the imagery of Europe became negative as a result. But at the start of the twentieth century, the self-assertion of Europe was still little short of bombastic.

A typical example from the public space of London will set the scene on the eve of the First World War. The Aldwych, east of Trafalgar Square in the City of Westminster, was rebuilt as part of a redevelopment in the early twentieth century. Statues to the left and right of the main entrance to Australia House (Figure 10.2) date from around 1914–15 and are signed by Harold Parker, a British-born but Australian-trained sculptor. The imagery is presumably a conjuncture of Australian and British elite tastes at the time, but needs to be seen in the context of high imperialism. Even though it represents Australia, it continues the Eurocentric

Figure 10.2   Statues outside Australia House, Aldwych, London, c. 1914

Othering and exoticism so typical of late-nineteenth-century continental portrayals. On the left, the scene is heroic and noble, with a seated woman, two labouring men below, a sheep, a bushel of wheat, and a cornucopia, all standing for the prosperity of Australia. On the right, the portrayal is rather more erotic, representing the awakening of the new continent. It is topped by a young woman with a naked torso and upstretched arms, rousing from slumber, which allows the artist to display her breasts to advantage and endow her with a facial expression of sexual ecstasy. There are two older men below, one still asleep but grasping a club (possibly even a cricket bat!), and the other blearily peering at a book as if to symbolize nascent learning. All the figures are white, of course, in these potent images of economic exploitation, hegemonic imperial condescension and sexual Othering. This is a rich image of the Australian continent, but it is also very much a part of the Othering of Europe in the age of empire, as yet unbowed by the disasters of the First World War.

Thus there was a clear continuity in European triumphalism from the nineteenth into the early twentieth century. But a sea change was about to take place in European representation, after which things would never quite be the same again: the Great War was to unhinge matters fundamentally, and forever.

The First World War and the Resurgence in the Interbellum

Despite some heroic incidents, the war disgraced Europe in terms of its own view of its standing in the world: the old continent had contrived to immerse itself and much of the rest of the world in a disastrous conflict with industrialized massacre, seemingly achieving very little for it. As other essays in this volume illustrate, after the Great War there occurred what has been called a crisis of European civilization. Any claim to European nobility and idealism was erased: 'the First World War shattered the self-confident belief of European civilization'.[6] Valéry, Spengler, Robert Curtius, Ortega y Gasset and many others led a depressing debate about what appeared to be the failure of European civilization.

In terms of the visual imagery, which emphasized and helped direct the debate, the horrifying images of the trenches, the mud, the corpses of men and horses, the blasted stumps of trees and buildings were the icons which most immediately represented the European war. Such despondent pictures were an indication of what Europe had finally come to: industrial-scale slaughter and destruction. The war graves sites, with their endless rows of identical markers to futile and fatal individual heroism and useless sacrifice, extended such negative impressions of the continent. And then came the war memorials, in every city, town and village in the countries of the belligerents.

One thinks automatically of the many iconic monuments in Flanders fields commemorating the dead of the First World War, none less famous than Reginald Blomfield's Menin Gate at Ypres, or less memorable than Edwin Lutyens' Memorial to the Missing of the Somme at Thiepval. A less well-known Belgian example appears in Figure 10.3: the Infantry Memorial of Brussels, in memory of the

Figure 10.3   Infantry war memorial, c. 1920, outside the Palais de Justice, Brussels

Belgian foot soldiers who fought in the world wars. It was designed by Edouard Vereycken, and stands near the massive bulk of the Palais de Justice in the Place Poelaert, with an impressive view over the city centre. Other war memorials adorn the surrounding space. This was no hastily erected moment: the granite pillar with its decorations was finally placed here in 1935. Like many other memorials all over the continent, after 1945 it also became a memorial for the dead of the Second World War. This one in Brussels is certainly a national moment: the soldiers are distinctively Belgian in their uniforms and helmets, and the dog-drawn machine-gun carriage is a most unusual if not idiosyncratic detail.[7]

Surprisingly, the resilience of the optimism of the European spirit proved greater than expected. The postwar depression about the crisis of European civilization was put into some perspective by the rapidity of the economic recovery which delivered the 'Roaring Twenties'; political uncertainty but lack of war, together with violently vacillating economic progress, allowed optimism to return to ideas of Europe. There were new schemes launched for organizing the continent, like those of Coudenhove-Kalergi and Briand, or Naumann's 'Mitteleuropa' and Masaryk's 'New Europe'.[8] They were invariably designed to prevent or limit future war, and thus implied a salutary note, but surprisingly many of them also began to reveal again a positive view of underlying European values, compared with other cultures, religions, races and continents, especially in the context of a revival of West European empires. Europe-assertion was on the return, despite the European capacity, empirically demonstrated in the First World War, to rip itself and others apart on an unprecedented scale.

Two examples of decorated architecture in large cities in northern Europe can assist in making these points. This return to identifying and approving European values can be seen in the fashion in many cities of Europe for decorating the doorways, windows and corbels with images portraying the continents, along with all the stereotyping which that involved. The first example is taken from the renowned Hotel Americain, whose bars and restaurants have had a place in Amsterdam's international literary-cultural life for many decades. The original hotel in the fashionable entertainment district of the Leidse Plein in Amsterdam was replaced in 1902 by a new Art Nouveau palace designed by the architects Willem Kromhout and H.G. Jansen, with Arab and gothic influences. It was extended towards the Leidse Kade in 1929, with a new wing by architect G.J. Rutgers, the decoration of which is the subject of Figure 10.4. There are ten larger-than-life-size figures carved into the fabric of the building, representing various parts of the world. The imagery was intended to suggest the internationalism of a modern hotel, and that its clients would be (assumed to be) sufficiently sophisticated and cosmopolitan to be familiar with most of the foreign parts personified in this way. Specific nations are probably not being portrayed here (as they are elsewhere in the city, for instance in the Magna Plaza, or old main Post Office, of the 1890s), and neither are they indicative of specific continents; nonetheless the group of four shown here, which are the four from the right end of the row of ten, are clearly meant to be associated with other parts of the world, ethnic types and nations.

Figure 10.4   Decorative figures, American Hotel, Amsterdam, 1929

From left to right, we see an African princess, a mustachioed and turbaned oarsman from the Pacific, a young Asian female, and a Chinese or 'Oriental' book-carrying mandarin or scholar. The Othering process is in full swing here, exoticizing other parts of the world in contrast to the European model.

The second of countless possible examples of this trend is an English set of bas-relief panels of commercial scenes and personifications of parts of the world on Abtech House, 18 Park Road, Leeds (Figure 10.5). It dates from the early part of the twentieth century, when this area, to the south of The Headrow and the main civic centre, was the financial district of this modern and vibrant city. It is clearly a commercial property, and there is a stone frieze by John Theulis across the whole building, just above the ground floor, emphasizing the international and indeed global nature of the business originally installed there, probably in the financial services or commercial sector. It consists of four panels. Over the main entrance, to the left, a coat of arms is supported by two semi-naked young women. Next, above the left-hand set of windows, there are Western stevedores with bales of goods, and a merchant or clerk in plain dress, being approached by a Chinese gentleman with a long moustache, a near-naked Negro carrying packages, and an Arab. European merchant vessels rest at anchor. These are not strictly speaking indicative of specific continents, but nonetheless represent Europe and the rest of the world, in parts. In the central niche is placed a hooded personification of Commerce herself, holding an orb for dominion and a Hermes' snaked sceptre which identifies her with that patron of trade. In the panel above the right windows there are two Western miners or engineers, with a steam locomotive above them. By contrast, to the left stands a group of North American Indians, with full feather bonnets and rawhide clothes. One has a musket, while the other points at the steam engine; there is a bison above them. On the right of this panel stands another Westerner, this time suggesting a cleric, with a kneeling figure in front of him carrying an urn; a palm tree waves above their heads. These tableaux

Figure 10.5   Commercial building decorated with parts of the world, Leeds, c. 1920

again reference Europe and the rest of the world, notably America, Africa and Asia, though not as specific continents. The themes are commerce, learning, science, religion, and their domination by the Western colonizers.

The ideology proclaimed by both these sets, in Amsterdam and Leeds, is unmistakable; it was continuing a tradition of Othering through marginalization. After a serious dent to European self-evaluation during and after the First World War, the Eurocentric thought processes of the turn of the century were being emphatically continued, and it can be seen all over the major cities of Europe. The visualized manifestations of this ideology conveyed and indeed reinforced the self-evident superiority of European civilization. This was particularly the case where there was a colonial connection, and that factor was directly present in most European cities in the Interbellum.

'Decolonization' was to occur in the decades immediately following the Second World War, and we are accustomed to think of the 1920s and 1930s as a period when imperial economic difficulties and outbreaks of nationalist resistance to colonial rule were the unmistakable writing on the wall, heralding the impending end of empire. While that view has a great deal to commend it, in many cases the

Interbellum was in fact experienced as a Golden Age of empire, especially in France, Britain and the Netherlands, but also in the colonies of Spain, Portugal, Italy, Denmark, Belgium and others. In the course of the First World War, the Russian Revolution and the Peace of Versailles, it is true that the Habsburg, the Romanov, the Ottoman, and the Hohenzollern empires were obliterated. Germany's enormous global empire and the rambling Ottoman territories were broken up and redistributed to the winners of the war, especially France and Britain, who added these new strategic, economic and political interests to their vast existing colonial empires. The Netherlands retained its extensive possessions, as did Belgium and the others; newcomers like the United States, Japan and Italy kept the competition on its toes. Empire was a major European concern in the 1920s and 1930s, even for those countries not directly involved. It was certainly experienced as an era in which the world was directed from the capitals of Europe, at a time when the United States and the USSR were not quite yet recognized as being the major powers on the earth's chequerboard. Certainly for the French, British and Dutch, their empires were absolutely central to their self-image and esteem. Hardly a family in these and several other European countries would not have had one or more members active in the trade, finance, civil administration or military operations connected with empire: especially in the middle classes, people were endlessly 'going out' and 'coming back', and empire dictated the rhythm of many lives and indeed the life of the nation. This was not only a political, strategic and economic concern: the cultural role of Europeans, teaching much of the rest of the world how to be civilized through the infrastructure of their empire, was also of immediate importance. This 'cultural imperialism' through religion, education, legal systems, and every other behavioural example allowed Europeans to consider themselves the enlighteners of the world, duty bound, willing or not: in short, the White Man's Burden. It justified the less attractive aspects of empire, but more importantly was a vital pillar of identity, and this patronizing mentality gave Europeans a large part of their *raison d'être*. In the period between the wars there were many upsets and calls for reform in the European empires, but the strategies of Orientalism and exoticism continued to bolster the self-esteem and identity of most of Europe's population in the interwar period.

All this was amply expressed in the decoration of public space, especially in the European capitals. Many of the major imperial institutes and museums, and the great colonial offices, had already been built before the First World War, but the imperializing trend in architecture continued apace, despite the setbacks of 1914–18. It was also an age in which architects favoured the adornment of their façades with iconography which reminded observers – indeed inspired them – to think on the grandiose achievements of the firm, office or government department involved, of the nation, or of the great European civilization which was so self-evidently the best in the world. The Amsterdam School of Architecture, which dominated Dutch monumental buildings from 1900 to 1940, was specifically dedicated to ornamenting the outside of its Art Deco buildings with meaningful sculpture, and indeed their impact on private and public housing was seminal before the crash of

1929.[9] This was the Dutch variant of a general trend in public-space architecture across Europe in the 1920s and indeed the 1930s: after the Italian example it might be called fascist, but it was felt equally in countries which energetically deny any connection with that label, such as England. For example, many factories, office blocks and public buildings of the 1920s and 1930s shared a masculine, monumental style, with façades adorned with decoration or iconography.

An example on a modest scale of this Orientalizing of Europe is a bas-relief sculpture, personifying gas, on the outer wall of the Gas and Electricity Board offices in Crouch End, London (Figure 10.6). This set of 1930s public buildings, centring on Hornsey Town Hall, was designed by R.H. Uren, and reveals the influence of the Dutch architect W.M. Dudok, whose early work was closely aligned with that of the Amsterdam School mentioned above. This image of gas personified as a beautiful young woman is also a depiction of Asia, which was where most oil came from in the 1930s (town-gas came from coal). In her left hand she has a horn of plenty, signifying nature's bounty, while in her right she has a flame signifying gas. Her torso is alluringly and gratuitously naked; her abdomen and legs are draped. A far-off and largely colonized continent is shown on this wall as a source of raw materials (fuel and agricultural produce) in an apparently sexually available, semi-naked, female representation. All these architectural adornments are in one sense simply pieces of decoration, but as with so much of the visual culture around us, they speak volumes about the world which created them, and which was reinforced by the imagery; the far-off colonized Asia is the Other in geographical, economic and sexual terms.

Figure 10.6 Bas-relief sculpture on the Gas Board building, Crouch End, London, 1937

Figure 10.7 Figures of Asia and Europe inside the Utrecht Post Office, designed by J. Crouwel, 1918–24

The Amsterdam School had adherents and commissions in other Dutch towns as well, in addition to its international influence. The main Post Office in Utrecht, designed by J. Crouwel and completed in 1924, is a fine example. Its interior is dominated by stunning parabola vaulting in glazed yellow brick and glass; the corbels supporting the soaring arches are in the form of imposing black life-size statues, personifications of the five continents (Australia included) and of trade. In Figure 10.7 on the left, Asia (where the Netherlands' main colonies lay), is standing over an elephant, and wears a coolie's hat with a strained expression. Despite the stylizing of Europe personified on the right, a considerable amount can be told from the presentation. He is standing on his traditional badge or emblem, the warhorse, indicating strength in arms; the figure itself is cloaked, wise looking, and authoritative. The whole building is a celebration of global diversity, brought together by the greatness of Dutch trade and empire. Such edifices are set firmly in a long tradition of empire buildings in the Netherlands which glorify the Dutch colonial regime based on both trade and charity.[10]

Many other buildings in Amsterdam itself celebrate the colonial heritage in Eurocentric terms, dating from the Interbellum. On the Vijzelstraat in the centre stands the literally massive block of 'De Bazel', named after its architect K.P.C. de Bazel, built in the early 1920s as the headquarters of the Dutch Trading Company, Nederlandsche Handel-Maatschappij (NHM). The NHM was the colonial arm of the Netherlands government, rather like the East India Company, for it was the nineteenth-century successor to the Dutch East India Company (Vereenigde Oostindische Compagnie) of the Golden Age. From its foundation by King Willem I in 1924, the NHM was permitted to farm a government monopoly of the cultivation of cash crops and their transport and trade back to Europe; for much of the nineteenth century these activities, known as the Culture System, poured colonial cash into the Dutch treasury, and were at least partly responsible for the prosperity and success of the Dutch in Europe. Their rapaciousness was much admired by other European imperial powers, who attempted to emulate the Dutch techniques of stripping their colonies so efficiently. After liberalization and denationalization measures in tune with the later part of the nineteenth century, the NHM became essentially a colonial bank, and the building has served several Dutch banking houses in recent decades, as a result of merger activity; it now happily houses the city archives.[11] For the NHM centenary of 1924, the opportunity was seized to erect this monument to Dutch colonialism, with large external sculptures of three of the military strong men of Dutch rule in Indonesia: Jan Pietersz. Coen, Herman Daendels and Johannes van Heutsz. On either side of the main entrance are female figures representing Asia and Europe, or, by association, the East Indies (Indonesia) and the Netherlands; the preliminary designs by the artist, Joseph Mendes da Costa, are shown in Figure 10.8. As with the finished pieces on the Vijzelstraat entrance, the artist's portrayal of the body language is revealing: Europe on the right has open eyes and outstretched palms, being generally more assertive than Insulinde or Asia, who is barefoot with eyes downcast, eroticized and submissive.[12] Unlike the finished sculptures, in these sketches they have other figures at their feet, sheltered in their long robes. These are references to the indigenous population of the East Indies, who are being offered protection by the great Dutch colonial regime, although their portrayal as extraterrestrial children or homunculi may look fundamentally strange to us, as well as redolent of a severe case of colonial condescension or White Man's Burden. In any case they were rejected by the commissioning directors because they might suggest oppression, and so the almost equally Eurocentric designs appear on the finished building without the little people. Across much of Europe, this kind of colonial propaganda in stone continued on from the nineteenth century and reached something of a climax in the 1920s and 1930s.[13] Even a non-belligerent country like the Netherlands had experienced a fundamental questioning of the European ideal after the First World War, but all the countries of Western Europe shared in this return to the bombast and arrogance of the 1890s New Imperialism and the self-image of Europe in the world which that implied. The various fascist or quasi-fascist regimes of the later 1930s could certainly empathize with that self-importance vis-à-vis the other continents, and indeed many of their buildings carried such images.

Figure 10.8 Joseph Mendes da Costa, designs for the main entrance of the De Bazel building, Amsterdam, c. 1925 (Photos: ABN-AMRO Historical Archives, Weesp NL)

The Second World War and After

When the advent of what would become the Second World War was beyond doubt, the visual representations of Europe took flight in different directions. The most obvious one was despair, and horror that the continent was going to be plunged yet again into internecine chaos with attendant persecution and slaughter. Europe had, as it were, done it again. It would be a global war, but particularly European in its origins and in much of its enactment. It was linked to the rise of militarist, fascist and related right-wing ultranationalist movements across Europe, some of which developed specific ideas about Europe, like the Nazi New Order; this evoked strong negative reactions from individuals and groups who espoused any idealistic notions about Europe. Thus two principal visions of Europe were projected: one by the Nazis and their ideological allies, and the other by those horrified and once again disillusioned at what their continent was becoming.

A Jewish perspective on this prospect was of course all the more poignant, in view of what was to come. A painting of 1939 by the German Jewish artist Felix Nussbaum, entitled 'European Vision', with the alternative title of 'The Refugee', expressed some of his horror of what Europe was becoming at that time (Figure 10.9). Nussbaum fled the Nazis to the Low Countries from Osnabrück (where a museum dedicated to his work, designed by Daniel Libeskind, now houses one of the two versions of the picture), but he was picked up there by the occupying forces, and died in Auschwitz in 1944. His painting shows a bleak despondency at European civilization. A refugee, representing Jewry, with stick and bag, sits alone in despair; on a table in a desolate room stands a globe showing a distended view of Europe (especially exaggerated in the version held in Osnabrück). Behind it, through an arch, we see leafless or even blasted winter trees, with carrion birds in the sky. This vision of cultural bankruptcy is about the persecution of the Jews, but it has a specifically European focus: this is the continent of the pogrom.

The envisaged Nazi 'New Order' was absolutely central to European ideology in the early 1940s, uncongenial though it may be to admit that. As far as visualization is concerned, one can hardly forget the Nazi posters based on maps of the continent, claiming the 'New Europe' as a German domain. Figure 10.10 shows one issued in occupied France, trying to unite Europe against the Bolshevik

Figure 10.9 Felix Nussbaum, 'European Vision', 1939 (Felix-Nussbaum-Haus, Osnabrück; by kind permission)

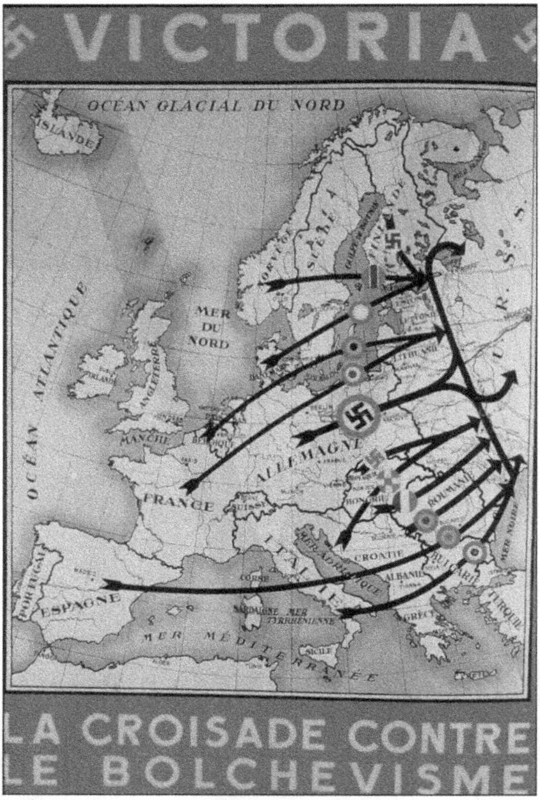

Figure 10.10   Poster: 'Victoria. La croisade contre le Bolshevisme', 1944

Other. Nearly all the nations of Europe (except Britain) are shown joined under Nazi leadership in a massed onslaught against Communist Russia. This is Europe envisaged as a like-minded unity led by fascist Germany, and its propaganda was widespread and powerful.

After the defeat of the fascists, there was a general humility about the Europe ideal, and very little talk of European 'civilization', other than a determination to adopt policies after the war which would prevent forever another of those disastrous internecine European civil wars which had characterized the cursed continent for centuries. There was still idealism there, in places, for example stemming from the island of Ventotene, with its renowned manifesto which eventually would contribute to setting up the first institutions of European integration. But contrite humility was the order of the day in the postwar gloom: Europe was not on the list of positive topics for discussion, and had little to offer the rest of the world any more, except in terms of salutary lessons about how not to conduct affairs. This phase of postwar negativity about Europe continued for some years, with the privations of postwar monetary reorganizations, ration books, drab fashions, painful reconstruction, handouts from America, and the advent of what would become the Cold War driving a wedge through Europe. The world was certainly not about to take sermons from Europe any more about high morals. Concurrently there took place what for many Europeans was the uncomfortable and even humiliating process of decolonization, as the European world empires were – to one extent or another – obliged to surrender their colonies, together with accompanying feelings of control and superiority. Europe was seen as a 'corpse' in 1945, devoid of qualities of civilization and humanity, and rapidly became 'a guilty continent'.[14]

An apt example of the gloom is a sculpture by the Dutchman Carel Kneulman, called 'The Europeans', made in 1950–51 and sited for many years near the Concertgebouw in Amsterdam (Figure 10.11). It shows Europeans as emaciated wanderers, full of holes and exhausted with old age. One carries a book, the

Figure 10.11 Carel Kneulman, 'The Europeans', 1949–50, Amsterdam, Stedelijk Museum (Photographer Gerrit Schreurs; by kind permission)

traditional symbol of Europe's wisdom and knowledge, but it has been of little use to her. Guilt pervades this highly negative, despondent image: it is quintessentially postwar, but is not so far removed from the despair of Nussbaum's pre-war vision of a sick, diseased continent in Figure 10.9.

Almost incredibly, however, it appears that even the horrors of the Second World War could be set aside and displaced in the European collective memory. The truly amazing economic recovery of Western Europe, which grew faster in the 1950s and 1960s than anywhere else in the world including America, generated a reemerging feeling of European self-assertion. After the war the mood was often one of austerity and belt-tightening, but by the mid-1950s almost everywhere in Western Europe was beginning to feel the effects of sustained economic prosperity. When economic fortune was accompanied by peace and political stability (which, perversely, is what the Cold War provided in Europe for forty years), then it was hardly surprising that an element of self-satisfaction and assertion crept back into the European self-image.

There was a new European confidence in those years; shame about Europe was either forgotten in the celebration of prosperity, suppressed as unspeakable, or unacknowledged by the emerging youth culture. Marshall Aid and the poster campaigns which led it were of some help in lifting public spirits: with American aid to start things off, Europe could fly again, especially in terms of world trade. Those posters expressed a positive side which would characterize official European imagery for a long time: it was of course pure propaganda, but it only exaggerated rather than invented an optimism which was in tune with a continent beginning to feel the pace of economic reconstruction. Figure 10.12[15] is taken from another campaign of those years, the European Movement, founded as an umbrella organization for pro-Europe groups. In a previous incarnation it helped to organize the seminal Congress of Europe in The Hague in 1948, and was instrumental in founding the Council of Europe in 1949. The European Movement was formally constituted in October 1948, and was from the start aware of the importance of visualizing its campaign for European unity: it flew a flag, in the form of a great letter 'E', at the Congress of Europe, and later changed its colour from red to green, which it retained. The poster shown in Figure 10.12 dates from the early 1950s, and announces, 'We are building a new Europe', showing a builders' scaffold in front of an edifice consisting of a multitude of European national flags, all forming a single structure. It is an early form of the 'unity in diversity' paradigm, and mirrors those Marshall Plan and other posters of the good ship Europe with, as its sails, the various national flags; there are several variants. Again, this is just as much a propaganda exercise as the 'agit-prop' Soviet posters of the same era, but there was a basis of truth in the sentiments they trumpeted, and their encouragement no doubt had some of the desired effect.

In the cathedral in Strasbourg, damaged during the Second World War, and long-term witness to unrelenting strife between Europe's nation-states, the optimists behind the Council of Europe arranged for a 'Europe window' in stained glass to be placed in the apse in 1956 (Figure 10.13). Designed by Max Ingrand

Figure 10.12   Poster: 'Wir bauen das neue Europa', 1950s (Collection 'Europese Beweging in Nederland en voorgangers, 1946–1986', National Archive, The Hague)

and installed on the eve of the signature of the Treaty of Rome, it portrays the Madonna and Child, but almost like a halo in the point of the arch there is a circle of twelve golden stars on a bluish background, the emblem adopted by the Council of Europe in 1955 (and later by the EC/EU). It associates the symbol of a uniting and distinctive Europe with the exalted Christian values of peace, charity and devotion. It would be harsh to call it Eurocentric, but hard to ignore that the postwar despair of Europe had to a large extent been dissipated by the mid-1950s.

However, we can see this postwar period as one of chastened or moderated Euro-assertion. There was less of the arrogant self-assurance of the Edwardian period before the First World War, when it never occurred to Europeans that there was the slightest doubt about European superiority. Now the United States was politically, militarily and economically a much great power in the world than the individual or even the potentially united European states, and then there was the looming presence of the Soviet Union. So Europe evidently no longer ruled the world, but at the same time, by the mid-1950s it did not need to feel so ashamed of itself any more.

Figure 10.13   Max Ingrand, Vitrail Européen, Strasbourg Cathedral, 1956

Conclusion

These images of Europe in the first half of the twentieth century, before the foundation of the EEC in 1957, have shown a considerable range of pride and disillusionment with the ideal of Europe, the personification of a continent. The disillusion is perhaps hardly surprising, given the occurrence of two world wars, the Great Depression and the Holocaust in those fifty years. More extraordinary, perhaps, is the almost unbelievable resurgence in pride in the European model, in European civilization, in those short interludes between the disasters that constituted Europe before 1957. The ebullience of Euro-assertion could always be relied upon, continuing to bounce back, despite periodic crushing blows. The Great War cut away European self-pride, and forced a crisis of conscience in the early 1920s; the Great Depression in the 1930s had a similar effect, as did the Second World War. Yet Eurocentric pretensions resurfaced between the wars, especially vis-à-vis the colonies, and again in the 1950s, on the coat-tails of a huge economic boom. The visual images explored here, alongside all the other sources, give us a clear and direct indication of these shifts and changes, perhaps more so than with any other kind of evidence. Visual sources are indeed indispensable.

Notes

1. This essay draws on a continuing project on visualizing Europe; see M. Wintle, *The Image of Europe: Visualizing Europe in Cartography and Iconography* (Cambridge, 2009); and in particular idem, 'Europe on Parade: World War I and the Changing Visual Representations of the Continent in the Twentieth Century', in M. Spiering and M. Wintle (eds), *Ideas of Europe since 1914: The Legacy of the First World War* (London, 2002), 105–29.
2. The field has been pioneered especially by the seminal work of D. Hay, *Europe: The Emergence of an Idea* (Edinburgh, 1957). See also Den Boer (et al.), *The History of the Idea of Europe* (Milton Keynes, 1993).
3. J.B. Harley, for example in 'Meaning and Ambiguity in Tudor Cartography', in Sarah Tyacke (ed.), *English Map Making 1500–1650* (London, 1983), was the principal proponent of this view of cartography, but his approach is now generally accepted.
4. Unless otherwise stated, the illustrations are the author's photographs.
5. See Den Boer (et al.), *The History of the Idea of Europe*, 51–58; and Wintle, *The Image of Europe*, 53–55.
6. M. Rodinson, *Europe and the Mystique of Islam* (Seattle and London, 1997), 71.
7. See J. Winter, *Sites of Memory, Sites of Mourning* (Cambridge, 1995), especially 79, 93, 111, 142, 223–27.
8. A survey of schemes and perceptions of Europe between the wars is provided by Peter Bugge in Den Boer (et al.), *The History of the Idea of Europe*, 83–143; see also the essay by Katiana Orlue in B. Stråth (ed.), *Europe and the Other and Europe as the Other* (Brussels and New York, 2000), 123–55.
9. See, for instance, M. Casciato, *The Amsterdam School* (Rotterdam, 1996).
10. In Amsterdam they range from the seventeenth-century Royal Palace on the Dam, with its west tympanum frieze of the four parts of the world bringing their tribute to the city, to the Central Station and the Rijksmuseum buildings of the 1880s.
11. M. Wintle, *An Economic and Social History of the Netherlands* (Cambridge, 2000), 214–25.
12. E. Vanvugt, *De maagd en de soldaat* (Amsterdam, 1998), 46–48.
13. The French example is well covered by R. Aldrich, *Vestiges of the Colonial Empire* (Basingstoke, 2005); the German by J. Zeller, *Kolonialdenkmäler und Geschichtsbewußtsein* (Frankfurt am Main, 2000).
14. R. Hoggart and D. Johnson, *An Idea of Europe* (London, 1987), 5 and 125–26.
15. I am grateful to my colleague Menno Spiering for bringing this image to my attention.

Chapter 11

EUROPE AND THE ARTISTIC PATRIMONY OF THE INTERWAR PERIOD

The International Institute of Intellectual Cooperation at the League of Nations

Annamaria Ducci

'Standing, now, on an immense sort of terrace of Elsinore that stretches from Basel to Cologne, bordered by the sands of Nieuport, the marshes of the Somme, the limestone of Champagne, the granites of Alsace – our Hamlet of Europe is watching millions of ghosts.'[1] Valéry's vision is a tragic one, of a desolate and gloomy European land. A pictorial vision, a bird's eye view, in which the immense geography of the continent seems to totter, becomes unstable, for the stone is juxtaposed with sand, mire, swamp. But the picture also implicitly refers to the works of humanity, to those changes that dotted the landscape and the history of Europe; the architecture breaks apart, falls, turns to rubble, turns once again into stone. So Hamlet contemplates not only the undoing of geographical boundaries, but also the fall of European history, which, in the imperishable memory of its own monuments, expresses itself.

A European Context

The tragedy of the Great War made clear what terrifying rifts might be produced by political and ethnic rivalry. The birth of the League of Nations in 1919 stood in this dramatic historical phase.[2] The league tried to assuage common anxieties: the issue was not only the maintenance of a new delicate balance, but also the discovery of a way of going back to the true spirit of cosmopolitanism, of going back to the lively exchanges between nations typifying the first decade of the twentieth century.[3]

At the heart of the political vision of the League of Nations was the concept of the 'free nation', on which the history of Europe had pivoted for over two centuries, in a sequence of dangerous, but always significant, tightrope walking. The history of Europe shows its extraordinary 'unity of diversities', which made it the homeland of freedom.[4] Yet the war altered everything and the very idea of the nation underwent a radical change. Looking at Europe after the Great War, one no longer sees a mosaic of different people defined by language, poetry and the arts, peacefully living together and respecting each other's freedom, but a disordered continent, with uncertain and fluctuating inner boundaries; a dying vision like that of Valéry's Hamlet.

As is well known, the United States did not join the League of Nations, even though the original idea of an international organization had been set forth by President Wilson in his famous 'Fourteen Points'. So the League of Nations, while counting among its members great extra-European nations such as Japan, was essentially made up in its decisive organs by European members,[5] and, in point of fact, the old continent, its geopolitical structure and its problems, always remained the League's central concern. Importantly, it can be said that the idea of the League of Nations was openly European because in the European way of belonging could be found a character at once national and universal: 'to be European is always to be at the same time pre-European (state, even state-nation) and post-European (global, worldwide)'.[6] To avoid disappearing, the old continent had to rethink and refound itself by using what represented its truest source of wealth: the harmonious unity of many cultures. The idea of Europe had to be reformulated, starting from its variegated identity.[7] Such a belief was strongly felt by the French members of the League of Nations, who were strongly influenced by the work of organizations such as the *Ligue des Droits de l'Homme* and by the work of liberal intellectuals and, more generally, of a pacifist and democratic national movement which, in 1929, reached its peak with Aristide Briand's pan-European project.[8] Remarkably, the French Foreign Minister's project still contained a deeply liberal and bourgeois conception of the state in which, nonetheless, the idea of national sovereignty was combined with pacifist perspectives. Such beliefs, furthermore, were coupled with a powerful concern to preserve the integrity of Europe from external threats, above all Bolshevism, with its oriental and theocratic traits, and a rising American culture, based on mass consumption and leading to a banalization of life.[9] It was easy to spot the latent ghosts dwelling in the old continent: social conflicts, the growth of nationalism, the drift towards to totalitarianism.

Beyond the noble declarations of principles, the League of Nations was also a 'place of national rivalries', where diplomatic strategies of governments of opposing political standpoints were put in place in order to keep the artificial balance established after the Great War. The League had an ambiguous, contradictory and uncertain character, to say the least, torn between a theoretical universalism and an openly conservative stance favouring the bourgeois idea of the nation-state. This weakness was soon perceived by the keenest intellectuals of the time, by the representatives of the League of Nations and its cultural organizations. For example, in 1933, Johan Huizinga defined nationalism as a 'caricature of patriotism'.[10] The author of the *Crise de l'esprit*, who had been named French representative at the Institut International de Coopération Intellectuelle (IICI),[11] was convinced that the crux of the matter lay in the concept of nation itself. Valéry went as far as to deconstruct it, defining the nation as a 'separation': 'nation means dissemblance, opposition, concurrence, jealousy, etc.' The very institution meant to overcome such an idea – the 'League of Nations' – was based on a theoretical paradox: 'League of Nations. This name stands for an absurdity; for it is the idea of nation (in the political-juridical sense) that one should take issue with.'[12]

The fact of a continent fragmented by nationalisms, as well as the internal contradictions of an elitist and excessively bureaucratized organization, were two of the main reasons for the failure of the League of Nations. On the geopolitical plane, the league was successful in solving minor controversies, while it showed itself ineffectual in major disputes, not least because the defection of the United States lessened its credibility. It remains true that the organization never took a precise stand against the disgraces of dictatorships: not only Nazi Germany, but also the Japanese invasion of Manchuria, or the colonization of Ethiopia by Fascist Italy. An effective withdrawal marked the actual defeat of the League of Nations before the outbreak of the Second World War.[13] After the war, some of the league's pacifist and federalist demands were put forward by the European Economic Community, while the activity of the cultural commissions of the League of Nations were carried out on the global plane by UNESCO.[14]

The Centrality of Culture: The IICI

The period from the 1920s to the mid-1930s was a phase of great intellectual activity for the League of Nations, within which several commissions with the purpose of encouraging cultural dialogue between peoples were created. Culture was considered the most appropriate instrument to fight against the growing ferment of nationalism and fight for the defence of the fundamental rights first laid out by the European Enlightenment, which would later be ratified by the Universal Declaration of Human Rights, promulgated by the UN in 1948.[15]

The main cultural organism of the League of Nations was indubitably the International Institute of Intellectual Cooperation (IICI), established in 1925.[16] The institute had been strongly desired by France, with the intention of opposing – at least on a cultural plane – an ever stronger Germany. Not only did the French government seek the creation of the IICI, but it also supported it financially and deeply influenced its agenda. It should be noted that the birth of the IICI came at that crucial moment of French history at which – following the shattering effects of the Dreyfus affair – the idea of the intellectual as the *homme engagé*, as political mediator, if not himself the inspirer of new ideologies, took hold.[17]

The original idea of creating a cultural organization of the League of Nations came from Léon Bourgeois, President of the Senate, a time-honoured pacifist and one of the spiritual fathers of the League of Nations, of which he was named President in 1920 – the year he received the Nobel peace prize. To another French politician, Julien Luchaire, General Inspector of Public Schools, we owe the programme for the creation of an organ of intellectual cooperation that would work 'for moral disarmament', on the assumption that 'universal peace … would never be attained if the national education of each people would not strive towards an ever deeper understanding of all other peoples'.[18]

Thanks to the action undertaken by the French, the IICI settled in Paris, where it obtained a prestigious location at the Palais-Royal.[19] The Parisian institute was a sub-organ of the Organization for Intellectual Cooperation (OCI), created in 1922 and based in Geneva, an intercultural organization of the League of Nations to which men such as Albert Einstein, Sigmund Freud, Thomas Mann, Gilbert Murray, Aldous Huxley, Paul Valéry, Jules Romains, Johan Huizinga, Giuseppe Prezzolini, and Francesco Ruffini – one of the twelve Italian intellectuals who refused to swear an oath to the Fascist regime – belonged. According to its founders, the IICI should have created a 'general republic of minds', a 'society of spirits'.[20] But while the values of peace and cultural exchange were intended at the IICI in a 'universal' sense and while it included representatives of extra-European countries, the ethical and cultural guidelines animating it were specifically European. As Emile Borel remarked in his speech at the congress on 'The Future of the European Spirit', organized by the IICI in 1933 and held in Paris, the same intellectual elite making up the institute was, by its nature, intimately European: 'It has been said that one of the great difficulties of our duty was in the relationship between elites and masses. It is certain that, although European elites have all the feelings that accompany nations, to which each one of us is attached, they are part of this greater entity that is Europe.'[21] European intellectuals rarely shared the purportedly nationalistic feelings of the masses; such a universalistic stand also inspired the members of the IICI, who felt the 'pedagogical' task of overcoming all sorts of particularisms in a European dimension, far from the broader anthropological cosmopolitanism, for example, of a Romain Rolland. It can be argued, as a consequence, that the IICI contributed not only to the preservation of Europe's identity, but also to the perpetuation of the myth of the 'superiority' of European culture.

It should be said that the identification of European with universal culture was a by-product of the idea of 'civilization'. Such a notion had flourished in Europe in the eighteenth century; from its original neutral meaning, it started, from the French Revolution onwards, to be thought of as a 'universal civilization', as the only possible civilization, since its nature was based on the ethical principles of universal rights.[22] In the first half of the twentieth century, the concept of civilization was at the centre of heated debates, which aimed to understand its ultimate meaning and its relations with connected and yet not identical terms such as *civilité* and *Kultur*. After the Great War, men such as Spengler, Demangeon and Toynbee rethought the historical meaning of civilization and its cyclical dynamics, assuming its inevitable 'decline'; to them, the decline of civilization was the decline of the Western world itself, a dramatic phenomenon against which Europe could and had to react by reconstructing its own geographical and cultural identity.

If the member states of the IICI coincided, in point of fact, with the founding members of the original nucleus of the Economic European Community, the idea of Europe they set forth coincided with an ideal, shared notion of the West – a theoretical paradox, reasserting the supremacy of European culture over those of other 'western' people.

There were uncertainties, of course, surrounding the very idea of the West and its historical and geographical meaning. The de facto coincidence of the West and the 'Atlantic' part of Europe was, for example, reasserted by the art historian Henri Focillon, who, together with Paul Valéry, represented France at the IICI.[23] In works such as *Art d'Occident* (1938) and the posthumous *L'an mil* (1952), he turned the 'West' into a category of historical analysis with the intention of overcoming the concept of race, which he saw as a dangerous tool of geographical determinism.[24] The West, according to Focillon, was neither the territory bordered by the Baltic Sea nor that facing the Mediterranean Sea; it was, on the contrary, the 'Franco-Lombard-Spanish bloc lapped by the Atlantic', since it was there, in this frontier facing the ocean, that the great cultural experiences, from the Middle Ages onwards, had taken place: 'The West, lapped by the Atlantic, is the basis of medieval and contemporary civilization, as Greece, lapped by the Mediterranean, is the basis of ancient civilization.'[25] In this 'Romance' bloc was to be found the true crib of humanism, the distinctive character of Europe; the western Middle Ages, starting in AD 1000, he defined as 'the West's arising awareness of being the new foyer of civilization, as well as a reaction against Germanism – amorphous or organized barbarity'.[26]

Focillon's interest in such issues started in the mid-1930s and grew and matured during two years of teaching at the Collège de France, alongside his friend Valéry. Both scholars reached the conclusion that the Atlantic West coincided with France alone. In reality, this was an equation referring to an important strand of nineteenth-century French historiography which had developed precisely in the art history focusing on the Middle Ages. From this angle, the architect Eugène Viollet-le-Duc's synthesis in his seventh *Entretien* (1863) is rather enlightening: 'In the West, on the contrary (*and when I speak of West I intend to speak but of France*), the dominant idea, the main idea, has been unity; *the arts have been one of the most powerful means for reaching such unity.*'[27]

The same axiom, linking culture to Europe, is deeply rooted in the idea of the Enlightenment as the diffusion of universal values, aiming at overcoming the prejudices of nature and race. In France, in particular, the foundations for a political interpretation of culture had been laid down. Henri de Saint-Simon explained it quite clearly in his *Essai sur la réorganisation de la société européenne*, written with Augustin Thierry in 1814, at the time when Metternich's Holy

Alliance was trying to reorganize a continent disrupted by the French Revolution and the Napoleonic wars.[28] What defined Europe's mission of civilization was precisely its 'lay' (*laic*) spirit, in which culture takes the place of religion and race.[29] This belief was retrieved at the beginning of the twentieth century by many French socialists. The Radical statesman Georges Clemenceau, who drew his inspiration from a kind of Proudhonian humanitarianism, conceived of culture as a fundamental element of the identity of a people, as well as a powerful – the most powerful – instrument to pursue social justice and achieve peace.[30] On such a basis, the historian Lucien Febvre[31] saw Europe as the '*patrie* of freedom', singling out the role of France as the mediating country between a Mediterranean 'latinity' and a barbaric north, as the beacon of civilization.[32]

This position, at once Euro- and Franco-centric, undoubtedly inspired the work of the IICI or, at least, of its French representatives – above all Valéry and Focillon – who then clearly referred to a long-standing intellectual tradition according to which France had a mission of 'civilization' and the role of 'guiding state' of the other countries of Europe, guarantor of both peace and harmony throughout the old continent; Paris would have been the capital – at least the cultural capital – of the great federal state led by the French nation. Victor Hugo's daring stance, on this point, is quite well known. In 1849, presiding over the Third Congress for Universal Peace in Paris, Hugo foretold a twentieth century during which the unity of Europe would become true, giving life to a single great federal nation inspired by peace and concord; this great country would be led by the France of universal rights. The 'myth of Paris', which was gaining strength in those years, was juxtaposed with the idea of a universal West in the name of culture and art:

> In the twentieth century there will be an extraordinary nation. This nation will be great, which will not prevent it from being free. It will be illustrious, rich, creative, pacific and friendly towards the whole of humanity ... Paris will be its capital, but its name will not be France: its name will be Europe. It will be called Europe in the twentieth century and, in the ensuing years, once further perfected, it shall be called humanity.[33]

The experience of the IICI ended, bitterly, with the Second World War and with the failure of the League of Nations. A progressive detachment from reality marked the activities of the IICI from the mid-1930s onwards in the face of totalitarianism. The debates, often heated, taking place within the Institute[34] had few significant political consequences but always remained relegated to a beautiful 'ivory tower', far from ongoing tragedies; the advocates of its original pacifist and democratic aspirations became increasingly disappointed by the powerlessness of the League of Nations. Such was the case of Focillon himself, who, in private correspondence, deplored the ineptness of the League: 'Not one single word in the League of Nations on the *Anschluss*! Not a single word about German blackmail!'[35] For the rest, the *savants* still gathering after 1933 were not able to go beyond the theoretical phrasing, idyllic and at times nostalgic, of a particularly abstract *humanisme*, as shown by the telling titles of the conferences promoted in those years: *L'Esprit, l'éthique et la guerre* (1934), *L'Art et la réalité. L'art et l'Etat* (1934), *La Formation de l'homme nouveau* (1935), *Vers un nouvel humanisme* (1936), and *Le Destin prochain des lettres* (1937).[36]

Popular Arts

The tragedy of the First World War had shown the fragility of cultural traditions which, just like states, could disappear from maps in a single blow; by such a token, the war cemented the romantic tradition of the 'culture of peoples'. According to the IICI, the realization of the European ideal should take place on the cultural plane through a dialectical exchange between national cultures, but to reach this point it was necessary to work on the notions of 'people' and 'popular culture'. The comparative study of popular arts could help to strengthen the idea of a united European culture, singling out, at once, the variegated differences existing within it.

The institute organized a memorable international congress of popular arts in Prague in the autumn of 1928.[37] The city was chosen for its strategic position from an ethnic and political point of view: as one of the speakers said, 'The capital of Czechoslovakia is the place where the Slavs get in touch with the Germans; at an equal distance from the northern and southern regions, it is a true crossroads of European cultures.'[38] The congress proceedings were published in French three years later.[39] Collected into two volumes and improved by a remarkable illustrative apparatus, the papers were organized in three sections. The first focused on theoretical questions and on the definition and the origins of popular art, with essays of exponents of the German, Balkan and 'Slav' areas, among whom were directors of ethnographic museums and scholars of prehistoric archaeology, as well as school teachers of applied arts. This first section was meant to analyse the juxtaposition of popular arts with primitive, prehistoric and infantile art, with the intention of using popular art to understand the anthropological reasons behind uneducated artistic production. The second section of the proceedings was organized on a geographical basis and included studies of national and local areas. Notwithstanding their openness to extra-European contexts, the studies were by scholars of the old continent whose folkloristic traditions had, for at least a century, been the object of literary and historical evaluation: Sweden, Switzerland and, especially, Russia, Poland, Czechoslovakia, Romania and Ukraine. The third section, the most dense, offered detailed overviews of objects organized in accordance with the traditional hierarchy of the arts: architecture (rural houses), sculptures on wood and metal, ceramics and fabrics (costumes, ornaments, rags). Confirming the anthropological character of the undertaking, the last two sub-sections integrated the exposition of 'artifacts' with studies of 'performances', the ephemeral expressions of popular culture: music, dance and theatre.

In 1928, the time seemed to be right for an exhibition of the state of research into European cultures. The colossal congress in Prague represented the first survey of a diversity of European experiences, the first attempt to assess a discipline that, since the previous century, had been perfecting itself and becoming more and more specialized. In the first decades of the twentieth century, mainly in France, Durkheim's new sociology was used in combination with the most ancient ethnographic and folkloristic research; for example, in André Varagnac's work, the future curator of the Musée des Arts et Traditions Populaires and then of the Musée des Antiquités Nationales.[40] In 1925, the Institut d'ethnologie of Paris was inaugurated, led by the likes of Rivet, Lévy-Bruhl and Mauss. In 1929, the Société du folklore français was founded, while, at the same time, studies *sur le terrain* multiplied in number, following the path paved by historical research.[41] Such activity, on the one hand, was about confronting distant and 'primitive' cultures and, on the other hand, of scientifically studying original aspects of an advanced country such as France by focusing on the lower classes and on the peripheries – both, up until then, ignored by a centralizing and elitist conception of knowledge.[42] This intellectual excitement reached its peak with the Universal Exhibition of 1937, when, in the new Palais de Chaillot, the Musée des Arts et Traditions populaires,[43] the renewed Musée de l'Homme and the Musée des Monuments français were grouped together – a combination which symbolized the unity of the anthropological, ethnological and artistic aspects of the study of man.

It comes as no surprise, then, that the conception underlying the Prague congress was mainly indebted to a Frenchman, the art historian Henri Focillon, who was also the author of the 'Introduction' to the proceedings. Focillon believed it was necessary to take away popular arts from the domain of nature in order to give them back to that of culture, understood as an open and dynamic system of relations. The study of popular arts, before dividing, united – he contended. From such a viewpoint, approaching a popular patrimony and studying the wealth of its traditions was tantamount to paying tribute to the moral aspect of man and his universality. Now, such a conviction was tied to a precise idea of people that had a French root, contrasting with the *Volk* of German Romantics. In fact, wrote Focillon, 'a people is an ancient or recent group, crystallized in a language and in a civilization; but such languages and civilizations grow rich from the outside, on pain of dying. History is made more by communications than conservations.'[44]

The idea of a people – or nation – as Focillon understood it was the one laid down by Ernest Renan. In the lesson he held at the Sorbonne on 11 March 1882, on the fundamental question '*Qu'est-ce qu'une nation?*', in the full climacteric of neo-positivism, Renan firmly rejected the coincidence of race and people: 'A nation is a soul, a spiritual principle ... through their different, and even opposite, faculties, nations work for the common oeuvre of civilization; all bring a note to this great concert of humanity which, in the end, is the highest ideal reality that we might reach.'[45] Renan's notion of 'people' remained the universalist conception of the French Revolution. In Renan, Focillon saw a means to correct the ethnic interpretation of the idea of 'people' and the dramatic drift he saw before his own eyes. Correspondingly, he summarized his ideas in a commemorative discourse on the great linguist, philologist and historian: '*Patrie* is not the determinism of blind forces, it is the spirit of freedom. Here we are in opposition to another doctrine, an unjust interpretation of obsolete and limited traits, Gobineau's, to which even Taine largely refers and, it must be said, modern German nationalists, too.'[46]

The Museum as the 'First Outline of European Self-Awareness'

Within the IICI, the idea of founding an international organization specifically dedicated to the museum took shape quite quickly. It is possible to reconstruct the main steps of its creation thanks to Focillon's Parisian archives, which contain an entire dossier on the IICI.[47] It is actually to him that we owe the first call for the creation of what would be the *Office International des Musées* (OIM) – a project published in 1927 in the OIM's review *Mouseion*.[48] Members of the first commission were, besides Focillon, the Belgian politician, Jules Destrée; the president of the Federal Commission of Fine Arts in Geneva, Daniel Baud-Bovy; the curator of the Musée du Cinquantenaire in Bruxelles, Jean Capart; the director of the Kupferstichkabinett in Berlin, Max Friedländer; the curator of the department of paintings, drawings and prints at the Louvre, Jean Guiffrey; the director of the Prado, Fernando Alvarez de Sotomayor; and Henri Verne, director of the National Museums of France.[49] The OIM was conceived of as the central organ, having the purpose of 'connecting with one another all the museums of the world' and of promoting the transmission of knowledge of works of art and monuments belonging to a supranational patrimony. The OIM was hence a kind of super-museum, the main task of which was to undertake 'federal' initiatives such as the documentation, the preservation and the exchange of works of art and reproductions. It can be said that it created a first, embryonic, 'European network of museums'. The birth of the OIM can be placed within wider discussions about the public role of museums and the definition of the new science of museology that was taking hold in Europe in the 1920s and 1930s.

The president of the OIM, from the start until his death in 1936, was Jules Destrée,[50] a key figure for understanding the cultural policy of the IICI. A proud Flemish man, a lawyer, a firm pacifist and an active deputy, he was a representative of late-nineteenth-century socialist humanitarianism who strongly believed that culture in general, and the arts in particular, could be catalysts of the self-awareness of a 'people'.[51] He was among the founders of Popular Universities, institutions which were meant to help the working classes by giving them an educational and aggregative role, and which in Belgium, as in France, were an important social phenomenon. Paul Valéry, paying tribute to Destrée, drew a subtle profile of him, praising the fact that he could combine, 'deep within himself, an intimate cult, that of art and that of the superior values of culture'.[52] His deep-seated interest in the arts, and his activity as a Flemish art historian,[53] helped him to become Minister of the Sciences and Arts in 1919 and, from then onwards, his commitment to the literacy and education of the poor and lower social classes was constant. Not surprisingly, Destrée adhered, from its founding, to the cultural initiatives of the League of Nations, aptly filling the role of spiritual guide of the Office, which also conceived the museum as an institution open to all.

Like Destrée, the young socialist Focillon had been educated in accordance with the Proudhonian idea that culture was the main springboard of social emancipation.[54] At the time of his entry into the IICI, in 1925, he already had considerable experience in the field of museums. Director of the Musée des Beaux Arts of Lyon between 1913 and 1923,[55] he had already laid out his idea of a public museum in 1921[56] which, for him, derived from the French Revolution; a museum open to all embodying the right of each individual to culture.[57] According to Focillon, the museum represented one of the fundamental institutions of social life, the basic structure of intellectual life in urban society; it was here that the connective tissue joining modernity to tradition was created and, importantly, that the specific values of a people blended with the 'universal' values of arts. He articulated such a belief, once again, in the programme of the OIM: the museum was 'an institution dedicated to intellectual cooperation', since it presented, at once, 'the genius of a nation and those of foreign civilizations'; it was, therefore, 'the best possible means of knowing a culture, in the most tangible manner', since, just like books, museums represented the best way to reconstruct the history of cultural relations and exchanges of ideas among peoples. In their own way, overcoming 'national questions, museums have been the first premonition of a European and world-wide self-awareness'.[58]

Europe and 'Patrimony'

The basic assumption animating the works of the IICI was that arts should play a privileged part in the understanding of cultures. Such a conviction went along with the rise of the inclusive and 'laic' conception of civilization described above; civilization made itself real and could be perceived in the artistic testimonies created by human intelligence. The activity of the IICI was also in tune, at the beginning of the twentieth century, with the widespread phenomenon known as the 'modern cult of monuments', as defined by the art historian Alois Riegl.[59] After the Industrial Revolution, Europe experienced an ever-growing interest for what was being called 'patrimony', a common – or public – good, understood at once as the 'historic monuments' of the past and as a source of education for future generations – a precious legacy that had to be loved and preserved.[60]

It must be said that in France, at the end of the nineteenth century, the idea of patrimony was influenced by a strongly nationalistic interpretation, finding one of its most convinced champions in Maurice Barrès, who dedicated most of his work as a writer and deputy to the exaltation of artistic patrimony, an unrelenting work that influenced generations of French intellectuals and artists. His idea of national patrimony presaged the modern idea of a 'disseminated museum', for it assumed that the artistic culture of a nation can be appreciated not in its museum-cemeteries, but in the environment marked by man. For Barrès, cultural patrimony was a notion that has to do with feelings, a sort of energy that flows as a vital flux from one end to the other of the *héxagone*, immediately recognizable and capable of reaching everyone. Yet, because of this irrational element, such a notion was particularly dangerous, leading to an ethnic interpretation of art and culture based on blood and race, which moved Barrès towards a point of view close to that of the *Action française*.[61]

Even Victor Hugo admitted that arts had a strong social dimension (*Utilité du beau*, 1860) and considered them a powerful lock-pick for catching the 'soul' of a civilization: 'One can hence reach deeper into the soul of the people and into the inner history of human societies by means of a literary rather than a political life.'[62] But because art could speak a universal language (prelinguistic and prepolitical), Hugo – who also was an active supporter of the policy of national patrimony[63] – recognized its role as an ideal binder among the people of that utopian European federation he was attempting to prefigure; in his opinion, Europe would be made, above all, through the exaltation of its imperishable monuments.[64]

In line with this rather more democratic French tradition was the policy of the Institut International de Coopération Intellectuelle, which recognized that artistic and historical monuments are a cultural patrimony with a universal value and that their protection was a common duty for all people. Following such an assumption, the OIM operated for the safeguarding of patrimony; one of its first steps was the creation of a Commission international des monuments historiques (1933), which was meant to protect the common patrimony of humanity, trying, on the European plane, what had already been done in France in 1930 for 'the protection of natural monuments and artistic, historic, scientific, legendary or picturesque sites' and laying down, for the first time, the notion of a 'site' of historic importance.[65] The OIM was directly involved in the most important initiatives in the field of restoration,[66] which, precisely in the early 1930s, led to the drafting of normative 'Charters': the Athens Charter for Restoration (1931), promoted and then published by the League of Nations;[67] the Italian Charter of 1932,[68] and, finally, the well-known 1933 Athens Charter.[69]

The theoretical programmes were soon followed by emergency operations. In 1936, during the Spanish Civil War, the first aerial bombings took place with devastating consequences for artistic patrimony, damaging the Prado.[70] The tragic events in Spain soon became a central concern for European public opinion, eliciting debates that grew in intensity over the years.[71] In 1939, the OIM printed a volume dedicated to *La protection des monuments et des oeuvres d'art en temps de guerre*,[72] that also contained a 'Project for an International Convention', centred on the idea of preventive protection.[73] But such a project, like the analogous *La protection des collections nationales d'art et d'histoire. Essai de réglementation internationale* (OIM, 1939), came too late, after the war had already defeated all efforts to cooperate.[74]

The IICI's organization for museums had taken upon itself, through an act of coordination, the works of the many national associations already active since the end of the previous century.[75] Its European scope aimed to counter cultural fundamentalisms, coupled with an appreciation of artistic diversities, and it turned the experience of the OIM into a fundamental episode of the history of museology and the protection of artistic patrimony. After the war, the legacy of the IICI was taken on by the organ officially created, in November 1945, within the Organization of the United Nations in New York; that is, UNESCO. The new organization was destined to perpetuate – on a global scale – the experiment of the preceding coalition, animated by the idea of a universal culture. Yet it is telling that UNESCO was set up, right from the start, in Paris and not in New York, thus asserting its ideal continuity with its predecessor.[76] During its first General Conference, in 1946, UNESCO took up, among other things, the task of reabsorbing the previous activities of the OIM, hence recognizing the role the latter had played in the field of museology and in the protection of patrimony.[77] Once again, the impetus to recreate an international office for museums came from Europe and in particular from France; it was, in fact, at the Louvre that, in November 1946, the first conference of the ICOM (International Council of Museums), a non-governmental organization of UNESCO, was held.[78]

Years later, the Cultural Convention for Europe, born within the European Council in 1954 and later absorbed by the European Museum Forum (EMF), listed, among its aims, the achievement of:

> a greater unity between its members for the purpose, among others, of safeguarding and realising the ideals and principles which are their common heritage, ... to pursue a policy of common action designed to safeguard and encourage the development of European culture, ... to foster among the nationals of all members, and of such other European states as may accede thereto, the study of the languages, history and civilisation of the others and of the civilisation which is common to them all.[79]

In this way, the experience of intellectual cooperation of the 1920s and the belief in cultural patrimony as a binding element of European nations survived the Second World War. From such a viewpoint, the founding fathers of the League of Nations had indicated the path towards that European cultural unity which seems today the greatest of all the challenges facing Europe.

Notes

1   P. Valéry, *La crise de l'esprit* (1919).
2. C.H. Ellis, *The Origin, Structure and Working of the League of Nations* (London, 1928) reissued in 2003; F.P. Walters, *A History of the League of Nations* (London, 1960); M. Marbeau, *La société des nations* (Paris, 2001); VV.AA., *The League of Nations in Retrospect* (Berlin and New York, 1983).
3. J.P. Azéma and M. Winock, *La IIIème république (1870–1940)* (Paris, 1976).
4. M. af Malmborg and B. Strâth (eds), *The Meaning of Europe: Variety and Contention within and among Nations* (New York and Oxford, 2002).
5. Great Britain, France, Italy and Japan were permanent members of the Council. Between 1926 and 1933, following the Locarno Treaties, even Germany was admitted and became one of

the most active members of the League of Nations: it was in fact with Stresemann that Briand launched, in 1929, his famous plan for the creation of the United States of Europe; J.-M. Guieu, 'Genève 1926: capitale de la paix? L'admission de l'Allemagne à la SDN', *Bulletin de l'Institut Pierre Renouvin* 12 (2001).

6.   F. Proust, 'Point de passage', *Revue des Sciences Humaines*, special issue *Mémoires de l'Europe* 3 (1993), 26.

7.   J.-L. Chabot, *Aux origines intellectuelles de l'Union européenne: l'idée d'Europe unie de 1919–1939* (Grenoble, 2005) ; J.-M. Guieu, C. Le Dréau, J. Raflik, L. Warlouzet, *Penser et construire l'Europe au XXe siècle, Historiographie, Bibliographie, Enjeux* (Paris, 2007); P. Stirk, 'Introduction: Crisis and Continuity in Interwar Europe', in idem (ed.), *European Unity in Context. The Interwar Period* (London and New York, 1989), 1–32.

8.   On the role of France in the League of Nations, see C. Manigand, *Les Français au service de la Société des Nations* (Bern, 2003); J.-M. Guieu, *Le rameau et le glaive, Les militants français pour la Société des Nations* (Paris, 2008); idem, 'L'Europe des militants français pour la Société des Nations', in K. Rücker and L. Warlouzet (eds), *Quelle(s) Europe(s)? Nouvelles approches en histoire de l'intégration européenne* (Brussels, 2006), 51–63.

9.   See R. Deswarte, *An American Future? Americanization and the Idea of Europe in the Inter-War Period*, unpublished paper.

10.   See his speech in *L'Avenir de l'Esprit européen* (Paris, 1933).

11.   On Valéry's intellectaul engagement in the IICI, see P. Roulin, *Paul Valéry. Témoin et juge du monde moderne* (Neuchâtel, 1964), 181–83.

12.   Quoted in A. Sanna, 'Sguardi sull'Europa', in C. Papparo (ed.), *Di là dalla storia. Paul Valéry: tempo, mondo, opera, individuo* (Macerata, 2007), 114.

13.   J.-M. Guieu, 'L'"insécurité collective". La Société des Nations et l'Europe dans l'entre-deux-guerres', *Bulletin de l'Institut Pierre Renouvin* 30 (2009), 21–43.

14.   P. Gerbet, *Le rêve d'un ordre mondial: de la SDN à l'ONU* (Paris, 1996).

15.   M.C. Giuntella, *Cooperazione intellettuale ed educazione alla pace nell'Europa della Società delle Nazioni* (Padova, 2001).

16.   J.-J. Renoliet, *L'UNESCO oubliée: La Société des Nations et la coopération intellectuelle (1919–1946)* (Paris, 1999). Also see *L'Institut International de Coopération Intellectuelle* (Paris, 1946); Pham-Thi-Tu, *La Coopération Intellectuelle sous la Société des Nations* (Geneva, 1962); C. Békri, *L'UNESCO, une entreprise erronée?* (Paris, 1991).

17.   P. Ory and J.-F. Sirinelli, *Les Intellectuels en France de l'Affaire Dreyfus à nos jours* (Paris, 1986).

18.   Luchaire would be the first secretary of the IICI; see Renoliet, *L'UNESCO oublié*, 14.

19.   Renoliet, *L'UNESCO oubliée*, 73–75.

20.   Institut de Coopération Intellectuelle, *Pour une société des esprits* (Geneva, 1933); Renoliet, *L'UNESCO oubliée*, 74.

21.   E. Borel, *L'Avenir de l'Esprit européen*, 299.

22.   M. Löwy, 'L'humanisme romantique allemand et l'Europe', in Madonna Desbazeille (ed.), *L'Europe, naissance d'une utopie?: genèse de l'idée d'Europe du XVIe au XIXe siècles* (Paris-Montréal, 1996), 165–72.

23.   On Focillon, see M. Waschek (ed.), *Relire Focillon* (Paris, 1998); VV.AA., *La vie des formes. Henri Focillon et les arts*, exhibition catalogue (Lyon and Paris, 2004); A. Ducci, A. Thomine, R. Varese (eds) *Focillon e l'Italia. Focillon et l'Italie* (Firenze, 2006); A. Ducci 'Henri Focillon', in P. Charron and J.-M. Guillouët (eds), *Dictionnaire d'histoire de l'art du moyen âge occidental* (Paris, 2009), 374–75.

24.   See Walter Cahn, 'L'art français et l'art allemand dans la pensée de Focillon', in Waschek, *Relire Focillon*, 27–51; and W. Sauerländer, 'En face des barbares et à l'écart des dévots. L'humanisme médiéval d'Henri Focillon', 53–74.

25.   Similar conclusions are reached by C. Petit-Dutaillis and P. Guinard, *L'essor des États d'Occident: France, Angleterre, Peninsule iberique* (Paris, 1944).

26.   H. Focillon, 'Autour de l'an mil, études archéologiques', *Annuaire du Collège de France* (1939), 1–4.

27. E. Viollet-le-Duc, *Entretien sur l'Architecture. Septième Entretien. Sur les principes de l'architecture occidentale au Moyen Age* (Paris, 1862–64).

28. F. Fichet, 'Réorganisation de la société européenne selon Saint-Simon et Augustin Thierry', in Desbazeille, *L'Europe*, 155–63.

29. As explained by Ossola: 'This demand, stressing the transformation thorugh the work of art, is essentially the civilizing vocation as opposed to political and ethnical search for a nature, that is to say a "specific patrimony" *contro la ricerca, biologica e politica*, of nature, i.e. a "specific genetic patrimony" that identifies and localizes', C. Ossola, 'Europa, Europa', in idem (ed.), *Europa: miti di identità* (Venice, 2001), xiii.

30. M. Winock, *Clémenceau* (Paris, 2007) and idem, *Les voix de la liberté: les écrivains engagés au XIX siècle* (Paris, 2001).

31. In *Civilisation. Évolution d'un mot et d'un groupe d'idées* (Paris, 1930). On the history of the meaning of term, the bibliography is almost endless; an essential text (that also takes into account the overlapping of 'civilization' and 'culture') still is the one by E. Benveniste, 'Civilization. Contribution à l'histoire du mot', in idem, *Problèmes de linguistique générale* (Paris, 1966), 336–45.

32. See the chapter by Vittorio Dini in this volume.

33. V. Hugo, 'Paris', in idem, *France et Belgique, Alpes et Pyrénées, Voyages et excursions, Paris* (Paris, 1955), 509–13.

34. This is testified by the *querelle* on the alleged racial origins of art opposing the Viennese pro-Nazi art historian Josef Strzygowski to the socialist Focillon; Josef Strzygowski, 'À Henri Focillon', in SDN/IICI, *Correspondance 4. Civilisations. Orient. Occident. Génie du Nord. Latinité* (Paris, 1935), 109–11; and, ibid., H. Focillon, 'À Joseph Strzygowski', 131–65; also see J. Arrechea Miguel, 'Focillon y Strzygowski o la lejana raíz del arte occidental', *Historia del arte* 7 (1993), 559–605.

35. In a letter dated 22 September 1938 to his Romanian friend Georges Opresco.

36. I am currently carrying out research into such publications.

37. Such initiative was to be followed by others: the Second International Congress of Popular Arts in Antwerp (1930) and the International Exposition of Popular Arts in Bern (1934).

38. A. Stransky, 'Projet d'organisation d'archives internationales de l'art populaire', in IICI, *Art populaire* (Paris, 1931), vol. 1, 29.

39. Ibid.

40. *Instinct et technique: remarques sur les conditions externes du comportement humain* (Paris, 1929) and *Définition du folklore* (Paris, 1938).

41. This was the aim, coherent with the *nouvelle histoire*, of the members of the Commission des recherches collectives, led by Lucien Febvre (1934), pushing for a decentralized research focusing on provinces.

42. R. Muchembled, *Culture populaire et culture des élites dans la France moderne (XVe–XVIIIe siècles)* (Paris, 1978).

43. M. Segalen, *Vie d'un musée. 1937–2005* (Paris, 2005).

44. H. Focillon, 'Introduction', in IICI, *Art populaire*, xi.

45. The quotes are from F. Mercury, *Renan* (Paris, 1990), 395–97.

46. H. Focillon, *Ernest Renan* (Lyon, 1923), 43.

47. C. Tissot, *Archives Henri Focillon (1881–1943). Inventaire* (Paris, 1998), 211–14.

48. H. Focillon, 'L'oeuvre de coopération intellectuelle et l'Office International des Musées', *Mouseion* 1 (1927), 3–10.

49. *Programme de l'Office International des Musées (Première réunion d'experts. Genève, 13 et 14 janvier 1927), Mouseion* 1 (1927), 11–16.

50. E. Foundoukidis, 'L'œuvre internationale de Jules Destrée dans le domaine des arts', *Mouseion* 33/34 (1936), 7–16.

51. J. Tordeur, *Jules Destrée le multiple* (Brussels, 1995).

52. P. Valéry, 'Hommage', *Journal des Tribunaux*, 10 Dec. 1933, quoted in F.B. and U. Crucitti, *Apollo tra le dune. Amicizie belghe di Paul Valéry* (Pisa, 1979), 55.

53. For example, his *Hugo van der Goes* (Brussels and Paris, 1914) and *Le Maître dit de Flémalle – Robert Campin* (Brussels and Paris, 1930).

54. A. Ducci, 'Entre art et politique. La formation parisienne, 1881–1913', in VV.AA., *La vie des formes*, 41–53.

55. C. Briend, 'Le conservateur', in VV.AA., *La vie des formes*, 99–109.

56. H. Focillon, 'La Conception moderne des musées', in *Actes du Congrès international d'histoire de l'art* (1921) (Paris, 1923), vol. 1, 85–94.

57. On this, see D. Poulot, *Musée, nation, patrimoine. 1789–1815* (Paris, 1997), 195–97.

58. Focillon, *L'oeuvre de coopération*, passim.

59. S. Scarrocchia, 'Introduzione' in A. Riegl, *Il culto moderno dei monumenti. Il suo carattere e i suoi inizi* (Bologna, 1985), 14–16; R. Recht, *Penser le patrimoine. Mise en scène et mise en ordre de l'art* (Paris, 1998), especially 86–89; S. Scarrocchia, 'Le concept moderne de monument et la valeur de l'ancien: pour une anthropologie de la conservation du patrimoine', *Revue de l'art* 145 (2004), 19–28.

60. J.-P. Babelon and A. Chastel, *La notion de patrimoine* (Paris, 1994); F. Choay, *L'Allégorie du patrimoine* (Paris, 1992), and her more recent *Le patrimoine en questions: anthologie pour un combat* (Paris, 2009).

61. See Barrès's *Du sang, de la volupté et la mort* (Paris, 1894), and his *Le Roman de l'énergie nationale* (Paris, 1897); Z. Sternhell, *Maurice Barrès et le nationalisme français* (Brussels, 1985).

62. Quoted in Savy, *L'Europe de Victor Hugo*.

63. R. Recht (ed.), *Victor Hugo et le débat patrimonial* (Paris, 2003).

64. Savy, *L'Europe de Victor Hugo*.

65. T. Gaehtgens, 'Présentation de la problématique du contexte, XIXe–XXe siècle', in F. Furet (ed.), *Patrimoine, temps, espace, patrimoine en place, patrimoine déplacé* (Paris, 1997), 47–65.

66. In 1930 the OIM promoted the Rome conference on methods of preservation and restoration of paintings; in 1939 it published the *Manuel de la conservation et de la restauration des peintures*, see A. Conti, *Manuale di restauro* (Turin, 1996), 56.

67. OIM, *La conservation des monuments d'art et d'histoire* (Paris, 1933).

68. Immediately published in *Mouseion* (1932), 17–18; see A. Aveta, 'La Carta italiana del restauro (1932)', in R. della Monica (ed.), *Carte, risoluzioni e documenti per la conservazione ed il restauro* (Pisa, 2006), 123–46.

69. For these, see G. Rocchi, *Istituzioni di restauro dei beni architettonici e ambientali* (Milan, 1994), 505–7; F. Choay, 'La Conférence d'Athènes et ses leçons', in della Monica, *Carte, risoluzioni*, 35–38.

70. A.C. Castellary, *El Museo del Prado y la guerra civil. Figueras-Ginebra, 1939* (Madrid, 1991).

71. See J. Renau, 'L'organisation de la défense du patrimoine artistique et historique espagnol pendant la guerre civile', *Mouseion* 39/40 (1937), 7–66. Also M. Daniel, 'Spain: Culture at War', in VV.AA., *Art and Power. Europe under the Dictators 1930–1945* (London, 1995), 63–68, who also insists on the critique of the League of Nations towards the National-Socialist Party and its responsibilities for the tragedies in Spain (68).

72. IOM, 'La protection des monuments et des oeuvres d'art en temps de guerre', *Mouseion* 47/48 (1939). Also see idem, 'Les mesures de protection prises dans différents pays contre les dangers de la guerre', *Mouseion*, suppl. Sep./Oct. 1939, 13–22; and idem, 'Les mesures de précaution prises dans divers pays pour protéger les monuments et œuvres d'art au cours de la guerre actuelle', *Mouseion* 49/50 (1939), 9–28.

73. See A.F. Panzera, *La tutela internazionale dei beni culturali in tempo di guerra* (Turin, 1993); and M. Frigo, *La protezione dei beni culturali nel diritto internazionale* (Milano, 1986).

74. Renoliet, *L'UNESCO oubliée*, 311.

75. As the British Isles' Museums Associations, the United States' American Association of Museums and the Deutscher Museumsbund.

76. On the difficult transition from the IICI to the UNESCO, see Renoliet, *L'UNESCO oublié*, 175–77.

77. J.-L. Luxen, 'La Convention du Patrimoine mondial (UNESCO): analyse critique', in della Monica, *Carte, risoluzioni*, 87–95.

78. P. Boylan, S.A. Baghli and Y. Herreman, *The International Council of Museums (ICOM) 1946–1996: Fifty Years in the Service of Museums and Their Development* (Paris, 1998).

79. *European Cultural Convention*, (European Treaty Series, No. 18), Paris, 19 Dec. 1954; also see D. Therond, 'Les Conventions du Conseil de l'Europe en matière de patrimoine culturel', in della Monica, *Carte, risoluzioni*, 57–64. According to its Declaration (1977), the EMF was meant 'to give a significant contribution to the understanding and safeguard of the European heritage … and to encourage exchange of ideas, information and experiences among museum professionals from countries included in the Council of Europe'. On this, see M. Negri (ed.), *Porte Aperte. L'accesso al patrimonio europeo nei musei* (Opening Doors. Access to the European Heritage in Museums) (Florence, 2003), and especally, idem, 'Introduzione', 3–8; and C. Bäumler and S. Gossner, 'Affrontare il patrimonio europeo. Il ruolo dei musei nel processo di creazione di un'identità europea', 39–44.

Chapter 12

HUIZINGA, INTELLECTUAL COOPERATION AND THE SPIRIT OF EUROPE, 1933–1945

>ᵗᵗᵗᵗᵗᵗᵗᵗᵗ<

Anne-Isabelle Richard

> What can we foresee, what should we think
> about the next likely guise of the European spirit?[1]
> – Paul Valery, *L'avenir de l'esprit européen*

This was the question that Paul Valéry posed to thirty European intellectuals assembled in Paris in October 1933.[2] The French Federal Committee for European Cooperation[3] had invited them to discuss the future of the European spirit at the International Institute of Intellectual Cooperation (IICI). The timing of this conference was pertinent. The experience of the First World War had led to many works about the decline of European culture in the immediate aftermath of the War.[4] The early 1930s saw a second wave of this type of work.[5] By 1933 the Great Depression had been raging for a few years and had affected even the strongest economies. Hitler had come to power and was about to announce Germany's withdrawal from the League of Nations. The nations of Europe tended 'to retreat behind their borders'.[6] What indeed was the future of the European spirit in these circumstances?

No exact definition of the 'European spirit' was attempted, as Julio Dantas put it: 'the European spirit still understood itself imperfectly'.[7] The existence of a European spirit was acknowledged by all, however.[8] In describing the 'European spirit', discussants drew on a repertoire of images and ideas, which included references to humanism, Enlightenment values and Christian morals.[9] As president of the meeting, Valéry pointed out in his opening address that, once attained, the European spirit would not automatically last. It had to be maintained in the face of certain political, economic and intellectual circumstances that were leading to anxiety and insecurity about the European spirit. Most intellectuals assembled identified the rising force of nationalism as an important source of this insecurity. Valéry went on to argue that a 'société de l'esprit' was an essential precondition for a viable 'société des nations' and for a peaceful future.[10] What then, should be the role, if any, of intellectuals in promulgating this 'société de l'esprit'?

The Dutch cultural historian, Johan Huizinga, who participated in the Paris meeting, can be regarded as a prime example of an intellectual imbued with European culture, who was part of an international intellectual network. He concurred with the majority at the meeting that to 'guérir notre pauvre monde, si riche et si infirme' a 'société de l'esprit' was needed.[11] While he firmly rejected nationalism, he considered patriotism a natural and benign phenomenon. In his thinking about the European spirit and the role of intellectuals in international society he drew strongly on his national background. Huizinga's thinking was very much informed by what he saw as the 'Dutch experience' in which moderation and moralism played an important role. This mindset led to a cautious attitude regarding the role of intellectuals in public life.

The question of 'Europe' and of a 'European spirit' greatly concerned intellectuals at this time of international crisis, a concern which was contemporaneous with political discontentment with a League-based internationalism. Focusing on the discussions at the IICI and the publications that followed from it, Huizinga will be used as a case study of one such intellectual. This essay will examine how the shared acceptance of the notion of a 'European spirit' could lead to different analyses regarding the role of the intellectual in society.

Huizinga's hesitant attitude to practical conceptions of 'Europe' and to the role of intellectuals in promulgating the European spirit will be analysed. Drawing on the framework of Dutch history and the Dutch foreign policy tradition, this article will then compare Huizinga's ideas with Dutch thinking about Europe in the interwar period and thus link Dutch 'sobriety and bourgeois mentality'[12] to the European spirit under threat from nationalism in the 1930s and early 1940s.[13] While Huizinga's thoughts regarding the role of the Netherlands in the world and his activities in the framework of intellectual cooperation have been studied,[14] his perception of Europe has not. Huizinga's attitude proves to be very similar to Dutch government discourse. As a result, a study of his thoughts expressed in this international context can help to elucidate both the development of, and the connection between, the thoughts of an eminent Dutch intellectual and the official Dutch position on Europe in the 1930s and 1940s. It then also sheds light on the extent to which the championing of a seemingly international cause, 'Europe', was compatible with an embrace of national ideas in foreign policy.

Intellectual Cooperation between
Passive Universalism and Universal Activism

The meeting on the future of the European spirit took place in the context of the series of meetings[15] organized by the International Committee on Intellectual Cooperation (ICIC), an organization working under the auspices of the League of Nations.[16] The aim of this organization was to strengthen intellectual collaboration and understanding, which in turn would reinforce the league's work for peace.[17] The ICIC was composed of eminent intellectuals who participated in a private capacity. While a geographical spread was sought, none of those involved represented their country officially. Nonetheless, many tended to – consciously or unconsciously – adopt the positions of their countries and take on an ambassadorial role.

The central concept of the meeting, the European spirit, which was seen as instrumental for a more peaceful future of Europe, has to be understood in the context of a surge of ideas of an 'international spirit' or an 'international mind' during this period. This notion of 'international mind' was explained by some of its proponents as a claim to transcend difference on an international level: to reconcile national interests with a universal vision of global society without sacrificing the uniqueness of the local.[18] The European spirit had similar connotations of transcending difference (on a regional scale) whilst respecting national traditions. More tangible, but also more 'political', ideas for economic or political cooperation, which were the common focal points of many European cooperation societies, were, quite deliberately, not discussed at the meeting. This distinction between the European spirit and more concrete European projects corresponded to the distinction that has been drawn between 'Europeanness' and 'Europeanism'.[19] The meeting was concerned with a general Europeanness. Whether this should develop into a tangible Europeanism was beyond the limits of the discussion. The majority thought (or hoped) that 'reason' would lead to a unified and peaceful Europe.[20]

The other central concept discussed at the meeting was nationalism. Nationalism was seen by many of the intellectuals assembled as the force that threatened the existence of a European spirit.[21] Like the European spirit, no definition of nationalism was attempted. Given the different conceptions of nationalism represented at the meeting – by intellectuals ranging from left-leaning liberals to sympathisers of the National Socialist regime – this would have been impossible. The lack of a clear understanding of what was meant by nationalism however made the distinction with patriotism problematic, leading at times to a conversation of the deaf.[22] The distinction between these contested terms, as it emerged, fitted in with a long tradition of equating patriotism with 'good' nationalism, and nationalism with 'bad' nationalism.[23] Huizinga later described the distinction between these two concepts as the difference between the will to safeguard what one cherishes and the desire to have one's nation prevail over and at the expense of others.[24] The identification of nationalism as a potential threat then did therefore not mean that everything national had to be overcome. The overarching view was that national cultures could enrich European culture without becoming diluted themselves.[25] The German and Italian participants, however, had a different conception of the European spirit and its future.[26] Espousing a form of anti-intellectualism, they rejected the role of reason and stressed the importance of force and nationalism.[27] The influence of domestic politics was evident in this position.

What should the role of intellectuals be in light of the nationalist threat to the European spirit?[28] The interwar period saw pressure on intellectuals from both the left and the right to face reality, take responsibility and become active for their cause.[29] At the same time an apolitical universalism advocated aloofness. The question of political engagement of intellectuals had been on the agenda of the ICIC for some years. On the one hand, the original aims of the commission were in a sense political. Defending universal humanist values and intellectual cooperation were not ends in themselves, but were means to attain the pre-eminent goal of the League of Nations, 'to create a state of mutual understanding between peoples', with peace as the result.[30] This could require the adoption of a political position. On the other hand, to ensure the participation of intellectuals from as many states as possible, political questions were best avoided. 'Intellectual cooperation must be universal and must, as much as possible, be independent of politics.'[31]

In the end it was this view that prevailed in the 1930s. The idea that it was not the role or the task of the intellectual to become involved in politics held great sway. The reasons for this were that, as Marie Curie pointed out, the experience of the First World War in which intellectuals had been on opposite sides of the battlefield, had to be avoided.[32] Secondly and perhaps more importantly, most of those involved saw the state of world affairs as a passing phase which did not require political engagement or activism by intellectuals.[33] The Organisation for Intellectual Cooperation (OIC)[34] therefore did not intervene to defend the universal ideals that it aspired to, nor the rights of intellectuals under threat from totalitarian regimes, thereby tacitly condoning the situation.

At the meeting in 1933, the question of whether intellectuals should take a proactive role in promulgating the European spirit and countering nationalism, or whether intellectuals would serve this spirit best if they refrained from any 'political' activity, framed the discussions. Following the OIC position, it had been agreed when the meeting was organized that politics was to remain beyond the discussions.[35] Paul Valéry for example gently scolded Aldous Huxley for wandering into the political domain.[36] However, at the end of the meeting, Jules Romains advocated a more active and 'political' position. He argued that avoiding politics led to 'academism', by which he meant talking without compromising oneself. Romains pointed out that avoiding politics did not mean that politics remained unconsidered, or that no position was adopted. Avoiding politics did not make intellectual cooperation apolitical.[37]

Despite the 'apolitical' stance adopted by the meeting on the European spirit, it was thought that the discussions about the future of the European spirit should be continued in a more permanent form. To this end a Société d'études européennes was founded. However, this society, of which Huizinga was one of the vice-presidents,[38] seems to have developed very little activity.[39]

Johan Huizinga, from Cultural Critic to Cultural Philosopher

Huizinga's engagement with the IICI, when already in his sixties, marked the beginning of his activities as a cultural critic. Up until then he had been renowned as the cultural historian who had written *The Waning of the Middle Ages* in 1919.[40] Huizinga's best-selling book, *In the Shadows of Tomorrow*, came out in 1935.[41] His last major work, *Homo Ludens*, was published in 1938.[42] By then, he had moved from being a cultural historian in the 1910s and 1920s to become a cultural critic in the 1930s, and a cultural philosopher in the late '30s and 1940s.[43] Huizinga had been a member of the Dutch national committee for intellectual cooperation since its conception in 1926.[44] In 1935 he became a member of the ICIC.[45] Although he told his wife that it was 'an incredible waste of time' resulting in '99% paper shuffling and only 1% useful result',[46] this 1 per cent was important enough for Huizinga to be very active in the Commission.[47] Not without foundation, Huizinga has been described as a cultural ambassador for the Netherlands.[48]

In the 1930s, Huizinga was very much part of the European republic of letters. This meant that he saw himself as a European of the spirit and as such a direct heir to the eighteenth century and the humanists.[49] His Europeanness was deeply embedded. In his contribution to the meeting in Paris and in his *Lettre à M. Julien Benda*, which he wrote shortly afterwards, Huizinga developed the main theme of his cultural criticism over the next few years.[50] This theme was very close to the consensus at the meeting: that Europe and, with it, European civilization, were under threat, and that only a reaffirmation of morality could save it from barbarity.

In his most important cultural critique, *In the Shadows of Tomorrow: A Diagnosis of the Mental Suffering of Our Time*, Huizinga further developed this theme.[51] He described what he saw as the ailments of contemporary society: moral decline, technocracy, 'heroism' and 'puerilism'. The 'door that gave access' to these weaknesses was nationalism. Although the book only claimed to be a diagnosis, Huizinga also indicated a (largely undefined) remedy: spiritual regeneration. This spiritual regeneration did not just apply to individuals but also to societies and states. As did many in the interwar period, Huizinga saw a special role for international law in preventing war. In line with Dutch views on international relations going back to Grotius, and reiterated by Huizinga's close friend the influential lawyer Cornelis van Vollenhove, Huizinga argued for an international moral standard.[52]

Applying spiritual regeneration to states did not mean that he advocated some form of European union at that time; his Europeanness did not entail Europeanism. Firstly, he was not convinced by the argument that political or economic reform leading to European cooperation would be a solution to the problems Europe faced. Only spiritual reform could go to the heart of society and have a real impact. Secondly, he was wary of compromising the diversity of nations which made the European spirit unique and worthwhile.

The corollary of this understanding of the idea of 'unity in diversity' was the idea that patriotism was perfectly natural and indeed benign. Whereas he was clear in his condemnation of contemporary nationalism, Huizinga accorded a prominent role to patriotism. He regarded attachment to one's own nation as a social instinct. Echoing Mazzini's idea that national movements worked for the greater good of humanity, Huizinga held that patriotism and Europeanness were not mutually exclusive.[53] One had to accept the binary tension which could make one 'national and European at the same time'.[54]

At the meeting in Paris, the French author of La trahison des clercs, Julien Benda, had questioned Huizinga about his attitude to patriotism. According to Benda, nations had to make sacrifices to cooperate. Benda considered Huizinga to be inconsistent by stressing patriotism and the importance of diversity while condemning nationalism.[55] Huizinga responded that whereas he thought that nations would not consciously make sacrifices, they would do so unconsciously; by getting to know each other and thus finding common ground, they would make sacrifices. Huizinga referred to the Dutch experience, at a crossroads between German, English and French culture, absorbing aspects of all those cultures, yet retaining its own character.[56] A comparison, including Benda's not-unambiguous Discours à la Nation européenne[57] and Huizinga's Lettre à M. Julien Benda, shows that their differences on this point were more differences of approach than differences of opinion.[58] As Huizinga put it himself, while he agreed with most of Benda's ideals, he asked Benda 'to mitigate the severity of [his] noble and pure precepts'.[59]

Despite his concern about the nationalism of the time, or perhaps even because of his concern, Huizinga had an ambivalent attitude to the political engagement of intellectuals. From an academic intellectual, specialized in cultural history, he became more and more a public intellectual. At times he engaged in the debates of the day but, in his role of public intellectual, he mostly commented on the general condition humaine. As rector of the University of Leiden he was confronted by anti-Semitic pamphlets written by the leader of a German delegation. He felt it was his obligation as rector to react immediately and ask the author to leave.[60] On the other hand, when asked in a personal capacity to support the Dutch Committee of Vigilance against national socialism, he refused.

Huizinga's reticence regarding political engagement for intellectuals seems to be explained by two considerations. On the one hand, there was the idea – comparable to Benda's approach in La trahison des clercs – that the only commitment suitable for intellectuals was the universal. When this was compromised, as it was by the anti-Semitic pamphlets incident, his function as rector required him to take action. On the other hand, he trusted that the threats posed to the European spirit would soon pass and that the pendulum would swing the other way. The unlimited nationalism of the annus horribilis of 1933 would soon appear 'absurd'.[61] If intellectuals committed themselves actively to certain causes, they would fuel the existing antagonisms and this situation in which extremisms thrived would only persist.

While this opinion was not uncommon among intellectuals in the 1930s –
Julien Benda also thought that the time for people wanting to unify Europe by
conquering it by force was over[62] – in Huizinga's case it seems to have been
heavily inspired by his understanding of Dutch history and his embeddedness in
the Netherlands.[63]

Huizinga and the Netherlands

Huizinga traced the roots of a national consciousness in the Netherlands not to
the Dutch Revolt, as was the common point of reference, but to the much earlier
and less antagonistic Burgundy period.[64] This was exemplary of Huizinga's
opinion of how identities developed. He emphasized the role of the law in creating
nations, and added that even if a primordial hostility had existed it could disappear
over time, as it had in the Scandinavian countries.[65] This also explains some of the
differences with Benda who saw identities developing in opposition to an 'Other'.[66]

According to Huizinga, the Dutch national character had changed little over
the ages. His understanding of the Dutch national character can be described as
representative of the self-understanding of the Dutch in that period.[67] According
to Huizinga, the Netherlands had always been a society of *burghers* with a down-
to-earth culture.[68] He argued that since the Dutch did not attach overriding value
to ideas, it was easier to respect differing opinions, while it also meant that the
Dutch were less likely to be swept away by fanaticism.[69] Especially after the First
World War, Huizinga became convinced that a certain amount of indifference and
mediocrity might be the price to pay for a peaceful and reasonably balanced
society. As Huizinga's biographer Krul puts it: 'the Dutch sense of reality could
prove useful in a world full of political agitation'.[70]

Huizinga saw the Netherlands as a go-between for the big nations of Europe.
He repeatedly emphasized the unique geographical and cultural position of the
Netherlands, between Britain, Germany and France, and influenced by all three
cultures.[71] In addition, as a believer in the power of international law, he thought
that the smaller countries of Europe had an important role to play in introducing
morals into international relations. Huizinga described the Netherlands as an
honest and disinterested nation that would provide the world with an example by
combining neutrality with membership of the league.[72]

This was a picture that fitted neatly into Dutch foreign-policy doctrine.[73] The
Dutch had followed a policy of strict neutrality since the nineteenth century. Being
a small state, with a large overseas empire, but without the means to defend itself
or its empire, the Netherlands counted on its strategic importance to the great
powers as a means of defence. Because of its positioning on the continent and the
importance of its trade, an independent Netherlands would benefit all great
powers and as a result no one would allow another power to take over the
Netherlands – or at least so the argument ran.[74] A second characteristic was
economically determined. From 1862 onwards the Netherlands had been a free-

trade nation with an open-door policy in the Dutch East Indies. By the early twentieth century, free trade and the gold standard had become enshrined dogmas that had to be upheld.[75] Finally, Dutch foreign policy was marked by an 'internationalist-idealist tradition'.[76] As the country of Grotius, the Dutch portrayed themselves as the great propagators of international law. After initial hesitations over the League of Nations, the enthusiasm for the league grew in the Netherlands, both in the popular and the official sphere. To the Dutch, the (theoretically) global character of the league was appealing. Given their extensive territories in South-East Asia and their more limited territories in the Caribbean, the Dutch considered themselves a middle-sized power with strategic interests across the world. Lacking a strong navy, international law and international organization were two of the few instruments the Dutch could actively use to defend their interests.

As may be clear from this very brief characterization of their foreign policy, initiatives for European cooperation did not sit very comfortably with the Dutch. It ran counter to neutrality, was often seen as inimical to free trade, could mean competition with the League of Nations and could compromise strategic interests outside of Europe. Nonetheless, a discourse on ideas for European cooperation did exist. Dutch advocates of European cooperation sought 'Europe' predominantly in economic reform. As elsewhere in Europe, organizations were set up that promoted European cooperation, including branches of Paneuropa and the Union Douanière Européenne.

While free trade had been the guiding principle in Dutch financial and economic circles, circumstances in the 1930s, especially after the Ottawa conference of 1932 and the failure of the World Economic Conference of 1933, were such that more and more of those involved in economic affairs sought other solutions. Regional ententes aimed at lowering tariffs or even producers' ententes were advocated as possible solutions.[77] Political schemes were less well developed in the Netherlands than in other European countries. The position of the Dutch East Indies was perceived by many as an insurmountable obstacle to political cooperation within Europe. However, because ideas for world federation became more and more unlikely, European federation was considered as a step in the right direction, and some political projects were floated.[78]

Comparing this Europeanist discourse to Huizinga's Europeanness, it is clear that they are quite far apart. Instead of emphasizing the 'reality' of economic and/ or political circumstances, Huizinga saw 'Europe' in the thirties as an intellectual and moral concept. Huizinga's view was quite similar to the official foreign policy discourse that prioritized neutrality, technical cooperation, international law and a moral quality in international affairs. The fact that Huizinga was close to members of the Dutch Foreign Office might well have reinforced his ideas.[79]

The neutrality of the Netherlands during the First World War meant that the nineteenth-century value system of the Dutch had remained essentially intact. Some even argued that it had been vindicated. Although world events were of course followed with great interest and anxiety, the Dutch foreign-policy elite felt relatively secure in their aloofness from world events, and did not fundamentally change its foreign policy outlook as described above. Huizinga betrayed similar sentiments when he contended that 'sobriety and bourgeois mentality' had saved the Dutch from the extremisms of the early twentieth century.[80] Like Erasmus, about whom Huizinga wrote a biography, the Dutch were 'too sensible and too moderate to be heroic'.[81] In such a context, intellectuals could, and indeed should perhaps, stay away from politics.

As long as the Netherlands remained neutral, Huizinga argued that Dutch intellectuals should also remain neutral and not do anything that might jeopardize the neutrality of the state. In his last contribution to a discussion at the IICI in 1939, Huizinga disagreed with the Brazilian physiologist and intellectual Miguel Ozório de Almeida, who argued that neutrality meant that intellectuals should seek truth and should then be able to comment on it openly.[82] Huizinga, on the contrary, almost elevated neutrality itself to a moral precept and followed his good friend and minister of Foreign Affairs, E.N. van Kleffens, in an absolute upholding of neutrality. In taking this 'neutral' position in what was one of his last exchanges with the international republic of letters, he combined arguments inspired by the official national position with the idea of a universal 'non-partisan' intellectual.

The German invasion of 1940 ended Dutch neutrality. These developments made Huizinga change his attitude and he became active in the intellectual resistance against the German occupation and national socialism. This change is also reflected in his last work, *Damaged World*, written in involuntary internal exile in the Groningen countryside.[83] Huizinga's analysis of the situation had become much darker: the Dutch mentality had not been resistant either. However, this shift did not mean that he abandoned his basic premise that the European spirit of civilization would resurface. He did move from his intellectual position to a more political position, his Europeanness becoming a cautious Europeanism. In *Damaged World* he pointed to a political form that could bring a solution: federation.[84] The independence of the constituent parts would be the safeguard against future descents into barbarism. Again, Huizinga was in step with official opinion. Dutch officials in exile in London evaluated political and economic cooperation more positively. Following up interwar negotiations that had led to the failed Ouchy Convention between the Netherlands and Belgium and Luxembourg, they conducted talks that would lead to the Benelux Customs Union.

What Huizinga would have thought about the European project, as it came about after the Second World War, will never be known, as he died on 1 February 1945, a few months before the Netherlands were liberated. *Damaged World* in which he pointed to a political form suggests, however, that Huizinga could have become a slightly reluctant supporter of European integration after the war, like many in the Netherlands.

Despite his culturally pessimistic works, for a long time, Huizinga retained a certain optimism or naivety that in the end the European spirit would overcome all difficulties. Generalizing his national, Dutch, experience he remained convinced that intellectuals should not commit themselves to a particular cause, except the universal, which according to Huizinga could be rooted in a neutral patriotism. As for so many, the experience of the Second World War changed his views. Huizinga, the intellectual, did commit himself actively against national socialism, and while he still accorded prime importance to moral regeneration, he started to look to more tangible means of securing the European spirit, and thus peace.

This chapter has used the discussions at the IICI and the case of Huizinga to address the concern of intellectuals for the future of the European spirit. At a time when concern for the future was widespread in European society, and while the concepts remained ill defined, the meeting was an attempt to establish what the role of intellectuals should and could be in those circumstances. Focusing on those who shared a liberal understanding of the European spirit,[85] two approaches were advocated. The first was defended by those who argued that intellectuals should refrain from engaging in 'reality' and who instead celebrated their Europeanness by focusing on the universal and the long-lasting. The case for the second approach was made by those who pointed out that an active Europeanism was necessary because adopting a neutral position resulted in condoning a situation that ran counter to the European spirit and universal values, and might eventually destroy the European spirit. At the meeting in Paris in 1933 and for several years to come, the first passive approach prevailed over intellectual activism.

The case of Huizinga and many of the other intellectuals at the IICI also showed that the pursuit of an internationalist cause in a private capacity by those ideally situated for it – polyglot intellectuals deeply imbued with European culture and part of international networks – did not automatically result in this internationalism trumping their national perspective.[86] If anything, their internationalism consisted of a generalization of a particular national culture.

Notes

1. Paul Valéry, Institut International de Coopération Intellectuelle, *L'avenir de l'esprit européen* (Paris, 1934), 12.
2. The conference took place between 16 and 18 October 1933. The conference proceedings were published as: Institut International de Coopération Intellectuelle, *L'avenir de l'esprit européen* (Paris, 1934).
3. While the French Federal Committee for European Cooperation (Comité fédéral de Coopération européenne), an organization that aimed to further European cooperation, was responsible for the organization and the choice of topic, the meeting and the publications that followed from it were thoroughly embedded in the work of the International Institute of Intellectual Cooperation (IICI). Therefore I will focus here on the IICI. To address the role of the French Committee for European Cooperation would go beyond the scope of this article. On the Committee, see: J.-M. Guieu, 'Le Comité fédéral de Coopération européenne: L'action méconnue d'une organisation internationale privée en faveur de l'union de l'Europe dans les années trente (1928–1940)', in S. Schirmann (ed.), *Organisations internationales et architectures européennes (1929–1939)* (Metz, 2003), 73–91.
4. For example: Oswald Spengler, *Der Untergang des Abendlandes: Umrisse einer Morphologie der Weltgeschichte* (Munich, 1918–22); Paul Valéry, *La crise de l'esprit* (Paris, 1919).

5. For example: José Ortega y Gasset, *La rebelión de las masas* (Madrid, 1930); Johan Huizinga, *In de schaduwen van morgen. Een diagnose van het geestelijk lijden van onzen tijd* (Haarlem, 1935).

6. Valéry, *L'avenir*, 12.

7. Dantas, ibid., 42.

8. For example: Valéry, ibid., 9; J. Dantas, ibid., 37; W. Martin, ibid., 154.

9. Valéry, ibid., 9–10; de la Brière, ibid., 88.

10. Valéry, ibid., 10–14.

11. 'To cure our poor world, so rich and yet so handicapped', J. Huizinga, ibid., 64.

12. J. Huizinga, *Nederlands geestesmerk, Verzamelde Werken (VW) Geschiedwetenschap en hedendaagsche cultuur VII* (Haarlem, 1950), 279–312, 287–88.

13. To avoid confusion: the 'European spirit' referred to here is not the nationalist, fascist or national-socialist version of 'European spirit'.

14. W.E. Krul, *Historicus tegen de tijd. Opstellen over werk en leven van J. Huizinga* (Groningen, 1990); A. van der Lem, *Het Eeuwige verbeeld in een afgehaald bed. Huizinga en de Nederlandse beschaving* (Amsterdam, 1997); H.L. Wesseling, 'Zoekt Prof. Huizinga eigenlijk niet zichzelf? Huizinga en de geest van de jaren dertig' (Amsterdam, 1996); H.L. Wesseling, 'From Cultural Historian to Cultural Critic: Johan Huizinga and the Spirit of the 1930s', *European Review* 10 (2002), 485–99. On intellectual cooperation in particular: C. de Voogd, 'Johan Huizinga en de Coopération intellectuelle internationale: een intellectueel ambassadeur van Nederland in de crisisjaren', *De Gids* 2 (2005), 159–69.

15. From 1931, several of these meetings were organized; topics included 'Goethe', 'The future of culture' and 'Contemporary art and reality'. Not all intellectuals invited to the meeting on the future of the European spirit were members of the ICIC. Per meeting, intellectuals with expertise relevant to the topic of the meeting were invited.

16. Intellectual cooperation in the context of the League of Nations went back to September 1921 when a French proposal for the creation of an organization for intellectual cooperation was adopted. In January 1922 the International Committee on Intellectual Cooperation (ICIC) was set up. For a list of the members of the Commission and their nationalities between 1922 and 1939, see: J.J. Renoliet, *L'UNESCO oubliée. La Société des nations et la coopération intellectuelle (1919–1946)* (Paris, 1999), 184–85. The commission was the first organism of what was to become the Organisation for Intellectual Cooperation (OIC). From 1923 onward, national commissions were formed in various countries. For a list, see: Renoliet, *L'UNESCO*, 280. In 1926 the International Institute of Intellectual Cooperation opened in Paris. After the Second World War, UNESCO succeeded the institute.

17. Renoliet, *L'UNESCO*. On transnational networks among intellectuals, see: C. Charle, J. Schriewer, P. Wagner (eds), *Transnational Intellectual Networks: Forms of Academic Knowledge and the Search for Cultural Identities* (Frankfurt, 2004). For cultural internationalism, see: A. Iriye, *Cultural Internationalism and World Order* (London, 1997).

18. J. Morefield, *Covenants without Swords: Idealist Liberalism and the Spirit of Empire*, (Princeton, 2005), 98, 113–35; J. Stapleton, 'The Classicist as a Liberal Intellectual: Gilbert Murray and Alfred Eckhard Zimmern', in C. Stray (ed.), *Gilbert Murray Re-assessed: Hellenism, Theatre and International Politics* (Oxford, 2007), 261–92.

19. R. Frank, C. Le Dréau, 'Introduction', ibid., *Le militantisme pour l'Europe. D'un après-guerre a l'autre (1919–1950) Cahiers Irice 1* (Paris, 2008), available at: http://irice.univ-paris1.fr/spip.php?article339, accessed on 14 April 2010. Jules Romains coined the term 'européisme' in 1915 and used it in a series of articles in American newspapers. These articles were published in 1933 as *Problèmes européens* (Paris, 1933). For the development of the term after 1945, see: B. Vayssière, 'La recherché face à un militantisme "supranational": le cas de l'union européenne des fédéralistes', in R. Frank, Ch. Le Dréau, *Le militantisme pour l'Europe. D'un après-guerre a l'autre (1919–1950) Cahiers Irice 1*, (Paris, 2008), available at: http://irice.univ-paris1.fr/spip.php?article347, accessed on 14 April 2010.

20. Several concepts, such as reason, morality and spirit were used to indicate a similar idea.

21. For example: Huizinga, *L'avenir*, 62.

22. To a certain extent the discussion between Huizinga and Benda following Huizinga's presentation seems to have suffered from this problem: Huizinga, Benda, ibid., 53, 67.
23. J. Breuilly, _Nationalism and the State_ (Manchester, 1993), 8.
24. J. Huizinga, 'Patriotisme en nationalisme in de Europeesche geschiedenis tot het einde der negentiende eeuw. Studium generale 1940' (1940), _VW IV_ (1949), 497–555 (497).
25. For example: P. Teleki, _L'avenir_, 91.
26. Thomas Mann excepted.
27. F. Coppola, ibid., 184–85; H. von Keyserling, ibid., 276. Hermann van Keyserling stressed the importance of the 'tellurgic forces' in this context.
28. For an analysis of the attitude of British intellectuals, see: S. Collini, _Absent Minds: Intellectuals in Britain_ (Oxford, 2006). For the situation in the Netherlands after the Second World War, see: L. Molenaar,'Wij kunnen het niet langer aan de politici overlaten ...' _De geschiedenis van het Verbond van Wetenschappelijke Onderzoekers (VWO) 1946–1980_ (Rijswijk, 1994).
29. See for example on the left: C. Prochasson, _Les intellectuels, le socialisme et la guerre, 1900–1938_ (Paris, 1993); J. Jennings and A. Kemp-Welch, _Intellectuals in Politics_. On the right: J.-L. Loubet del Bayle, _Les non-conformistes des années trente. Une tentative de renouvellement de la pensée politique française_ (Paris, 1969); O. Dard, _Le rendez-vous manqué des relèves des années 1930_ (Paris, 2002).
30. Leon Bourgeois cited in Renoliet, _L'UNESCO_, 120.
31. Gilbert Murray: 'La coopération intellectuelle doit être universelle et autant que possible indépendante de la politique.' UNESCO, ICIC, Com.Ex. 11th session, 20 December 1933, b. 544.
32. UNESCO, ICIC, Com.Ex. 11th session, 20 December 1933, b. 544. During the First World War there were many instances in which intellectuals let national solidarity prevail over universal humanist values. A famous example is the 'Aufruf an die Kulturwelt' by 93 German academics and the response by 117 British scholars in October 1914. J. von Ungern-Sternberg, _Der Aufruf an die Kulturwelt: Das Manifest der 93 und die Anfänge der Kulturpropaganda im Ersten Weltkrieg_ (Stuttgart, 1996); 'Reply to German Professors. Reasoned Statement by British Scholars' (_The Times_, 21 October 1914). The attempt to publish a counter pamphlet in Germany, the 'Aufruf an die Europäer' by Georg Friedrich Nicolai, Albert Einstein and Wilhelm Förster, only counted one signature beyond the authors. G.F. Nicolai, _Biologie des Krieges_ (1917). See also: H. Pogge von Strandmann, 'The Role of British and German Historians in Mobilizing Public Opinion in 1914', in B. Stuchtey, P. Wende (eds), _British and German Historiography, 1750–1950: Traditions, Perceptions and Transfers_ (Oxford, 2000), 335–72. For the Netherlands, see: M.J. Riemens, _Een vergeten hoofdstuk, De Nederlandsche Anti-Oorlog Raad en het Nederlands pacifisme tijdens de Eerste Wereldoorlog_ (Groningen, 1995).
33. Renoliet, _L'UNESCO_, 121–25.
34. See note 16.
35. M. Riemens however classifies the universal aspirations voiced at the meeting 'by the formerly apolitical intellectuals' as political. M. Riemens, _Passie voor de vrede: de evolutie van de internationale politieke cultuur in de jaren 1880–1940 en het recipiëren door Nederland_ (Groningen, 2005), 294.
36. Valéry, _L'avenir_, 143.
37. J. Romains, ibid., 298. For a similar argument, see: P. Nizan, _Les chiens de garde_ (1932). J. Jennings, 'Of Treason Blindness and Silence: Dilemmas of the Intellectual in Modern France', in Jennings and Kemp-Welch, _Intellectuals in Politics: From the Dreyfus Affair to Salman Rushdie_ (London, 1997), 65–85.
38. Valéry was elected president, Bodrero, Cantacuzene, Huizinga, Keyserling and de Madariaga vice-presidents.
39. No references to this society were found in the IICI files in the UNESCO archive in Paris, nor in any of the literature on the subject.
40. J. Huizinga, _Herfsttij der middeleeuwen studie over levens- en gedachtenvormen der veertiende en vijftiende eeuw in Frankrijk en de Nederlanden_ (Haarlem, 1919).
41. Huizinga, _In de schaduwen van morgen_.
42. J. Huizinga, _Homo Ludens: proeve eener bepaling van het spelelement der cultuur_ (Haarlem, 1938).

43. Wesseling, 'From Cultural Historian to Cultural Critic', 486.
44. National Archief, Den Haag, Ministerie van Buitenlandse Zaken: A-dossiers, 1815–1940 nummer toegang 2.05.03, inventarisnummer 1521.
45. And not in 1933 as Anton van der Lem suggests in Van der Lem, *Het Eeuwige verbeeld*, 180. After the death of Professor H.A. Lorentz (1923 secretary, 1925 president of the ICIC), Mr. B.J.C. Loder became a member of the ICIC in 1932. Huizinga then in turn succeeded Loder in 1935, after he had retired for health reasons. NL-HaNA, BuZa / A-dossiers tot 1940, 2.05.03, inv. Nr. 1522. See also Riemens, *Passie voor de vrede*, 269.
46. Letter J. Huizinga-A. Scholvinck, 3 Jul. 1937, in L. Hanssen, W.E. Krul, A. van der Lem (eds), *J. Huizinga. Briefwisseling III 1934–1945* (Utrecht, 1991).
47. De Voogd, 'Johan Huizinga', 159.
48. Ibid., 162.
49. Huizinga, *L'avenir*, 62.
50. J. Huizinga, 'Lettre à M. Julien Benda' (1934), *VW VII* (1950), 269–78. Henri Bonnet, the director of the IICI, had at first suggested that Huizinga respond to a letter by Hans Kelsen on the philosophy of law or to a letter by Sigmund Freud and Albert Einstein on 'Why War?', but Huizinga had already started work on a letter on the European question. UNESCO, IICI, F II, 1, letter H. Bonnet-H. Kelsen, 7 Nov. 1933, letter H. Bonnet-J. Huizinga, 17 Nov. 1933, letter H. Bonnet-H. Kelsen, 21 Nov. 1933.
51. J. Huizinga, 'In de schaduwen van morgen', *VW VII*, 313–428.
52. Ibid.; Wesseling, 'From Cultural Historian to Cultural Critic', 493.
53. G. Mazzini. *Doveri dell'uomo* (1960). For an analysis of Young Europe, see: R. Sarti, 'Giuseppe Mazzini and Young Europe', in C. Bayly, E. Biagini (eds), *Guiseppe Mazzini and the Globalization of Democratic Nationalism, 1830–1920* (London, 2008), vol. 152, 275–97 (275).
54. Huizinga, 'Lettre à M. Julien Benda', 275.
55. Benda, *L'avenir*, 65–67. For a study of Benda's views on Europe, see: J.W. Müller, 'Julien Benda's Anti-Passionate Europe', *European Journal of Political Theory* 5 (2006), 125–37. Müller, however, seems to be unaware of the meeting at the IICI and the inherent 'Europeanness' of the European spirit and Benda's ideas about European cooperation.
56. Huizinga, *L'avenir*, 69.
57. J. Benda, *Discours à la Nation européenne* (Paris, 1933).
58. On the ambiguities in Benda's ideas about Europe, see P. Engel, 'Julien Benda's Thoughtful Europe', in L. Morena and M. Ferraris, *Europa!* in *The Monist* 92 (2009).
59. Huizinga, 'Lettre à M. Julien Benda'.
60. This was the so-called 'Von Leers affaire'. De Voogd points out that Huizinga's position in this affair raised his profile as a 'brave intellectual'. IICI circles, Lucien Febvre and Marc Bloch all took note of these developments. De Voogd, 'Johan Huizinga', 160. For an analysis of the event, see: W. Otterspeer, 'Huizinga before the Abyss: The von Leers Incident at the University of Leiden, April 1933', *Journal of Medieval and Early Modern Studies* 27 (1997), 385–444.
61. Huizinga, 'Lettre à M. Julien Benda', 278.
62. Benda, *Discours à la nation européenne*, 37.
63. 'Geistige Lebensform', Van der Lem, *Het Eeuwige verbeeld*, 316.
64. Krul, *Historicus tegen de tijd*, 244. There is an interesting comparison to be made with the Belgian historian Henri Pirenne. Pirenne used the Burgundy period to prove the inevitability of the Belgian nation. H. Pirenne, *Histoire de Belgique* (1900). Huizinga did not agree with this interpretation based on historical determinism. For a full discussion of Huizinga's aversion to historical determinism related to state and nation, see the introduction by W.E. Krul to J. Huizinga, *Verspreide opstellen over de geschiedenis van Nederland* (Alphen a/d Rijn, 1982), 22–23; and W. Krul, 'In the Mirror of van Eyck: Johan Huizinga's Autun of the Middle Ages', *Journal of Medieval and Early Modern Studies* 27 (1997), 353–85.
65. Huizinga, 'Lettre à M. Julien Benda', 274.
66. Ibid., 276.

67. For a study of Dutch culture and identity, see: R. van Ginkel, *Op zoek naar eigenheid. Denkbeelden en discussies over cultuur en identiteit in Nederland* (Den Haag, 1999).

68. Krul, *Historicus tegen de tijd*, 248; Huizinga, *Nederland's geestesmerk*, 287–88.

69. Ibid., 290.

70. Krul, *Historicus tegen de tijd*, 248; Huizinga, 'Twee worstelaars met den Engel', *VW IV*, 441–97 (469).

71. Huizinga, 'How Holland Became a Nation', *VW II*, 266–83 (282); 'Die Mittlerstellung der Niederlande zwischen West- und Mitteleuropa', *VW II*, 284–303; 'Discours', 268; and 'Nederland's geestesmerk', 291. See for the larger argument: Krul, *Historicus tegen de tijd*, 249.

72. Huizinga, *VW II*, 281.

73. J.J.C. Voorhoeve, *Peace, Profits and Principles: A Study of Dutch Foreign Policy* (The Hague, 1979); E.H. Kossmann, 'De deugden van een kleine staat', in N.C.F. van Sas, *De kracht van Nederland, internationale positie en buitenlands beleid* (Haarlem, 1991), 36–41; M. Kuitenbrouwer, 'Het imperialisme van een kleine mogendheid', in N.C.F. van Sas, *De kracht van Nederland, internationale positie en buitenlands beleid* (Haarlem, 1991), 42–71. For a further development of Voorhoeve's thesis, see R. van Diepen, *Voor Volkenbond en Vrede. Nederland en het streven naar een nieuwe wereldorde 1919–1946* (Amsterdam, 1999).

74. See also: W. Klinkert, G. Teitler, 'Nederland van neutraliteit naar bondgenootschap. Het veiligheids- en defensiebeleid in de twintigste eeuw', in B. de Graaff, D. Hellema and B. van der Zwan (eds), *De Nederlandse buitenlandse politiek in de twintigste eeuw* (Amsterdam, 2003), 9–36.

75. In the literature it has now been established beyond doubt that the Netherlands should have devalued earlier than it did: J.L. van Zanden, *De dans om de gouden standard. Economisch beleid in de depressie van de jaren dertig* (Amsterdam, 1988). On free trade, see: H.A.M. Klemann, *Tussen Reich en Empire. De economische betrekkingen van Nederland met zijn belangrijkste handelspartners: Duitsland, Groot-Brittannië en België en de Nederlandse handelspolitiek 1929–1936* (Amsterdam, 1990); E.S.A. Bloemen, 'Tussen vrijhandel en protectie. Colijn en de internationale economische congressen, 1927–1933', in J. de Bruijn and H. J. Langeveld (eds), *Colijn. Bouwstenen voor een biografie* (Kampen, 1994), 235–59; R.T. Griffiths, '"Free Traders" in a Protectionist World: The Foreign Policy of the Netherlands, 1930–1950 (with particular reference to Europe)', in S. Groenveld and M. Wintle (eds) *Britain and the Netherlands: State and Trade, Government and the Economy in Britain and the Netherlands since the Middle Ages* (Zutphen, 1988), 152–68.

76. Voorhoeve, *Peace, Profits and Principles*, 49–52. For a further analysis of this tradition, see: P. Malcontent and F. Baudet, 'The Dutchman's Burden? Nederland en de internationale rechtsorde in de twintigste eeuw', in B. de Graaff, D. Hellema and B. van der Zwan (eds), *De Nederlandse buitenlandse politiek in de twintigste eeuw* (Amsterdam, 2003), 69–104.

77. Gemeentearchief Rotterdam, Plate, 422, 17, Rapport sommaire sur le travail du Comité National néerlandais de l'EDE, 22 Jun. 1930; Philips Company Archive, Eindhoven, Paneuropa Nederland, letter J.L. van der Valk–A.F. Philips, 21 Mar. 1932.

78. T. Mulder, 'De Vereenigde Staten van Europa', *Europa!* 1, 4, October 1932.

79. De Voogd, 'Johan Huizinga', 168.

80. Huizinga, *Nederland's geestesmerk*, 287–88.

81. Huizinga, 'Erasmus', *VW VI*, 3–195 (184); Van der Lem, *Het Eeuwige verbeeld*, 120.

82. Letter M. Ozorio de Almeida, 16 Sept. 1939, IICI, A I, 51.

83. Between 7 August 1942 and 30 October 1942, Huizinga was a 'Schutzhäftling' in the internment camp in Sint Michielsgestel. He was then released under the condition that he would not return to the west of the Netherlands.

84. J. Huizinga, *Geschonden Wereld. Een beschouwing over de kansen op herstel van onze beschaving, VW, VII*, 477–606 (601–2).

85. Liberal as opposed to national socialist or fascist understandings.

86. On the complementary relationship between internationalism and nationalism in an interstate context, see: M. Herren, *Hintertüren zur Macht. Internationalismus und modernisierungsorientierte Aussenpolitik in Belgien, der Schweiz und den USA* (Munich, 2000).

Chapter 13

THE IDEA OF EUROPEAN UNITY IN HEINRICH MANN'S POLITICAL ESSAYS OF THE 1920s AND EARLY 1930s

>⚬⚬⚬<

Ernest Schonfield

Heinrich Mann (1871–1950) and his brother Thomas Mann (1875–1955) were the two most prominent German intellectuals of the interwar period. Their collected essays and speeches of the 1920s and early 1930s bear witness to a sustained political commitment in support of Weimar democracy and Franco-German understanding, as 'unofficial cultural ambassadors of the Republic'.[1] Both writers called for resistance against national socialism, both before Hitler seized power, and afterwards, when they were in exile. This chapter will focus primarily on Heinrich Mann's ideas about European unity during the years of the Weimar Republic, 1918–33. Throughout the 1920s, Heinrich Mann's principal political aim was the promotion of a Franco-German entente in order to secure peace in Europe. To pursue this aim, he engaged in forms of cultural diplomacy which included lecture tours, essay writing and political lobbying. He knew that German nationalism was the biggest threat to peace and he spoke out against it continuously. From 1931 until he was forced into exile in February 1933, he acted as president of the Literature Section of the Prussian Academy of the Arts in Berlin, using this position to rally opposition against Hitler. Once Hitler gained power, Heinrich Mann knew that war was inevitable. In exile in France from 1933 to 1940 he attempted to coordinate anti-Fascist resistance amongst German exiles, becoming chairman of the official Committee for the Establishment of a German Popular Front. When Germany invaded France in 1940, he escaped to California where he remained until his death in 1950. The main focus of this essay will be on Heinrich Mann's essays of the 1920s, the decade in which a peaceful settlement still seemed possible. It will also be necessary to refer to the work of Thomas Mann during this period, because any assessment of Heinrich Mann's public engagement requires an understanding of Thomas Mann's own public activity, and vice versa. The achievements of the two brothers in the fields of literature and politics can be seen as complementary: as Thomas Mann put it in a letter of 23 April 1925, there was a 'division of labour' between them.[2] I will therefore begin by setting out the two brothers' political positions in the years before 1920.

Democracy, Internationalism and the First World War

The brothers Mann were not always united in their support of democracy and internationalism. In their twenties, they spent a year (1895–96) working for the nationalist and conservative monthly magazine *Das Zwanzigste Jahrhundert* (The Twentieth Century), with Heinrich Mann working as the editor. Initially, then, both brothers were politically strongly conservative. Their cultural reference points were, however, modern and European (Nietzsche, Bourget, Flaubert, Maupassant). Over the following decade, Heinrich Mann in particular spent much of his time in Italy. Around 1904–5, and partly as a result of his reading of French literature (Zola, Rousseau) he adopted a liberal and republican stance. When the First World War broke out, therefore, the two brothers soon found themselves in opposing political camps. Thomas Mann was quick to promote the German nationalist cause. In his essay 'Gedanken im Kriege' (Thoughts in War) of September 1914, Thomas Mann countered *Entente* propaganda which depicted Germany as internally divided between high culture and military aggression, by denying that such a division existed. Thomas Mann argued that the true conflict was that between Germanic, Romantic 'culture' and the superficial Enlightenment reasoning of democratic Western 'civilization'. He claimed that Germanic 'culture' implied a tribal sense of unity, and a profound acceptance of life's brutality, and that it therefore included the ruthless military pragmatism of *Realpolitik*. Western 'civilization', on the other hand, was too intellectual – it only led to scepticism and dissolution. Whilst Thomas Mann spoke out in favour of the war, Heinrich Mann spoke out against it. The major essay, 'Zola', published in November 1915, ostensibly celebrated Zola's uncompromising critique of French militarism, but this criticism clearly also applied to the militarism, and war guilt, of the German Empire of the time. Heinrich Mann's essay also characterized the German intellectuals who had rallied to the nationalist cause as self-serving opportunists. This insult was clearly directed at Thomas Mann, and it led to a very public split between the brothers, which lasted until they were reconciled in 1922. Thomas Mann spent the rest of the war years producing a mammoth volume of essays, *Betrachtungen eines Unpolitischen* (Reflections of an Unpolitical Man). It was completed in March 1918 and published in October of that year, when the war was already lost. The book was an elaboration of the opposition between German 'culture' (defined in terms of Romanticism, monarchism and unpolitical education) and Western 'civilization' (defined in terms of democratic republicanism) which he had already set out in 'Gedanken im

Kriege', but it was also a detailed self-justification, highly polemical in tone, in response to the accusations made in 1915 by Romain Rolland and by his own brother, that his patriotism was a form of opportunism.[3] Much of the book's criticism is directed at the so-called 'Zivilisationsliterat', a pro-Western intellectual and apologist for Western-style 'civilization'. This figure, who clearly resembles Heinrich Mann, stands accused of doctrinaire narrowness and superficial humanitarianism. Thus, in 1918, Thomas Mann's position, despite the title of his book, remained conservative and nationalist. Thomas Mann's political conversion to the twin causes of democracy and internationalism did not occur until after the German foreign minister, Walther Rathenau, was assassinated by a right-wing extremist on 24 June 1922. Only after this point did Thomas Mann finally come to realize that the greatest threat to the cultural values which he cherished was nationalist violence. At first he may only have been a 'Vernunftrepublikaner' – a republican due to necessity rather than conviction – but in fact his gradual shift towards democratic centrism in the mid-1920s parallels that of Gustav Stresemann, who was chancellor in 1923 and then foreign minister from 1924 to 1929. As T.J. Reed has shown, by the mid-1920s Thomas Mann, like Stresemann who also set out from an initially conservative position at the end of the war, had become 'a devoted servant of the Republic'.[4]

Whereas Thomas Mann always emphasized his identification with German cultural greats such as Wagner, Schopenhauer and Nietzsche, Heinrich Mann felt a much stronger affinity with Italian and French humanism. Under the influence of Zola, from around 1905 onwards, Heinrich Mann attempted to combine art and politics in his own literary works. From this point on, Heinrich Mann's political position was pro-democratic and pro-European – a position which Thomas Mann was only to adopt almost two decades later. In his novel *Die kleine Stadt* (The Small Town) (1909), Heinrich Mann provides a utopian fable of grass-roots European democracy. The novel is set in a provincial town (Palestrina) in Italy, where the arrival of an opera company triggers a battle between politically progressive and reactionary forces within the town. After much political intrigue, the Enlightenment ideals of reason and democracy win the day. The novel pays tribute to the political values of the Enlightenment and the Italian Risorgimento of the nineteenth century.[5] But Mann was keenly aware of the strength of anti-democratic forces within Germany itself. His next major work, *Der Untertan* (The Loyal Subject) – completed 1914, but then banned; first published in book form 1918 – was a brilliant satire of Wilhelmine Germany, focusing on the career of a conservative opportunist, the self-serving factory owner Diederich Heßling. As in the previous novel, there is a battle between progress and reaction, only this time it is the reactionaries who triumph.

When the war broke out, Heinrich Mann quickly turned to writing essays as a means to promote peace and democratic reform in Germany. In his 'Zola' essay of 1915 he celebrated the figure of the intellectual who defends freedom of thought by promoting real, political freedom. So whilst Thomas Mann spent the war writing essays in defence of German nationalism, Heinrich Mann's concern was to promote democracy and reconciliation among the warring European powers. The 1916 essay 'Der Europäer' (The European) is Heinrich Mann's first major pronouncement in favour of European cooperation. In it, he condemns the racial discourse which claims that Europeans belong to different races, arguing that Europeans are related both racially and in terms of their cultural and intellectual history. Despite this, Heinrich Mann does not entirely reject racial discourse; on the contrary, his essay is full of it. Indeed, like many of his political essays, 'The European' contains some strange contradictions between progressive and conservative positions.[6] Alongside his emphasis on Enlightenment values, Heinrich Mann expresses the fear that Europe could be overwhelmed by the irrational Asian continent.[7] He also proclaims Europe's civilizing mission in the world in imperialist terms, defending the domination of 'foreign races' by the Roman Empire and the British East India Company.[8]

When Germany lost the war in 1918, the result was the creation of the Weimar Republic, the democratic state that Heinrich Mann had hoped and fought for. And yet the new peace seemed fragile at best. In the years immediately after the First World War, several observers commented that there was an 'iron curtain' which divided Germany from the West.[9] Despite attempts to bring about a lasting settlement, Europe was divided and politically unstable, especially in terms of the hostile diplomatic relations between France and Germany. In October 1921, talks between foreign ministers Walther Rathenau and Louis Loucheur led to the Wiesbaden agreement which modified the schedule of reparations payments. But this agreement proved to be unpopular in both countries, and in June 1922 Rathenau was killed. If peace in Europe was to be maintained, Franco-German relations would have to be radically improved. This challenge – to improve Franco-German relations with a view to European political harmony and stability – was taken up by a handful of intellectuals. In Germany, the most prominent of these intellectuals was the novelist Heinrich Mann. In recognizing the need for European unity, Heinrich Mann was decades ahead of most of his compatriots: the only other prominent German intellectual to promote the cause of European federalization to a comparable extent around this time was Kurt Tucholsky.[10]

Attempts at Mediation during the Crisis of 1923

In 1920 Heinrich Mann became friends with Count Richard Coudenhove-Kalergi. A doctor of philosophy and the son of an Austro-Hungarian diplomat, Coudenhove-Kalergi spent the period between the wars lobbying ceaselessly for European integration.[11] His most important work is *Pan-Europa*, first published in Vienna in 1923. In the preface to this book, Coudenhove-Kalergi announces that Europe is in danger of being overtaken by the rest of the world, and risks falling victim either to Russian military domination, or to American economic domination.[12] According to Coudenhove-Kalergi, Europe's only hope was to organize itself into a political and economic federation of states.[13] Coudenhove-

Kalergi built up a pan-European movement in order to promote the cause of European unity; at its peak in the late 1920s, it numbered several thousand members.[14] When Heinrich Mann met Coudenhove in 1920, their shared interest in promoting a European federation soon led to a close friendship. The two men spent several summer holidays together, and their essays of the early 1920s on the European question show strong similarities.[15] Coudenhove's 1921 short text 'Heinrich Mann as Politician', too, bears witness to this period of collaboration between the two men.[16]

Their hopes for European reconciliation soon ran aground against the crisis of 1923. On 11 January 1923, the French government under Poincaré sent in troops to occupy the Ruhr. In Germany, the occupation caused outrage, and the German policy of passive resistance was supported by parties from across the political spectrum. In the divided years of the Weimar Republic, this was no mean feat, and as one American observer remarked: 'Only two people have been able to bring about German unity … Bismarck and Poincaré.'[17] With anti-French sentiment at a peak, the promotion of Franco-German understanding must have seemed like a lost cause. However, this crisis provoked a vigorous response from Heinrich Mann. In his view, the real enemy was not the French but the wealthy industrialists from both countries who had profited from the war and who were now profiting from the inflation crisis caused by the policy of passive resistance in the Ruhr. While the inflation wiped out the savings of the middle classes, it enabled industrialists with foreign holdings to liquidate their debts and expand their empires further. Thus the inflation increased the tendency towards cartelization and monopolization of the German economy.[18] Because of this phenomenon, Heinrich Mann became convinced that economic cooperation by itself would not be enough to bring the two nations closer together; on the contrary, he saw industrialists as profiteering from the war and fanning the flames of nationalism. Between April and October 1923, Heinrich Mann wrote a series of five short texts which were published in various French and German periodicals including the *Nouvelle Revue Française* and the *Neue Rundschau*, and which were later published in book form in the same year.[19] The five texts have appeared in print under various titles. Their original titles are as follows: (1) 'Ihr müßt wollen' (You have to want it) [April 1923];[20] (2) 'Europa. Reich über den Reichen' (Europe. State above States) [May 1923];[21] (3) 'Coopération économique seulement?' (first published in German as 'Deutschland und Frankreich') [June 1923];[22] (4) 'Dresdner Rede' (Dresden Speech) [August 1923];[23] and (5) 'Diktatur der Vernunft' (Dictatorship of Reason) [October 1923], an open letter to the Chancellor Gustav Stresemann.[24]

In all of these texts, the key argument is that monopoly capitalism represents a danger to peace and democracy in Europe. In response to Jacques Rivière's call (in April 1923) for an economic alliance between France and Germany,[25] Heinrich Mann pointed out that the new German state was finding it increasingly difficult to control the super-rich captains of industry, who were forming cartels which were capable of holding the state to ransom.[26] Chief among these new industrial barons was Hugo Stinnes (1870–1924), who formed a trust with the industrialists

Emil Kirdorf and Carl-Friedrich von Siemens.[27] Stinnes was indeed favourably disposed to the idea of a right-wing dictatorship.[28] Heinrich Mann, in the May 1923 essay 'Europe: State above States', argues that industrialists such as Stinnes had effectively taken control of the state away from the middle classes: 'The war was the surest means to select the most avaricious individuals. Now it is no longer the bourgeoisie itself which is in power, but only the greediest of them. They have swallowed up the middle classes.'[29] Despite the vocabulary, Mann's critique here has little in common with Marxism. In fact, Mann's outrage at the consequences of the German inflation led him to assume a radically anti-materialist, idealist position. For him, European harmony could only be achieved by intellectual and spiritual endeavour, not economic cooperation. Disappointed by the trade unions' support of a nationalist programme of passive resistance, Mann argued that the unions were too materialistic, too mired in questions of wage increases, to represent a force for genuine political change: 'The belief that economics is everything and that man is determined by economics rather than economics by man, is shared by both industrialists and trade unions. But you cannot defeat an enemy if you share his way of thinking.'[30] At this time, Heinrich Mann regarded intellectuals as the most progressive social force, and not as exponents of an ideological superstructure. Unlike Marx, Mann even exempts intellectuals from the bourgeoisie, claiming that they represent an independent group who remain apart from class interests.[31] Having thus dismissed both bourgeoisie and proletariat, Mann concludes his essay 'Europe: State above States' with a call for intellectuals to found a new church, a church of European unity, loosely modelled on the medieval Catholic church: 'For the purposes of our church, everything depends on our faith being unshakeable. The faith is called Europe, its sacred doctrine is its unity. These must stand firm. Criticism of this faith cannot be permitted; intellectuals and men of criticism will have to restrain themselves.'[32]

In his desperation, Heinrich Mann the intellectual calls for an organization in which criticism and reasoned debate will be forbidden. Mann's conception here owes much to the French writer Pierre Drieu la Rochelle, who later became a Fascist and a Nazi collaborator. As Paul Michael Lützeler points out, Heinrich Mann has become entangled here in anti-democratic, irrationalist ideology, showing how confused his ideas were under the pressure of the inflation crisis of 1923. It is almost as if, in his attempt to counter the nationalist mythology of the conservative revolutionaries, Heinrich Mann has raised his belief in European spirit to the level of an absolutist doctrine.[33] It is important to note, though, that Heinrich Mann later recognized this himself: when he revised this essay for publication in 1929, he removed this entire section. Even so, it is clear that in the midst of this major political crisis, Mann's concern to protect democracy led him to use some anti-democratic rhetoric. But his point was that economic cooperation alone was not enough to ensure European peace, since some of the main economic actors (the industrialists) were themselves anti-democratic. In order to achieve the goal of a European federation, economic ties were not enough. The political will had to be forthcoming too, and it was up to politicians and intellectuals to ensure that this would be so. Thus, in his response to Jacques Rivière, he writes: '[Franco-German] understanding under the rule of economic autocrats would not be a success. Economic closeness is not always a guarantee of peace.'[34] This does not mean that Mann was against European economic integration, as Lützeler claims.[35] Heinrich Mann did want close economic cooperation. But he wanted it to be subordinate to political partnerships, not the other way around.

This becomes clear in his letter to Stresemann in October. On 26 September 1923, the stalemate between Germany and France over the occupation of the Ruhr was ended when Stresemann announced the termination of passive resistance. Mann was so encouraged by Stresemann's action that he wrote an open letter to him, published on 11 October 1923 in the *Vossische Zeitung* (Berlin). In this letter, he congratulates Stresemann on having saved Germany from anarchy by giving up the policy of resistance, but insists that this can only be the first step. He urges Stresemann to negotiate personally with Poincaré in order to build a lasting solution.[36] He also begs Stresemann to curb the power of the plutocrats and 'rich traitors' who are trying to install a right-wing dictatorship (the industrial magnate Stinnes is implied here). Heinrich Mann argues that Germany and France can only survive and assert themselves against global empires if they work towards economic unity: 'Germany and France can only survive as an economic unity. Only in this way can they assert themselves against global empires.'[37] And Mann concludes the letter by asking Stresemann to arm the republic against the plutocrats, if necessary by nationalizing their property. Critics have commented that Heinrich Mann's call for a 'dictatorship of reason' is highly self-contradictory, given his attachment to democracy. But, as Karin Gunnemann argues, surely this call should be understood 'more as a moral imperative in a desperate situation than as an order to transfer political leadership to an intellectual power elite'.[38]

A United States of Europe

In 1924, Heinrich Mann published the essay 'V S E' in the *Vossische Zeitung*; it calls for a 'United States of Europe' (Vereinigte Staaten Europas).[39] This essay represents the high point of Heinrich Mann's engagement with Coudenhove-Kalergi. The first part of the essay repeats the key tenets of the Pan-European Movement: the current discord between European nations will lead to Europe's downfall; the continent is doomed to become an 'economic colony' of America or a 'military colony' of Asia; the only hope for European nations is to form a political federation; only when acting in concert with one another can they hope to assert themselves on the world stage. Nationalism became a religion in the nineteenth century, and this was a necessary development so that modern states could be formed. Nationalism has been misused, but he does not want nationalism to disappear entirely, since it is acceptable as an extended form of personal pride, as the expression of a people's self-respect. However, the concept of nationalism needs to be extended once again in order to include all the peoples of Europe. The Christian rhetoric of 'Europe: State above States' (1923) is still present, but it has been toned down to a minimum, as the essay calls for a new form of non-institutional Christianity, one 'without dogma' which would restore spiritual unity amongst Europeans.[40] More pragmatically, Mann quotes Aristide Briand, pointing out that the political will for such a federation already exists in France.

In the second half of 'V S E', Heinrich Mann expresses his support for Coudenhove's model of a pan-European federation of states with a transnational parliament. He even argues that Germany, of all European countries, has the most to gain from such a federation. However, Mann also carefully differentiates his position from Coudenhove's:

> The strongest arguments against Coudenhove's plan are England and Russia. He wants to exclude them, at least provisionally: Russia, until it is governed on a parliamentary basis; England, until it becomes once again an entirely European state, independent of its dominions. The reply to this is that neither Spain nor Italy are governed on a parliamentary basis, and Pan-Europe cannot do without Russia for its supplies of food. Separate England from Europe? Treat it as a power external to Europe? On this question one would have to consult one's confederates, and learn that of every ten books that are translated into French, nine are English. Cultural attraction is just as important for Pan-Europe as economic attraction. Europe's inner cohesion should derive from shared emotional and intellectual values. We should reconnect with Europe as a spiritual value, as it once was for the Greeks who fought against Asia. But if the land of Shakespeare were missing, this Europe would no longer be worthy of the name.[41]

This is a more inclusive vision of Europe than Coudenhove's. The concluding rhetoric of 'V S E' evokes Coudenhove's image of a pan-European parliament placed above the national parliaments: nation-states will continue to exercise sovereignty, but only on a restricted basis. However, the essay's conclusion gives further indication of Heinrich Mann's divergence from Coudenhove: Mann warns against politicians who represent a 'high-earning elite' whose interests are opposed to those of the majority of European people. And the final words of the essay commemorate the death of the French Socialist leader Jean Jaurès (1859–1914), who attempted to avert the First World War through diplomatic means and who was shot by a French nationalist assassin in 1914. Thus, Heinrich Mann criticizes big business, and portrays the Socialist Jaurès as a martyr to the cause of European unity; such sentiments were bound to distance him from Coudenhove, who regarded industrialists as important potential sponsors of Pan-Europa.

In years between 1924 and 1927, the opinions of Heinrich Mann and Coudenhove continued to diverge. Although Mann was far from being a socialist, his willingness to entertain certain socialist ideas was bound to offend Coudenhove, who hoped to achieve European unification from above, with the help of statesmen, heads of government, and leading industrialists. Whilst Coudenhove regarded the industrialists as useful allies, Heinrich Mann viewed them as a threat to German democracy. In Mann's view, the industrialists' inflationary profiteering had destabilized the German bourgeoisie, causing it to withdraw its support for the Republic. By 1927, he had come to the conclusion that the pan-European project had become the tool of businessmen and power politics. Undeterred by the break with Heinrich Mann, Coudenhove courted Thomas Mann instead, with a considerable degree of success.[42]

Acting as an unofficial cultural ambassador, Thomas Mann spent a week in Paris in late January 1926, making public appearances and meeting French intellectuals. He also met up with Coudenhove-Kalergi. The details of this visit are recorded in his travel diary *Pariser Rechenschaft* (An Account of Paris) (1926). Thomas Mann's description of Coudenhove combines admiration and scepticism: 'His manner and his words announce his unshakeable faith in a political idea. I am not convinced that this idea is entirely flawless, but he knows how to represent and propagate it with the greatest energy, both in person and through his writings.'[43] Thomas Mann's attitude to the prospect of a pan-European union was characteristically more pragmatic than Heinrich's. Thus, in a speech made at a conference on 20 January 1926, Thomas Mann stresses that Germany could gain a great deal of political influence if it were to enter into a federation of states: 'Germany shall join the confederation of peoples: not only because it sees that in the council of peoples it shall be able to regain the influence it deserves, but also because of the intellectual and moral reasons which I have tried to sketch out in my lecture.'[44] In a letter of 17 September 1926, however, Thomas Mann warns Coudenhove not to underestimate the strength of German nationalism, and notes prophetically that this 'godforsaken piety' may yet prove victorious.[45] One of the high points of Thomas Mann's public engagements on behalf of the Pan-Europa Movement was a speech he made in Berlin in 1930: 'The Trees in the Garden. A Speech for Pan-Europa'. In this text, Thomas Mann criticizes German nationalists who claim that patriotism and internationalism are irreconcilable opposites. According to Thomas Mann, both instinct and reason are essential for life, and it is therefore necessary to combine base, nationalist instincts with the higher principle of reason which calls for an international form of organization.[46]

The Locarno treaties of 1925, in which Britain and Italy guaranteed France against a German attack and vice versa, were regarded as a new sign of hope for European harmony. Heinrich Mann referred to this new 'spirit of Locarno' in an essay of 1927 in which he called for 'Ein geistiges Locarno' (A Locarno of the spirit). Once again, Heinrich Mann distances himself from Coudenhove by including Russia in his model of a new Europe. Mann argues that Germany is uniquely suited to act as a mediator because of its geographical position in the centre of Europe. Therefore, Germany's new role will be to facilitate a dialogue between East and West:

> I see Germany as a born mediator. To mention only the two most important nations of continental Europe, we cannot allow Russia and France to be distant from us, not the one more than the other. How could they be distant? We are the country in the centre of Europe. The first consequence of this is that we must feel ourselves to be

European at least as much as others, and feel ourselves responsible for this Europe. And it is thus also clear to me that we have to hold the middle ground between our neighbours in East and West, and not only in geographical terms.[47]

Heinrich Mann expresses this same idea, that Germany should mediate between France and Russia, again in another speech of 1927 made in Paris, in French, where he regrets his inability to speak Russian.[48] This view of Germany as the natural mediator between East and West was also expressed by Thomas Mann in the same year; it appears in the essay 'Lübeck als geistige Lebensform' (Lübeck as a spiritual concept of life) (1927), showing that the two brothers' political views were now closer than they had been for years.

Unfortunately, the tide was against the peacemakers. The world economic crisis of 1929 resulted in a surge of German nationalism, propelling Hitler ever closer to power. In 1931, Heinrich Mann visited Aristide Briand in Paris.[49] He later described Briand at the meeting as a shadow of his former self.[50] In late 1932, with Germany on the verge of dictatorship, Mann wrote his final essay before he fled into exile: 'Das Bekenntnis zum Übernationalen' (Confession to Supranationalism). It was published in the last uncensored edition of *Die Neue Rundschau* in December 1932.[51] In this essay, Mann argues that German nationalism was noble and pure, but only prior to the existence of a German nation-state in 1871. In the early phases of nationalism, the movement was directed against the absolutism of the monarchy. But, since unification, nationalism was used by a militaristic German state as an excuse for economic exploitation and war. Mann argues that nationalism is irrational because it refuses to tolerate rational argument, and facilitates the manipulation of the individual by the state. It is worth noting Mann's continuing ambivalence about concrete economic and political questions: on the one hand, he quotes the opinion of the French Minister of Finance Joseph Caillaux that European economic integration should precede political integration,[52] and he demands a shared unit of currency for France and Germany.[53] On the other hand, he still continues his criticism of 'outmoded' economic leaders,[54] and implies that socialism has a role to play in uniting people of different countries.[55] Despite these continuing contradictions, the ending of this essay is rhetorically brilliant, as Mann demands that individuals should pledge their allegiance to the idea of a federal Europe. Mann dictates the words of this European pledge as follows:

> I want a supra-national state; not just a general European federation of states, but without delay, the first step towards this goal: a federal state of Germany and France; because only this state promises a natural development of existing conditions and freedom for people. A single country can no longer sustain itself in Europe today, neither economically, nor politically, and especially not morally. Several countries, ones which are supranationally associated, are capable of making their citizens better and happier. No one can serve one isolated country; whoever claims otherwise is lying. There are only interconnected interests and service to them.[56]

Heinrich Mann was excluded from the Prussian Academy of the Arts on 15 February 1933. He fled Germany on 21 February 1933. His first country of exile was France, where he continued to publish essays in the *Dépêche de Toulouse* in which he denounced German Fascism and supported the popular front in France. He also tried to coordinate a popular front amongst German exiles, and made radio broadcasts against Hitler (as Thomas Mann was later to do from his American exile). In the period between 1933 and 1939, he produced nearly four hundred essays and speeches, and participated in numerous congresses and committees, whilst also finding time to complete his magnum opus, a fictional account of the life of King Henri IV of France.[57] Paul Michael Lützeler argues that Heinrich Mann's involvement with the popular front brought about a shift in his concept of Europe. According to Lützeler, Heinrich Mann's previous viewpoint was that European unity could only be based upon a strong bilateral union between Germany and France. Now, however, he included the Soviet Union in his scheme for a united Europe, at the core of which would be France, Germany and the USSR.[58] In my view, Lützeler's account here is a little too schematic: it ignores Heinrich Mann's previous assertion of Germany's importance as a mediator between France and Russia, which is the keynote of Mann's essays of 1927. However, Lützeler is correct in discerning an increasing shift in Heinrich Mann's thought in favour of including the Soviet Union at the core of any European solution. Mann even stressed that this new Europe should have more of a socialist basis. In a short text of August 1941, he expressed his hope that, after the war, Great Britain and the Soviet Union would recognize the need for a joint European federation along broadly socialist lines:

> A federal Europe will have to be, perhaps in various gradations, a socialist one; and a socialist one can only be federal. Future wars can only be prevented if the entire world attains a condition which is politically and socially similar. If this war leads to one Europe based on class dominance and another Europe based on a community of the people, then the cause of peace will be lost in advance … The natural calling of Germany, as the centre of the continent, is to mediate and not to rule.[59]

It is clear, then, that Heinrich Mann's ideas about Germany's role as a mediator between Russia and the West shifted, but did not change radically between 1927 and 1941.

In 1940 Heinrich Mann fled to the United States. He spent the final decade of his life in California, financially assisted by his (by now) more famous brother Thomas Mann. In the spring of 1949, Heinrich Mann was offered the post of president of the German Academy of Arts in East Berlin. After some initial hesitation (he knew and mistrusted Walter Ulbricht), he accepted the offer, but his visa was delayed. His ship back to Europe was due to leave on 28 April 1950, but he died on 11 March 1950 at his home in Santa Monica. He never learned about the postwar politicians who laid the foundations for the European Union, such as Jean Monnet, Robert Schuman and Walter Hallstein.[60]

Conclusion

It should be stressed that Heinrich Mann overestimated the power of intellectuals like himself to change the world. He still remains, however, one of the key cultural figures who helped to prepare Germany's path to democracy and European federalism. His significance in Germany is comparable to that of his mentor Zola in France: like Zola, he inaugurated the modern social novel in his own country; and, like Zola, his political engagement was exemplary. The Mann brothers' fear of German nationalism also proved to be fully justified. Nationalism in Britain and France in the 1920s and 1930s was a potent force, yet Heinrich Mann and Thomas Mann grasped, with wonderful acuteness, the monstrous potential that was inherent in German nationalism, which was of a different order from its British and French counterparts. Several of Heinrich Mann's basic arguments still hold true. His concept of 'supranationalism' anticipates more recent debates about 'post-national citizenship', based upon an acceptance of universal human rights. In _Inventing Europe_ (1995), Gerard Delanty argues that 'post-national citizenship' should be determined by residence, not by nationality or birth, and that 'it is crucial to break the connection between citizenship and nationality, both intellectually and constitutionally'.[61] Thus, like Heinrich Mann, Delanty argues that notions of sovereignty and citizenship need to be redefined in order for the European Union to succeed. Mann was ultimately correct in his repeated assertions that it was in the interest of all European citizens to try to rise above nationalism, and he was also a pioneer in trying to conceptualize ways to move beyond narrow, chauvinistic definitions of national identity. His emphasis on Franco-German understanding is still relevant today: arguably, if the European Union is to emerge successfully from the current economic crisis, this can only be on the condition of continuing close political cooperation between France and Germany.

Notes

1. N. Hamilton, _The Brothers Mann: The Lives of Heinrich and Thomas Mann 1871–1950 and 1875–1955_ (London, 1978), 206.
2. Ibid., 213.
3. T.J. Reed, _Thomas Mann: The Uses of Tradition_, 2nd edn (Oxford, 1996), 190.
4. Ibid., 292.
5. E. Segelcke, '"Die kleine Stadt" als Hohelied der Demokratie. Heinrich Manns Naturrechtsidee im geschichtsphilosophischen Kontext von französischer Aufklärung und italienischem Risorgimento', _Heinrich-Mann-Jahrbuch_ 5 (1987), 1–28.
6. Siegfried Sudhof, 'Heinrich Mann und der europäische Gedanken', in K. Matthias (ed.), _Heinrich Mann 1871/1971. Bestandsaufnahme und Untersuchung. Ergebnisse der Heinrich-Mann-Tagung in Lübeck_ (Munich, 1973), 147–62 (152).
7. H. Mann, _Essays_ (Hamburg, 1960), 554–60 (555–56).
8. Ibid., 554–55.
9. G.A. Craig, _Germany 1866–1945_ (Oxford, 1987), 442.

10. I. King, 'Kurt Tucholsky as Prophet of European Unity', *German Life and Letters* 54 (2001), 164–72.

11. See the chapter on Richard Coudenhove-Kalergi in this volume by Anita Prettenthaler-Ziegerhofer.

12. R. Coudenhove-Kalergi, *Pan-Europa* (1923), 2nd edn (Vienna and Leipzig, 1924), xi.

13. Ibid., 27.

14. P.M. Lützeler, *Die Schriftsteller und Europa. Von der Romantik bis zur Gegenwart* (Munich, 1992), 315.

15. Sudhof, 'Heinrich Mann und der europäische Gedanken', 156.

16. Coudenhove-Kalergi, 'Heinrich Mann als Politiker', in idem, *Krise der Weltanschauung* (Vienna, 1923), 127–32.

17. J. Joll, *Europe since 1870: An International History*, 3rd edn (Harmondsworth, 1985), 284.

18. Ibid., 285.

19. The five essays are collected in H. Mann, *Diktatur der Vernunft* (Berlin, 1923). They are also published in revised form in H. Mann, *Sieben Jahre. Chronik der Gedanken und Vorgänge* (Berlin, Vienna and Leipzig, 1929), 96–163. Four are also published in H. Mann, *Essays* (Hamburg, 1960), 443–95.

20. H. Mann, 'Ihr müßt wollen' (April 1923), in *Diktatur der Vernunft*, 17–21. Also published as 'I. Das Sterben der geistigen Schicht' in *Sieben Jahre*, 96–101, and in *Essays*, 443–47.

21. H. Mann, 'Europa. Reich über den Reichen', *Neue Rundschau* 34/2 (1923), 577–602; also in *Diktatur der Vernunft*, 22–54. Also published in a shortened and revised version under the chapter headings 'II. Wirtschaft 1923' and 'III. Anfänge Europas', in *Sieben Jahre*, 101–28, and in *Essays* (1960), 448–73. The essay also appeared in French as 'Europe, État supréme', *Europe* 2 (1923), 129ff.

22. H. Mann, 'Coopération économique seulement?', *La Nouvelle Revue Française* 10/119 (1923), 248–53. First published in German as 'Deutschland und Frankreich. Antwort an Jacques Rivière', in *Neue Rundschau* 34/2 (1923), 769–77. Also as 'Deutschland und Frankreich (Juni 1923)' in *Diktatur der Vernunft*, 55–65. Also as 'IV. Noch ein Krieg mit Frankreich. Antwort nach Frankreich, Juni 1923', in *Sieben Jahre*, 129–41. Not published in *Essays* (1960).

23. H. Mann, 'Dresdner Rede, gehalten zur Feier der Verfassung, am 11. August 1923 in der Staatsoper', in *Diktatur der Vernunft*, 66–75. Also as 'V. Wir feiern die Verfassung' in *Sieben Jahre*, 141–52, and in *Essays* (1960), 485–95.

24. Also as 'Herr Reichskanzler!' in *Diktatur der Vernunft*, 7–16. Also as 'VI. Sie gehen bis zum Verrat' in *Sieben Jahre*, 153–63. Also as 'Diktatur der Vernunft' in *Essays* (1960), 474–84.

25. J. Rivière, 'Pour une entente économique avec l'Allemagne', *La Nouvelle Revue Française* 10/115 (1923), 725–35.

26. For details of this exchange of views, see P.M. Lützeler, 'Heinrich Mann 1923: Die Europa-Idee zwischen Pragmatik und Religionsersatz', *Heinrich-Mann-Jahrbuch* 7 (1989), 85–104.

27. B. Widdig, *Culture and Inflation in Weimar Germany* (Berkeley, 2001), 137. Heinrich Mann also provided a fictionalized account of Hugo Stinnes in his dystopian novella 'Kobes' of the same year.

28. See K.V. Gunnemann, *Heinrich Mann's Novels and Essays: The Artist as Political Educator* (Rochester, 2002), 109.

29. H. Mann, *Essays*, 458.

30. H. Mann, *Diktatur der Vernunft*, 39. Mann deleted this passage when he revised the essay for publication in 1929, suggesting that he had changed his mind about the trade unions.

31. Lützeler, 'Heinrich Mann 1923', 92.

32. Mann, *Diktatur der Vernunft*, 49.

33. Lützeler, *Die Schriftsteller*, 301.

34. Mann, *Diktatur der Vernunft*, 60.

35. Lützeler, 'Heinrich Mann 1923', 94.

36. Mann, *Essays*, 480.

37. Ibid., 481.

38. Gunnemann, *Heinrich Mann's Novels and Essays*, 111.
39. Mann, 1956. 'V S E' [1st publ. 1924], in Heinrich Mann, *Ausgewählte Werke in Einzelbänden*, A. Kantorowicz (ed.), Berlin: Aufbau, vol. 12: *Essays* vol. 2, 275–85.
40. Mann, 'V S E', 279.
41. Ibid., 282.
42. Lützeler, *Die Schriftsteller und Europa*, 318–19.
43. T. Mann, *Gesammelte Werke* (Frankfurt am Main, 1974), vol. 11, 46.
44. Ibid., 22.
45. Cited in Hamilton, *The Brothers Mann*, 217.
46. Mann, *Gesammelte Werke*, vol. 11, 868.
47. Mann, *Essays* (1956), vol. 2, 347.
48. Ibid., 362.
49. Briand had taken up Coudenhove's ideas, but his policy of reconciliation with Germany foundered after the death of Stresemann in 1929.
50. H. Mann, *Ein Zeitalter wird besichtigt* (Düsseldorf, 1974), 296–97.
51. Gunnemann, *Heinrich Mann's Novels and Essays*, 172–74.
52. Mann, *Essays*, 637.
53. Ibid., 638.
54. Ibid., 641.
55. Ibid., 643.
56. Ibid., 643–44.
57. W. Jasper, *Der Bruder. Heinrich Mann: Eine Biographie* (Munich, 1992), 280.
58. Lützeler, *Die Schriftsteller*, 373–474.
59. Cited in Jasper, *Der Bruder*, 317.
60. P.M. Lützeler, 'Heinrich Manns Europa-Ideen im Exil', *Heinrich-Mann-Jahrbuch* 3 (1985), 79–92.
61. G. Delanty, *Inventing Europe: Idea, Identity, Reality* (Basingstoke, 1995), 162.

Chapter 14

LUCIEN FEBVRE AND THE IDEA OF EUROPE

Vittorio Dini

As a modern and contemporary historian, Lucien Febvre had long planned to write one or more books on the history of Europe. In fact, already in 1925, he added two titles to the plan for the book series edited by Henri Berr: *Europe and the European Mind in the Sixteenth Century: Nationalism, Imperialism and Universalism*, and *Europe and the Universe at the End of the Eighteenth Century*. The books were never published; but, at a crucial time, between 1944 and 1945, Febvre delivered a course of twenty-eight lessons at the Collège de France, and the following academic year he offered another course at the Libre Université de Bruxelles – a manuscript of which was published some fifty years later in France, Germany and Italy. In his lessons, Febvre tackled the question of Europe from the perspective of a new historiography, the foundations of which he himself, Marc Bloch and the young Fernand Braudel were then laying, and which – after his experience with the *Revue de Synthèse* and, with Henri Berr, the *Semaines de Synthèse* – led to the founding of the journal that marked a revolution in contemporary historiography: the *Annales*. His search for a history which was neither diplomatic nor political, but a history of culture, ran alongside the political imperative of the dramatic needs created by the war.

In the lessons at the Collège de France, Febvre set forth an inquiry into the genesis of Europe and of European 'civilization':

> Here I do not offer you, I cannot offer you, chapters of a static history, wise and well balanced chapters of a handbook on Europe. I offer you something on which you should reflect; on which you should meditate … Europe is not a political entity of which one can easily and usefully write an external, methodical and classic and unproblematic history. Europe is a civilization.[1]

Importantly, Febvre had already edited a special number of the *Semaine de Synthèse*
– one of the few published in the 1930s – precisely on the concept of 'civilization'
which is central to grasp his vision of Europe.

Febvre's history of the idea of Europe was conceived as the construction of an
identity – an aspect to which he dedicated twenty lessons – and as the construction
of a myth. He did this bearing in mind one specific element:

> European civilization was a Mediterranean civilization, and therefore, our duty, here,
> today, is to scrutinize the basis, to establish the foundations of this Mediterranean
> culture, of this Mediterranean civilization, of this Mediterranean fatherland which
> remained for such a long time the fatherland of those men who, over an extended
> period, prepared for us the bed of culture in which we calmly rest ... in spite of
> everything ... with the unconscious serenity of a man who falls asleep in Pompeii,
> calmly, in his own house, while the lava is already sliding down the slopes of the
> Vesuvius.[2]

In lessons twenty-one to twenty-three, finally, Febvre analysed the actual birth of
Europe as 'consciousness'. Here, we also find the problem of the continent's crisis,
determined by two essential elements of modernity: the nation and nationalism
(lesson twenty-three). Crisis, nation and nationalism were all elements which in
the same years were central in the reflections of other European historians like
Federico Chadod, Johann Huizinga and Ernest Curtius.

That some of Febvre's main ideas, as well as his main approach, represent a
useful and seminal point of departure, going well beyond the historical
circumstances he found himself in, is proven by the many references still made to
his text. Giorgio Napolitano, a convinced Europeanist, member of the European
Parliament, president of its Commission for Constitutional Affairs and, since May
2006, president of the Italian Republic, has often referred to Febvre's course. In
2003 he went as far as to dedicate to it an entire section of the introduction to a
collection of essays on Europe's political unity, written during the crisis of the
project for a European Constitution: 'A precious historical reflection: Febvre and
Chabod'.[3] Extensively quoting Febvre's text, Napolitano highlighted how at the
end of the war, precisely when to speak about a united Europe seemed impossible,
two of its greatest historians, Febvre and Chabod, went against the current, against
the mystification that the tragedy of Fascism and Nazism had created. Offering a
picture of Europe's history as the 'genesis of a civilization', Febvre outlined,
according to Napolitano, answers and solutions that still today are 'incredibly
enlightening', 'impressing by their topicality' and for the way in which, discussing
the question of Europe's borders, they defined it in terms of 'civilization'.[4] In the
words of Napolitano himself:

> The fresco of the 'genesis of a civilization' which Febvre has left us with and with
> which he identifies Europe is a powerful one. It goes from the Greek world and
> Hellenism to the Roman Empire; from Carolingian Europe to eighteenth-century
> Europe; it still represents today one of the most illuminating reconstructions of

the shaping of that identity about which Euro-sceptics still doubtfully, and often vacuously, wonder, trying to deny that one might recognize it and uphold its value. The reference to the history and the idea of Europe, to its constitutive elements and its unitary profile, remains essential to strengthen Europe's consciousness, to give it awareness of the idealistic foundations upon which, in our time, has stood the undertaking of the gradual unification of Europe.[5]

Time and again, Napolitano referred to Febvre's text in official speeches, stressing the originality of the historian's work as well as his relevance for the predicaments of today's Europe.[6] On one occasion, in 2010 at the Sorbonne, he focused on the historical and conceptual relationship of Europe with the idea of civilization and its 'genesis' laid out by Febvre. For Napolitano, by finding the roots of European civilization in the early Middle Ages and yet denying its mere identification with the Carolingian Empire, the French historian usefully problematized the issue of Europe's origins. In fact, by seeking the origins of its civilization in the beginnings of the second millennium, in the flourishing of its cities, Febvre ended up stressing the importance of diversity within European civilization; by underplaying the importance of the unity represented by the empire, he decoupled Europe's unity from politics, showing the need to look at Europe's culture and at the diversities within it. On such basis, Febvre could claim that 'European unity is not uniformity; in the history of Europe, the chapter on diversities remains as important as the one on resemblances'. Napolitano has remarked that such a view would later be shared by Braudel as well as another important intellectual and Europeanist, Bronislaw Geremek, for whom, 'the diversity of national cultures remains the richest resource for Europe'.[7]

Europe as a Civilization

'Is Europe an outdated concept or is it fundamental for the progress of the world?' Febvre's was by no means a rhetorical question, asked at the presentation of his 1944–45 course a few days after the liberation of Paris. At the time, the historian was contemplating the personal losses of the war: 'many are absent at the roll-call. In particular M.B. [Marc Bloch]. What a pity! What a frightful scarcity of men', he wrote on 15 November 1944 in a laconic note to his pupil Fernand Braudel, at the time detained in Lübeck.[8] The concept of Europe brought back to mind a dramatically defeated ideal rather than a luminous project of free men belonging to the democratic and enlightened Western tradition. Even worse, it seemed, as Marc Ferro writes in the postscript to the French edition of Febvre's course, it was a prohibited reference since it was connected to the collaborationist ideology of Pierre Laval's Franco-Hitlerian *Nouvelle Europe*. In short, circumstances challenged the core of the democratic vision of Europe that Febvre saw magisterially crystallized in a passage by Montesquieu: 'If I knew something useful to my family but not to my homeland, I would try to forget it. If I knew something useful to my homeland and detrimental to Europe, or else to Europe and detrimental to humanity, I would consider it a crime.'[9]

If his was not meant to be, and could not be, a well-ordered detached history of Europe, what Febvre had in mind was a more ambitious aim: to tackle the concept, cleansing it of myths and falsifications by referring to those same categories that, up until then, had moved Febvre himself in his own research, all of which fitted into the conceptual frame of 'civilization' – a concept, for Febvre, full of seminal ambivalences. What the war had destroyed had to be rebuilt; above all, the notion of Europe as the home of liberty, the 'Europe-refuge which has served as an alibi, in the last half a century, to the men tired of conflicts and national rivalries'.[10] It was necessary to turn back to the teachings of his friend and mentor Henri Pirenne and to his *History of Europe*, which had also been conceived in a particular situation, during his confinement in Thuringia in the First World War. At the same time, it was necessary to resort to Michelet's rhetorical art in order to attain the strength to convince his listeners and offer them, in those difficult days, an ethic even more than a history lesson.

The course programme, outlined in the first lesson, is of capital importance and enshrines the core of Febvre's thesis. If he mainly defined Europe in negative terms – what Europe is 'not' – the Spinozian dictum *omnis determinatio est negatio* seems in this case quite appropriate. It is an original reading of Europe's identity:

> I call Europe not a continent, nor a geographical division of the globe, nor a racial section of white humanity, since no anthropologist, no ethnologist … has ever dared to speak of a European race to replace the most extraordinary range of ethnic diversities with an imaginary unity and a merely conventional – or propagandistic – racial purity. I call Europe, simply, a historical unity, an incontestable, undeniable history, a unity which was created in a well-defined period; it is a recent unity, a historical unity. We know exactly when it appeared in history, since Europe, in this sense, as we define it, as we study it, is the creation of the Middle Ages; a historical unity which, as with all other historical unities, is made up of diversities, of pieces, of shards torn from preceding historical unities, these, in turn, themselves torn to pieces, made of shards, of fragments of preceding unities.[11]

Throughout his course, Febvre insisted on the importance of such diversities. He stressed the impossibility of any simplistic juxtaposition of the Greek and Roman worlds – both contributing to create modern Europe and yet so different from it – and pointed to the divide separating the Roman Empire and Europe – a Europe born out of the collapse of Rome. Similarly, he assumed that, while stemming from the Carolingian Empire, 'the heart' of Europe, the continent should not be simplistically identified with it. Europe, for Febvre, was an overlapping of historical layers, all important, all living alongside and within one another, none truly dominant and none that could be considered the main root of Europe. The continent was characterized by its complexity, in its historical development, it was itself a process. Europe was not only the product of its past, it was its history – as Febvre would say. Such a historical unity was, for the great French historian, a 'real and living notion', producing a system of 'solidarities among nations which carried, within themselves, an ideal or, at least, a common civilization'. In this sense, Europe could be said to stem from the 'participation of quite different peoples, some Mediterranean, the others oceanic, Nordic or Oriental, which have known different destinies', 'but which have all contributed to its common civilization'. From here Febvre derived his polemic against the notion of European boundaries based on the wrongful assumption that Europe is a continent: 'The borders of Europe are the borders of European civilization. But the borders of European civilization are not fixed. They are moving boundaries which never cease to shift and, generally speaking, to move eastwards.'[12]

For Febvre, then, Europe is a civilization, and, as such, far from being 'a fatality', it is 'a human value'.[13] In opposition to the idea of race, it is a choice, moral as well as political:

> Europe is not a geographical notion that can stand to scrutiny. Europe is an ideal, a dream, for which men die by the thousands. Europe is a cultural notion (but to speak of Europe today is more or less to speak of a dream). Europe is an extension of extendable territories, continuously extendable and which enlarge in point of fact not only towards the East (since, where is, today the barrier of the Urals), but also, take notice, towards the West, in spite of the boundaries of the ocean.[14]

In the same lesson, the ninth, on 'Europe and Christianity' – in which, strangely enough, Novalis was never quoted though *Die Christenheit oder Europa* was clearly in the background – Febvre adds these remarkable ideas on the historical relationship between civilization and barbarism:

> Union, sum, fusion; since the barbarians had gradually been Romanized and Christianized while the ancient Romans were fully barbarized, the result of such a meeting of quite different elements in their origins, but which ended up being quite similar, issued, in the end, in a common civilization, a civilization that must be called European but which, if you asked its name, would not answer "Europe". It would answer "Christianity".[15]

Some eighty years have passed since Lucien Febvre inspired the first issue of the *Semaine de synthèse*, on *Civilisation. Le mot et l'idée*, published in 1930 and never republished – not even in France.[16] And yet, from then onwards, there has barely been an essay or a book that has not made reference to that wide, intelligent and well-documented analysis of the concept. This is because of the innovative method that it used, because of its interdisciplinary character, because of the intertwining of various perspectives of the history of ideas, anthropology and sociology, because of the presence of quantitative as well as qualitative research and, last but not least, because of the original results which it yielded by considering the concept of civilization in historical terms – as part of a *longue durée* – and with a well-defined theoretical and historical grounding.

European civilization – thus defined – argued Febvre, had a specific set of connotations, seemingly spatial, but truly cultural, historical and anthropological. As for its historical and political aspects, Febvre relied on the thesis of Marc Bloch, for whom Europe arose 'precisely when the Roman Empire crumbled'.[17] In the conclusion, the substance of Europe is confirmed, the essence of Europe, its 'humane' character that only a cultural and psychological history can grasp. In these fundamental pages, asking himself 'when is Europe', Febvre answered that it was not simply the time when we became accustomed to labelling different countries with the same name, placing together 'Mediterranean and Nordic countries' or when, during relatively brief periods, men such as Charlemagne were able to group them together under the same rule. On the contrary, according to Febvre, we can only talk of Europe when a certain number of Western men, with a central role within society because of their intellectual, political, artistic or economic influence, have felt European themselves, when the fact of being European, rather than Christian or even English, German, French or Italian, became for them of capital importance in defining who they were and when this way of representing themselves made them different from and opposed to other men who were not Europeans. This, for Febvre, 'gave them a feeling of pride, of dignity and soon of superiority, which has, indeed, turned them into Europeans'. While Febvre never denied the importance of political factors, of the political organization of Europe into different spaces, he considered it nonetheless a secondary aspect. What really counted was 'the cultural plane' thanks to which there was a cultural Europe before a diplomatic and political one; such a 'Europe of the learned' was first and foremost a reality of the mind, a 'spiritual entity'. Yet, Febvre went on, 'every civilization naturally tends to become an organization. And this was also the case with the European civilization'. The outcome was the rise of a political Europe through the work of diplomats and statesmen, above all through the balance of powers stemming from the Westphalia Treaty. What is remarkable is that Febvre identified such a history, rooted in the representations and images of its men, this 'psychological history', with the beginning of Europe; political facts, he argued, 'count and are even a priority', but 'they crumble quite quickly when they are not sustained by other elements – psychological and moral ones'.[18]

Europe and the Nations

While the myth of Europe was gaining shape within the universalistic frame of the Enlightenment, another myth pervaded the minds of Europe's citizens, deeply penetrating their psychological history, namely, the myth of the nation, constructed on the solid basis of the political and historical realities of modern states – or, rather, of nation-states. The territorial reference is juxtaposed with the psychological and moral ones of nationalities, leading to nationalism. The modern concept of the nation, argued Febvre, contrary to the Greek notion, referring to a hypothetical reality, was instead 'infused with necessity': 'The nation has an existence which the homeland does not have in the same measure'. A man, argued Febvre, might not love his country, and even though he might be labelled an evil person or a heretic, nobody can actually force him to become a patriot deep within; yet argued Febvre, the case of the nation is quite different:

> I cannot but belong *de facto* to a nation, because of the simple fact of my own birth ... belonging to a nation is a necessary thing or, rather, it has something of the biological, in some way, and of the psychological, since the nation powerfully shapes the individuals within it; from this it follows that for a nation to exist it is necessary that a people be aware of being a community of origin, [sharing] cultural traditions and interests, which are accepted and wanted as the condition of the vocation of each person belonging to the nation. All this is something quite different from the notion of people of the seventeenth century and to the conceptions before then.[19]

Considering the relationship between the 'state-nation' on the one hand and Europe on the other, Febvre argued that when reading history books it almost seems that all history was made by states alone and that the history of Europe was simply that of the nations which were part of it; furthermore, he argued, the list of states reminded a squeezed box: 'sometimes it gets shorter, at other times it gets longer'.[20] But it is a dangerous list, continued Febvre, since it turned Europe into nothing more than a label, a geographical place. And yet, 'nation-states kill Europe – Europe as a political reality, the reality of an ideal, of course – exactly because states are always there to bar that reality from gaining a body; and behind the states are the nations'.[21] Such a standpoint explains the historian's startling claim at the end of the twenty-third lesson:

> In the eighteenth century, at the time when Europe was flourishing, Europeanism was a pure vision of the mind. All reasoned as if on the earth there were only men, free men, disembodied ... All reasoned as if states did not exist ... and, after all, wasn't it true that kings had been won over by philosophy? For too long innovators had written about imaginary travels and travels to the moon. They continued to do so, and there was nothing in their speculations. If another storm should arrive, they would have melted into smoke. And the storm arrived and the NATION blew, followed, soon after, by NATIONALITY.[22]

In an intelligent review of Febvre's book, with the telling title *Europe Killed by the States*, the historian Adriano Prosperi has focused on a fundamental question: 'It is not by chance that Febvre's train of thought is tied to honour and patria', he argues. Recalling Febvre's debt to Bloch for the idea that Europe was born out of the ashes of the Roman Empire, Prosperi stresses how he draws from there the principle of a philosophy of history according to which 'Europe is born when the empire crumbles; no matter which empire, whether the Roman one, on which the theoreticians of Fascist Europeanism had insisted, or the German and Nazi one that had led to the ruin of the whole continent'. The history of Europe always had its turning points at the end of empires; always at precise, critical, historical moments. Comparing Febvre's with Chabod's ideas, the ones he laid out in his course in 1943/44 on the history of the idea of Europe, Prosperi stresses how even for the Italian historian '[t]he wealth of European society lay in its differences'. The relationship between Europe, freedom and diversity lies precisely in the opposition to an 'empire', to the desire to unite and deny those differences in the name of Europe – at least that of the Fascist regimes, an idea celebrated in a famous conference in 1932 held in Rome, at the Istituto Volta.

Already in 1932, Febvre pointed to the role of nations in relation to Europe. In the 1944/45 course, in the last lesson, he quoted his previous essay:

> In point of fact, along with national interests, side by side with political traditions I see in today's Europe no less substantial and disturbing realities, in terms of their instability; that is, nations. Those nations that history gladly analyzes but never – or almost never – summarises. If it tried to do so, if it tried to embark on such a delicate yet fascinating task ... probably we would realize quite soon that it is easier to speak to humanity than it is to speak of the nation of Europe.[23]

The problem of nations and nationalism was, then, already part of Lucien Febvre's researches in historical semantics. What is surprising, it should be added, is the absence of any reference to a classic work on the issue, to Ernest Renan's *What is a Nation?* (1882).[24]

The theme of the nation was taken up again by Febvre in two courses at the Collège de France between 1945 and 1947, and then, once more, ten years later, with a view to drafting a book. The courses were on 'Honour' and 'Patria' – which was the motto of the French navy – and were inspired by a tragic episode. In 1942, close to the shores of Oran, an officer of the French navy lost his life at sea, trying to defend the ideal behind one of the two words; at the same time, another officer, his brother, was fighting on the opposite side to defend the other ideal; so, argued Febvre, these two words, a 'symbol of unity, the words that inspire the feeling of cohesion and of belonging of the French people, became, at a given moment, words of division, words of a deep-seated division'.[25] The two young men were the sons of one of Febvre's assistants, Henriette Psichari, his secretary for the editing of the *Encyclopédie française*,[26] of which only a few volumes were written.

It is important to relate the course on Europe to the courses on 'Honour' and 'Fatherland' since in these we find a clarification of Febvre's ideas on the nation. In answering the question of what a nation is, he highlighted two elements. The first one is that one cannot but belong to a nation; a person might repudiate his nation, hate it, just as a nation might exclude from its bosom an individual; in both cases that person will necessarily become part of another nation. In this sense, the nation attends to a need, a sheer necessity, 'a fact'. The second element is 'psychological', for it intervenes in the relationship between the individual and society at large: 'The nation is not made up of individuals, but of groups (families, corporations, schools, churches), groups that it helps to unify and that it subordinates to common aims.' In this sense, argued Febvre, the nation represents the 'passage to a wider community', where the bonds of empathy can be found, allowing the creation of 'a mentality', a 'national consciousness', which is rooted in a specific territory. For Febvre there was no such thing but, rather, a 'state consciousness':

> There is a patriotic, national consciousness, which is in part made up of history, in part made up of an ideal. The nation is the rise of a consciousness that constantly acts upon an ideal which in turn acts continually on history. A history lived in common determines the rise of consciousness; and this rise of consciousness marks the representation of history, the meaning of history, the course itself of history. The nation is, at once, a fact one is subject to and a willed fact. From there it derives its strength.[27]

Of course, today's historical and political debate on nations and nationalism is much more complex, thanks to the works of Ernest Gellner, Eric Hobsbawm, Anthony D. Smith, John Breuilly, Etienne Balibar, Immanuel Wallerstein, Jürgen Habermas, Edward Said and the scholars of postcolonialism.[28] However, Febvre's analysis and diagnosis of the relationship between the nation and Europe still maintains all of its validity and shows its up-to-datedness in the face of an ever growing and obvious crisis of the nation-state. The complexity of social relationships, in relation to the development of processes such as that of mass migration or European integration have pushed many to analyse the theme anew. On the other hand, even today the myth of the nation turns almost always to the identity-related excesses of nationalism. The defining of a more rational and open form of identity and collective belonging, such as – for example – Habermas's constitutional patriotism,[29] is surely a more complex solution on the theoretical plane and seems even more difficult to turn into a reality in the minds of citizens and in the workings of institutions.

Europe, remarked Febvre, contains within itself a notion of crisis: this becomes an ever more frequent and pressing notion from the 1920s onwards. Once again, Febvre took the idea form Marc Bloch,[30] who in turn referred to Costantino Argetoriano, a remarkable Romanian statesman. The latter read a paper at the conference at the Istituto Volta on the 'Teachings to Draw from our Conference', in which he claimed that 'Europe is a notion of crisis. It is the fear of failure that has created it; it is an economic notion. The more the crisis is acute, the more the notion of Europe gains strength.' Following such assumption, Argetoriano claimed that by solving the economic problems, the urge for a united Europe would diminish. The idea of a united Europe met the strong opposition of nationalists, and only necessity, above all economic necessity, could turn it into a feasible project. From such a standpoint, all measures diminishing the need for Europe by improving the economic situation of its states actually reduced the possibility of Europe becoming a political reality. Therefore, if paradoxically, all partial attempts to unite Europe, for example through common trade policies, went 'in the opposite direction of total unification'.[31] Clearly, Argetoriano did not limit himself to the formulation of a definition of 'Europe as a notion of crisis', but he gave intelligent reasons for it; furthermore, he related the question of the method used in the understanding of Europe with that of its content, asking the members of the seminar whether 'they consider the definition of Europe on a natural and geographical or a moral and historical basis. Depending on the adoption of either one of the two, the notion of Europe becomes wider or narrower.'[32] Marc Bloch's essay on the 'Problems of Europe' was not only relevant for the reference he made to Argetoriano's idea of 'Europe as a notion of crisis', but also because he added that one might well speak of 'a notion of panic'.[33]

It is necessary to stress – and Febvre returned to the point several times during his course – that Europe is a confused notion, especially at times of crisis when desperation forces historians down dangerous paths:

> Europe is a balance of powers, a balance of strengths, a balance of rival states. Europe is an ideal fatherland, the ideal country of liberal eighteenth-century élites. Europe is an enemy, the enemy of nations and, above all, of the French nation, of the great nation – a model to other liberal countries. Europe is a desperate remedy because there has never been so much talking of Europe as after the Versailles Treaty, between 1920 and today; at this time Europe has shown itself to be a notion of crisis … Europe: it seems too great a reality, since the word Europe refers not to one but many different political and cultural unities, or too small, because it is impossible to refer to Europe without referring to the whole universe.[34]

Therefore 'crisis' has the sense of decline, a catastrophe which is opposed to hope – the one we find in Peguy's utopian and solid *Mystère de l'espérance*, with which Febvre ends his course.[35]

Conclusion

Febvre returned to the theme of Europe as a civilization years later, at a conference in Strasbourg in March 1953 on the 'Crisis of Civilization and Europe's Future'. Already in the title, all the strings are tied into a single knot: civilization, crisis and Europe. But the historical climacteric was then radically different, and the analysis of a careful historian had to register such changes. The war was long past; Fascism and Nazism had been defeated and the hopes for Europe and its future had dramatically improved. Above all, in 1953, Febvre could stress the importance of science, technology and scientific progress in history. These, he argued, created a different language and set new forms of communication – Febvre went as far as to foresee the transformation of television[36] – which contributed to the birth of a new mentality, of a new culture. Even in such a renewed enquiry, Febvre found inspiration in a short and dense article by Marc Bloch written in 1938, which he quoted: 'One could say that humanity has waited for our time to give itself inventions for which each problem disturbs the economy, and therefore its social and consequently its political structure'.[37] It is a great event, a great transformation: 'Now, at this moment, we are part of a *formidable revolution*. An unprecedented revolution.' This was Febvre's radical and firm statement, thus radicalizing Bloch's position. And yet the spirit of his statement remained the same as the one animating his course on Europe; the historical perspective was still the same as the one expressed in the conclusions of that course: 'to make Europe means three things, to accept three aims: the first one, that mesmerizes, is a political-administrative aim; the next, over which we draw a veil, is an economic-financial one; the third one, that we treat as an *hors d'oeuvre* or a dessert, is a cultural aim'.[38]

Seventy years have passed since Febvre taught his course; of those aims, the second one has been resiliently pursued and has produced some positive results – although the 2008 crisis questions many of its goals. As for the political-administrative aims, modest but not meaningless steps forward have been made. As for the cultural goal, civilization, much still needs to be done. For Febvre, today, instead of the motto 'we must be good Europeans', we should use the following:

> from Europeans, from good Europeans, we must try to become good midwives of civilization. Our fathers might have said, and have said: "let's try to be good godfathers of nationality" … Good midwives of civilization is instead the formula that appeals to us. To not enslave; to not subdue with force. To not assimilate. To help others to expand. To be the good gardeners that do not force nature but who help the plants, European plants, extra-European plants, to grow, develop and ripen their good fruits.[39]

Notes

1. Quoted in B. Mazon, 'Introduction', in L. Febvre, *L'Europe. Genèse d'une civilisation* (Paris, 1999), 19.
2. Febvre, *L'Europe*, 65.
3. G. Napolitano, *Europa politica. Il difficile approdo di un lungo percorso* (Roma, 2003), 39–43.
4. Ibid.
5. Idem, 'Lectio Magistralis del Presidente della Repubblica in occasione del conferimento della Laurea honoris causa dell'Università Complutense', Madrid, 29 January 2007. The text and those of the other speeches by Giorgio Napolitano quoted are on the web page of the Presidency of the Italian Republic.
6. Idem, 'Eredità del passato e sfide del futuro: Turchia e Europa nei nuovi equilibri del mondo globale', Ankara, 18 November 2009.
7. Idem, 'Ringraziamento del Presidente Giorgio Napolitano alla Cerimonia di Conferimento del dottorato Honoris Causa', Paris, 28 September 2010.
8. Quoted in B. Mazon, 'Introduction', 23.
9. Febvre, *L'Europe*, 387–88.
10. Ibid., 48.
11. Ibid., 37.
12. Ibid., 128.
13. Ibid., 83.
14. Ibid., 132–33.
15. Ibid., 134.

16. L. Febvre, M. Mauss, É. Tonnelat, A. Niceforo, L. Weber and H. Berr, *Civilisation. Le mot et l'idée* (Paris, 1930); on this, see my introduction to the forthcoming Italian edition, translated by Paolo Primi.

17. Febvre, *L'Europe*, 73. The exact expression used by Marc Bloch is: 'Europe, I think, arose precisely when the Roman Empire fell', review to 'Barbagallo, Il Medioevo', *Annales d'histoire économique et sociale* 8 (1935), 476; Bloch's thesis is also referred to by Febvre in lessons five and six.

18. Febvre, *L'Europe*, 404.

19. Ibid., 271.

20. Ibid., 277.

21. Ibid.

22. Ibid., 254. Emphasis in the text.

23. Ibid., 315. The essay he quoted from was L. Febvre, 'De la France à l'Europe. Histoires, psychologies et physiologies nationales', *Annales d'histoire économique et sociale* 4 (1932), 207.

24. E. Renan, *Qu'est-ce qu'une Nation? Et autres écrits politiques* (Paris, 1996); Renan made an interesting remark on the nature of what he named, interestingly, 'social capital', on page 240: 'A nation is a soul, a spiritual principle. Two things, which in truth are but one, constitute this soul or spiritual principle. One lies in the past, one in the present. One is the possession in common of a rich legacy of memories; the other is present-day consent, the desire to live together, the will to perpetuate the value of the heritage that one has received in an undivided form. Man, Gentlemen, does not improvise. The nation, like the individual, is the culmination of a long past of endeavours, sacrifice, and devotion. Of all cults, that of the ancestors is the most legitimate, for the ancestors have made us what we are. A heroic past, great men, glory (by which I understand genuine glory), this is the social capital upon which one bases a national idea.' And the famous statement, a few pages on, '[a] nation's existence is, if you will pardon the metaphor, a daily plebiscite, just as an individual's existence is a perpetual affirmation of life'.

25. C. Donzelli, 'Prefazione all'edizione italiana', in L. Febvre, *Onore e patria* (Rome, 1997), viii.

26. On this project, see E. Roudinesco and P. Schöttler, 'Lucien Febvre à la rencontre de Jacques Lacan', *Genèses* 13 (1937), 139–50, which confirms the many interests of the great French historian.

27. L. Febvre, *Honnoeur et patrie* (Paris, 1996), 147; also see the working notes for the book that will never come to light on pages 181–84.

28. See F. Tuccari, *La nazione* (Rome and Bari, 2000); for the history of the idea of nation, in which much space is given to German political thought, see N. Merker, *Il sangue e la terra. Due secoli di idee sulla nazione* (Rome, 2000). A good anthology is the one edited by V.P. Pecora, *Nations and Identity* (Malden-Oxford, 2001). For a critical review of the most recent approaches to nationalism, U. Özkirimli, *Theories of Nationalism: A Critical Introduction* (Basingstoke, 2010).

29. J. Habermas, 'Citizenship and National Identity: Some Reflections on the Future of Europe', *Praxis International* 12 (1992), 1–19.

30. M. Bloch, 'Problèmes d'Europe', in idem, *Histoire et historiens* (Paris, 1995), 133–44.

31. C. Argetoiano, 'Relazione di S.E. Argetoiano', in Reale Accademia d'Italia, *Convegno di scienze morali e storiche, 14–20 novembre 1932* (Rome, 1933), i, 644.

32. Idem, 'Osservazione di S.E. Argetoiano', in *Convegno di scienze morali e storiche*, i. 112.

33. Bloch, 'Problèmes d'Europe', 134.

34. Febvre, *L'Europe*, 307 and 315. The same monition is repeated in the twenty-eighth lesson (307), and in the postscript (388): 'EUROPE: a word-fetish, it will be said, a word-remedy. A word of salvation that echoes everywhere: let us make Europe, fast. Let us immediately create the European republic. Let us create the nations of a Europe the provinces of which will be our sovereign states. And Europe becomes a notion of crisis. The last hope of the passengers that the tempest pushes, on a wild sea, towards an almost sure shipwreck, in the anguish of night ...' Emphasis in the text.

35. Ibid., 317.

36. Lucien Febvre, 'Quand la télévision sera d'usage courant, ou s'arrêtera notre champ visuel?', *Rivista di storia della storiografia moderna* 1–2 (1993), 127–35; also see the foreword by M. Wessel, 'Lucien Febvre et l'Europe. L'avenir d'une civilisation', ibid., 123–26. Also see Wessel's essays 'Lucien Febvre et l'Europe. Aux frontieres de l'histoire', *Yearbook of European Studies* 4 (1991), 203–16; and idem, 'Honneur ou patrie? Lucien Febvre et la question du sentiment National' 25 (1996), *Genèses*, 128–42.

37. Febvre, 'Quand la télévision …', 129; in footnote 4, Wessel points out that the quote is actually a re-wording of Bloch's ideas in the special issue of *Europe* on 'Les techniques, la science et l'évolution humaine' 47 (1938), 495; Bloch's essay, 'Technique et évolution sociale. Réflexions d'une historien' is now in Marc Bloch, *Mélanges historiques* (Paris, 1963), ii, 833–38.

38. Febvre, *L'Europe*, 305.

39. Ibid., 307.

Part IV

LOOKING TO THE FUTURE

The forty years between the end of the First World War and the Treaty of Rome encapsulate a particularly gloomy period of European history. Europe before the European Community was a continent characterized overwhelmingly by war, the threat of war, militarism, political extremism, economic chaos and social misery. The interwar and war eras gave rise to dark forebodings of the future. Even the postwar period, which witnessed the replacement of the League of Nations by the United Nations and finally came to terms with nationalism as a threat to peace in Europe, was haunted by the growing nuclear weapons rivalry between the United States of America and the Soviet Union in the new age of bipolarity. In this sense, we may construe the European project of the 1950s as both a rejection of this dark past and a concerted attempt to break with it by removing the causes of war and going beyond the traditional concepts of 'nation' and 'state' which – fused together – were deemed largely responsible for man's inability to live in a condition of perpetual peace; that is, to live by politics and law rather than war. This diagnosis of the causes of war led ineluctably to a widespread and penetrating critique of the so-called 'nation-state' itself and its operative principle – national sovereignty – and to various international, intergovernmental, supranational or federal plans for Europe's future.

Such federalism was particularly prominent in Italy, as Matthew D'Auria shows (Chapter 15). In January 1918, the young economist and journalist Luigi Einaudi wrote a letter to the Italian newspaper *Il Corriere della Sera* foreseeing the miserable failure of the League of Nations. The letter firmly stated that since the league did not undermine the absolute sovereignty of its member states, it failed to counter the true and ultimate cause of war – that is, the division of the world into independent states. Furthermore, Einaudi also maintained that the need to overcome such a division had been increased by growing international economic interdependence, which had created a dangerous discrepancy between the formal political independence and the actual economic interdependence of all countries. In other words, economics had literally outgrown the boundaries of the nation-state, so that what had once been the cradle of modern economic progress had now turned into a harmful fetter on Europe's development. From this standpoint, Einaudi could then argue that the ongoing war was simply the manifestation of the natural tendency of Europe to unite politically, given that its economic unity had been achieved already. According to Einaudi, the solution to Europe's predicament lay in a federation based on the model of the United States, where all member states had given up their independence and accepted the rule of a central government. The solution, therefore, did not consist in an improvement of the existing deficiencies of the European system of nation-states, nor was it to be found in Europe's past or in a common historical or cultural nexus. On the contrary, the answer was to be sought in a model which had never really existed in Europe and which was epitomized by the United States. Europe's future lay neither in its past nor in its present; the continent could only have a future if it denied these and adopted a form of political organization which was associated with an extra-European power. Precisely such an organization of political space had given the United States the strength to decide Europe's own destiny. Einaudi repeatedly asserted the beliefs that he had expressed in 1918, maintaining the need for a European federation which would overcome the discrepancy between the 'space of politics' and the 'space of economics'. He did so even as the first president of the Italian Republic and until his death in 1961. Moreover, his ideas deeply influenced those of Italian federalists from Spinelli and Rossi – who found inspiration for their famous *Ventotene Manifesto* in Einaudi's letters – to contemporary political thinkers.[1]

Italian intellectuals such as Einaudi stood within a European tradition of federalism, analysed by Michael Burgess in Chapter 16.[2] Mindful of the historical context in which intellectuals acted, Burgess investigates the emergence of a separate, distinct federalist critique of the causes of war through the works of men such as Lord Lothian, Lionel Robbins, Altiero Spinelli and Jean Monnet. Although this survey of the ideas of Europe's main federalist thinkers of the time accepts the classical distinction between the interwar, wartime and postwar eras, it highlights, at the same time, fundamental continuities of ideas, events, *dramatis personae* and circumstances. By such a token, the three periods – 1917–39, 1939–45 and 1945–57 – reveal shifts of emphasis but also a fundamental continuity and persistence of federal thinking that straddled all three eras. A focus upon the continuity and persistence of the federal idea between 1917 and 1957 is tantamount to a revisionist history of the building of Europe. It is in some ways an alternative version of mainstream European history, giving a specialized unity to the period and emphasizing the importance of political and economic ideas which bore no institutional fruit in Europe before the Second World War but which, nonetheless, represented the necessary intellectual premises on which the European Community was built.

Notes

1. M. D'Auria, 'The Ventotene Manifesto: The Crisis of the Nation State and the Political Identity of Europe', in M. Spiering and M. Wintle (eds), *European Identity and the Second World War* (London, 2011), 141–58.

2. See also M. Burgess (ed.), *Federalism and Federation in Western Europe* (London, 1986); idem, *The British Tradition of Federalism* (London, 1995); idem, 'The British Tradition of Federalism: Nature, Meaning and Significance', in Stanley Henig (ed.), *Federalism and the British* (London, 2007), 35–61; idem, *Federalism and European Union: The Building of Europe, 1950–2000* (London, 2000); R. Mayne and J. Pinder, *Federal Union: The Pioneers, a History of Federal Union* (London, 1990); J. Pinder, 'Federalism and the Beginnings of the European Union', in K. Larres (ed.), *A Companion to Europe since 1945* (Oxford, 2009), 25–44.

Chapter 15

JUNIUS AND THE 'PRESIDENT PROFESSOR'

Luigi Einaudi's European Federalism

>︵︵

Matthew D'Auria

> It is necessary to destroy the ideas that have originated the war. Among such
> ideas, productive of evil if taken to their extreme consequences, the dogma of
> sovereignty, *absolute and perfect in itself*, is especially malefic.[1]
> Luigi Einaudi, 'Il dogma della sovranità'

On 5 January 1918, while Woodrow Wilson, Edward Grey and Edward House
were talking of peace and the end of all wars, a letter was published in the *Corriere
della Sera*, one of the most respected and widely read Italian newspapers. Signed
Junius, the letter was, in the words of the editor-in-chief Luigi Albertini, a 'cold
shower on the idealism of all those who fight so that humanity might see better
days'.[2] The letter predicted that the project of the League of Nations, which
President Wilson would officially announce only three days later, would fail
miserably since, just as the other peace projects discussed in those days, it rested
on a dangerous contradiction:

> Most people, when discussing the 'League of Nations', think of a sort of perpetual
> alliance or confederation of states, the purpose of which is to keep harmony among
> the member states, defend them against foreign aggression and reach some common
> aim of moral and material civilization. Everybody implicitly admits that the allied
> or confederate states must remain fully sovereign and independent, and that a true
> super-state with direct sovereignty over the citizens of the various states, with the
> right to levy its own taxes, maintain a super-national army distinct from national
> armies, with its own administration distinct from the national administrations,

should not be created. They want, yes, the United States of Europe, but each nation must be independent.[3]

The arguments put forward could hardly be clearer; while politicians and intellectuals sought a united Europe as the only possible means against future wars, few were actually prepared to limit the freedom of their own country. Thus, argued *Junius*, most of the projects were mere chimeras, for the unity they sought would dissolve when diverging interests would finally arise among the member states. Between the end of the war and the early 1920s, the *Corriere* published other letters by *Junius*.[4] Behind the pseudonym was the future president of the Italian Republic, Luigi Einaudi. At the time a known and respected journalist and a professor of economics, Einaudi believed that the division of Europe into independent states was the last cause of war and that only a true federation, in which the sovereignty of each state was definitively surrendered to a supranational organism, could ensure a lasting peace.

Einaudi's interest in the cause of European unity dated back as far as 1897, when a naval force of French, British, Germans and Italians intervened in the Thirty Days' War between Greece and the Ottoman Empire; although the involvement was simply meant to save a precarious balance of power, the episode was hailed nonetheless by William Thomas Steed, writing in his *Review of Reviews*, as the birth of the United States of Europe, no longer the dream of philosophers and enthusiasts but a union which could effectively decide war and peace. Commenting on Steed's article, the young Einaudi felt he could not entirely share the British federalists' optimism since, if it was true that European forces had effectively imposed peace, it was also obvious that this was the outcome of a fleeting agreement, a play of fate which had little to do with European unity; anticipating some of his later arguments, Einaudi already pointed out that conflicts remained possible as long as the right to wage war, in the legal theory of the time a prerogative of state sovereignty, remained untouched.[5]

If we exclude a parenthesis during the interwar period imposed by Fascist rule, it can be said that Einaudi's interest in the projects of European unity remained with him throughout his life. It can also be argued that he remained faithful to many of the ideas he wrote down in the *Junius* letters and that his federalist aims remained largely the same throughout his career; because of this, in 1947, in a polemic with Benedetto Croce on the Allies' peace treaty, he could easily support his view by referring to his 1918 letters.[6] Even during his presidency, between 1948 and 1955, he often intervened with notes, remarks and texts in the debates on the Schuman Plan and the European Defence Community with arguments recalling those used in the *Corriere* some forty years earlier.[7] In a sense, this was due to the fact that the thesis he laid out in 1918, deeply contrasting with the cultural context, were strongly ahead of their time so that in the early 1950s some of the problems they singled out and some of the solutions they offered still seemed valid. Nevertheless, if the core of his vision of a European federation remained the same, some of its elements did change over time, with Einaudi shifting from a 'federalist' to a 'functionalist' standpoint before returning to his initial stance – a wavering that, as we shall see, was in part a consequence of Einaudi's changing confidence in Europe's ruling classes.

Analysing the unvarying as well as the changing elements of the federalist ideas of such an acute observer, through writings spanning from 1918 to the early 1950s, may well shed light on some of the changes to the society Einaudi lived in and tried to understand. Yet there is another important reason for looking at his works. In 1920 the *Junius* letters were collected in a volume published by Laterza, which some twenty years later Einaudi himself sent to his old acquaintance Ernesto Rossi.[8] At that time Rossi was 'confinato' on the island of Ventotene by the Fascist government for his involvement with the liberal-socialist movement 'Giustizia e Libertà'. It was there that the letters soon fell into the hands of one of Rossi's friends, a man who was to become the father of modern Italian federalism and one of the most prominent contributors to the process of European integration: Altiero Spinelli. The letters were eagerly read and soon the far reaching implications of Einaudi's federalism became a powerful stimulus for Spinelli's own ideas and, as he himself later wrote in his autobiography, 'started to fructify' in his own and in Rossi's minds, paving the way to some of the most innovative and influential ideas on European unity in those years.[9] It is precisely because of their influence on the *Ventotene Manifesto*, surely one of the most important documents of European federalist thought, that Einaudi's ideas may offer us several hints for a better understanding of Italian federalism and of its merits as well as its faults.[10]

A Liberal Education

The first of four sons of a civil servant, Luigi Einaudi was born in the village of Carrù, near the town of Cuneo, in 1874;[11] after his father's death, in 1888, he moved to his mother's hometown and from there to Savona and Turin where he attended secondary school specializing in classical studies. He enrolled at the University of Turin where he read law and economics, and graduated in jurisprudence in 1895 with merit; shortly afterwards, he became a teaching assistant and researcher, working with the economist Salvatore Cognetti de Martiis until he was appointed professor of Finance at the University of Turin in 1902. During those years, publishing many influential works on economic theory, economic history and international finance, Einaudi also contributed to *La Riforma Sociale* and to the *Critica Sociale*, the journal of the socialist leader Filippo Turati, and came into contact with the economist Pasquale Jannaccone, the political theorist Gioele Solari and, later on, with Vilfredo Pareto. Meanwhile, Einaudi continued his activity as a journalist, writing – literally – hundreds of articles for Albertini's *Corriere della Sera* and gaining a renown which allowed him to become financial correspondent of *The Economist*. In the early 1920s he looked at the rise of Fascism with a certain sympathy for some of the economic reforms undertaken, and yet he immediately understood the dangers of Mussolini's

'constitutional reforms'.[12] In 1924 the murder of the socialist leader Giacomo
Matteotti by the Fascist squads finally and firmly moved Einaudi into the camp of
Mussolini's enemies and prompted him to write a famous article perorating the
return to liberal-democracy.[13] He then joined the *Unione Nazionale* organized by
Giovanni Amendola, a movement uniting all MPs opposing Mussolini, and he
even signed the *Manifesto degli intellettuali anti-fascisti* drafted by Croce – which he
did at the cost of his university post. After the armistice and the German
occupation of northern Italy in September 1943, Einaudi fled to Switzerland,
where he resumed his activity against Fascism. There, he came into contact with
several exiled opponents of the Fascist and Nazi regimes and met once again his
old acquaintance Ernesto Rossi; thanks to him, Einaudi was introduced to Altiero
Spinelli and became involved in the discussions of the many members of federalist
movements then living in Switzerland.[14] At the end of the war he was called by
Prime Minister Ivanoe Bonomi to lead the newborn *Banca d'Italia*, and the
following year he was elected to the new Republican parliament with the liberal
Unione Democratica Nazionale, and onto the *Commissione dei Settancinque* to draft
the project for the new Constitution. In May 1948, Einaudi became president of
the Republic – the 'President Professor', as he would later be called – an
appointment he held until 1955, when he went back to his writings, until he died,
in Rome, on 30 August 1961.

As is always the case with prolific and original thinkers, to classify the political
thought of Luigi Einaudi is far from easy and perhaps any labelling would
excessively simplify the set of ideas he matured over sixty years of intellectual and
political life;[15] in his career he combined, in different and changing ways, concerns
which would properly fit in both the liberal and the socialist field. During his
youth, living in the capital of Italian industry, Einaudi developed a strong
consideration for the working class that remained with him throughout his life.
Praising 'the beauty of struggle', in a work of 1923, and attacking 'scientific
socialism' for degenerating into collectivism and communism, he believed in what
he called a 'socialist feeling', which helped Italian workers 'raise their heads' and
'think, discuss, read';[16] according to Einaudi, the capacity of socialism to
emancipate the workers and give them back their dignity was its most praiseworthy
element, and one that Italy surely needed. From this angle, class struggle had first
and foremost a moral and pedagogic significance.[17] This sympathy for the working
class, nonetheless, went hand in hand with a strong distrust of workers' parties
and trade unions, which kept calling for strong state intervention in the nation's
economy, and which Einaudi saw, as most liberals would, as the antechamber of
authoritarianism.

Unlike Croce's liberalism, which he criticized for its abstract Hegelianism,[18]
Einaudi's liberal ideas were indebted to the works of Mill, Marshall and Smith,
which gave his political stance a strong pragmatic component: 'In the face of
actual problems', he wrote, revealingly, 'the economist can never be a free trader,
intervener or a socialist at all costs.'[19] Refuting all dry utilitarianism, he strongly
believed, as did Hayek and von Mises, that there could be freedom only if

citizens were capable of making decisions for themselves, accepting the consequences and being responsible for them;[20] people had to 'experience' freedom in order to become aware of their worth through their actions. If Einaudi argued that no authority could ever hinge on individual autonomy without turning the state from the keeper of freedom into its worst enemy, his was not a mere denial of the role of politics, nor was it an unconditional praise of a free market.[21] It was a mistake to assume that liberalism implied the absence of state authority; just as misleading was the idea that liberals neglected the issue of social inequality. Remarkably, one of the tasks Einaudi gave politics was precisely to reduce the distance which nature or chance placed between men: 'each man', he wrote in 1957, 'must initially be placed in the same situation as every other, so that he may conquer that moral, economic and political place that is proper to his intellectual attitudes, to his moral character, to his working energy, courage and perseverance'.[22] One way of doing this, other than through free education accessible to all, was by removing the unfair privileges that in a free-trade system were caused by capitalistic monopolies and which, stifling competition, destroyed the spring of economic and moral progress. In a way, Einaudi's liberalism was sharply set against the logic of the status quo that made it possible for the stronger to use the state to protect his privileges at the expense of the weaker. Following on from this, he recognized in his later years that the desire for freedom and the need to cooperate 'force man to be, from time to time and even at once, socialist and liberal'; with the one no longer the mere denial of the other, these two 'spiritual principles' were finally conceived by Einaudi in terms of a seminal antagonism stemming from a difficult search for a balance between freedom and justice.[23]

Einaudi's liberalism, in itself so difficult to classify because of its blend of progressive and conservative elements, constituted the shifting frame within which he defined his own European federalism.[24] Bearing this in mind, the necessary starting point for understanding his ideas on Europe is the conception of peace and of war he expounded in the *Junius* letters, in which he rejected the 'negative' conception of peace as the mere absence of war. Following one of the basic arguments of Kant's *Project for Perpetual Peace* (1795), Einaudi maintained that if peace were to be the outcome of treaties and alliances from which a state could drop out, or of a balance of powers that could falter at any moment, then it would be nothing more than an uncertain truce. Peace, he believed, had to be the definitive and actual impossibility of all armed conflicts; this would only be reached by eradicating the ultimate cause of all conflicts which, contrary to the opinion commonly held, was not founded on economic, religious or ideological differences. For Einaudi, in fact, the rush for new markets, the contrasts between rich and poor countries and even the folly of despots, were only superficial causes. His claim was instead that the ultimate reason for all conflicts lay in the anarchic nature of international society, based on the formal independence and the absolute sovereignty of each single nation. By putting at the fore the issue central to classical political philosophy of the relationship between absolute freedom and violence,

Einaudi reached the logical conclusion that in so far as states were independent, they were in a condition of potential war, one against the other.

A System of States

According to Einaudi, when reasoning on the nature of international society, one had to admit that the principle of sovereignty created an inherently violent system of states in which war was unavoidable. The 'diabolical power' of absolute sovereignty lay in the fact that it forced states towards continuous territorial expansion for strategic as well as economic reasons.[25] Only by conquering its neighbours, argued Einaudi, could a state be safe and independent; and yet, by extending its borders, it eventually found new neighbours which immediately turned into threatening enemies. International anarchy simply created a never-ending war – actual or potential. At the same time, political independence did not simply require a state to have the means to defend itself and to attack its enemies – which, in the end, were one and the same thing; it also involved the economic self-sufficiency necessary for a state's own defence. Looking at the First World War from this standpoint, Einaudi argued that it was precisely the perverse logic of absolute sovereignty that moved German generals and politicians to seek hegemony in Europe and create the Fichtean 'closed commercial state'. Nonetheless, their mistake was that the takeover of Europe could never be enough: 'The Empire must possess within its boundaries not only iron, but even cotton and grain and gum and copper and all the other necessary things to wage war and to live in peace.' It was obvious, said Einaudi, that even in the largest and richest territory some goods would be missing; when pushed to its logical conclusion, then, 'full and absolute sovereignty can only be attained by ruling the entire world'.[26] The folly of sovereignty was that, while pleading for the independence and the freedom of nation-states, it condemned them to live a miserable and violent existence – like that of free men in a Hobbesian state of nature.

Not only was absolute sovereignty the antithesis of peace because it created an anarchic system; it was also a principle based on a dangerous misconception: 'the isolated state, sovereign because self-sufficient, is a deception of imagination; it cannot be real'.[27] Just as men could only live in a society, he argued, so states could not exist independently of each other:

> The truth lies in the ties between, not the sovereignty of, the states. The truth is the interdependence of free people, not their absolute independence. A thousand signs manifest the truth that people are dependent on one another, that they are not absolute sovereigns and judges, with no limits, of their own fates, that they cannot make their will prevail regardless of those of others. To the truth of the national idea that 'We belong to ourselves', we must add the truth of the community of nations: 'We also belong to others'.[28]

Given the nature of their modern economies, states could not ignore the reality of international interdependence just as they could no longer refrain from exchanging goods and raw materials, or cooperating in scientific progress, without 'falling back into barbarity'.[29] Looking at Europe, Einaudi remarked that the need for international cooperation had increased in the second half of the nineteenth century to unprecedented levels thanks to staggering technological innovation. He also found a confirmation of the increase of interdependence in the ever-growing number of treaties that states signed in order to regulate international matters. However, such agreements not only proved the growing need for cooperation; more importantly, they also confirmed that a constant erosion of national sovereignty was taking place. What were in fact international postal agreements or treaties on international transport, asked Einaudi, 'if not renunciations of full and absolute sovereignty, substantial abdications, even if masked, on the part of parliaments to legislate according to their own will within the limits of the national territory?'[30] Underlying these arguments was the assumption that the interdependence tying European nations to one another simply caused an increasing inability, for each state taken individually, to regulate and control what took place within its borders, finally emptying the idea of state independence of any meaning. In light of this, while international anarchy was and remained the ultimate cause of war, the widening gulf between the legal independence and the economic interdependence of European states was increasing the risk of conflicts. In fact, the expansion of international trade and finance, with its effects on national economies, was often perceived by politicians and wider public opinion as a deadly threat to be fought with import duties and barriers; the paradox, for the liberal Einaudi, was that such policies not only ended up impoverishing the people of Europe, but also set them one against the other by appealing to economic nationalism, turning an opportunity for improving the lives of millions into a cause of hatred. Thus, Einaudi could argue that large economic spaces, integrated by technological improvements, had to be ruled by a single political authority. As he put it, in the age of railways, sea and air navigation, telegraphs and telephones, the 'anachronistic sovereign state', with its limited territories, simply had to disappear.[31] In passing, it should be noted that Einaudi's liberal assumption that closed and small economic spaces were no longer advantageous or even possible was at the time an original idea that came to be shared from the mid-1920s to the early 1930s by many liberals, socialists and radicals – such as Laski, Delaisi and Nitti – before becoming an important argument for the advocates of European unity.[32]

Examining the causes of the First World War from such a stand, Einaudi's explanation came to be based on the structural changes that the international community was undergoing and, above all, on the discrepancy between the formal independence and actual interdependence of the states of Europe. The conclusions he reached were that the war itself had been a sort of violent and tragic attempt to adjust the space of politics to the space of economics: 'The ongoing war', he wrote, 'is the condemnation of European unity imposed through force by an ambitious empire; but it is also the bloody effort involved in the creation of a political form of a superior order.'[33] Einaudi used the very same explanation some thirty years later, arguing that even the Second World War could be understood as an attempt to solve the European conundrum by unifying the continent – a tragic attempt made at the cost of millions of lives, and which had failed because of Europe's love of freedom.[34] Both wars, therefore, had been 'fought in vain', since they did not end the 'anachronistic' division of Europe. In 1914 just as in 1939 and, again, in 1947, Europeans were facing a dangerous crossroads; the question was not whether or not Europe should unite – that was unavoidable; the question was how would unification occur, 'by the sword of Satan or by that of God'.[35] At stake was the capacity of Europe to compete with the rising world powers and to maintain its role in the world and its own independence. Developing some of the ideas in Seeley's *The Expansion of England* (1883) and in the essays edited by Lionel Curtis in *The Commonwealth of Nations* (1916),[36] Einaudi argued that just as the free cities and the small principalities of Italy in the sixteenth century had to disappear because they could no longer fight against the great Spanish and French monarchies, European states would have to disappear too, since they could no longer compete, economically or militarily, with the United States and the USSR.[37]

Already in his *Junius* letters, Einaudi had reached the conclusion that the only solution for Europe, the only one that could grant a lasting peace, was to abandon the 'deadly dogma of absolute sovereignty' and unite in a single political entity.[38] Reasoning in terms of a domestic analogy, quite in line with his liberal standpoint, he claimed that just as the modern state, gaining control over all means of violence, assured peace to its citizens, a supranational organization could prevent conflict among European states by gaining control, definitively and without reserve, over the means of waging war. The price states would pay for peace would be their own absolute sovereignty, which Einaudi, referring to the ideas in Treitschke's *Politik* (1899), fittingly defined as the faculty 'to declare war and sign peace'.[39] In a 1948 essay, the domestic analogy was even more explicit: 'As the state, with policemen, judges and jailers, keeps at bay thieves and murderers, so it is necessary that a power above the state, a super-state, keeps at bay the states aiming to attack, ravish and plunder others … He who wants peace must want the federation of states, the creation of an authority above that of single sovereign states.'[40] From a pact of association, placing the goods of its members in common, a pact of subjugation had to follow, an agreement in which all members renounced their right to use force and accepted the power of a third superior party.[41] Based on such an insight, looking at the project of the League of Nations, Einaudi remarked in 1918 that the latter simply sought a 'confederation' which left untouched the complete independence of its member states and, with this, the actual cause of war. At best, Wilson's project could only delay the outbreak of a new conflict; at worst, it could actually arouse new disagreements among its members: 'the efforts made to create a league of nations, which remain sovereign, would create nothing, the unthinkable, [and would] increase and poison the reasons for discord. To the existing causes of bloody fighting would be added jealousies resulting in the division of common expenses [and] rage against the defaulting or recalcitrant states.'[42] Because it left intact the sovereignty of its member states, the project of the League of Nations could not achieve its ambitious aims.

European Federalism

To make his point clearly, Einaudi used the historical example of the birth of the United States of America and, developing some of Hamilton's ideas in *The Federalist Papers* (1788), he made his case rest on the difference between the 1776 and 1787 Constitutions; while the first one gave birth to a confederation of thirteen states, each with its sovereignty and independence, the second one no longer spoke of an agreement of independent governments; the 1787 Constitution derived its legitimacy from the 'act of will of the whole people, which created a new, different and superior state to the old states'. By such a token, 'for the "agreement" among sovereign states to regulate "some" subjects of common interest is substituted "the act of sovereignty of the entire American people", which creates a new state, gives it a constitution and which superimposes itself, in a much wider sphere, on the old states'.[43] For Einaudi, the gulf separating the two constitutions was immense both in form as well as in consequence: 'under the first one, the new union soon threatened to dissolve; under the second one the United States became a giant'.[44] It was only thanks to the 1787 Constitution, fusing the sovereignties of the thirteen colonies into a single political space, that the United States were able to suppress war within their own immense territory. On the basis of this historical example, Einaudi set forth a clear distinction between 'confederation' and 'federation', showing the advantages of the latter over the former. He insisted once again on this distinction while reviewing an important book published in 1918 by his colleague and friend, Attilio Cabiati,[45] and by the founder of FIAT, Giovanni Agnelli, calling for a European federation.[46] History, he argued, repeatedly showed the impossibility of achieving results through a simple league of nations; the confederation of cities in ancient Greece, the Holy Roman Empire, the Holy Alliance, as well as the American Confederation, were all destined to fail since 'no state can exist where a central authority with its own financial means and its own army is missing'.[47] It was necessary, therefore, for Europe to create a federation in which states would remain free to follow their own inclinations in all except some specific fields such as 'foreign policy, the armed forces and the navy, federal finance and tariff policy'.[48] A constitution would have assigned these competences to a central authority, on the example of what happened in federal states.

While Einaudi remained faithful to this idea from the *Junius* writings to his Presidency of the Republic, always insisting that war was the inevitable outcome of international anarchy and that the only solution was a federation of European states, the means he conceived for reaching this ambitious aim changed over the years, even adopting a stance usually defined by scholars as 'functionalistic'.[49] The starting point for such a turn was a 1919 article which Einaudi started by stressing that political ingenuity, passion, rhetorical capacities, great visions and learning were all necessary skills for politicians in making their decisions in their 'government of men'; yet, went on Einaudi, once such decisions were taken and aims set, then technical abilities, administrative skills and scientific knowledge became fundamental, and politicians were forced to place the 'government of things' in the hands of 'technicians'.[50] Well aware that too sharp a distinction between 'government of men' and 'government of things' was misleading, Einaudi believed nonetheless that there was a difference between the political decision of creating an international postal union and the administrative decision made by a technical commission to put in place the most efficient system for sending and receiving letters abroad. Growing international interdependence had caused a mushrooming of 'international administrations', which proved at once that politicians had to abdicate state sovereignty and that technicians and experts were essential in administering international issues.

For Einaudi, what was truly remarkable was that the many existing interstate commissions continued their work during the war and even after. The reason for their successes, he argued, was that, once created, their officers ignored the instructions of governments and relied on their own abilities to achieve the aim of the organization. An interesting example of this was the European Commission for the Danube created in 1867 which, gaining an ever-growing authority, had become the 'true image of an abstract state, supranational, without its own territory and yet capable of effective action in the interest of the people'.[51] Furthermore, the fact that many of an increasing number of international commissions were under the direct control of the League of Nations allowed Einaudi to hope that the latter would soon start to coordinate their activities – a relatively easy task since it involved the 'government of things'. While such commissions would have a real impact on the lives of millions, their decisions would nonetheless be beyond the influence of nations' politicians or of international public opinion, which 'does not take much of an interest'; in this way they would take the authority they needed or even 'usurp it' to achieve their aims, becoming in the end even capable 'of governing men'.[52] With the increase of this interstate administration of 'things', the 'sovereignty of single states would undoubtedly be weakened', and legislators and common citizens would realize that there was a superior organization above them 'with its own life'[53] and a strong 'superstate' able to suppress wars 'among states apparently independent, but truly dependent' from one another.[54]

Einaudi repeated these same ideas – clearly forerunning David Mytrany's theories – in several other articles, even praising the work of the League of Nations before the Fascist tide forced him to take up less controversial issues.[55] It is quite plausible to assume that, between 1919 and 1925, in the face of the growing antagonism among European nations and the rise of authoritarian movements, Einaudi must have realized that the defeat of national sovereignty was out of reach. As he understood already in May 1919, while little trust could be given to politicians promising to remain faithful to a league of nations after the bloodshed of the Great War, the success of the international administration of roads, railways, harbours and canals was something that could be hoped for: 'Europeans are not willing to give up the national principle on the altar of the League of Nations,' he wrote, 'but they can work out the advantages of a supranational government of material goods, of the mere instruments of economic life.'[56] If this might seem a step back from the federalist ideal of universal peace,[57] it was in truth a strategic move based on an awareness that little trust could be placed at the time in Europe's politicians or in the wider public opinion. After 1943, once he had recovered his confidence, it became obvious that Einaudi's 'functionalist' approach was just meant to push forward a series of international agreements to force states onto the path of federation by increasing juridical ties among them. As he explained in a 1952 essay on the European Defence Community, functionalist agreements were acceptable only inasmuch as they fixed 'short deadlines' for the next step towards a 'political federation'.[58] The very idea of a 'functionalist federation', for Einaudi, was an 'intellectual mystification' that could never create a truly lasting peace.[59]

It is clear that the federalism Einaudi depicted in his writings revealed at once a number of flaws as well as several strong points. While the content of the ideas he laid out in the *Junius* letters were beyond doubt ahead of their time, it would be misleading to assume that his were the only works in Italy calling for a European federation; on the contrary, the book by the liberal politician Ettore Ponti, *La Guerra dei popoli e la futura federazione europea* (1915), the writings of Guglielmo Ferrero, Alessandro Levi and Gaetano Salvemini, as well as Cabiati and Agnelli's book, all written before the end of the war, testify to a strong interest in the project of European unity.[60] Nonetheless, the originality of Einaudi's ideas and the clarity of his arguments make his *Junius* letters stand apart. Sharing with the British federalists of the 1920s and 1930s the same intellectual grounding – Hamilton's *Federalist Papers* and Seeley's and Curtis's works – Einaudi anticipated some of their theses which, in turn, were to have a deep and lasting impact on Italian federalism.[61] Just as Philip Kerr argued in *The Prevention of War* (1922) and in his famous *Pacifism Is Not Enough* (1935) that war was the outcome of international anarchy and could be averted only by limiting national sovereignty, so did Einaudi in 1918; just as Lionel Robbins made clear in *Economic Planning and World Order* (1937) that economic interdependence, deeply contrasting with national sovereignty, required an international federation, so did the *Junius* letters. Even Einaudi's writings of 1919–1924, belonging to his 'functionalist phase', were amazingly original. Leonard Woolf's *International Government* (1916) and Jan C. Smuts's *The League of Nations: A Practical Suggestion* (1918)[62] spoke about the importance of functional factors in international integration, but they never depicted a relationship between technical administration and political integration, in contrast to Einaudi, who anticipated some of the arguments in David Mitrany's influential *The Progress of International Government* (1933).

One of the most relevant elements of Einaudi's theory was the idea that international, above all economic, integration created an ever-expanding unity which contrasted sharply with the fixed spaces of the nation-state. Although it is not immediately obvious, the line of thought running from Benjamin Constant to Richard Cobden, and, in Italy, to Carlo Cattaneo, which assumed that the development of international economic relations paved the way to world peace, was actually called into question. Although Einaudi favourably reviewed Norman Angell's famous work *The Great Illusion* (1909), which was one example of such a line of thought, after the outbreak of war he changed his stand and reached the conclusion that the idea that economic liberalism brought peace, while economic nationalism brought war, was in itself misleading.[63] He recognized that ever-growing economic interdependence could in theory create advantages for workers, producers and consumers, yet it was obvious that this was not occurring; on the contrary, the growing discrepancy between the ever-wider space of economics and the fixed boundary of the nation-state deprived the latter of the ability to govern its own economy, forcing it to close its borders to foreign trade and finance – an option Cobdenites had not foreseen. As a result, the benefits of interdependence were denied, while economic nationalism increased attrition among European states, showing that the growth of international commerce was not in itself sufficient to assure peace, and demonstrating that the political unity of Europe was necessary. What is important for us is that Einaudi provided a new understanding of the causes of war, seeing it as an attempt – if tragic and appalling – to bridge the gap between a continental, unified economic space, and its political division into nation-states; in this respect, his great merit is shifting the analysis from the relationship between single states, and from economic, ideological and religious causes, to the structure of the European state system, which he came to conceive of as a single entity. To him, it was all too obvious that if the cause of war was supranational, the measures used to end war also had to be supranational.[64]

In spite of these great merits, when looking at the distinction Einaudi made between federation and confederation, and comparing it with the model he constantly referred to, that of Alexander Hamilton, the shortcomings of his theory become clear. In *The Federalist Papers*, in fact, Hamilton depicted, on the one hand, a multifaceted relationship between each member state and the central government in which the juridical personality of the single state did not melt into a super-state but lived alongside it; on the other hand, he assumed the existence of a complex articulation of political authority within the boundaries of each federated unity, where cities and counties were something more than mere administrative units. Hamilton's federalism, therefore, implied a partial transfer of sovereignty, above as well as below state level, seeking a sort of territorially based checking of political authority which went alongside a more classical functional one. Looking at Einaudi's writings, it is clear that such an insight was completely absent, at least in the *Junius* letters; what might actually be argued instead is that Einaudi at the time was calling for a super-state of greater scope in which all pre-existing political units would become 'mere provinces' of the central government.[65] The widening of the space of the state was Einaudi's major concern, while the articulation of political authority within it was inadequately understood. It is quite plausible that the experience of Fascism moved him to conceive, in addition, of an 'internal' understanding of federalism, as emerges from some of his 1944 and 1945 writings,[66] and yet internal and external aspects were never integrated into a full theory of federalism which would have properly turned it, in Cattaneo's words, into 'a theory of freedom'.[67]

A second important drawback of Einaudi's work lies in the ambiguity of his critique of national sovereignty, which he actually made while calling for the safeguard of 'the principle of nationality'.[68] Possibly a legacy of the Risorgimento, where nation and Europe were not only compatible but even depended on each other, such an apparent contradiction emerged in many of his works.[69] Interestingly, in some of his earlier writings, Einaudi even claimed that the creation of federations of ethnically homogeneous countries was the road to follow in order to avoid wars and improve Europe's economy, while preserving national diversity.[70] Such an option, which proffered an easy solution to the problem of political legitimacy, was soon abandoned by Einaudi in favour of a more radical federalism calling for the unification of the whole continent.[71] However, this option obviously left unanswered the question of how to combine the feeling of belonging to a nation, which Einaudi recognized as natural, and the need to unite politically, which he thought necessary. The only solution set forth was the decoupling of nation and state with the aim of saving the former and changing the latter, a solution which clearly underestimated the problem of the legitimacy of the European federation. Focusing on the economic, juridical and even institutional aspects of unification, and neglecting the cultural, social and historical issues involved, Einaudi's federalism was misleading in so far as it assumed that a federation would found its legitimacy, ex post, on the results it attained.

Conclusion

Einaudi unduly overlooked the fact that political authority requires some sense of belonging that goes beyond – and comes before – any mere calculation of convenience; nationalism was able to create such feeling. In spite of these limitations, it is beyond doubt that Einaudi had the merit of introducing the study of modern federalist thought in Italy, along with ideas and intuitions, the originality of which can hardly be overestimated.[72] What is truly remarkable, when reading the *Junius* letters as well as the writings of the 'President Professor', is that many arguments, such as the need to redefine national sovereignty or to overcome the growing discrepancy between political and economic spaces, are today assumptions commonly held by diplomats, politicians and 'eurocrats'. In the same way, even the limitations and contradictions of Einaudi's thought are still present in the programmes of federalist movements across Europe, above all the difficulty of overcoming a soulless federalism unaware of the emotions and feelings of the peoples of Europe. It is for these reasons, because they ask questions still worth asking, that Einaudi's works are of interest, and it is to them we should turn to understand and measure the progress federalism has made from where Einaudi left it.

Notes

1. Junius [L. Einaudi], 'Il dogma della sovranità e l'idea della Società delle Nazioni' (1918), in idem, *La guerra e l'Unità europea* (Milan, 1948), 25. Italics in the text.
2. L. Albertini, *Epistolario, 1911–1926. Vol. II, La Grande Guerra* (Milan, 1968), 845.
3. Junius [L. Einaudi], 'La Società delle Nazioni è un ideale possibile?', in Einaudi, *La guerra e*, 12–13.
4. The use of the pseudonym is explained by Einaudi himself in his 'Prefazione', in L. Einaudi, *Cronache economiche e politiche di un trentennio (1893–1925)* (Turin, 1965), vol. 4, xxxiv.
5. L. Einaudi, 'Un sacerdote della stampa e gli Stati Uniti d'Europa' (1897), now in idem, *Il buongoverno. Saggi di economia e politica* (Bari, 1973), vol. 2, 633–35; see also U. Morelli, *Contro il mito dello stato sovrano. Luigi Einaudi e l'unità europea* (Milano, 1990), 17–22.
6. L. Einaudi, 'La guerra e l'unità europea' (1947), in idem, *La guerra e l'Unità europea*, 124.
7. L. Einaudi, *Lo scrittoio del Presidente* (Turin, 1956), 47–97.
8. G. Fanello Marcucci, 'Rossi ed Einaudi, due vite in dialogo', in L. Strik Lievers (ed.), *Ernesto Rossi, Economista, federalista, radicale* (Venice, 2001), 235–44.
9. A. Spinelli, *Come ho tentato di diventare saggio* (Bologna, 1999), 307; acknowledging his intellectual debt to Einaudi, in the copy of the *Ventotene Manifesto* he sent him, Rossi wrote: 'To *Junius* who, in the distant 1918, sowed in Italy the first federalist ideas for which we fight today', quoted in Norberto Bobbio 'Luigi Einaudi federalista', *Nuova Antologia* 2188 (Oct.–Dec. 1993), 271.
10. On the *Ventotene Manifesto*, see M. D'Auria, 'The Ventotene Manifesto: The Crisis of the Nation State and the Political Identity of Europe', in M. Spiering and M. Wintle (eds), *European Identity and the Second World War* (London, 2011), 141–58.
11. On Einaudi's life, see R. Faucci, *Luigi Einaudi* (Turin, 1986); and G. Limiti, *Il Presidente professore: Luigi Einaudi al Quirinale* (Milan, 2001).
12. L. Einaudi, 'Risanamento economico e finanziario dell'Italia nel discorso del ministro delle finanze a Milano' (1923), in idem, *Cronache economiche*, vol. 7, 233–38.
13. L. Einaudi, 'Stato liberale e stato organico fascista' (1924), in idem, *Cronache economiche*, vol. 7, 794–98.
14. Faucci, *Luigi Einaudi*, 317–23; C. Cressati, *L'Europa necessaria. Il federalismo liberale di Luigi Einaudi* (Turin, 1992), 81–96.
15. For Einaudi's political ideas, N. Bobbio, 'Il pensiero politico di Luigi Einaudi', *Annali della Fondazione Luigi Einaudi*, 8 (1974), 183–215; also A. Giordano, *Il pensiero politico di Luigi Einaudi* (Genoa, 2006); and F. Forte, *Luigi Einaudi: Il mercato e il buongoverno* (Turin, 1982), 190–250.
16. L. Einaudi, 'La bellezza della lotta' (1923), in idem, *Il buongoverno*, vol. 2, 523.
17. N. Bobbio, *Profilo ideologico del novecento italiano* (Turin, 1986), 90.
18. L. Einaudi, 'Liberismo e Liberalismo' (1931), in idem, *Il Buongoverno* (Bari, 1973), vol. 1, 218–29.
19. Ibid., 222; also Bobbio, *Profilo ideologico*, 88–90.
20. A. Zanfarino, 'Liberalismo e liberismo. Il confronto Croce-Einaudi', *Studi e note di economia* 2 (1996), 14–16.
21. Einaudi, 'Discorso elementare sulle somiglianze e sulle dissonanze fra liberalismo e socialismo', in idem, *Prediche inutili. Dispensa quarta* (Turin, 1957), 216.
22. Ibid., 209.
23. Ibid., 236; also see Forte, *Luigi Einaudi*, 227–28.

24. On Einaudi's federalism, see Cressati, *L'Europa necessaria*; Morelli, *Contro il mito*; A. Quadrio Curzio and C. Rotondi, 'Luigi Einaudi: il disegno istituzionale ed economico per l'Europa', *Atti dei Convegni Lincei*, 2005, n. 214, 163–94; and Bobbio, 'Luigi Einaudi federalista'.

25. Einaudi, 'Il dogma della sovranità', 27.

26. Ibid., 27–28; also L. Einaudi, 'Fiume, la Società delle Nazioni ed il dogma della sovranità' (1919), in idem, *Lettere politiche* (Bari, 1920), 164; see S. Pistone, 'Le critiche di Einaudi e di Agnelli e Cabiati alla Società delle Nazioni nel 1918', in idem (ed.), *L'idea dell'unificazione europea dalla prima alla seconda guerra mondiale* (Turin, 1975), 28–29.

27. Einaudi, 'Il dogma della sovranità', 29.

28. Ibid., 28. Also, L. Einaudi, 'Le cause dello scisma e le tendenze verso una intesa dei popoli di. lingua inglese' (1918), in idem, *Gli ideali di un economista* (Firenze, 1921), 176–77.

29. Einaudi, 'Il dogma della sovranità', 29.

30. Ibid., 30.

31. L. Einaudi, 'The Nature of a World Peace', in *Annals of the American Academy of Political and Social Science* 210 (1940), 66; also see idem, 'La unificazione del mercato europeo', in F. Parri (et al.), *Europa federata* (Milan, 1947), 55–66.

32. H. Laski, *Nationalism and the Future of Civilization* (London, 1932), 25; F. Delaisi, 'L'union économique européenne, est-elle possible?', *Le monde nouveau*, 15 October 1926; F.S. Nitti, *La pace* (Turin, 1925), 205–6; also see J.-L. Chabot, *L'idee d'Europe unie de 1919 à 1939* (Grenoble, 1978), 336–41.

33. Einaudi, 'La Società delle Nazioni', 22; also see his 1940 'The Nature of a World Peace', 66–67.

34. Einaudi, 'La guerra e l'Unità europea', 124–25.

35. Ibid., 125; 'Without knowing, Anglo-Americans have fought for the same cause as Hitler's: the unification of Europe', L. Einaudi, [Contro la «Resa incondizionata»] (1943?), in idem, *Riflessioni di un liberale sulla democrazia* (Florence, 2001), 38.

36. See *Annali della fondazione Luigi Einaudi* 20 (1986), 30–34; also Morelli, *Contro il mito*, 24–26; see Einaudi's review of Curtis' book in *Riforma Sociale* 29 (Jan.–Feb. 1918), 105–7. The idea that in the future the world would be divided among a small number of large powers was already in L. Einaudi, 'Unioni politiche e unioni doganali', *Minerva. Rivista delle riviste*, 1916, n. 3, 97.

37. The idea that the future belonged to political unities of continental size was often used in the interwar period to justify the call for a European federation; not least, it was used by Coudenhove-Kalergi in his *Pan-Europa* (Vienna, 1923), 23. See Anita Prettenthaler-Ziegerhofer's contribution to this volume.

38. Einaudi, 'Il dogma della sovranità', 33.

39. Ibid., 24; see Morelli, *Contro il mito*, 30–31; also see Einaudi's essay on Treitschke, 'L'idea dello stato come forza' (1918), in idem, *Gli ideali di un economista*, 163–78.

40. Luigi Einaudi, 'Chi vuole la pace', in idem, *La guerra e l'Unità europea*, 137.

41. On this point, see N. Bobbio, *Teoria generale della politica* (Turin, 1999), 483–88.

42. Einaudi, 'La società delle Nazioni è un ideale', 16–17.

43. Ibid., 14.

44. Ivi.

45. R. Marchionatti, 'Luigi Einaudi ed Attilio Cabiati. Appunti su un'amicizia e un sodalizio intellettuale', *Atti dei Convegni Lincei*, 214 (2005), 335–44.

46. G. Agnelli and A. Cabiati, *Federazione europea o Lega delle Nazioni?* (1918), (Pordenone, 1995). The two authors, quite remarkably, quoted the *Junius* letters to compare federation and confederation (55–56). On this important work, see Pistone, 'Le critiche di Einaudi e di Agnelli e Cabiati alla Società delle Nazioni'.

47. L. Einaudi, 'Federazione Europea o Società delle Nazioni' (1918), in idem, *Gli ideali di un economista*, 196.

48. Ibid. To this rather sharp and clear distinction between federation and confederation Einaudi remained faithful throughout his carrier, so that even during his presidency, in 1952, he repeated almost verbatim the same arguments; see Veterano [Luigi Einaudi], 'Tipi e connotati

della federazione. Discorrendo di Comunità europea di difesa' (1952), in idem, *Lo scrittoio del Presidente*, 62–63.

49. Quadrio Curzio and Rotondi, 'Luigi Einaudi', 171–73, 186–90. Also Morelli, *Contro il mito*, 71–94.

50. L. Einaudi, 'La Società delle Nazioni e il governo delle cose' (1919), in idem, *Gli ideali di un economista*, 219–27.

51. Ibid., 222.

52. Ibid., 227.

53. Ibid., 226.

54. Ibid., 227.

55. Einaudi, 'Fiume, la Società delle Nazioni', 159–67; Luigi Einaudi, 'Avvertenza' (1921), in idem, *Gli ideali di un economista*, 7; Luigi Einaudi, 'Sacrificio fecondo' (1924), in idem, *Cronache*, vol. 7, 823–26.

56. Einaudi, 'Fiume, la Società delle Nazioni', 166.

57. Ibid., 159.

58. Einaudi, 'Tipi e connotati', 65.

59. Ibid., 67.

60. For the Italian federalist literature of the time, see C. Malandrino, *Socialismo e libertà. Autonomie, federalismo, Europa da Rosselli a Silone* (Milan, 1990), 22–55; for the European one, Carl H. Pegg, *Evolution of the European Idea, 1914–1932* (Chapel Hill, 1983), 8–39; and Chabot, *L'idee d'Europe unie*.

61. On the influence of British thinkers on Italian federalism, see J. Pinder, 'Il federalismo in Gran Bretagna e in Italia: i radicali e la tradizione liberale inglese', *Il federalista* 31 (1989), 92–118; also see Michael Burgess's essay in this volume.

62. For an overview, see V.-Y. Ghébali, 'The League of Nations and Functionalism', in A. J. Richard Groom and P. Taylor, *Functionalism: Theory and Practice in International Relations* (London, 1975), 141–61.

63. See Einaudi's presentation to Norman Angell's, 'La grande illusione: guerre di ieri e guerre di oggi', *La riforma sociale* 23 (1912), 265–66. On Angell's work, D. Biocca, 'Il pacifismo e La Grande Illusione di Norman Angell', *Studi Storici*, 1980, n. 3, 595–607.

64. M. Albertini, *Il federalismo* (Milan, 1993), 231.

65. Einaudi, 'La Società delle Nazioni è un ideale', 13.

66. Junius [L. Einaudi], 'Via il prefetto!' (1944), in idem, *Il buongoverno*, 54–62; L. Einaudi, 'La sovranità è indivisibile?' (1945), *Annali della Fondazione Luigi Einaudi*, n. 23, 1994, 565–67.

67. C. Cattaneo, 'Lettera a L. Frapolli' (1851), in idem, *Epistolario di Carlo Cattaneo* (Florence, 1952), vol. 2, 122.

68. See for example Einaudi, 'Fiume, la Società delle Nazioni', 159–67; Einaudi, 'La Guerra e l'unità europea', 131.

69. On the influence of the ideas of the Risorgimento on Einaudi, Limiti, *Il Presidente professore*, 127–36.

70. Einaudi, 'Unioni politiche', 97–99.

71. Einaudi, 'Federazione Europea o Società delle Nazione', 195–203.

72. Sergio Pistone, *L'Italia e l'unità europea* (Turin, 1982), 52.

Chapter 16

FEDERATE OR PERISH

*The Continuity and Persistence of the Federal Idea in Europe,
1917–1957*

⫷⫸

Michael Burgess

Introduction: Looking Back

The two singular events that serve to define and give shape to our images and ideas of Europe in this volume of essays are the end of the First World War and the Treaty of Rome; the latter launched the European Economic Community (EEC) in March 1957 and it came into operation in January 1958. To the extent that the former represented in essence a nineteenth-century European conflagration, its outbreak in many ways signified the birth of the twentieth century in 1914, while in hindsight the emergence in 1958 of the EEC – after another essentially European civil war ended in 1945 – marked the beginning of a distinctly new era of inter-state relations in Europe.

In retrospect, the forty years between these two events encapsulated a particularly dark, dismal and gloomy period of European history that is appropriately summarized in the menacing title of Mark Mazower's *Dark Continent: Europe's Twentieth Century*.[1] Europe before the EEC, then, was a continent characterized overwhelmingly by war, the threat of war, militarism, political extremism, economic chaos and social misery. It was a Europe where the roots of liberal democracy remained shallow and the role of government contested and uncertain. This was the Europe characterized in 1939 by the sceptical E.H. Carr, whose aptly titled *The Twenty Years Crisis* was a realist's survey of international relations between the wars that questioned the initial optimistic assumptions and public expectations of Wilsonian reasoning and diplomacy manifested in the principle of national self-determination and the League of Nations.[2] What the mass publics of the European states gradually came to experience was a diffuse but deep-seated sense of crisis, 'not merely the severity of the crisis' but a pervading idea 'that the crisis was, so to speak, permanent'.[3] Looking back from the vantage point of half a century of successful European integration, it is easy for us today to forget how far the interwar years, the wartime period and the early postwar years, that together constitute our framework of analysis during 1917/18–1957, represented dark forebodings of the future. Even the postwar period, which witnessed the replacement of the League of Nations by the United Nations and finally came to terms with nationalism as a threat to peace in Europe, was haunted by the growing nuclear weapons rivalry between the United States of America and the Soviet Union in the new age of bipolarity. The sheer scale and magnitude of these extremely difficult circumstances – of the curious mixture of initial hopes melting gradually into solemn pessimism, and the highly unpromising conditions that confronted those who thought in terms of a future for Europe that would constitute a lasting peace order – are now often hard to appreciate.

In this sense we may construe the European project of the 1950s as both a rejection of this dark past and a concerted attempt to break with it by removing the causes of war and going beyond the traditional concepts of 'nation' and 'state' that – fused together – were deemed largely responsible for man's inability to live in a condition of perpetual peace, that is, to live by politics and law rather than war. This diagnosis of the causes of war led ineluctably to a widespread penetrating critique of the so-called 'nation-state' itself and its operative principle – national sovereignty. And it is precisely with this question of national sovereignty and the international order of states that we must locate our point of departure in this chapter. This is because they are construed here as the bedrock of virtually all of the intellectual analyses of what was wrong with this 'dark continent'. They are also the basis upon which the federal idea and the emergence of a separate, distinct federalist critique of the causes of war first appeared and grew ever stronger during the historical period under review. As we shall see, the basic premise of the federalists' arguments about Europe's 'propensity for war' was that war itself was a condition of the international system of states. War, in short, was immanent in Europe. Consequently if the state was allowed to pursue so-called 'national interests' in a world of national sovereignties where there was no recognized legal order but only the condition of an anarchy of state interests and preferences, Europe would forever be at war with itself.

Looking back, then, we can see that there are three distinct periods that historians conventionally identify as a convenient framework of analysis, namely, the interwar, the wartime and the postwar eras. And it is interesting how far these three divisions that mark off one period from another are each defined by war – the First World War and the Second World War. It is almost as if history was really only about war rather than the larger study of how people routinely live their lives and organize their social, economic and political forms of peaceful association. On this reckoning history was actually only an interlude between the regular recourse to arms. It is important to remember, then, that in extrapolating periods in history we compress, distort and oversimplify in our explanatory interpretations.

When we consider 'Europe before the European Community' we would be wise to remember that the interpretation of separate distinct historical periods may obscure and even conceal fundamental continuities of ideas, events, *dramatis personae* and circumstances. This is certainly the case with the federal idea and the men and women who worked consistently together throughout this period towards the forging of a new European peace order that would be a new federal order. Mindful of these precautions, my chapter will be divided into a broad survey of the federal idea during the three periods identified above to reveal shifts of emphasis but a fundamental continuity and persistence of federal thinking that straddled all three eras. I will begin with the interwar period between 1918 and 1939.

The Interwar Years

It is customary for most studies of federal ideas and movements in Europe during this period to refer to the Pan-European Union of Count Richard Coudenhove-Kalergi that was formed in 1923. Led by an Austro-Hungarian aristocrat, this organization was essentially a propagandist pressure group with headquarters in Vienna, from where its publishing house sent out a regular series of pan-European literature that advocated a federal Europe. Although construed by the political establishment as variously naïve, idealistic and utopian, the great merit of Coudenhove-Kalergi's activism lay in his diagnosis of the ills of Europe, as carefully sketched out in his *Pan-Europe*, first published in 1926.[4] Here he set out Europe's problems in 'an intercontinental, global framework', construing Europe both 'from within and without' which was 'the essence of his Pan-Europeanism'.[5] Looking at Europe's internal weaknesses and external vulnerabilities enabled him to present the case for federal union, as it were, in the round, as one of 'peace, security and even survival *vis-à-vis* the external world, as well as a resolution of Europe's domestic problems'.[6] His approach enabled him to predict several things: the decline of Europe in world affairs; the threat of nationalism; the redundancy of the nation-state; the ultimate failure of the League of Nations; and perpetual conflict in Europe if it remained economically and politically disunited. However, if he had explained *why* Europe needed federal union he did not adequately explain precisely *how* this would come about or *what* it would look like. His political strategy was flawed and his institutional conception of a federal Europe was anaemic.

It is easy to appreciate why, at the time, professional diplomats might have dismissed such a man and a movement as hopelessly impractical and wildly optimistic, but in the light of what we now know about Europe today we can probably afford to be more generous to his legacy. His idealism can now be viewed as prophetic.[7] He was a man of imagination – a man ahead of his time. Consequently, it is, I think, important to note that when we survey the past to look again at the ideas, proposals and activities of previous federalist thinkers and practitioners dedicated to the cause of European unity we need constantly to reappraise their contributions in the light of contemporary developments. In this way we are able to reassess them and their political goals and strategies in a more measured, even-handed way. What might have seemed far-fetched and hopelessly impractical fifty or eighty years ago is often construed in a very different way to modern minds today. In short, what was yesterday's practical impossibility is today's conventional practice. And no better example of this exists than the current European Union.

Turning to other examples of the political expression of the federal idea during these years, it is also important to look much closer to home and focus our attention upon the specifically British contribution to the continuity and persistence of the federal idea. Here it is necessary for us to situate British federal ideas about Europe firmly in the context of the nineteenth and twentieth centuries – a continuity confirmed by the links that connected 'Empire, Ireland and Europe' wrought by revised elite perceptions of international change.[8] This conceptual and empirical continuity of federal ideas was clearly established by the activities and influences of key British political figures and public men, and the emergence of a series of political organizations that symbolized the need for fundamental far-reaching practical policy reassessments and adjustments to British imperial, foreign and domestic policies. Central to these developments were Lionel Curtis, Frederick Scott Oliver and Philip Kerr (later Lord Lothian) who themselves became an integral part of the larger British tradition of federalism stretching back to the Imperial Federation League (1884–93), the creation of the Imperial Federation (Defence) Committee in 1894, the Round Table Movement established in 1910 and the Federal Union that would eventually emerge during 1938–39.[9]

For the purposes of this chapter I want to concentrate upon just one of these political figures, namely Philip Kerr, who became Lord Lothian in 1930 having inherited the title of Marquis of Lothian from his cousin. Lothian is of special interest in the interwar years, not so much for his political influence upon the decision makers of his day as for his intellectual diagnosis of international relations in Europe and the federal prescription at which he arrived. As we shall see, the structure of his analysis retains a contemporary significance for what it reminds us about the nature of power politics.

Kerr's early career in South Africa working for the Inter-colonial Council for the Transvaal and Orange River Colony brought him into direct contact with people, such as Robert Brand and Lionel Curtis, who had originally gone out to work for Lord Alfred Milner when he was High Commissioner there. Rubbing shoulders with colleagues like these, part of whose purpose was to forge a scheme for the federal union of the South African colonies, which became known as the Selborne Memorandum, exposed him first to the federal idea for South Africa and then to the closer union of the British Empire itself. On his return to the United Kingdom, Kerr joined his former colleagues in setting up the Round Table movement during 1909–10, became the editor of the quarterly journal, *Round Table*, and worked actively in the cause of educating British and colonial public opinion about the need for constitutional reform.[10] Unlike his compatriot, Curtis, who had a mystical faith in the British Empire and an almost doctrinaire commitment to the cause of imperial federation, Kerr was much less sanguine about grand constitutional schemes designed to fit the empire into practices that had suited the U.K. and the self-governing colonies in the past, but he did share Curtis's interest in a major reorganization of the imperial structure and he concurred about the need for a common policy in defence and foreign affairs.

This practical experience in a political movement that promoted federal ideas in British imperial affairs convinced Kerr that only when international circumstances had changed, and there had been a long period of discussion between the British and colonial governments, were concrete proposals and practical initiatives liable to be well received. The crisis that the Round Tablers had been waiting for arrived in 1914 with the onset of the First World War. Here at last was an opportunity to confront the basic lacuna in the British imperial system. In 1916 Curtis published *The Problem of the Commonwealth*, which reiterated the urgent need for a common foreign policy.[11] With Lord Alfred Milner, the Round Table's inspiration and idol, entering Lloyd George's Cabinet in 1916, and both Philip Kerr and Waldorf Astor joining the Prime Minister's 'Garden Suburb' in the same year, the prospects for the federal idea at the forthcoming Imperial War Conference to be summoned in 1917 seemed highly promising.

In hindsight we now know that no supreme federal organ emerged from this episode. The conference did produce the Imperial War Cabinet with (briefly) executive powers in which all autonomous governments were represented, but it only just outlasted the war to represent the empire at the Versailles Peace Conference. With it faded the vision of a common imperial government. It would indeed be difficult to take issue with Ged Martin's conclusion: '1917 marked both the greatest triumph and the final defeat of the imperial federation movement.'[12]

The British imperial dimension to Lothian's intellectual thinking brought about by his personal experience with South African affairs was later complemented by his practical acquaintance with India. In 1931 he accepted the post of Under Secretary at the India Office in the National Government reshuffled after the general election of that year, and this represented his 'most significant intervention in the practical work of government'.[13] But if South Africa and India together enabled Lothian to bring the federal idea into sharper focus in his mind, they were not the original source that drove him to contemplate this idea for Europe. For this we have to turn elsewhere. It was much earlier in May 1921, after he left the Prime Minister's Office, that he devoted much of his time to a systematic postwar study of international politics. 'The conceptual nucleus', as Andrea Bosco has put it, 'of his federalist conception of international relations' is contained in *The Prevention of War*, a work containing three lectures that Lothian delivered at the Institute of Political Studies in Williamstown, Massachusetts, in August 1922.[14] Here Lothian drew upon his personal experience of monitoring the Peace Conference at Versailles in 1919:

In these pages appear the lessons of the American federalists, such as Alexander
Hamilton, John Jay, and James Madison, and also of Immanuel Kant, refracted
through Lothian's experience of practical international politics in Paris. Theory
and experience are combined, offering the reader an analysis of the international
situation and of its possible development towards federalism.[15]

Bosco's textual exegesis of Lothian's two main works on federalism, *The Prevention
of War* in 1922, and his more famous Burge Memorial Lecture, *Pacifism is not
Enough, nor Patriotism Either*, delivered at Lincoln's Inn in May 1935, allow us to
identify the structure of his argument – based upon the diagnosis of the problem
– and the potential remedy for abolishing the causes of war in Europe and
ultimately in the world. I have distilled the elements of Lothian's federalist thought
in the following way, that will take us from his diagnosis to his remedy: the
division of humanity into separate sovereign states; the absence of an international
government and a rule of law; the shortcomings of international diplomacy; the
condition of permanent war due to the search for security; the reliance upon a
military definition of reality: arms races, military alliances and military planning;
the prevailing conception of national self-determination that was narrow and
selfish, and unable to rise above the frontiers of the state; the idea that the state
remained a necessity because man remained 'selfish, greedy, intolerant, imperfect
and quarrelsome' but in order to harness it to the cause of peace it must be
elevated to the supra-national level; the notion that man must externalize the
internal conditions of law and order in the state; and the claim that the only
remedy for preventing war was to pool national sovereignty in a federal system
that could guarantee a qualitative condition of peace: a federation of nations
would establish peace and liberty. Lothian reached his goal of creating a new
federation of nations by a form of logical reasoning that John Pinder has referred
to as a 'combination of ideas and experiences' that enabled him to develop 'the
most powerful analysis of the federal principle and its relevance to the international
system to appear from any writer in any country during the interwar period'.[16]
Pinder's assessment of Lothian the federalist is both subtle and complex, precisely
because it accurately portrays the strengths, weaknesses and limitations of his
federalist thinking as well as the sensitivities of his essentially fragile character.

Lothian's career in the public service ended with his appointment as British
Ambassador to Washington in September 1939. He died in December 1940, but
not before playing a leading role in helping to form the Federal Union in November
1938.[17] Energetically driven by three young federalist activists – Derek Rawnsley,
Charles Kimber and Patrick Ransome – the new political pressure group set out to
promote the cause of peace and unity in Europe as the storm clouds gathered
across the 'dark continent' in 1939.[18] The initial driving force behind the Federal
Union was the prevention of war, but once Hitler's aggression began in Poland it
gradually turned its attention to the reconstruction of a postwar Europe based
upon the federal idea. However, the federal idea could easily accommodate a wide
variety of interpretations in terms of both the scope and depth of its practical

application. Indeed, Mayne and Pinder remarked that at the beginning neither Kimber nor Rawnsley had any clear notion of precisely what 'federalism' meant.[19]

Lothian had also been somewhat reticent about prescribing any blueprint for Europe. He appeared consistently to rely upon imperial federation up until the First World War destroyed it as a practical proposition, and 'the only proposal of a more specific nature' that he put forward in *Pacifism is not Enough* was to return to 'the underlying idea at Paris in 1919 … that the United States, France and the British Empire' should provide a surrogate stabilizing force in the way that the British had done in the nineteenth century. Pinder concluded that 'he seems to have regarded federation essentially as a project to be based on partnership between the British Empire (as it still was) and the USA.' It was left to the English-speaking nations to bring about 'a much larger idea', namely, 'the integration of the English-speaking world'. Translated into practical terms in the late 1930s, this meant informal cooperation between the British Commonwealth and the United States.[20]

With Europe on the brink of war it was the publication of Clarence Streit's *Union Now* and W.B. Curry's *The Case For Federal Union* that signalled the last clarion call for a novel response to the era of national sovereignty, international brinkmanship and another European conflagration.[21] Curry's paperback rapidly became a runaway best-seller, with a hundred thousand copies sold within six months.[22] Streit's diagnosis of the world's ills and his advocacy of a federal union spearheaded by the United States of America that would bind fifteen democracies together was certainly a bold initiative that seemed prima facie to be a last desperate attempt to prevent war, but given the isolationist predisposition and the very enormity of the power resources of the United States, it was hopelessly impractical in the prevailing circumstances. Literature like this had its followers, but it also raised serious questions of federal political strategy: should the goal be world federation or should efforts be directed toward the immediate objective of union in Europe? Would the projected federal union turn out to be an Anglo-American Atlantic union or was it likely that the British Commonwealth could be mobilized to fulfil its perceived destiny as the successor to the British Empire?

These fundamental divergences of aims and strategies were later to become the source of serious strains and tensions within the Federal Union, but its very existence symbolized the underlying shift from the Empire and Ireland to Europe in the British tradition of federalism. The significance of this was not then fully appreciated with war beckoning but it was to become increasingly apparent both during and after the Second World War.

The War Years

The continuity and persistence of the federal idea during the war years is confirmed by the energetic activities of the British Federal Union but also by the role of the resistance movements across a Europe at war. When we contemplate what in an earlier work I have called the European Community's 'federal heritage', we would be well advised to recall the important observation made by Walter Lipgens in his monumental work on the history of postwar European integration: Europe's growing self-awareness 'should not be construed as simply a continuation of earlier European plans for unification'. Such schemes and plans for political unity had been drawn up repeatedly in past centuries but remained, with few exceptions, mere paper projects with no real chance of policy implementation. However, the intellectual self-examination 'initially begun ... during the First World War', which led eventually to a cultural and political revival of ideas advocating European unification, 'arose from a passionately renewed awareness ... of the centuries-old unity of European civilisation and values'.[23] In short, the movement for European unification in all of its cultural and political manifestations was both a highly self-conscious and a uniquely twentieth-century phenomenon.

Naturally the intellectual and historical lineage of this movement can be traced back many centuries, probably at least to the Enlightenment, but for practical reasons in terms of an embryonic self-conscious political movement Lipgens' emphasis upon the impact of war in the twentieth century seems incontestable. The compelling drive to reorganize European interstate relations after 1918 possesses both a qualitative and a quantitative distinction from previous public expressions and sentiments for closer European unity. It is clear, then, that among the long- and short-term factors assisting the centripetal forces towards unification were: the horrors of what military technology could inflict upon human beings; the rise of the United States; the impact of the Russian Revolution; the spread of Fascism; and a myriad of economic and social changes. Together these ideas and events amounted to a crisis of European values, often linked to perceptions of the decline of Europe itself, which provided fertile soil for the nourishment of the unification movement.[24]

In the last twenty years much research has been devoted to the examination of plans for European integration during the years between 1939 and 1945, and we are now in a better position to understand both the origins and the influence of such ideas.[25] Both the threat of war and the Second World War itself spurred political elites and intellectuals to reconsider ways and means to prevent Europe from tearing itself asunder at regular intervals. Government elites by and large sought merely the destruction of totalitarian states, but there was also a formidable body of European intellectual opinion whose vision transcended this immediate priority. It was among the members of the anti-Fascist European resistance that the federal idea was largely nurtured as the answer to Europe's destiny. For them the defeat of Hitler was only the first step. It offered a golden opportunity for Europeans to return to fundamental organizational questions. What was the best way to organize human relations? What form should political authority take? How could the modern state be reconstructed or should it simply be transcended and replaced by a radically different mode of relations between states? The Franco-German conflict was only the most visible and persistent manifestation of nation-state rivalries in Europe. In order permanently to remove the very basis of military conflict, resistance thinkers directed their intellectual challenge towards the perceived cause of war itself: the nation-state.

Let us briefly paint the federal idea here on a broad canvas. It consists of radically different conceptions of Europe and divergent political strategies. What does, however, seem to be common ground among these rival conceptions and strategies is shared experiences of war. Among the intellectual resistance movements this factor runs continuously throughout their agonizing journey towards the new reconstructed Europe. In his splendid work *The Intellectual Resistance in Europe*, James Wilkinson put it this way:

> The Resistance spirit was a blend of defiance and idealism ... for Europe's intellectuals, in particular, the Resistance experience gave to politics a moral dimension ... This sense of moral mission continued undiminished after the Liberation of 1945. Guided by their vision of a 'spiritual revolution', Resistance intellectuals sought to initiate a process of renewal in which they themselves would play a leading role. Projects that had been conceived and elaborated in the underground were now discussed with growing confidence. The Resistance offered a model for the social order to be erected after the war – one in which individual freedom would coexist with social justice, human dignity would be accorded new respect, and the bonds formed in the underground would encourage trust and openness among citizens from all classes. These hopes were widely shared. The catastrophe that had engulfed the continent for six years seemed to assure a radical break with the past and to make a fresh start imperative.[26]

They learned that just as the Fascist juggernaut had demonstrated how supposedly immutable European structures could be swept away, so the defeat of Hitler and Mussolini could open the way for their vision to become reality. Old state structures and petty sovereignties were not part of God's law for the universe. At the end of the Second World War almost anything must have seemed possible.

The resistance belief in man's capacity to control events and to shape his own destiny ensured that former national loyalties and the obedience to the old state would not be integral to their ideas about the reconstruction of Europe. Reverence for the old state seemed inappropriate. It had collapsed almost everywhere in Continental Europe in the face of the Nazi Blitzkrieg. In their quest for a better and peaceful society, many in the resistance had fought Hitler not for the old nation-states but rather for a new European society. For them, the defeat of totalitarianism and the creation of a 'United Sates of Europe' in its place went hand in hand. To allow the old nation-states to recover and regain their former positions in a world of international rivalry would be to re-create the very conditions of war and totalitarian rule.[27]

Written by a small nucleus of Italian federalists led by Altiero Spinelli and Ernesto Rossi, these views and assumptions were lucidly expressed in the famous *Ventotene Manifesto* of 1941, which was one of the first resistance declarations devoted to European unification.[28] In it, Spinelli observed that the collapse of most European states had already 'reduced most peoples of the Continent to a common fate' but that public attitudes were 'already much more favourable toward a new, federative European order'. The brutal experience of the previous decade had 'opened the eyes of the unbelievers'.[29] Much later, he recalled that the anti-Fascist resistance 'accepted that it would be preferable to give a federal structure to Europe since this would also solve the problem of co-existence in peace and freedom with Germany'.[30]

But the appeal of federalism in resistance thought and experience also derived from their mode of operation. And it was not confined solely to Spinelli's conception of a federal future for Europe. There were important rival conceptions of a federal Europe based upon socioeconomic preferences that were also influential. If the essence of social change – of altering people's minds and perceptions – lay in the moral conversion of society, then the resistance organization itself epitomized the federal idea in practice. 'The Resistance appeared to many of its adherents as a forerunner of a true federation.'[31] And if we reflect for a moment upon the role of the underground as a framework for international cooperation during the war, it becomes clear why this should be so:

> The intellectuals' ideal, inspired by their Resistance experience, was a network of local voluntary associations, vehicles of direct democracy, united within a European federation. The old nation-states bellicose and unresponsive to the needs of their citizens, were to be superseded at both a lower and a higher level by more responsible institutions ... local autonomy and international cooperation would form a complementary whole ... such groups would ... continue to follow the 'natural' pattern of free human associations ... The intellectuals' desire for flexibility in government reflected a concern for remaining close to life.[32]

This understanding was much more along the lines of the French Proudhonian school of federalist thinking, and remained an important but relatively less effective approach in practical terms compared to Spinelli's later political strategy. The *Ventotene Manifesto* elaborated the idea of a federal Europe as the panacea for virtually all of the outstanding problems that would confront postwar statesmen. And Spinelli, who became the leading spokesman for the federalist cause in Europe, always retained the resistance-based capacity to argue that the common people, if allowed to determine themselves, would inevitably gravitate towards unity in cooperation. It was obsolete state structures and the selfish, anachronistic values of states' elites and vested interests, which impeded this natural movement. People's basic needs, whether in Italy, France or Denmark, were fundamentally the same. And contemporary problems were essentially common problems necessitating common solutions. All that was needed was a solid institutional structure to allow this common elaboration to develop and determine itself.

This short survey of the emergence of the federal idea in European resistance thought, sketched out above, does not of course do justice to the various nuances of opinion and the real differences that existed among those federalists who sought to rebuild Europe after 1945. But their agreement on basic principles remains more striking and more significant than their personal controversies. And although the resistance programme – and the spiritual revolution which it symbolized – was effectively defeated and abandoned by the postwar conservative restoration, the federal idea did not disappear with it. On the contrary, it survived in the plethora of interest groups that sprouted across Western Europe after 1945, and it was sustained in the *European Union of Federalists* (UEF) founded in Basle in December 1946.

Meanwhile the Federal Union had been consolidating its position in the U.K. Immediately before war was declared in September 1939, its membership had doubled to two thousand, with 'a score of local branches organising meetings and debates. A newsletter was at the press and an International committee had been formed, with contacts in France, Belgium, the Netherlands and Switzerland.'[33] By the spring of 1940 there were 'more than 120 Federal Union groups', but Mayne and Pinder noted that by April of that year there were 253 local branches with more than ten thousand members.[34] This period of the 'phoney war' represented the apogee of the Federal Union's membership, with the later war years witnessing a haemorrhage of members until its revival in 1944 when 4,727 were registered, many of them Service personnel attracted by the paperback book, *Federate or Perish*, published in that year and written by John S. Hoyland, Principal of Woodbrooke, the Quaker College.[35]

The war years are not the most suitable period to furnish an overall assessment of the Federal Union's achievements but it is clear that, as Mayne and Pinder have remarked, for a 'small, idealistic movement' its 'influence exceeded its actual power', and it 'helped to create the climate of opinion in which the War Cabinet could confidently make its historic offer of union to France' in 1940.[36] Moreover, what the Federal Union lacked in the quantity of its membership, it more than made up for in the quality of the adherents to the cause of federation: Lionel Curtis; Lord Lothian; C.E.M. Joad; Barbara Wootton; Wickham Steed; Arnold Toynbee; R.W.G. Mackay, MP; Sir William Beveridge; J.B. Priestley; Friedrich von Hayek; H.N. Brailsford; Ivor Jennings; Lionel Robbins; Clement Atlee; Ernest Bevin; and Sir Archibald Sinclair.[37] The Federal Union could claim significant support from all sides of the British party-political spectrum, the professions of law, journalism and teaching, and the wider realms of the arts, including music and writing. It represented a catch-all political movement that cut across the traditional party divide to embrace influential members of British society in the quest to find a durable peace order for Europe, based upon the federal idea. And as we shall soon discover, it had an entirely unexpected impact upon the postwar era when many among the political elites and mass publics across Europe sought to take stock of the wartime experience and reconstruct the continent upon a different dynamic than national sovereignty.

The Postwar Years

The years between 1945 and 1957 witnessed the beginnings of a most remarkable change in our perception and understanding of national sovereignty. It occurred only gradually at the level of political and economic elite understanding of the need for a radical rethinking and reappraisal of the role of the nation-state in postwar Western Europe. In the immediate aftermath of the end of the Second World War, the widespread economic chaos, social dislocation and political uncertainties were addressed by the conventional mode of international cooperation and coordination as demonstrated typically by the proposals of the United States for Lend-Lease arrangements, Marshall Aid, the creation of the United Nations (UN), the Organisation for European Economic Cooperation (OEEC), the Council of Europe and the North Atlantic Treaty Organization (NATO). Together these institutions and arrangements were representative of the restoration of the international states system that had at its core the revival and recognition of the nation-state. The period 1945–50 therefore suggests in many ways a return to the fundamental conditions of the interwar period in the extent to which it symbolized the recovery of the nation-state and the reassertion of national sovereignty.

During the late 1940s, however, there was a parallel, if less prominent, history to be written. Alongside the more visible cornerstones of the new international order there existed another historical legacy that had endured. It, too, had survived the human oppression and persecution wrought by the nation-state. This was the intellectual resistance. In his seminal article on European federation in resistance political thought, Lipgens explained the appeal of the federal idea for the future of Europe:

> The true character of the resistance movements was that of an intellectual resistance … the Resistance writings … were not marginal efforts, produced in addition to military actions by a few intellectuals. On the contrary, for years, during which other forms of opposition were hardly possible, these *were* the Resistance. The most important function of the movements could only be to formulate ethical and political principles that would help people to live through the totalitarian experience, and that would strengthen their opposition to it … These principles were supported by specific plans for a better future … These proposals contained demands for a thorough limiting of the state's authority, for the possibility of self-government in districts and regions, for regional federalism as opposed to the centralised nation state … From this central idea – namely the struggle against sovereignty – and from the experience with the League of Nations derived concern with the manner in which an effective European Federation should be constituted.[38]

These remarks and observations about an alternative vision for the reconstruction of postwar Western Europe serve to remind us that the federal idea, which was nourished and strengthened in the war years, was also actively promoted during the early years of peace. Indeed, one scholar has noted that in 1948 in France alone there were seventeen European federalist groups, each with between fifty and four thousand members.[39]

It is true nonetheless that the resistance predictions of the immediate postwar circumstances first outlined in the *Ventotene Manifesto* simply did not occur. The victorious superpowers did not arrive, as the resistance hoped they would, as supporters in the fight against nationalism and the recovery of the nation-state. Indeed, they flatly opposed the goal of a European federal union. It is true that the United States eventually came to support Jean Monnet and the European Community project in the 1950s, but in the early postwar years this was still only an idea. Moreover, many federalists underestimated the rapidity with which people reaccustomed themselves to thinking in terms of nation-states. This reality that confronted them underpinned many of the strategic and doctrinal controversies that served to rupture the early postwar federalist movement. Once the Second World War had ended, how could federalism be translated into practical action? Indeed, in the radically changed circumstances of postwar Europe, was not the very idea of the resistance itself a contradiction? How could its political ideals and experience, sustained by the war itself, be effectively preserved and persistently pursued after 1945?

The critical issue confronting resistance intellectuals at this time was that of political strategy. In fact it was on this very issue during 1945–47 that the Movimento Federalista Europeo (MFE), originally formed as early as August 1943 in Italy, split between those who wanted to campaign for the European peoples to be mobilized as a genuine popular opposition movement, dedicated to forcing the hands of national governments, and those who preferred to channel their energies into supporting political parties and governments known to be in favour of federalist solutions. Prominent among those who supported the latter strategy, Altiero Spinelli was convinced that it was much more important to win over the leaders of the progressive parties than to try to mobilize the masses. In an open letter to those who attended the MFE Conference in January 1946, he warned them to come to terms with the harsh postwar realities: 'if we do not want to become a small clique of people with our heads in the clouds, we must frankly acknowledge that our prediction and consequently our programme have proved to be mistaken'.[40] This example of the MFE's strategic dilemma in postwar Europe underlines the fundamental difficulties that confronted the various resistance movements when they sought to translate their federalist vision into reality. For the federalists, these early years were tantamount to a period of reevaluation and reassessment.[41]

Leaving aside the various ideological and strategic political splits and realignments that characterized the postwar federalist movements, we should not forget the pervasive influences of federalist thought upon practical policy making at this time. In a famous public speech on 9 May 1950, the French Foreign Minister, Robert Schuman, declared the goal of a united Europe:

Europe will not be made all at once, or according to a single plan. It will be built through concrete achievements which first create a *de facto* solidarity. The coming together of the nations of Europe requires the elimination of the age-old opposition of France and Germany. Any action taken must in the first place concern these two countries ... The pooling of coal and steel production should immediately provide for the setting up of common foundations for economic development *as a first step* in the *federation of Europe* ... this proposal will lead to the realisation of the first concrete foundation of a *European federation* indispensable to the preservation of peace.[42]

If we look closely at the eventful years between 1952 and 1954 it is clear that the introduction of a radically new dynamic in interstate relations was occasioned by the attempt to launch two remarkable projects that had enormous implications for postwar West European integration. A complex combination of international and domestic events and circumstances in the aftermath of the Schuman Declaration of May 1950, and the creation of the European Coal and Steel Community (ECSC) in July 1952, catapulted the far-reaching proposals for a European Defence Community (EDC) and a European Political Community (EPC) to the forefront of West European politics. Given their colossal constitutional and political implications, these events were truly astonishing.

The ECSC itself emerged from Jean Monnet's long personal journey that corresponded with the framework of analysis utilized here. Like Spinelli, though much older, he had lived through the First World War, the interwar period and the Second World War so that both of them belonged to an age far older than the European Community. Monnet was convinced that his own experiences – as Deputy Secretary-General of the League of Nations from 1919 until 1923, as a leading member of the Washington-based British Supply Council during the Second World War, and as the architect in 1947 of the eponymous Monnet Plan for the modernization of postwar French industry and agriculture – had equipped him to understand both the possibilities and limitations of international cooperation in a Europe that cried out for a lasting peace order. Monnet and his small band of friends and advisors – Pierre Uri, Etienne Hirsch and Paul Reuter – were responsible for the original idea, the political initiative and the blueprint of the ECSC.[43] Together with the pooling of coal and steel production, the new institutional architecture of the ECSC would for the first time combine 'supranational' with conventional international features so that, in the words of William Diebold, it was 'a major federal measure of economic integration'.[44] Historians appear to have an open verdict on the successes and failures of this first real experiment in European integration in the 1950s, but its radical originality cannot be denied. The practical political experience of bringing six separate sovereign nation-states together to work in an unprecedented supranational decision-making context was itself a remarkable achievement. The ECSC symbolized the end of the era when national sovereignty monopolized relations between states.

Conversely the collapse of the EDC and the EPC projects in August 1954, when the French National Assembly jettisoned the EDC treaty, persuaded some historians and other commentators to earmark the period 1945–1954 as the end of the so-called 'federalist phase' of early postwar European integration and cooperation. This conclusion, however, was mistaken. The abortive attempt to build political Europe in the early 1950s was, as Monnet himself acknowledged in his *Memoirs*, both hasty and premature. But recent research has shown that the federal idea continued to live on in the next incremental steps designed in the Treaty of Rome (1957) to create a customs union that would evolve eventually into a common market. The federal idea did not expire with the commitment to 'an ever closer union among European peoples'. Rather it displayed a continuous and persistent presence during the next half-century of economic and political integration and cooperation.[45]

Conclusion: The Life and Times of the Federal Idea

In this short chapter I have suggested that the life and times of the federal idea in the context of Europe before the European Community (1917/18–1957) have been related for our purposes to the quest for a lasting peace order. Perhaps this empirical focus upon the international relations dimension to the federal idea in its Kantian sense should not surprise us because the only practical European example that Europeans had of a successful federal enterprise during these years was Switzerland. Absent this model, and they understandably looked to the United States as their historical template. As the founding fathers of the American Constitution, Alexander Hamilton, John Jay and James Madison were understandably cited regularly as often being the chief inspiration for the building of a federal Europe. Today it is the European Union that is looked upon by the world as the future model for a federal union of states and citizens, if not exactly for a federation.

Looking back to our Introduction, it is clear that a focus upon the continuity and persistence of the federal idea during 1917–1957 is tantamount to a revisionist history of the building of Europe. It is in some ways an alternative version of mainstream European history, giving a specialized unity to the period and emphasizing the importance of political and economic ideas, none of which bore any institutional fruit in Europe before the Second World War. It also gives visibility and unaccustomed weight to largely unfamiliar *dramatis personae*. The likes of Lord Lothian, Lionel Curtis, Lionel Robbins, Altiero Spinelli and Jean Monnet are not the usual cast of characters (Monnet excepted) liable to be put in the European and international spotlight when most people think of twentieth-century European history.

But there is one particular aspect of the adventures of the federal idea to which we must call attention in our conclusion, and that is the neglected and little-known continuity between the British and Continental European traditions of federalism. It is significant because it links the Federal Union of the 1930s and 1940s to the European Union of the 1970s and 1980s in a most circuitous and unexpected fashion. The importance of the British federalist literature that emanated from the Federal Union lay in the crucial role it played in the conversion of Altiero Spinelli to the federalist cause during his confinement between 1937 and 1943 on the island of Ventotene, Italy, where he received copies of writings by Lionel Robbins and Friedrich Hayek in addition to those that he already had by Luigi Einaudi, a prominent Italian liberal and distinguished Professor of Economics at the University of Turin. This literature left such a major impression on him that he acknowledged British federal ideas to be the intellectual origins of his own federalist thinking. The basic assumptions and principles of these ideas were subsequently preserved and woven into his overall political strategy, thereby confirming the links between the intellectual influences of the 1930s and 1940s and those of the 1980s when he successfully championed the Draft Treaty on European Union in the European Parliament. Through Spinelli, then, British federal ideas have made a significant intellectual contribution to the unification of Europe in a curious and quite remarkable manner scarcely known outside of federalist circles.[46]

The subject of the continuity and persistence of the federal idea in Europe during 1917–1957 causes us to ponder whether a study like this should be conducted by historians or political scientists. Interestingly, while much of the research for the period 1918–1945 has been conducted largely by historians, Mark Mazower has remarked that until quite recently they have 'mostly left the subject of post-war western Europe to social scientists'. Consequently he claims that 'it is still hard to see this as a period of history rather than as a series of contemporary social, political and economic issues', although 'they *have* started to write on post-war reconstruction and the USA's contribution to it'.[47]

Summing up, it is impossible for the younger generations of today fully to comprehend the traumatic impact of the Second World War – let alone its predecessor – upon Europe and its population. The horror and brutality of it can only be imperfectly transmitted via films, recorded speech, memoirs and scholarship. Indeed, as new generations replace old generations and memories fade, it has become increasingly difficult to defend the European idea, particularly in the U.K. The sources of its inspiration are easily forgotten. Postwar generations see only a European Union of bickering, churlish nation-states, in a seemingly divided Europe, obsessed with short-term economic trade-offs. Some progressive Europeans argue that we need a new external threat – a new 'Aunt Sally' – that can reinvigorate the European idea and remind us of our shared values and common aims. But the idea of a federal Europe, being much older than the European Union, retains its original moral basis in reason and humanity as the directing force for the piecemeal construction of a Europe of peoples as well as states.

Fortunately it is no longer necessary to proclaim that Europe must 'federate or perish', for Europe has already become a new federal model in the new millennium. The continuity and persistence of the federal idea has no better legacy.

Notes

1. M. Mazower, *Dark Continent: Europe's Twentieth Century* (London, 1999).
2. E.H. Carr, *The Twenty Years Crisis, 1919–1939* (London, 1939).
3. P.M.R. Stirk, 'Introduction: Crisis and Continuity in Interwar Europe', in idem (ed.), *European Unity in Context: The Interwar Period* (London, 1989), 10–11.
4. R.N. Coudenhove-Kalergi, *Pan-Europe* (New York, 1926).
5. R. White, 'The Europeanism of Coudenhove-Kalergi', in Stirk, *European Unity in Context*, 31.
6. Ibid.
7. White concluded that *Pan-Europe* had 'an original and prophetic quality','The Europeanism of Coudenhove-Kalergi', 39–40.
8. The role of Ireland in relation to the British Empire and Europe is crucial as a connecting link to the British tradition of federalism. See M. Burgess, 'Empire, Ireland and Europe: A Century of British Federal Ideas', in idem (ed.), *Federalism and Federation in Western Europe* (London, 1986).
9. For a detailed survey, see M. Burgess, *The British Tradition of Federalism* (London, 1995) and the recent essay titled 'The British Tradition of Federalism: Nature, Meaning and Significance', in S. Henig (ed.), *Federalism and the British* (London, 2007), 35–61.
10. For further details, see J.E. Kendle, *The Round Table Movement and Imperial Union* (Toronto, 1975).
11. L. Curtis, *The Problem of the Commonwealth* (London, 1916). For further details about Curtis and his federal political ideas, see D. Lavin, *From Empire to International Commonwealth: A Biography of Lionel Curtis* (Oxford, 1995).
12. G. Martin, 'The Idea of Imperial Federation', in R. Hyam and G. Martin (eds), *Reappraisals in British Imperial History* (London, 1975), 134.
13. G. Douds, 'Lothian and the Indian Federation', in J. Turner (ed.), *The Larger Idea: Lord Lothian and the Problem of National Sovereignty* (London, 1988), 67.
14. A. Bosco, 'National Sovereignty and Peace: Lord Lothian's Federalist Thought', in Turner (ed.), *The Larger Idea*, 108–23.
15. Ibid., 108.
16. See J. Pinder, 'Prophet not without Honour: Lothian and the Federal Idea', in J. Turner (ed.), *The Larger Idea*, 139. This essay was a later version of the original article of the same title published in *The Round Table* 286 (1983), 207–20.
17. See A. Bosco, 'Lothian, Curtis, Kimber and the Federal Union, 1938–1940', *Journal of Contemporary History* 23 (1988), 465–502.
18. On the formation and the early years of the Federal Union, see R. Mayne and J. Pinder, *Federal Union: The Pioneers – A History of Federal Union* (Basingstoke, 1990), 5–49.
19. Ibid., 8.
20. Pinder, 'Prophet not without Honour', 141.
21. W.B. Curry, *The Case For Federal Union* (Harmondsworth, 1939).
22. Mayne and Pinder, *Federal Union*, 18.
23. W. Lipgens, *A History of European Integration, 1945–1947: The Formation of the European Unity Movement* (Oxford, 1982), v. 1, 18.
24. Ibid., 1–92.
25. See W. De Gruyther, *Continental Plans for European Integration, 1919–1945* (Berlin, 1985), 456–555, in the series, *Documents on European Integration*, W. Lipgens (ed.), v. 1; and P.H. Bell and J. Pinder, 'British Plans for European Union, 1939–1945', in *Documents on European Integration: Plans for European Union in Great Britain and in Exile, 1939–1945*, W. Lipgens (ed.), v. 2, 23–275.
26. J.D. Wilkinson, *The Intellectual Resistance in Europe* (London, 1981), 1.
27. This point has been underlined in W. Lipgens, 'European Federation in the Political Thought of Resistance Movements during World War II', *Central European History* 1 (1968), 5–19.
28. Lipgens, *A History of European Integration*, v. 1, 108–11.
29. Extract quoted from Wilkinson, *Intellectual Resistance*, 174.

30. A. Spinelli, 'European Union in the Resistance', *Government and Opposition* 2 (1966–67), 325.
31. Wilkinson, *Intellectual Resistance*, 173.
32. Ibid., 268.
33. Mayne and Pinder, *Federal Union*, 15.
34. Ibid., 23–25.
35. Ibid., 32. See J.S. Hoyland, *Federate or Perish* (London, 1944).
36. Mayne and Pinder, *Federal Union*, 33.
37. Ibid., 11–16.
38. Lipgens, 'European Federation in the Political Thought of Resistance Movements', 7–11.
39. See I. Greilsammer, 'Some Observations on European Federalism', in, D.J. Elazar (ed.), *Federalism and Political Integration* (Tel Aviv, 1979), 108.
40. Lipgens, *A History of European Integration*, 278.
41. For a detailed analysis of the MFE, see Lipgens, *A History of European Integration*, 3–17, 274–78 and 628–33.
42. 'The Schuman Declaration', in Brent F. Nelsen and Alexander C.-G. Stubb (eds), *The European Union: Readings on the Theory and Practice of European Integration* (London, 1994), 11–12.
43. J. Monnet, *Memoirs* (New York, 1978), 292–317.
44. W. Diebold, 'The Relevance of Federalism to Western European Economic Integration' in A. W. Macmahon (ed.), *Federalism: Mature and Emergent* (New York, 1962), 441.
45. For a detailed survey of the persistence of the federal idea in the 1950s, see J. Pinder, 'The Influence of the European Federalists in the 1950s', in T.B. Olesen (ed.) *Interdependence versus Integration: Denmark, Scandinavia and Western Europe, 1945–1960* (Odense, 1997), 220–40.
46. See J. Pinder, *Altiero Spinelli and the British Federalists: Writings by Beveridge, Robbins and Spinelli, 1937–1943* (London, 1998); and more recently L. Levi, 'Altiero Spinelli and European Federalism: The British Influence', in Henig, *Federalism and the British*, 62–83.
47. For further reading, see Mazower, *Dark Continent*, 478.

Conclusion

EUROPE BETWEEN A CRISIS OF CULTURE AND POLITICAL REGENERATION

>≈≺

Mark Hewitson

Cooperation and integration in Europe between 1917 and 1957, contrary to the case put forward recently by Ludger Kühnhardt, took place in the context of a continuous series of internal and external crises, which disrupted the established conventions and procedures of national policy making.[1] Faced with the prospect of economic dislocation and decline, ideological conflict and dictatorship, diplomatic antagonism and industrialized warfare, intellectuals, publicists, politicians, officials and ministers considered European solutions to terrifying new problems, at the same time as conducting domestic experiments (democratization, state intervention, welfare, economic planning and redistributive taxation), reaching bilateral or multilateral agreements (the Locarno Treaty, the Franco-German trade treaty of 1927, the International Steel Cartel, the Marshall Plan, GATT and Bretton Woods) and participating in international organizations (the League of Nations, UN, NATO and OEEC). The writers and thinkers examined in this volume, along with many others, helped to give policy makers a sense that 'Europe' existed, with an 'identity' of its own, and that it faced a set of momentous crises, some of which could – and should – be addressed at a European level.

Kühnhardt's claim, in so far as it applies to the period before 1957, is that the EEC and 'all crises in European integration since 1957' 'were possible only because the original post-1945 crisis had been resolved with far-sightedness'.[2] 1945 constituted a potential 'crisis of' future integration which, because it was resolved successfully, ensured that subsequent setbacks were merely 'crises in' integration, 'related to difficulties in implementing certain policy objectives or goals without implying that the failure in achieving these objectives could derail the integration process as such or unravel its rationale and legitimacy'.[3] 'It is widely accepted that the Treaties of Rome and the creation of the European Economic Community in 1957 became the definite European responses to the end of World War II and the renaissance of parliamentary democracy in Western Europe after 1945,' he continues: 'It seems to be fair to say that "1957" was the European answer to "1945".'[4] By contrast, this study argues that 'crisis' in Europe was much longer-lived and more continuous and, as a consequence, European cooperation and integration during the late 1940s, 1950s and beyond were less well defined and less securely anchored than Kühnhardt suggests.[5] The principal threats confronting European policy makers after 1917 were domestic or global, it seemed, requiring internal and international solutions: two 'world' wars; communism at home and abroad; 'totalitarianism' in the Soviet Union and, by extension, in Eastern Europe; nationalism and 'authoritarianism', sympathy for which – opinion polls made plain – had not simply disappeared in 1945; colonialism and decolonization, prompting a reappraisal of European states' global role and resulting in internecine conflicts – with up to one million killed in India in 1947, and 750,000 in Algeria from 1954 to 1962 – with profound effects in the metropolis; and the shift towards extra-European superpowers, with their armies on European soil and their nuclear weapons trained on European targets. Most of these threats existed before and after 1945, issuing in a fundamental reform of European nation-states and international organizations. European integration was, in part, entangled in such wider processes of transformation and, in part, grafted onto them. It was not, as a result, as firmly rooted as Kühnhardt implies.

Much of the literature on European integration assumes that 1945 was a critical juncture in – and frequently a primary cause of – a course of events or process which led to the creation of unprecedented supranational institutions. This is even true of those scholars influenced by the work of Alan Milward on the rescue of the nation-state and the reconstruction of national economies, who have, it could be held, come to constitute the most influential historical approach to integration.[6] In general, such historians usually begin in 1944–45, or 1939–41, with defeat or a supposed 'zero hour'. Yet it could be contended that they overstate the scope and significance of economic reconstruction, overlooking the fact that a state such as Belgium might have been a net contributor of aid in the late 1940s despite participating in the Economic Recovery Program (Marshall Plan), and that even German industry had retained much of its plant, its large companies and their detailed plans for the postwar era.[7] Similarly, state bureaucracies, although purged of high-level 'collaborators', usually remained in place, as the transition from the Third Republic via the Vichy regime to the Fourth Republic demonstrated.[8] Many agencies and cadres of the state did not collapse, and returning or reemerging political elites and parties were quick to dispel fears of a potential power vacuum. Consequently, officials', politicians' and ministers' priorities and horizons were not merely dictated by day-to-day exigencies, but were also characterized by a historical understanding of the crises of the interwar era, which they had been able to reflect upon in internal or external exile.[9] Policy makers were not simply motivated by the need to restore the nation-state and rebuild economies, as the foundation of future welfare states; they were guided by longer-standing concerns, such as a desire to strengthen Europe against extra-European Great Powers, to compensate for or halt the loss of empire, to reverse economic decline, to escape the worst effects of nationalism, to stop the spread of communism and to prevent a lapse or relapse into dictatorship, as had occurred in Greece, Spain and Portugal.[10] All of these problems were connected to persuasive narratives about Europe. They ought to be addressed, it appeared to many leaders in the 1920s and in the 1940s and 1950s, on a European or international level. In this respect, the decision makers and commentators of the interwar and postwar eras were not as different as they might seem, in spite of the existence of influential advocates of supranational institutions within continental administrations after 1945, but not beforehand.[11] The most important decisions in both periods were taken, as Milward rightly suggests, by governments pursuing clearly defined national interests, which tended to favour various forms of economic integration, since such forms were agreeable to most parties, and to rule out integration – or the delegation of sovereignty to new institutions – in the spheres of diplomacy and defence, not least because these spheres were considered to safeguard states' autonomy, and in other areas of government, including social policy, education, law and order, which were barely discussed. Cooperation and integration failed in the 1920s and early 30s, but succeeded in the 1950s, because the Weimar Republic – one of the parties in the main Franco-German relationship – succumbed to dictatorship, whereas the Federal Republic of Germany and the Fourth Republic did not.

The two other principal approaches to the early stages of European integration – namely, 'federalism' and 'neo-functionalism' – both tend to overlook similarities between the 1920s and 1950s, with 'federalists' contending that more practical-minded proponents of supranationalism had entered government after the Second World War, partly as a consequence of the federalism of the resistance movements, and with 'neo-functionalists' assuming that practical projects had increasingly replaced utopian ideas of integration.[12] This study proposes that the supposed 'intellectualism' of pro-European circles was characteristic of the entire period between 1917 and 1957, existing alongside initiatives within governments to facilitate cooperation and bring about integration on a European level.[13] Prominent intellectuals and publicists appealed to 'Europe' and put forward a panoply of solutions to variously defined European questions, many of which, like Carl Schmitt's '*nomos* of the earth' in 1950, continued to contain mystical elements or unrealizable objectives.[14] Since policy makers in the 1920s and 1950s were attempting to achieve more narrowly defined goals – a lowering of tariffs, the supply of credit, agreed quotas in the steel industry, recognition of borders, a consensual basis for rearmament – which were especially pressing in the wake of the two world wars, they were not deflected from their task by the diversity of descriptions of, and prescriptions for, Europe nor by the frequent disjunction of intellectuals, the European movements and governments.[15] Thus, the prominence of Marxist and existentialist thinkers in the French public sphere after 1945 appears to have had little bearing on the incidence or success of initiatives for European integration within government.[16] Although postwar movements such as the Union Européenne des Fédéralistes counted more deputies and ministers in their ranks than had their interwar counterparts, they seem to have been peripheral to the critical decisions which led to the founding of the Council of Europe, the ECSC, the EEC and Euratom, and to the failure to ratify the EDC and EPC.[17] Transnational networks of Christian and Social Democrats appear to have been more influential, but largely as a means of explaining and preparing the ground for policies which had been devised, adopted and proposed by governments themselves.[18] What was more important in both 'postwar' periods, it could be argued, was the sense of policy makers that they were facing crises – economic decline, the threat of war, nationalism, communism, dictatorship and decolonization – with obvious European components and with European or 'Western' – part-American, part-European – solutions. Here, intellectuals were significant in defining the terms of debate and helping to sustain the idea, even after 1945, that specifically European initiatives should be launched as well as international or American ones.[19]

Appeals and allusions to 'Europe' became much more salient as a result of the supposed 'self-destruction' of the First World War, after which extra-European powers such as the United States and the Soviet Union seemed to challenge the continent's ascendancy.[20] In the years before the Great War, nation-states appeared to have become less and less constrained in their external actions, with transnational economic ties obscured by the mythology of national markets and commercial competition, and with alliances between states usually secret and unenforceable, given the demise of the Concert of Europe.[21] The First World War and its aftermath at once promoted such processes of nationalization, increasing state intervention and engendering radical nationalist movements and autarkic dictatorships, at the same time as highlighting the necessity of international cooperation and institutions, including the League of Nations.[22] Fearing the consequences of national rivalries, protectionism, and ideological and military conflicts, governments since 1917 have concluded numerous bilateral, multilateral and international agreements and formed various international organizations. The fact that many of these agreements and institutions have been European, despite a proclivity towards American-led international organizations after 1945, derives in considerable part from a deep-rooted mythology of Europe, popularized during the interwar and postwar eras. In limited spheres, governments have been able to justify a transfer of powers, competencies or sovereignty to European – rather than multilateral or international – institutions. Although leaders and intellectuals have failed to agree on the necessity and form of a European polity, on appropriate spheres of activity for European institutions or on the territorial extent of Europe, they have nonetheless found it easier to imagine and to set up supranational European organizations than other regional or global ones.[23] Such 'integration' – a term coined by American Marshall planners in the late 1940s as a vaguer analogue of 'union' – was possible in the 1920s, as an outgrowth of Franco-German reconciliation; it found echoes in Churchill's eve-of-defeat offer of a Franco-British Union, partly based on a draft by Monnet and Pleven to the ministry of Paul Reynaud on 16 June 1940, and it came into being with the signing of the Treaty of Paris, founding the ECSC, in 1951.[24] It rested less on convergence between European states, whose economic, social, cultural and political differences had been exacerbated by the national and ideological conflicts of the interwar and war years, than on a shared sense of a common European plight and set of needs.[25]

Such feelings and perceptions had proved to be durable, but they were also defensive and unstable, linked to a series of enduring crises which threatened to reawaken national antipathies, as seemed to be the case in respect of the German question (the Saar, partition, eastern borders, rearmament, industrial 'hegemony'), or which risked subsuming 'Europe' altogether, as in the struggle against communism, during the onset of the Cold War, in relations with the United States and through the workings of global capitalism and free trade.[26] Intellectuals and other publicists contributed to such potential instability by defining 'Europe' negatively, broadly agreeing on what it differed from and what it was opposed to, not what it consisted of or stood for. This defensive justification of European unity remained a source of potential weakness during the pressing external crises of the 1940s and 1950s and during later internal ones, when the binding force of an outside threat had disappeared. 'Europeanism', or an affiliation with Europe resting on a putatively common set of values or interests, was often subordinate, in the minds of opinion and decision makers, to national interests and, in the realm of foreign policy and defence, to other international commitments. In the discussion and negotiation of a European Defence Community, contemporaries were able to witness the rapid resurfacing of anti-German sentiment, unambiguous displays of national rivalry – with Anthony Eden only agreeing to station British troops in Germany under the aegis of NATO – and a demonstration of the primacy of allegiance to the United States, as the Cold War worsened.[27] While it is true that national interests and international commitments sometimes coincided with European integration, they were not bound to do so, as could be seen during acts of national self-assertion – for instance, the U.K.'s opposition to 'federalism' in 1949–51 and 1955–58, or France's precipitation of the 'empty chair crisis' between June 1965 and January 1966 – and periods of international crisis, whether the unpredictable corollary of decolonization (the partition of India, the Suez crisis in 1956, the Algerian War) or the Cold War (the Berlin blockade in 1948–49, the Korean War, Soviet intervention in the GDR in 1953 and Hungary in 1956, the second Berlin crisis of 1958).[28]

At such moments, it was not clear whether national and international crises would also become crises of European integration, in Kühnhardt's sense. Certainly, limited, hard-fought *acquis communautaires* in the areas of coal and steel production, nuclear power and the regulation and running of a common market seemed insecure and reversible until the 1960s, at the earliest, in the face of the global and domestic conflicts which had helped to produce them. Most of the conditions which had complicated attempts at European cooperation in the 1920s – the changing policies of the United States and the menace of U.S. isolationism, Soviet expansionism and the strength of home-grown communism, the Janus-faced nature of the Franco-German relationship, the shifting conceptions and realities of geopolitics and the uncertain role of European states in the world, and the unpredictable consequences of nationalism, imperialism and world war – remained in place in the late 1940s and 1950s. 'Europe' in these circumstances was still in danger, but it was also, thanks to the efforts of intellectuals, publicists and others, a point of reference, attachment and refuge.

Notes

1. L. Kühnhardt (ed.), *Crises in European Integration: Challenge and Response, 1945–2005* (Oxford, 2009), 1–18.
2. Ibid., 6.
3. Ibid., 1–2.
4. Ibid., 4–5.
5. For a similar approach to a connected theme, see C. Levy and M. Roseman (eds), *Three Postwar Eras in Comparison: Western Europe, 1918–1945–1989* (Basingstoke, 2002).
6. On Milward, see Introduction, note 20. Also, A.S. Milward, 'Allegiance: The Past and the Future', *Journal of European Integration History* 1 (1995), 7–19. Many studies of national governments have been influenced by Milward: see, for instance, much of the literature on the U.K.; J.W. Young, *Britain and European Unity, 1945–1992* (London, 1993), 1–52; W. Kaiser, *Using Europe, Abusing the Europeans: Britain and European Integration, 1945–1963* (Basingstoke, 1997); D. Gowland and A. Turner, *Reluctant Europeans: Britain and European Integration, 1945–1998* (London, 1999); and idem and A. Wright, *Britain and European Integration since 1945* (London, 2009); S. George, *Britain and European Integration since 1945* (Oxford, 1992); N.J. Crowson, *The Conservative Party and European Integration since 1945: At the Heart of Europe?* (London, 2009), 14–44, 71–104.
7. On Belgium, see D.C. Reymen, 'The Economic Effects of the Marshall Plan Revisited', in J. Agnew and J.N. Entrikin (eds), *The Marshall Plan Today: Model and Metaphor* (London, 2004), 82–126. On Germany, W. Abelshauser, 'Kriegswirtschaft und Wirtschaftswunder: Deutschlands wirtschaftliche Mobilisierung für den Zweiten Weltkrieg und die Folgen für die Nachkriegszeit', *Vierteljahreshefte für Zeitgeschichte* 47 (1999), 503–38; N. Finszch and J. Martschukat (eds), *Different Restorations: Reconstruction and 'Wiederaufbau' in the United States and Germany, 1865–1945–1989* (Oxford, 1996); S. Reich, *The Fruits of Fascism: Postwar Prosperity in Historical Perspective* (Ithaca, 1990); J. Gimbel, *Science, Technology and Reparations: Exploitation and Plunder in Postwar Germany* (Stanford, 1990); V.R. Berghahn, *The Americanization of West German Industry, 1945–1973* (Oxford, 1986); R.G. Stokes, *Divide and Prosper: The Heirs of I.G. Farben under Allied Authority, 1945–1951* (Berkeley, 1988); P. Hayes, *Industry and Ideology: IG Farben in the Nazi Era* (Cambridge, 1987), 213–384; W. Abelshauser et al., *German Industry and Global Enterprise: BASF* (Cambridge, 2009), 332–61; N. Gregor, *Daimler-Benz in the Third Reich* (New Haven, 1998), 76–108, 218–46; S. Tolliday, 'Enterprise and State in the West German *Wirtschaftswunder*: Volkswagen and the Automobile Industry, 1939–1962', *Business History Review* 69 (1995), 273–350.
8. R.O. Paxton, *Vichy France: Old Guard and New Order, 1940–1944* (New York, 1972); S. Fishman et al. (eds), *France at War: Vichy and the Historians* (Oxford, 2000); R. Gildea, *Marianne in Chains: In Search of the German Occupation, 1940–1945* (New York, 2002); J. Jackson, *France: The Dark Years, 1940–1944* (Oxford, 2003); S. Kitson, 'From Enthusiasm to Disenchantment: The French

Police and the Vichy Regime, 1940–1944', *Contemporary European History* 11 (2002), 371–90. See also Introduction, note 19.

9. A. Glees, *Exile Politics during the Second World War: The German Social Democrats in Britain* (Oxford, 1982); D. Orlow, 'Delayed Reaction: Democracy, Nationalism and the SPD, 1945–1966', *German Studies Review* 16 (1993), 77–102; A. Rödder, *Die deutschen sozialistischen Exilgruppen in Grossbritannien* (Hanover, 1968); J. Herf, *Divided Memory* (Harvard, 1997), 13–68; E. Lacina, *Emigration 1933–1945* (Stuttgart, 1982); S.M. Di Scala, *Renewing Italian Socialism* (Oxford, 1988), 3–32; W. Kaiser, *Christian Democracy and the Origins of European Union* (Cambridge, 2007), 119–90; and idem, 'Cooperation of European Catholic Politicians in Exile in Britain and the USA during the Second World War', *Journal of Contemporary History* 35 (2000), 439–65; I. Tombs, 'Une identité européenne assiégée? Les exiles socialistes à Londres, 1939–1945', *Revue d'histoire moderne et contemporaine* 46 (1999), 263–79; W. Loth, *Sozialismus und Internationalismus. Die französischen Sozialisten und Nachkriegsordnung Europas, 1940–1950* (Stuttgart, 1977); C.W. Nettelbeck, *Forever French: Exile in the United States, 1939–1945* (Oxford, 1991); N. Atkin, *The Forgotten French: Exiles in the British Isles, 1940–1944* (Manchester, 2003); J.P. and M. Cointet, *La France à Londres, 1940–1943* (Brussels, 1990); G. Adams, *Political Ecumenism: Catholics, Jews and Protestants in de Gaulle's Free France, 1940–1945* (Montreal, 2006); M. Conway and J. Gotovitch (eds), *Europe in Exile: European Exile Communities in Britain, 1940–1945* (New York, 2001).

10. G. Sapelli, *Southern Europe since 1945: Tradition and Modernity in Portugal, Spain, Italy, Greece and Turkey* (London, 1995); J. Kurth and J. Petras, *Mediterranean Paradoxes: The Politics and Social Structure of Southern Europe* (Oxford, 1994); K. Featherstone, *Political Change in Greece: Before and after the Colonels* (Basingstoke, 1987); S. Payne, *The Franco Regime, 1936–1975* (Madison, 1987); J.J. Linz and A. Stepan, *Democratic Transition and Consolidation* (Baltimore, 1996), 3–86; J.J. Linz and A. Stepan (eds), *The Breakdown of Democratic Regimes* (Baltimore, 1978), vols 1–2.

11. Compare Chapters 2 and 3.

12. A. Wiener and T. Diez, *European Integration Theory* (2003), 25–66, 125–43, and B. Rosamond, *Theories of European Integration* (2000), 20–73. Also, Chapter 3, notes 1–4.

13. J.-L. Chabot, *Aux origines intellectuelles de l'Union européenne: l'idée d'Europe unie de 1919 à 1939* (Grenoble, 2005), 325.

14. See Chapters 7 and 8.

15. Chapters 1, 2 and 4.

16. Compare D. Drake, *Intellectuals and Politics in Postwar France* (Basingstoke, 2002), and M. Winock, *Le siècle des intellectuelles* (Paris, 1997), who argue for the dominance of Sartre, and C. Parsons, *A Certain Idea of Europe* (Ithaca, 2003), who demonstrates – with some overstatement – the influence of pro-Community voices in government.

17. Chapter 3.

18. On the significance of such networks, see W. Kaiser, *Christian Democracy and the Origins of European Union* (Cambridge, 2007); G. Bossuat, 'Les euro-socialistes de la SFIO: Réseaux et influences', in idem (ed.), *Inventer l'Europe* (Berne, 2003), 409–29. On actual decision making, see Chapters 2 and 3 for further reading.

19. On U.S.-dominated conceptions of the 'West', including Germany, see P.T. Jackson, *Civilizing the Enemy: German Reconstruction and the Invention of the West* (Ann Arbor, 2006).

20. See, especially, the essays in M. Spiering and M.J. Wintle (eds), *Ideas of Europe since 1914* (Basingstoke, 2002), as well as in this volume.

21. F.H. Hinsley, *Power and the Pursuit of Peace* (Cambridge, 1967), remains the classic account. See also the vast literature on the causes of the First World War: A. Mombauer, *The Origins of the First World War* (London, 2002).

22. Above all, Z.S. Steiner, *The Lights That Failed: European International History, 1919–1933* (Oxford, 2007), on the League of Nations and international relations; and M. Mazower, *Dark Continent: Europe's Twentieth Century* (London, 2000), on radicalization, amongst many others.

23. On American-led internationalism and internationalisation, see J.M. Cooper, Jr. (ed.), *Reconsidering Woodrow Wilson: Progressivism, Internationalism, War and Peace* (Baltimore, 2008); D.F. Schmitz, *The Triumph of Internationalism: Franklin D. Roosevelt and a World in Crisis,*

1933–1941 (Washington, D.C., 2007); E.E. Spalding, *The First Cold Warrior: Harry Truman, Containment and the Remaking of Liberal Internationalism* (Kentucky, 2006).

24. See Chapters 2 and 3. On the Franco-British Union, see A. Shlaim, 'Prelude to Downfall: The British Offer of Union to France, June 1940', *Journal of Contemporary History* 9 (1974), 27–63, who stresses that the offer was born of desperation, although having 'a respectable intellectual parentage'; D.W.J. Johnson, 'Britain and France in 1940', *Transactions of the Royal Historical Society* 22 (1972), 141–57; R. Mayne et al. (eds), *Cross Channel Currents: 100 Years of Entente Cordiale* (London, 2004), 87–108; D. Reynolds, *In Command of History: Churchill Fighting and Writing the Second World War* (New York, 2005), 168–69; R. Jenkins, *Churchill* (London, 2002), 619–20.

25. On convergence, see especially Hartmut Kaelble, *Sozialgeschichte Europas 1945 bis zur Gegenwart* (Munich, 2007); idem, *A Social History of Western Europe, 1880–1980* (Oxford, 1990); idem, *Nachbarn am Rhein: Entfremdung und Annäherung der französischen und deutschen Gesellschaft seit 1880* (Munich, 1991); idem, *Social Mobility in the Nineteenth and Twentieth Centuries: Europe and America in Comparative Perspective* (New York, 1986); idem (ed.), *The European Way* (New York, 2004). Most historians of twentieth-century Europe have emphasized divergences and conflicts, from Eric Hobsbawm, *An Age of Extremes: The Short Twentieth Century, 1914–1991* (London, 1994), 21–224, to Bernard Wasserstein, *Barbarism and Civilization: A History of Europe in Our Time* (Oxford, 2007), 80–519.

26. N. Lewkowicz, *The German Question and the International Order, 1943–1948* (Basingstoke, 2010); P. Alter, *The German Question and Europe: A History* (London, 2000); J. McAllister, *No Exit: America and the German Problem, 1943–1954* (Ithaca, 2002). On a global Cold War, see, in particular, John Gaddis, *We Now Know: Rethinking Cold War History* (Oxford, 1998); and idem, *The Cold War: A New History* (London, 2006).

27. D.C. Large, 'Grand Illusions: The United States, the Federal Republic of Germany and the European Defence Community, 1950–1954', in J.M. Diefendorf et al. (eds), *American Policy and the Reconstruction of West Germany*, 375–94; L. Köllner et al., *Die EVG-Phase* (Munich, 1990); H.E. Volkmann and W. Schwengler (eds), *Die Europäische Verteidigungsgemeinschaft* (Boppard, 1985); T.P. Ireland, *Creating the Entangling Alliance* (Westport, Conn., 1981); F.H. Heller and J.R. Gillingham (eds), *NATO: The Founding of the Atlantic Alliance and the Integration of Europe* (New York, 1992); A. Grosser, *The Western Alliance* (London, 1980); S. Dockrill, *Britain's Policy for West German Rearmament* (Cambridge, 1991); and P. Winand, *Eisenhower, Kennedy and the United States of Europe* (New York, 1993). W. Loth, 'Die EWG und das Projekt der Europäischen Politischen Gesellschaft', in R. Hudemann (ed.), *Europa im Blick der Historiker* (Munich, 1995). 191–201, argues – unconvincingly – against this line, positing that the EDC failed because it was not supranational enough.

28. In addition to the literature on the U.K. above, see J. Palayret et al. (eds), *Visions, Votes and Vetoes: The Empty Chair Crisis and the Luxembourg Compromise Forty Years On* (Berne, 2006); N.P. Ludlow, *The European Community and the Crises of the 1960s: Negotiating the Gaullist Challenge* (London, 2007); idem, *Dealing with Britain: The Six and the First UK Application to the EEC* (Cambridge, 1997). On international crises, see A. Shlaim, *The United States and the Berlin Blockade, 1948–1949* (Berkeley, 1983); D.F.Harrington, 'The Berlin Blockade Revisited', *The International History Review* 6 (1984), 88–112; P. Lowe, *The Korean War* (New York, 2000); W. Stueck, *The Korean War: An International History* (Princeton, 1995); L.S. Kaplan, 'The Korean War and US Foreign Relations: The Case of NATO', in F.H. Heller (ed.), *The Korean War* (Lawrence, Kans., 1977); R.G. Hughes, *Britain, Germany and the Cold War: The Search for Détente, 1949–1967* (London, 2007), 6–89; G. Schmidt (ed.), *Zwischen Bündnissicherung und priviligierter Partnerschaft. Die deutsch-britische Beziehungen und die Vereinigten Staaten von Amerika 1955–1963* (Bochum, 1995); R. Steininger et al. (eds), *Die doppelte Eindämmung. Europäische Sicherheit und deutsche Frage in den Fünfzigern* (Munich, 1993); J.M. Schick, *The Berlin Crisis, 1958–1962* (Philadelphia, 1971); J. Arenth, *Der Westen tut nichts! Transatlantische Kooperation während der zweiten Berlin-Krise (1958–1962)* (Frankfurt, 1993); C. Bremen, *Die Eisenhower-Administration und die zweite Berlin-Krise 1958–1961* (Berlin, 1998). On decolonization, see F. Heinlein, *British*

Government Policy and Decolonisation, 1945–1963 (London, 2002); R. Hyam, *Britain's Declining Empire: The Road to Decolonisation, 1918–1968* (Cambridge, 2007); N. White, *Decolonisation: The British Experience since 1945* (London, 1999); J. Darwin, *Britain and Decolonisation* (New York, 1988); R.F. Betts, *France and Decolonisation, 1900–1960* (London, 1991); M. Connelly, *A Diplomatic Revolution: Algeria's Fight for Independence and the Origins of the Post-Cold War Era* (Oxford, 2002); I.M. Wall, *France, the United States and the Algerian War* (Berkeley, 2001); T. Shaw, *Eden, Suez and the Mass Media: Propaganda and Persuasion during the Suez Crisis* (London, 2009); J. Pearson, *Sir Anthony Eden and the Suez Crisis: Reluctant Gamble* (Basingstoke, 2002); W.S. Lucas, *Divided We Stand: Britain, the United States and the Suez Crisis* (London, 1991); D. Carlton, *Britain and the Suez Crisis* (Oxford, 1989); S.C. Smith (ed.), *Reassessing Suez 1956* (Aldershot, 2008).

NOTES ON CONTRIBUTORS

Michael Burgess is Professor of Politics and International Relations at the University of Kent, where he is the Director of the Centre for Federal Studies. He has written extensively on the theory and the history of European integration. Among his latest works are *State Territoriality and the European Union* (London, 2006), edited with H. Vollaard; *Comparative Federalism: Theory and Practice* (London, 2005); *Federalism and Europe: The Building of Europe* (London, 2000); and *The British Tradition of Federalism* (London, 1995).

Vittorio Cotesta is Professor of Sociology at the Università Roma III. He is currently working on images and perceptions of Europe. Among his latest publications are *Images du monde et société globale* (Quebec, 2006); 'Europe: Common Values and Identity', in M. Ferrari Occhionero and M. Nocenzi (eds), *Europe between Memory and Change: Towards the Construction of a European Society* (Rome, 2006); and *Società globale e diritti umani* (Rome, 2008).

Matthew D'Auria is completing his doctoral studies at the Centre for European Studies at University College London, where he has taught European history and social and political thought. A historian of political ideas, he is working on the relationship between nationalism and internationalism in the history of European political thought. Among his publications are 'L'Europa dei federalisti italiani. Storia e prassi di un'idea' with Massimo Pendenza in Vittorio Cotesta (ed.), *Immagini d'Europa* (Rome, 2010). He is currently a Research Fellow at the University of Salerno.

Vittorio Dini is Professor of History of Political Ideas at the University of Salerno, where he also is the Director of the Department of Sociology and Political Studies. Among his many publications are an edited volume on *Individualismo, Assolutismo e democrazia* (Naples, 1992); and *Il governo della prudenza* (Milan, 2000).

Annamaria Ducci gained her doctorate at the University of Pisa. She was subsequently awarded a Getty Postdoctoral Fellowship, allowing her to pursue her research interest at the Institut National d'Histoire de l'Art, which led to the publication of several essays on nineteenth- and twentieth-century history of art. She is currently working at the University of Arezzo.

Dina Gusejnova holds a doctoral degree from the University of Cambridge. From 2009 to 2011, she was a Collegiate Assistant Professor in the Social Sciences at the University of Chicago, before joining the History Department at University College London as a Leverhulme Early Career Fellow. She has published, amongst other things, 'Concepts of Culture and Technology in Germany, 1916–1933', *Journal of European Studies* 36 (2006); and 'Olympian or Pathologist? Cassirer, Gundolf and the Hero Myth', in Paul Bishop and R.H. Stephenson (eds), *Cultural Studies and the Symbolic* (Glasgow, 2008).

Mark Hewitson is a Senior Lecturer in German History and Politics and Chair of the Centre for European Studies at University College London. His publications include books on *National Identity and Political Thought in Germany* (Oxford, 2000); *Germany and the Causes of the First World War* (Berg, 2004); *Nationalism in Germany, 1848–1866* (Basingstoke, 2010); and *What is a Nation? Europe, 1789–1914* (Oxford, 2006), edited jointly with Timothy Baycroft. He is currently working on a book entitled *The People's Wars: German Images and Experiences of Conflict, 1792–1918*.

Lukasz Mikołajewski is now completing his doctoral research at the European University Institute in Florence. His thesis deals with the images of Europe in 'Kultura', the Polish émigré literary-political magazine published in Paris in the years 1948–2000.

Anita Prettenthaler-Ziegerhofer is Professor of Contemporary History at the Institute of Austrian Legal History and Development of European Law at the University of Graz. She has published extensively on the history of European integration. Among her latest publications are *Botschafter Europas: Richard Nikolaus Coudenhove-Kalergi und die Paneuropa-Bewegung in den zwanziger und dreißiger Jahre* (Vienna, 2004); and *Europäische Integrationsgeschichte: Unter besonderer Berücksichtigung der österreichischen Integration* (Innsbruck, 2007). Her main research fields are the history of European Union, the development of European constitutionalism, and gender studies.

Anne-Isabelle Richard is a postdoctoral researcher at the University of Utrecht in the Netherlands. She was awarded a Ph.D. by the University of Cambridge in 2010. She is currently working on a book project, provisionally entitled 'Colonialism and the European movement in France and the Netherlands in the interwar period', which draws upon her doctoral dissertation. Her research interests address the interaction between world and European history from the late nineteenth century onwards.

Ernest Schonfield was educated at the University of Sussex and University College London. His doctoral thesis, *Art and its Uses in Thomas Mann's Felix Krull*, was published in 2008. His research interests include modern German prose fiction and drama; he is also part-time Lecturer in Comparative Literature at King's College London.

Ionut Untea is completing his doctoral studies at the Ecole Pratique des Hautes Etudes, Paris. Among his latest publications are 'A Heretical Political Theology: Carl Schmitt and the Hobbesian Concept of Representation', *International Journal of Humanities*, 6 (2009), and 'Public and Private Regular Bodies and their Souls: Materialism and Mortalism in the Political Theory of Thomas Hobbes' in *Anatomy and the Organization of Knowledge, 1500–1850* (London, 2012), edited by Matthew Landers and Brian Muñoz.

Jan Vermeiren is Lecturer in Modern European History at the University of Essex. His publications include 'The "Rebirth of Greater Germany": The Austro-German Alliance and the Outbreak of War' in H. Jones et al. (eds), *Untold War: New Perspectives in First World War Studies* (Boston, 2008); and 'Germany, Austria, and the Idea of the German Nation, 1871–1914', *History Compass* 9/3 (2011). He is currently working on a book on the Dual Alliance at War for Cambridge University Press.

Michael Wintle holds the Chair of European History at the University of Amsterdam, where he directs the degree programmes in European Studies. Among his many publications on the history of Europe are *The Idea of a United Europe*, edited with Jamal Shalin (London, 2000); *Imagining Europe* (Brussels, 2008), of which he is the editor; and *Ideas of Europe since 1914* (London, 2002), edited with Menno Spiering.

SELECT BIBLIOGRAPHY

Albertini, M., *Il federalismo* (Milan, 1993).

Alter, P., *The German Question and Europe: A History* (London, 2000).

Bachoud, A., J. Cuesta and M. Trebitsch (eds), *Les intellectuals et l'Europe de 1945 à nos jours* (Paris, 2000).

Bariéty, J., *Les relations franco-allemands après la Première Guerre Mondiale* (Paris, 1977).

Barraclough, G., *European Unity in Thought and Practice* (Oxford, 1963).

Becker, J. and F. Knipping (eds), *Power in Europe? Great Britain, France, Italy and Germany in a Postwar World 1945–1950* (Berlin, 1986).

Bell, P.M.H., *France and Britain, 1900–1940: Entente and Estrangement* (London, 1996).

Bessel, R. and D. Schumann (eds), *Life after Death: Approaches to a Cultural and Social History of Europe during the 1940s and 1950s* (Cambridge, 2003).

Bessel, R., *Germany 1945: From War to Peace* (London, 2010).

———, *Germany after the First World War* (Oxford, 1995).

Bobbio, N., *Ideological Profile of the Twentieth Century in Italy* (Princeton, 1995).

Boer, D. et al., *The History of the Idea of Europe* (Milton Keynes, 1993).

Bosco, A. (ed.), *The Federal Idea*, 2 vols (1991–1992).

Bossuat, G. and G. Saunier (eds), *Inventer l'Europe. Histoire nouvelle des groupes d'influence et des acteurs de l'unité européenne* (Brussels, 2003).

Boyce, R., *The Great Interwar Crisis and the Collapse of Globalization* (Basingstoke, 2009).

Brugmans, H., *Europe: Dream, Adventure, Reality* (Brussels, 1987).

———, *L'idee européenne 1920–1970*, 3rd edn (Bruges, 1970).

Burgard, O., *Das gemeinsame Europa – von der politischen Utopie zum außenpolitischen Programm: Meinungsaustausch und Zusammenarbeit proeuropäischer Verbände in Deutschland und Frankreich, 1924–1933* (Frankfurt am Main, 2000).

Burgess, M. (ed.), *Federalism and Federation in Western Europe* (London, 1986).

———, *Federalism and the European Union: The Building of Europe, 1950—2000* (London, 2000).

———, *The British Tradition of Federalism*, (London, 1995).

Burgess, S. and G. Edwards, 'The Six Plus One: British Policy-Making and the Question of European Economic Integration, 1955', *International Affairs* 64 (1988), 393–413.

Burke, P., *The French Historical Revolution: The Annales School, 1929–1989* (Stanford, 1990).

Bussière, E. (ed.), *Europa. L'idée et l'identité européennes de l'antiquité grecque au XXe siècle* (Anvers, 2001).

———, 'Premiers schemas européens et économie internationale Durant l'entre-deux-guerres', *Relations internationales* 123 (2005), 51–68.

———, *La France, la Belgique et l'organisation économique de l'Europe* (Paris, 1991).

Calleo, D., *The German Problem Reconsidered* (Oxford, 1978).

Chabod, F., *Storia dell'idea Europa* (Bari, 1961).

Chabot, J.-L., *Aux origines intellectuelles de l'Union européenne: l'idée d'Europe unie de 1919 à 1939* (Grenoble, 2005).

Checkel, J.T., and Katzenstein, P.J. (eds), *European Identity* (2009).

Collini, S., *Absent Minds: Intellectuals in Britain* (Oxford, 2006).

Conway, M. and J. Gotovitch (eds), *Europe in Exile: European Exile Communities in Britain, 1940–1945* (New York, 2001).

———, 'The Rise and Fall of Western Europe's Democratic Age, 1945–1973', *Contemporary European History* 13 (2004), 67–88.

——— and K.K. Patel (eds), *Europeanization in the Twentieth Century: Historical Approaches* (Basingstoke, 2010).

Conze, V., *Das Europa der Deutschen. Ideen von Europa in Deutschland zwischen Reichstradition und Westorientierung (1920–1970)* (Munich, 2005).

Cooper, J.M. Jr. (ed.), *Reconsidering Woodrow Wilson: Progressivism, Internationalism, War and Peace* (Baltimore, 2008).

Darnton, R., 'Intellectual and Cultural History', in M. Kammen (ed.), *The Past Before Us* (Ithaca, 1980).

Davies, N., 'The Idea of Europe', in idem, *Europe East and West* (London, 2007), 5–21.

———, *Europe: A History* (Oxford, 1996).

Dedman, M., *The Origins and Development of the European Union, 1945–2008* (London, 2009)

De Gruyther, W., *Continental Plans for European Integration, 1919–1945* (Berlin, 1985).

Deighton, A. (ed.), *Building Postwar Europe* (Basingstoke, 1995).

———, *The Impossible Peace: Britain, the Division of Germany, and the Origins of the Cold War* (Oxford, 1990).

Delanty, G., *Inventing Europe: Idea, Identity, Reality* (Basingstoke, 1995).

DePorte, A.W., *Europe between the Superpowers: The Enduring Balance* (New Haven, 1986).

Derrida, J., *The Other Heading: Reflections on Today's Europe* (1992).

Desbazeille, M. (ed.), *L'Europe, naissance d'une utopie?: genèse de l'idée d'Europe du XVIe au XIXe siècles* (Paris-Montréal, 1996).

Dinan, D., (ed.), *Origins and Evolution of the European Union* (2006).

———, 'The History of European Integration: From Integration History to the History of Integrated Europe', in W. Loth (ed.), *Experiencing Europe*, 17–32.

———, *Europe Recast: A History of European Union* (2004).

Di Nolfo, E. (ed.), *Power in Europe? Great Britain, France, Germany and Italy and the Origins of the EEC, 1952–1957* (Berlin, 1992).

Di Scala, S.M. and S. Mastellane, *European Political Thought, 1815–1989* (Boulder, Colo., 1998).

Drake, D. *Intellectuals and Politics in Postwar France* (Basingstoke, 2002).

Duchhardt, H. and Istvan Nemeth (eds), *Der Europa-Gedanke in Ungarn und Deutschland in der Zwischenkriegszeit* (Mainz, 2005).

Duroselle, J.-B., *L'idée d'Europe dans l'histoire* (Paris, 1965).

————, *La Décadence, 1932–1939* (Paris, 1979).

Elisha, A., *Aristide Briand, la paix mondiale et l'union européenne* (Louvain, 2003).

Ellwood, D.W., *Rebuilding Europe: Western Europe, America and Postwar Reconstruction* (London, 1992).

Elvert, J., *Die Europäische Integration* (Darmstadt, 2006).

Febvre, L., *L'Europe. Genèse d'une civilisation* (Paris, 1999).

Frank, R. (ed.), *Les identités européennes au XXᵉ siècle* (Paris, 2004).

Frisby, D. and M. Featherstone, *Simmel on Culture* (London, 1998).

Fulbrook, M., *German National Identity after the Holocaust* (Cambridge, 1999).

Fussell, P., *The Great War and Modern Memory* (Oxford, 1975).

Garton Ash, T., *In Europe's Name: Germany and the Divided Continent* (London, 1993).

Gay, P., *Weimar Culture* (London, 1968).

Geppert, D. (ed.), *The Postwar Challenge: Cultural, Social and Political Change in Western Europe, 1945–58* (Oxford, 2002).

Germond, C. and H. Türk (eds), *A History of Franco-German Relations in Europe* (Basingstoke, 2008).

Gilbert, M., *Surpassing Realism: The Politics of European Integration since 1945* (Lanham, MD, 2003).

Gildea, R., *Marianne in Chains: In Search of the German Occupation, 1940–1945* (New York, 2002).

Gillingham, J., 'A Theoretical Vacuum: European Integration and Historical Research Today', *Journal of European Integration History* 14/1 (2008), 27–34.

————, *Coal, Steel and the Rebirth of Europe, 1945–1955* (Cambridge, 1991).

————, *European Integration, 1950–2003: Superstate or New Market Economy* (Cambridge, 2003).

Girault, R. (ed.), *Identité et conscience européenne au XXᵉ siècle* (Paris, 1994).

————, (ed.), *Les Europe des Européens* (Paris, 1993).

————, and G. Bossuat (eds), *Europe brisée, Europe retrouvée. Nouvelles réflexions sur l'unité européenne au XXᵉ siècle* (Paris, 1994).

————, 'Das Europa der Historiker', in Hudemann et al. (eds), *Europa im Blick der Historiker*, 55–90.

Gowland, D. and A. Turner, *Reluctant Europeans: Britain and European Integration, 1945–1998* (London, 1999).

Griffiths, R.T. (ed.), *The Netherlands and the Integration of Europe* (Amsterdam, 1990).

Guerrina, R., *Europe: History, Ideas and Ideologies* (London, 2002).

Guieu, J.-M., 'L'Europe des militants français pour la Société des Nations', in K. Rücker and L. Warlouzet (eds), *Quelle(s) Europe(s)? Nouvelles approches en histoire de l'intégration européenne* (Brussels, 2006), 51–63.

Guieu, J.-M., C. Le Dréau, J. Raflik and L. Warlouzet, *Penser et construire l'Europe au XXe siècle, Historiographie, Bibliographie, Enjeux* (Paris, 2007).

Haas, E.B., *The Uniting of Europe: Political, Social and Economic Forces 1950–1957*, 3rd edn (Notre Dame, Ind., 2004).

Habermas, J., *The Postnational Constellation: Political Essays* (Cambridge, 2001).

Hay, D., *Europe: The Emergence of an Idea* (Edinburgh, 1957).

Heater, D., *The Idea of European Unity* (Leicester, 1992)

Henig, S. (ed.), *Federalism and the British*, (London 2007).

Herrmann, R.K., et al. (eds), *Transnational Identities: Becoming European in the EU* (Lanham, MD, 2004).

Hess, J., 'Europagedanke und nationaler Revisionismus. Überlegungen zu ihrer Verknüpfung in der Weimarer Republik am Beispiel Wilhelm Heiles', *Historische Zeitschrift* 225 (1977), 572–622.

Hinsley, F.H., *Power and the Pursuit of Peace* (Cambridge, 1967).

Hobsbawm, E., *An Age of Extremes: The Short Twentieth Century, 1914–1991* (London, 1994).

Hogan, M.J., *The Marshall Plan: America, Britain and the Reconstruction of Western Europe, 1947–1952* (Cambridge, 1987).

Hoggart, R. and Douglas Johnson, *An Idea of Europe* (London, 1987).

Holl, K., 'Europapolitik um Vorfeld der deutschen Regierungspolitik. Zur Tätigkeit proeuropäischer Organisationen in der Weimarer Republik', *Historische Zeitschrift* 219 (1974), 33–94.

Hudemann, R. et al. (eds), *Europa im Blick der Historiker* (Munich, 1995).

Hynes, S., *War Imagined: The First World War and English Culture* (London, 1992).

Jackson, J., *France: The Dark Years, 1940–1944* (Oxford, 2003).

Jackson, P.T., *Civilizing the Enemy: German Reconstruction and the Invention of the West* (Ann Arbor, 2006).

Jaeckle, E., *Die Idee Europa* (Berlin, 1988).

Judt, T., *Past Imperfect: French Intellectuals, 1944–1956* (Berkeley, 1992).

———, *A Grand Illusion: An Essay on Europe* (London, 1997).

———, *Postwar: A History of Europe since 1945* (London, 2005).

Kaelble, H., *Europäer über Europa. Die Entstehung des europäischen Selbstverständnisses im 19. und 20. Jahrhundert* (Frankfurt, 2001).

Kaiser, W., *Christian Democracy and the Origins of European Union* (Cambridge, 2007).

———, *Using Europe, Abusing the Europeans: Britain and European Integration, 1945–1963* (Basingstoke, 1997).

Kaiser, W., et al. (eds), *The History of the European Union: Origins of a Trans- and Supranational Polity* (London, 2009).

Karmis, D., and W. Norman (eds), *Theories of Federalism: A Reader* (Basingstoke, 2005).

Kelley, D.R., *The Descent of Ideas: A History of Intellectual History* (London, 2002).

Kendle, J.E., *The Round Table Movement and Imperial Union* (Toronto, 1975).

Koselleck, R., *The Practice of Conceptual History* (Stanford, 2002).

Kühnhardt, L. (ed.), *Crises in European Integration: Challenge and Response, 1945–2005* (Oxford, 2009).

LaCapra, D., *Rethinking Intellectual History* (Ithaca, 1983).

Lacroix, J., and K. Nikolaïdes (eds), *European Stories: Intellectual Debates on Europe in National Contexts* (Oxford, 2010).

Lane, T. and M. Wolanski, *Poland and European Integration: The Ideas and Movements of Polish Exiles in the West, 1939–91* (Basingstoke, 2009).

Laursen, J., 'Towards a Supranational History', *Journal of European Integration History* 8 (2002), 5–17.

Lepenies, W., *Between Literature and Science: The Rise of Sociology* (Cambridge, 1988).

Levy, C. and M. Roseman (eds), *Three Postwar Eras in Comparison: Western Europe, 1918–1945–1989* (Basingstoke, 2002).

Lewkowicz, N., *The German Question and the International Order, 1943–1948* (Basingstoke, 2010).

Lichtheim, G., *Europe in the Twentieth Century* (London, 1972).

Lipgens, W., 'European Federation in the Political Thought of Resistance Movements during World War II', *Central European History* 1 (1968), 5–19.

————, *A History of European Integration, 1945–1947* (Oxford, 1982).

————, *Die Anfänge der europäischen Einigungspolitik 1945–1950* (Stuttgart, 1977).

————, *Europa-Föderationspläne der Widerstandsbewegungen 1940–1945* (Munich, 1968).

Liulevicius, V.G., *The German Myth of the East, 1800 to the Present* (Oxford, 2009).

Loth, W. (ed.), *Experiencing Europe: 50 Years of European Construction, 1957–2007* (Baden-Baden, 2009).

Loth, W., 'Explaining European Integration: The Contributions from Historians', *Journal of European Integration History* 14/1 (2008), 9–26.

————, *Der Weg nach Europa. Geschichte der europäischen Integration 1939–1957* (Göttingen, 1996).

————, *Sozialismus und Internationalismus. Die französischen Sozialisten und Nachkriegsordnung Europas, 1940–1950* (Stuttgart, 1977).

Loubet, J.-L. del Bayle, *Les non-conformistes des années trente. Une tentative de renouvellement de la pensée politique française* (Paris, 1969).

Lovett, A.W., 'The United States and the Schuman Plan', *Historical Journal* 39 (1996), 425–55.

Ludlow, N.P., 'Widening, Deepening and Opening Out: Towards a Fourth Decade of European Integration History', in W. Loth (ed.), *Experiencing Europe*, 33–44.

————, *Dealing with Britain: The Six and the First UK Application to the EEC* (Cambridge, 1997).

Lützeler, P.M., *Die Schriftsteller und Europa. Von der Romantik bis zur Gegenwart* (Munich, 1992).

Lundestad, G., *'Empire' by Integration: The United States and European Integration, 1945–1997* (Oxford, 1998).

Maier, C., *Recasting Bourgeois Europe: Stabilisation in France, Germany and Italy in the Decade after World War I* (Princeton, 1975).

Malandrino, C., *Socialismo e libertà. Autonomie, federalismo, Europa da Rosselli a Silone* (Milan, 1990).

Mallinson, W., *From Neutrality to Commitment: Dutch Foreign Policy, NATO and European Integration* (London, 2010).

Marbeau, M., *La société des nations* (Paris, 2001).

Martin, G., 'The Idea of Imperial Federation', in R. Hyam and G. Martin (eds), *Reappraisals in British Imperial History* (London, 1975).

Mayne, R. and J. Pinder, *Federal Union: The Pioneers, a History of Federal Union* (London, 1990).

Mazower, M., *Dark Continent: Europe's Twentieth Century* (London, 1999).

McAllister, J., *No Exit: America and the German Problem, 1943–1954* (Ithaca, 2002).

McCormick, J., *Europeanism* (Oxford, 2010).

Mikkeli, H., *Europe as an Idea and an Identity* (Basingstoke, 1998).

Milward, A.S., *The European Rescue of the Nation-State* (London, 1992).

————, *The Reconstruction of Western Europe, 1945–51* (London, 1984).

Milward, A.S. and V. Sorensen (eds), *The Frontier of National Sovereignty: History and Theory* (London, 1992).

Morelli, U., *Contro il mito dello stato sovrano. Luigi Einaudi e l'unità europea* (Milan, 1990).

Morin, E., *Penser l'Europe* (Paris, 1987).

Moses, D.A., *German Intellectuals and the Nazi Past* (Cambridge, 2007).

Müller, G., 'Europa' als Konzept adlig-bürgerlicher Elitendiskurse', in H. Reif (ed.) *Adel und Bürgertum in Deutschland II. Entwicklungslinien und Wendepunkte im 20. Jahrhundert* (Berlin, 2001), 235–69.

————, *Europäische Gesellschaftsbeziehungen nach dem Ersten Weltkrieg. Das Deutsch-Französische Studienkomitee und der Europäische Kulturbund* (Munich, 2005).

Müller, J.-W., *A Dangerous Mind: Carl Schmitt's Post-War European Thought* (New Haven and London, 2003).

Müller, J.-W. (ed.), *German Ideologies since 1945: Studies in the Political Thought and Culture of the Bonn Republic* (Basingstoke, 2003).

Nelson, B., et al. (eds), *The Idea of Europe* (1992).

Okey, R., 'Central Europe/Eastern Europe: Behind the Definitions', *Past and Present* 137 (1992), 102–33.

Pagden, A., *The Idea of Europe: From Antiquity to the European Union* (Cambridge, 2002).

Parsons, C., *A Certain Idea of Europe* (Ithaca, 2003).

Payne, S., *A History of Fascism, 1914–1945* (London, 1996).

Pegg, C.H., *Evolution of the European Idea, 1914–1932* (Chapel Hill, 1983).

Pernhorst, C., *Das paneuropäische Verfassungsmodell des Grafen Richard N. Coudenhove-Kalergi* (Baden-Baden, 2008).

Pinder, J., 'Federalism and the Beginnings of the European Union', in K. Larres (ed.), *A Companion to Europe since 1945* (Oxford, 2009), 25–44.

————, *Altiero Spinelli and the British Federalists: Writings by Beveridge, Robbins and Spinelli, 1937–1943* (London, 1998).

Pistone, S., *L'Italia e l'unità europea* (Turin, 1982).

Power, M.S., *Jacques Maritain, Christian Democrat, and the Quest for a New Commonwealth* (Lampeter, 1992).

Prettenthaler-Ziegerhofer, A., *Europäische Integrationsgeschichte. Unter besonderer Berücksichtigung der österreichischen Integration* (Innsbruck, 2007).

Prochasson, C., *Les intellectuals, le socialisme et la guerre, 1900–1938* (Paris, 1993).

Raley, H.C., *José Ortega y Gasset: Philosopher of European Unity* (Alabama, 1971).

Réau, E. du (ed.), *Europe des elites? Europe des peoples? La construction de l'espace européenne 1945–1960* (Paris, 1998).

————, 'La France et l'Europe d'Aristide Briand à Robert Schuman. Naissance, déclin et redéploiement d'une politique étrangere (1929–1950)', *Revue d'histoire moderne et contemporaine* 42 (1995).

————, *L'Europe en construction. Le second vingtième siècle*, 2nd edn (Paris, 2007).

————, *La construction européenne au XXe siècle. Fondements, enjeux, defies* (Nantes, 2007).

————, *L'idée d'Europe au XXe siècle. Des mythes aux réalités* (Brussels, 1996).

Reynolds, D. (ed.), *The Origins of the Cold War in Europe* (New Haven, 1994).

————, *One World Divisible* (London, 2000).

Ringer, F., 'The Intellectual Field, Intellectual History and the Sociology of Knowledge', *Theory and Society* 19 (1990), 269–334.

Rödder, A., *Stresemanns Erbe. Julius Curtius und die deutsche Aussenpolitik 1929–1931* (Paderborn, 1996).

Rosamond, B., *Theories of European Integration* (Basingstoke, 2000).

Rupnik, J., 'Central Europe or Mitteleuropa?', *Daedalus* 119 (1990), 249–78.

Salewski, M., 'Europa: Idée und Wirklichkeit in der nationalsozialistischen Weltanschauung und politischen Praxis', in O. Franz (ed.), *Europas Mitte* (Göttingen, 1987), 85–106.

Schmitz, D.F., *The Triumph of Internationalism: Franklin D. Roosevelt and a World in Crisis, 1933–1941* (Washington, D.C., 2007).

Schöpflin, G. and N. Wood (eds), *In Search of Central Europe* (New York, 1994).

Schulze, H., *States, Nations and Nationalism* (Oxford, 1996).

Schwabe, K. (ed.), *Die Anfänge des Schuman-Plans* (Baden-Baden, 1988).

Shennan, A., *Rethinking France: Plans for Renewal, 1940–1946* (Oxford, 1989).

Skinner, Q., *Visions of Politics. Vol. 1. Regarding Method* (Cambridge, 2002).

Spiering, M. and M. Wintle (eds), *Ideas of Europe since 1914: The Legacy of the First World War* (Basingstoke, 2002).

Steiner, Z.S., *The Lights That Failed: European International History, 1919–1933* (Oxford, 2007).

Stirk, P.M.R. (ed.), *Mitteleuropa: History and Prospects* (Edinburgh, 1994).

Stirk, P.M.R., 'Authoritarian and National Socialist Conceptions of Nation, State, and Europe', in idem (ed.), *European Unity in Context: The Interwar Period* (London, 1989), 125–48.

———, *A History of European Integration since 1914* (London, 1996).

———, *European Unity in Context: The Interwar Period* (London, 1989).

———, *Twentieth-Century German Political Thought* (Edinburgh, 2006).

Stråth, B. (ed.), *Europe and the Other and Europe as the Other* (Brusssels and New York, 2000).

Streim, G., 'Deutscher Geist und europäische Kultur. Die "europäische Idee" in der Kriegspublizistik von Rudolf Borchardt, Hugo von Hofmannsthal und Rudolf Pannwitz', *Germanisch-romanische Monatsschrift*, N.F. 46 (1996), 174–97.

Swedberg, R., 'The Idea of "Europe" and the Origin of the European Union: A Sociological Approach', *Zeitschrift für Soziologie* 23 (1994), 378–87.

Théry, F., *Construire l'Europe dans les Années Vingt: L'Action de l'Union Paneuropéenne sur la Scène Franco-Allemande, 1924–1932* (Geneva, 1998).

Todorova, M.N., *Imagining the Balkans* (Oxford, 1997).

Tombs, I., 'Une identité européenne assiégée? Les exiles socialistes à Londres, 1939–1945', *Revue d'histoire moderne et contemporaine* 46 (1999), 263–79.

Turner, J. (ed.), *The Larger Idea: Lord Lothian and the Problem of National Sovereignty* (London, 1988).

Urbach, K. (ed.), *European Aristocracies and the Radical Right 1918–1939* (Oxford, 2008).

Urwin, D.W., *The Community of Europe: A History of European Integration since 1945* (London, 1994).

Vinen, R., *A History in Fragments: Europe in the Twentieth Century* (London, 2000).

Walters, F.P., *A History of the League of Nations* (London, 1960).

Wasserstein, B., *Barbarism and Civilization: A History of Europe in Our Time* (Oxford, 2007).

White, H., *The Content of the Form* (Baltimore, 1987).

Wiener, A. and T. Diez, *European Integration Theory* (Oxford, 2003).

Wilson, K., and J. van der Dussen (eds), *The History of the Idea of Europe* (London, 1993).

Winock, Michel, *La IIIème république (1870–1940)* (Paris, 1976).

———, *Le Siècle des intellectuelles* (Paris, 2006).

Wintle, M.J. (ed.), *Culture and Identity in Europe* (Aldershot, 1996).

———, *The Image of Europe: Visualizing Europe in Cartography and Iconography* (Cambridge, 2009).

Woolf, S., 'Europe and its Historians', *Contemporary European History* 12 (2003), 323–37.

Young, J.W., *Britain and European Unity, 1945–1992* (London, 1993).

———, *Cold War Europe: A Political History* (London, 1991).

INDEX

www.ingramcontent.com/pod-product-compliance
Lightning Source LLC
Chambersburg PA
CBHW060023030426

42334CB00019B/2160